THE ONE YEAR®

Devotions for Girls Starring Women of the Bible

KATRINA CASSEL

Tyndale House Publishers, Inc.
Carol Stream, Illinois

Visit Tyndale's website for kids at www.tyndale.com/kids.

The One Year Devotions for Girls Starring Women of the Bible

Designed by Jacqueline L. Nuñez

For manufacturing information regarding this product, please call 1-800-323-9400.

ISBN 978-1-4143-3874-3

Printed in the United States of America

17 16 15 14 13 12 11
7 6 5 4 3 2 1

To . . .

Rick: best friend and guide

Tyler: firstborn

Jessica: firstborn princess

Adam: warrior in the making

Jasmine: my joy and song

Kaleb and Kayla: chosen ones. I thank God he brought you safely to us.

A special thanks to the Tyndale team—Katara, Erin, and Elizabeth—whose touch transformed this book, and to Teresa for her helpful suggestions and corrections.

Eve: Created in God's Image

God created human beings in his own image. In the image of God he created them; male and female he created them.

GENESIS 1:27

Eve: the first woman. Made in the image of God. Many times people overlook how special she was as one of God's first creations, and they remember her failure instead. People remember that Eve listened to the serpent, ate the forbidden fruit, and gave some to Adam to eat. They remember that Adam and Eve had to leave the Garden of Eden and their lives got harder. But Eve was more than just the one who ate the fruit. Eve was the first woman, created by God in his own image.

What exactly does it mean that Eve was created in God's image? It means she was a reflection of God's glory. She had the ability to love, to be faithful, to show kindness, and to do many of the other things God does. It doesn't mean she physically resembled God, although God did design her and create her in a way that he said was very good (Genesis 1:31).

Eve was the second human created, but she wasn't second best or a second-class citizen. In fact, God designed her in a way that was unique and individual. Of course, since there were no other women and there was only Adam for Eve to compare herself to, Eve didn't play the comparison game. There were no fashion magazines filled with thin models to make Eve feel fat or outdated. There were no TV shows to make her feel her life wasn't as good as someone else's. And because she hadn't yet eaten the forbidden fruit and she saw only good, it probably wouldn't have occurred to her that she could be anything other than the way she was.

Eve was exactly as God wanted her to be. He designed her and created her in a marvelous way. Just like Eve, you are a one-of-a-kind girl created in God's image, an individual with unique looks and personality. And that's something worth celebrating.

thinking it through

Maybe being you doesn't seem all that exciting. "What's special about me?" you might be asking. Lots. God has created you in his own image (Genesis 1:26-27). God created you to be unique and amazing (Psalm 139:14). God has a special plan for you (Jeremiah 29:11). And God calls *you* by name (Isaiah 43:1).

Choose one truth above to think about today. Write down the Scripture verse and tape it to your mirror or locker to give yourself confidence throughout the day.

thinking it through

You have your own unique personality. It's the one God created just for you. That doesn't mean you can't strive to be a better person, but don't try to change who God made you to be. Ask God to show you the ways he has made you—and other people—unique and special, in his image.

Eve: One of a Kind

You made all the delicate, inner parts of my body and knit me together in my mother's womb. Thank you for making me so wonderfully complex! Your workmanship is marvelous—how well I know it.

PSALM 139:13-14

We don't know much about Eve other than that she was the first woman, created in God's image and part of his amazing plan. We don't know if she was outgoing or quiet, musical, artistic, or logical. But we can be assured that she had her own unique looks, personality, and abilities. Those are things God gives to each of his wonderful creations. Things he gave you.

There is no one on earth who has your same combination of looks, personality, talents, and abilities. You have been individually designed and specially made by God. Ephesians 2:10 says, "We are God's workmanship, created in Christ Jesus to do good works, which God prepared in advance for us to do" (NIV). God already knows his plan for you and created you to be just who you need to be in order to live out that plan. So determine now that you will go ahead and be what God created you to be—the talented, still growing, still maturing young woman that you are.

In these changing years, it may be especially hard to know who you really are and who God made you to be. One minute you feel happy; the next minute you feel blue. Today your best friend promises to be your friend for life, but by the end of the week she's found a new girl to be her best friend. Life is constantly changing around you—and you might be changing too—but it's important to remember that God made you the way you are and he can help you shine just the way he created you.

Eve: Set Apart for God

I knew you before I formed you in your mother's womb. Before you were born I set you apart and appointed you as my prophet to the nations.

JEREMIAH 1:5

God had a special plan for Eve. She was the first woman and the first mother. When God created Adam and Eve, he told them to have children and to fill the earth with people all created in his image.

In today's verse, God tells Jeremiah that he set him apart to be a prophet before Jeremiah was ever born. "Of course," you say, "being a prophet is important, but I'm just me. I'm not going to be a prophet. Or the mother of all living people like Eve."

Jeremiah 1:5 is as true for you as it was for Jeremiah—minus the prophet part, of course. Fill your own name in the verse: "___________, I knew you before I formed you. . . . Before you were born I set you apart." The end of the verse is different for each of us. Maybe it says, "I set you apart to teach people or to be a leader." Perhaps it says, "I set you apart to show the world how great I am through music, art, or dance." You don't know yet what you'll do in your adult life, but be assured, God has something special for you—then and now. The things you are learning now will be a part of what God has for you later.

Take a look at the things you know how to do, enjoy doing, and do well. Are you using them every day to serve God and help others? If not, today's the day to start.

thinking it through

Think of one way to serve God today. It may be as easy as cooking supper with your mom or helping a friend with her math homework. Ask God to show you other ways you can use your abilities and interests to help others this week.

Eve: Your Own Special Talents

"I know the plans I have for you," says the LORD. "They are plans for good and not for disaster, to give you a future and a hope."
JEREMIAH 29:11

Certainly Eve didn't realize how important her role was as first woman and first mother. After all, she had never known anything different. But she was important. God gave her all she needed to fulfill his plan for her.

And God has given you all you need to fulfill the wonderful plan he has for you. God has equipped you with your personality and talents to help you become what he wants you to be.

Just as there are many different personalities, there is a variety of talents. Maybe you have an eye for art and you can see patterns others miss or capture images with your camera or paints. You might have a way with words. Whether it's writing poetry or solving a word puzzle, your word power leads the way. Or you might have good coordination. Sports and physical activities come easily for you. Movement feels natural. Maybe God has given you an ear for music or a flair for the dramatic. Whether you are composing or performing, your creativity shines through. Do you enjoy meeting new people and making sure everyone around you is having a good time? Maybe you use your "people skills" to get people organized and motivated to work. Or maybe you enjoy studying science or figuring out new gadgets. You might have a knack for technology. Maybe you enjoy baking cookies or redecorating your room or doing other "domestic" activities. Whatever talents you have, know that God has created you to use them for him, others, and yourself.

thinking it through

What talents has God given you? Remember, no one talent is greater or lesser than others. The important thing is that you take what God has given you and use it for him and those around you. Can you think of a way you are using these talents in your life right now? Thank God for making your talents part of his plan for you.

Eve: Be Who God Created You to Be

Now, O Jacob, listen to the LORD who created you. O Israel, the one who formed you says, "Do not be afraid, for I have ransomed you. I have called you by name; you are mine."

ISAIAH 43:1

Can you imagine what it was like for Adam and Eve to walk and talk with God in the Garden of Eden? What would it be like to have God call you by name? Well, God does call you by name, just not usually aloud like he did with Adam and Eve. He knows your name, he knows your likes and dislikes, and he knows your strengths and weaknesses.

God knows all those things about you because he created you. Sometimes when girls don't like who God made them to be, they try to make themselves into someone else. They may cover up their true selves by trying to be the class clown and being disruptive for attention or by making themselves the beauty queen in order to hide their true feelings. They may fall in with the wrong crowd. There are lots of wrong ways to deal with bad feelings about yourself—some are more obvious, like smoking, drinking alcohol, or doing drugs. But others can be more subtle, like letting thoughts about food take over your mind or hanging out with friends who aren't good influences or getting too involved with guys.

The better thing is to accept who God made you to be. Then practice the talents you do have so you can become even better at the things God has made you to do. Take another look at yesterday's Thinking It Through. Which talents did you think of? If you couldn't think of one, keep trying. God blessed you with talents, strengths, and abilities. Ask a parent or Sunday school teacher to help you identify your strong areas. Then use those abilities for God.

thinking it through

When you use your talents to help someone else, you are reflecting God's love to him or her, and that is part of being created in God's image. Get together with a friend or family member, and brainstorm three ways you might use the talents you've been given. Then choose one idea off your list, and take the next step to make that happen. Thank God that he made you and that he knows everything about you.

Eve: Your Own Story

God looked over all he had made, and he saw that it was very good! And evening passed and morning came, marking the sixth day.

GENESIS 1:31

God finished his work of creation by forming Adam and Eve. Then he looked around and declared everything good. Not okay or average, but *good*. And you are part of that creation! You are created in God's image just as Eve was. The only difference is that Eve started out as an adult and didn't have to go through braces or giving an oral report, or even dealing with siblings' first dates.

Do you ever feel like God made a mistake when he created you? Do you ever wonder, *Where is my flawless face or perfect skin? Where is my head for math or my bubbly personality?* The cool thing is that God gave each person just what she needs to do what he plans for her. God doesn't have a second set of not-as-good plans for those who have disabilities, are from broken homes, or have other challenges.

Why did God allow some people to be born with difficulties while others seem to breeze through life? Only he knows. Have you read or seen any of the Chronicles of Narnia books or movies? In one of the books, *The Horse and His Boy*, Aslan (the lion, who's a little bit like Jesus in the world of Narnia), tells the character Shasta, "Child . . . I am telling you your story, not hers. No one is told any story but their own." You can only live the plan God has for you. Take a look at who God created you to be, and then be the best you that you can be.

thinking it through

Can you think of anything you are doing because someone else thinks you should, or to get someone to like you better? Ask God for courage to do the things you're gifted at and interested in—whether or not your friends are doing them.

When God created you, he called you good. Write down three of your personality traits or physical features that you like. Then write down one thing you've been tempted to wish you could change. Thank God for *all* of them!

January 7

Eve: Partnership with God

God, who has called you into fellowship with his Son Jesus Christ our Lord, is faithful.

1 CORINTHIANS 1:9, NIV

The greatest privilege Eve had was getting to spend time with God in the Garden. Genesis 3:8 says that the husband and wife heard God walking in the Garden "when the cool evening breezes were blowing." That was when God spent time walking and talking with Adam and Eve.

Sometimes I wish I could physically walk with God. I'd like to ask him why some things happened in my life that were hurtful or made no sense to me. I'd like to ask for his opinion on some decisions I need to make. It would be great to have him tell me specifically what he wants me to do in coming years. Adam and Eve were truly blessed to have the opportunity to meet personally with God in the Garden.

Do you have some things you'd like to talk over with God? The Bible says God has called you into fellowship with his Son, Jesus Christ. What exactly does it mean to have fellowship with God? The biblical (Greek) word for fellowship is *koinonia*, which means a living, loving, shared relationship with another person. This means you can talk with God just like you talk with your friends.

But fellowship with God is only through Jesus. There is no other way to be close to God, to talk to God, or to listen to God than through Jesus. Jesus says in John 14:6, "I am the way, the truth, and the life. No one can come to the Father except through me."

God wants to partner with you because he loves you. You can know God is with you each step of your journey and that he cares about you more than anyone else does. God cares about your victories and your defeats, your sad times and happy times. Whatever matters to you matters to God.

thinking it through

Choose one of the following ways to fellowship with God today:

- Talk to God on your way to school or as you get ready for class.
- Write a letter to God telling him about the best or worst part of your day.
- Read a chapter from the book of Psalms in the Bible aloud at bedtime.

If you want to fellowship with God but have never thought about starting a relationship with Jesus before, talk to God about it. Then tell a parent or an adult from church so that person can help you know where to begin.

Quiz Time

On January 4, we talked about the talents that God has given each of us. Not sure of your talent? Take the quiz below.

1. It's party time. What do you do?
   A. Design posters and decorations
   B. Teach everyone some cool new games
   C. Choose the music
   D. Make sure everyone is having fun
   E. Organize people to get jobs done
   F. Figure out how to set up cool disco lights
   G. Write a catchy invitation to get everyone to attend
   H. Figure out the party cost and make sure there is enough money
   I. Prepare the food

2. It's time to plan the family vacation. What do you want to do?
   A. Sketch scenery
   B. Horseback ride, ski, or surf
   C. Find a quiet place to play your guitar
   D. Meet new people
   E. Tour the White House or Senate
   F. Explore the Museum of Science and Technology
   G. Visit the home of a famous author
   H. Plan the route
   I. Help make your rustic cabin more like home

3. Which school elective would you choose?
   A. Art
   B. Physical education or cheerleading
   C. Chorus or drama
   D. Mentoring program (being a good role model)
   E. Speech
   F. Computer lab
   G. School newspaper or yearbook
   H. Statistics and probabilities
   I. Home economics (cooking, sewing, etc.)

4. What do you see yourself doing in fifteen years?
   A. Working in an art studio
   B. Coaching girls' basketball
   C. Teaching music and drama in a high school
   D. Counseling people
   E. Running a business or being mayor of my town

F. Working in a lab or teaching science
G. Writing mysteries or poetry
H. Working as an accountant or math teacher
I. Being an interior decorator or a cake decorator

How many do you have of each letter circled?

A ___ B ___ C ___ D ___ E ___ F ___ G ___ H ___ I ___

It's okay if you have several different letters circled. You are still exploring all your talents and deciding what you like the most.

Mostly:

A. You have an eye for art. Whether it's drawing, ceramics, or watercolor, your artistic ability shines through.
B. You have good coordination. Sports and physical activities come easily for you.
C. You have an ear for music or a flair for the dramatic. Expressing yourself in music or words is important to you.
D. You have a way with people. Whether it's classmates, children, or older adults, you relate to people and understand their feelings.
E. You have leadership ability. You can get people organized and motivated to work.
F. You have a good understanding of science and technology. New gadgets and concepts fascinate you.
G. You have a way with words. Whether it's reading or writing, you love the way words come together to form poems, stories, and ideas.
H. You reason and make good deductions. You are good with numbers and see the patterns in the world others might miss.
I. You like to cook, sew, and do other domestic things. You may design costumes, decorate cakes, or cook for a living.

thinking it through

Eve was fooled by what the serpent said. It sounded right, so she believed it. Sometimes you hear things at school or on TV that sound right but may not be. How can you know? Remember that you can read God's Word for the answers you need (Psalm 119:105). Think of one person (a parent, pastor, older friend, or adult you trust) who you could ask to help you. Talk to that person the next time you're not sure about something you heard.

Eve: Listening to the Wrong Voice

The woman was convinced. She saw that the tree was beautiful and its fruit looked delicious, and she wanted the wisdom it would give her. So she took some of the fruit and ate it. Then she gave some to her husband, who was with her, and he ate it, too.

GENESIS 3:6

God said, "You can have it all but this one thing."

Satan, speaking through the serpent, said, "God just doesn't want you to have something good."

Eve listened to the wrong voice and made the choice to eat from the tree that God said not to eat from. God could have put up an electric fence or a Do Not Touch sign, but he wanted Adam and Eve to *choose* obedience.

What could Eve have done differently when the serpent came along? She might have asked God about what the serpent said. What would have happened if Eve had said to the serpent, "Let me ask God about this when I talk with him in a little while"? Would the serpent have left and returned later to try again? Would it have just made up more lies that sounded true?

We'll never know what might have happened. But Eve made her choice, and the result is that we are all born with the tendency to disobey God. We may not be visited by a serpent, but we are still tempted to sin and often give in to our weaknesses. Thankfully Eve's choice to sin isn't the end of the story.

The most amazing thing about Eve's story is that even though she sinned and had to leave the Garden, God had a plan to make things right for her—and us. And God blessed her and allowed her to be the mother of all people. God is a God of second chances.

Eve: God's Messages

Every word of God proves true. He is a shield to all who come to him for protection.

PROVERBS 30:5

You hear messages every day. "Have it your way." "Be all that you can be." "Just do it." The problem is that sometimes the messages you hear aren't the right ones to listen to. They encourage people to live for their own pleasure or gain.

It was the serpent's message that tripped Eve up in the Garden. God had told Adam and Eve that if they ate the fruit of the tree of the knowledge of good and evil, they would die. But the serpent said, "You won't die." Eve believed the serpent's lie because it was what she wanted to hear: "It's okay to go ahead and eat from that tree. God's limits are pointless."

That same kind of thinking is around today. Just listen to what your classmates or neighbors talk about. Do they talk about living for God or living for themselves? Do their plans include ways to serve God and get the most out of church, or do they brag about going behind their parents' backs to go to a party on the weekend? Do they talk about pushing God's boundaries with their boyfriends or using their bodies in a way that is pleasing to God?

Listen to the messages your favorite TV shows give you. You might hear that it's okay to disobey as long as it turns out okay in the end or that it's okay to lie about where you are going as long as it's for a good cause or that it's okay to make fun of others since they make fun of you or that rules are made to be bent or broken.

But God's messages, not your favorite TV shows, are the standard for right living. God's messages are the way to live an abundant life. God's messages are the ones that lead to peace and joy.

thinking it through

Pay attention to the conversations around you today. What are the messages you are hearing? As you watch your favorite TV show, think about the messages it gives. How do they compare to what God says in the Bible? Can you think of any verses that have a different message?

Ask God to help you figure out which messages are good to listen to and which ones you should block out.

thinking it through

What can you do when temptations pop into your head?

- Pray it through. Ask God to take away the thoughts from your mind.
- Say it through. Memorize today's verse and say it often when you are tempted.
- Sing it through. Listen to praise music and sing along.
- Talk it through with a close Christian friend or parent, or write in a journal.
- Walk away. Remove yourself from the temptation.

Eve: A Way Out

The temptations in your life are no different from what others experience. And God is faithful. He will not allow the temptation to be more than you can stand. When you are tempted, he will show you a way out so that you can endure.

1 CORINTHIANS 10:13

The serpent tempted Eve. He pointed out the delicious fruit to her. He made her think she was really missing out on something. Being tempted is not wrong. Eve sinned when she acted on the temptation and took the first bite.

You probably face a lot of temptations every day. That is part of being human. You may be tempted to

- say something rude to an unkind classmate;
- look at someone's test paper
- disobey your mom's instructions to set the table; or
- tell a lie.

Those things are sinful, but being tempted to do them isn't wrong. You will be tempted as long as you live on this earth. The things you see and hear at school or on the Internet may tempt you. Sometimes it's easy to go along with what others are doing even when you know it's wrong. The right thing to do is to walk away, but that's not always easy.

Imagine you are at a friend's house, and her older brother says he has a DVD you will love. The problem is that the movie is rated PG-13 and your parents have told you that you may not watch anything above PG. It's a really popular movie, and you feel left out when others discuss it. You know your parents would probably never find out, but you'd know. What should you do?

There are several right choices. You could go home and do something with your family. You could suggest watching another movie. You could suggest doing something outside. You could ask your friend to come to your house.

With every temptation, God will give you a way out. You just need to look for it.

Eve: Happiness through Obedience

Temptation comes from our own desires, which entice us and drag us away. These desires give birth to sinful actions. And when sin is allowed to grow, it gives birth to death.

JAMES 1:14-15

God told Eve she could eat from any tree except for one. She had many choices, each delicious. But the serpent made Eve think she was missing out on something. He made her believe that God was denying her something she deserved.

Your parents have rules that keep you safe. You have limits as to where you are allowed to go and how late you can stay. God has rules to keep his children safe too. Sometimes it might seem like you are missing out. The girls who go to parties, flirt with boys, gossip, and break the school's rules seem to have more fun. The problem is that some kinds of fun leave you feeling empty inside. You can never disobey God's rules and experience peace and joy.

Does it seem like something is missing in your life? Does it seem like those who aren't following God have it all? If you feel, like Eve did, that God is keeping something good from you, ask him to show you how he is giving you the rich and satisfying life he promised. If you have a Bible close by, look up Deuteronomy 6:5, Colossians 1:10, and 1 Peter 2:21. These three verses give you a purpose for life: to love God, to know God, and to follow Jesus' steps. Following God's purpose for your life will bring you more than you can imagine.

True happiness is found only by obeying God's rules. God promised that the Christian life would be rich and satisfying (John 10:10). Don't get bogged down by what you can't have or can't do; look for what you can have in Christ.

thinking it through

As you go through your daily routine today or tomorrow, keep a list of all the good things God has given you or done for you. At the end of the day, thank God for everything on your list.

thinking it through

Not always sure what the right choice is? That's okay. God knew you would have that problem, so he gave you the Holy Spirit to guide you. Pay attention to the choices you face today and tomorrow. Ask the Holy Spirit to help you make the right choice each time.

Eve: Making the Right Choice

The instructions of the LORD are perfect, reviving the soul. The decrees of the LORD are trustworthy, making wise the simple.

PSALM 19:7

One choice: to eat or not to eat. The rest of Eve's life was determined by that single wrong choice she made in the garden. Maybe the choice didn't seem like a big deal to her. After all, what difference did it make if she ate an apple from this tree or a pear from that tree? But it made a big difference. It meant that she had gone against God's command. Sin had entered the world.

The choices you make each day may not have as much of a dramatic impact on your life as the choice Eve made, but you still face the decision every day whether to do what God says is right. The decisions you make each day affect tomorrow. They determine who you are becoming as you journey toward adulthood, even when adulthood seems so far away.

It's only by honoring God in the daily decisions of life that you will become all God plans for you to be. But following God isn't a chore. Listening to his instructions will give you wisdom and peace!

Eve: Peer Pressure

Imitate God, therefore, in everything you do, because you are his dear children. Live a life filled with love, following the example of Christ. He loved us and offered himself as a sacrifice for us, a pleasing aroma to God.
EPHESIANS 5:1-2

The serpent tempted Eve, but most of the time we don't need any help making wrong choices. We choose chocolate over carrots and the Internet over math homework. Sometimes we make poor choices because we listen to others rather than God. Like Adam did. After Eve ate the fruit, she gave some to Adam, and he ate it too. The serpent didn't tempt him. He followed Eve's example.

Have you ever been in Adam's shoes? You did what someone suggested without thinking it through? Maybe you snubbed the new kid because everyone else did. Or perhaps you bought a certain kind of shoes because they were what all your friends were buying. Or you might have watched a certain movie because everyone else thought it was cool. When you do those kinds of things, you are giving in to peer pressure.

But peer pressure isn't always bad. In fact, it can be good. Like when all your friends decide to meet at a friend's house to study for a test. Or when someone decides to help with a church project and everyone else goes along with it. You can use positive peer pressure to make a difference. You could sell homemade cookies or jewelry to raise money for a cause you support, or you could collect hats and scarves for homeless people to wear during the cold winter months. There are a few ways to avoid negative peer pressure and start some positive peer pressure instead.

thinking it through

Does peer pressure affect you? Whether it's a small decision like what color shirt to buy or a big decision like whether to shoplift, stand up for yourself. Look to God for guidance, and ask a parent or youth leader for help.

Try using positive peer pressure to make a difference. Think of something you can do to help someone else. Then ask a friend to help you, and together, spread the news about your idea. See how many people you can get involved.

thinking it through

Think of three things in your life that you are thankful for and write them on a piece of paper. Carry the paper around with you this week. Every time you start to feel discontent about something, pull out the paper to remind yourself of the things God has given you. Say a quick thank you to God each time.

Eve: Be Content

Don't love money; be satisfied with what you have. For God has said, "I will never fail you. I will never abandon you."

HEBREWS 13:5

One way to keep from giving in to temptation is to be content. Be satisfied with your possessions, your talents, and your own unique personality. Eve was happy with all the good things God had given her in the Garden—until Satan came along and pointed out the one thing she didn't have—the forbidden fruit. Up until then she enjoyed living with Adam in the Garden surrounded by all the animals, plants, and fruit that God had created.

If you are content with who you are and what you have, then you won't be jealous of others who seem to have everything. You won't wish for the latest iPod or cell phone that your best friend has. You won't covet your classmate's leading role in the play or solo in the spring musical. It won't matter that a teammate broke the record for the one-hundred-meter butterfly that you set last season. Even your sister getting the outfit you wanted won't be all that important.

Instead of looking outward at what you don't have, look inward at all God has given you. You have been offered friendship by God's own Son. You are chosen by God to be part of a wonderful plan that he has for you. You have your own unique personality, strengths, and talents. You have clothes, food, and a place to live. And you probably have plenty of "stuff," too. Just look around your room.

When you play the comparison game, it's easy to want more than you have. But when your heart is filled with gratitude to God for all he's given you and all he's done for you, it takes away the bad feelings about what you don't have. Then you can be content with who you are and what you have. And you won't be tempted, like Eve, to go for that one thing you don't have.

Puzzle Page

We've been learning a lot from Eve's story about obeying God. The book of Proverbs has some good advice for us. Use the Box Code below to help you decode the verse.

	A	C	D	E	G
	H	I	K	L	M
	N	O	P	R	S
	T	U	W	Y	Q

____ ____ ____ ____ ____ ____ ____ ____ ____ ____ LORD

with ____ ____ ____ your ____ ____ ____ ____ ____;

____ ____ not ____ ____ ____ ____ ____ ____ on

____ ____ ____ ____ ____ ____ ____ understanding.

____ ____ ____ ____ ____ ____ ____ ____ ____ ____ ____

in all ____ ____ ____ ____ ____, and ____ ____

____ ____ ____ ____ ____ ____ ____ ____ ____ ____ ____

____ ____ ____ ____ ____ ____ ____ ____ ____ to ____ ____ ____ ____.

When you seek God, he will show you which choices are the right ones. You will know which path to take. How can you seek God today?

Answer: Trust in the LORD with all your heart; do not depend on your own understanding. Seek his will in all you do, and he will show you which path to take. (Proverbs 3:5-6)

thinking it through

Sometimes we don't understand why God does the things he does, but our job is to obey and be willing to follow God's plans. Hebrews 11:7 tells us, "It was by faith that Noah built a large boat." This verse was written more than two thousand years after Noah and Mrs. Noah lived. If someone were to write about you thousands of years in the future, what do you think you would be remembered for?

Mrs. Noah: Acting in Faith

I will confirm my covenant with you. So enter the boat—you and your wife and your sons and their wives.

GENESIS 6:18

We don't know her name, and we often don't give her much thought, but Mrs. Noah is an important part of the Flood story. In some ways her life was probably not much different from a wife and mother's life today. She cared for her husband and three sons. She fed, rocked, and clothed her sons and watched them grow up. She loved her husband and took care of their home. Life went on pretty much the same day after day.

Then came the day Noah got the message from the Lord. God was tired of people's sinful ways. He was going to send a flood to destroy the earth and start over with just Noah's family. God gave Noah specific instructions on how to build a boat to keep his family and pairs of animals safe during the Flood.

For one hundred years, Noah dedicated himself to building the ark. His sons were probably involved in helping with preparing the wood and building. What did Mrs. Noah do? Probably the same thing she had been doing—feeding, clothing, and caring for her husband and sons. But she also must have wondered about the message her husband received from the Lord. Was it really true? How would she explain to her friends or neighbors why her husband was building a huge boat? What would she say to those who questioned God's message and laughed at her family?

Mrs. Noah might have told her friends what God had said about destroying the earth, which probably didn't make her very popular. Or perhaps she was already unpopular for following God when other people ignored him, so she didn't even have friends to tell about God's message.

Mrs. Noah may have had some doubts and questions, but she responded to God's message in faith and helped ready her family for their unusual journey.

Mrs. Noah: When Other People Make Fun

If someone asks about your Christian hope, always be ready to explain it. But do this in a gentle and respectful way. Keep your conscience clear. Then if people speak against you, they will be ashamed when they see what a good life you live because you belong to Christ. Remember, it is better to suffer for doing good, if that is what God wants, than to suffer for doing wrong!

1 PETER 3:15-17

God told Noah to build, so he did. And Mrs. Noah went about her daily chores tending to her family. Although the Bible doesn't say so, we can assume that she was a godly and brave woman. Why? Because of the teasing and mean comments she must have endured during the years when Noah was building the boat.

If you've ever had to put up with unkindness and teasing at school or church for a few weeks or even a year, you know how hard that can be. Now imagine putting up with it for 120 years! People lived much longer in Noah's day. He was six hundred years old when he boarded the ark. He and his wife had probably spent the past one hundred years listening to people say things like, "A flood? You have to be kidding." (Keep in mind it had never rained before this.) "Who are you to judge us?" "Ha. Ha. Looks like Noah's gone a little loopy."

How did the Noah family respond to the meanness? They stayed busy with God's work. There was a lot to do—boards to cut, a boat to build, food to store, and of course the animals to gather. When the teasing came, Noah, his wife, and their sons probably reminded each other of all God had done for them in the past and of his promise to spare them when he destroyed the whole world. As long as they were doing God's will, the Noah family could stand strong against ridicule, knowing that they were a part of the new world God was planning.

thinking it through

The more you are like Jesus, the less you will be like others around you. And the less you are like them, the more likely they will be to make fun of you for your beliefs. But when you are doing the things you know are right, it's easier to face being teased.

How does 1 Peter 3:15 say to answer people who question your faith? Have you ever had to "suffer for doing good" (verse 17)? Why is it worthwhile to follow God, even if you risk getting made fun of?

thinking it through

Have your parents ever made a decision that was hard for you to accept? Maybe they moved and you had to leave everything behind. Maybe they changed churches, so you had to change too. How did you react to the changes? How can you support your parents in doing what God wants them to do?

Maybe you're the one who feels God calling you to do something. Can you think of something God may want you to do? How can your friends or parents support you in it?

Mrs. Noah: Living Out God's Plan

When everything was ready, the LORD said to Noah, "Go into the boat with all your family, for among all the people of the earth, I can see that you alone are righteous."

GENESIS 7:1

God chose Noah to build an ark, save his family, and begin again in a new world. Even though God chose Noah, Mrs. Noah shared his mission. Before boarding the ark, she had already helped Noah through hard years of farming (Genesis 5:29) and then one hundred years of boat building. During the years of preparations, she raised her sons to believe in God and to believe his message that a flood was coming. She taught them to live differently from others their age.

Once aboard the ark, Mrs. Noah set up housekeeping on her new floating home. That must have been quite a job. She had to feed her family using the food they'd gathered and brought aboard. She probably became assistant zookeeper for the year they were on the ark also. If people didn't get along, she might have had to become the peacekeeper, too. Can you imagine being on a boat with your family for over a year—no way to get away for a few hours or to meet a friend at the mall? No way to phone, text, or e-mail anyone else. In fact, there wasn't anyone else left. If you got tired of the food onboard, you couldn't just grab a pizza from the nearby pizza place. There was no Chinese takeout either.

Mrs. Noah was able to support her husband in living out God's plan because she shared his belief in God and what God was going to accomplish through her family. Mrs. Noah survived the hard years and was able to see God's plan fulfilled when she stepped onto dry land and saw the rainbow God put in the sky as a promise never to destroy the world with a flood again.

Mrs. Noah: Facing Changes

Leave the boat, all of you—you and your wife, and your sons and their wives.

GENESIS 8:16

Change is hard, and a move can be a stressful event in family life. The Noah family faced both. Not only did they float around on the ark for over a year, but also a flood destroyed everything they knew. All their neighbors were gone; all the plants and animals not onboard were destroyed.

Mrs. Noah climbed onto the ark, knowing life would never be the same again but trusting in God and his plan. After forty days of rain, it took months for things to dry out enough for the Noah family to step off the ark onto dry land. Can you imagine what it would have been like to once again be on land after living in their houseboat for so long? Imagine how excited the animals would have been to roam free again.

But everything had changed. Now it was only Mr. and Mrs. Noah and their three sons and three daughters-in-law, along with the animals that had been on the ark with them. It was up to them to rebuild the new world.

The challenges were great, but they trusted that God's ways are always best, and they started their new lives with that in mind.

Maybe you are facing changes in your life. They may feel as overwhelming as boarding an ark and floating away from all you know. Perhaps you are facing a move to a new home or a new school or both. Maybe your family is changing in ways that are hard for you. Maybe you are no longer friends with someone you used to be really close to. Remember that God knows what you are going through. He is with you. Even if things around you are overwhelming, he can fill your heart with peace just as he did for Mrs. Noah.

thinking it through

Your life is changing as you grow up. Some changes are good, like getting more privileges. Other changes may be uncomfortable or upsetting. What is the biggest change you have gone through? A move? A new school? A new sibling? The loss of a family member? How did you deal with the change? Did any one person or any one Bible verse help you?

Isaiah 26:3 says that God gives us peace when we trust him. How can that help you to handle the changes you've faced or the changes you are facing?

thinking it through

The Bible tells us that we should let our good deeds shine so people will praise God and want to know more about him. Write out Matthew 5:16 on a note card or slip of paper. Find an old flashlight in your house and tape the verse to the handle. Then put the flashlight on your desk or dresser to remind yourself that you are a light for God. Ask God to show you how to shine for him each day.

Mrs. Noah: A Bright Light

Let your good deeds shine out for all to see, so that everyone will praise your heavenly Father.

MATTHEW 5:16

God looked down on the world he had created and saw that people's hearts were full of darkness. Then he saw a light. The Noah family. The only family of God-followers in an ungodly world. It must have been difficult for the Noah family to live by God's rules when not one other person was doing it, but they did what was right and it came to God's attention.

If you've ever turned on a flashlight during the day, you probably didn't notice much difference. But turn on that same flashlight in the dark, and it lights up the area around you. Even the smallest light pierces the darkness. And that's how it was with the Noah family.

God wants us to be lights in our world today. What does that really mean? It means living in a way that points to God. When you are a light, other people will see it and wonder what is different about you. It might mean being kind to someone who is unkind to you, reacting fairly when someone else is unfair, or walking away when someone wants to start an argument.

You can also encourage others who are shining for God. Have you ever noticed a friend do something especially kind or selfless or courageous? Thank God for that person, and then write an encouraging note to let your friend know how he or she is being a light for God.

Remember that even a tiny flashlight shows up in the dark. When you live your life in a way that pleases God, other people will notice.

Mrs. Noah: Live Enthusiastically

Work willingly at whatever you do, as though you were working for the Lord rather than for people.
COLOSSIANS 3:23

God told Noah to build the ark and save his family. He told him just how to do it, and "Noah did everything exactly as God had commanded him" (Genesis 6:22). Noah knew what his calling was, and he followed it wholeheartedly. Mrs. Noah had her own work to do to prepare, and she did that work willingly.

You aren't called to build an ark or prepare a floating zoo, but God does have a plan for your life. You can live life fully and passionately, knowing this is true. People with no plan have no direction, but people who know God has something special in mind for them can live confidently and with purpose.

What does God want you to do right now? Be enthusiastic about life. Tackle it head-on. If you read the devotions about Eve earlier this month, you'll remember that we looked at your talents and how to use them for God now. Think about what you are good at and do it with all your heart.

Noah was a farmer, and that is what he did until God called him to do something else. Then he became a boat builder and zookeeper. When the flood was over and his family was once again on dry land, he returned to farming. It was what he knew how to do and what he was good at.

What are you good at? What are your strengths? Are you friendly? Look for new people at church or in your neighborhood and welcome them. Can you sing? Join the church youth choir. Do you draw? Offer to design posters for an upcoming event in your community.

Take whatever God has given you and use it for him. Live enthusiastically and confidently this week.

thinking it through

Read today's verse at the top of the page. How could working for God rather than people change the way you do things? Does it make you want to work harder or not as hard? Why? This week, think about what it means to work for God in everything you do.

thinking it through

The Bible says that everyone has sinned (Romans 3:23). Sin has a penalty—not getting to live with God in heaven for eternity (Romans 6:23). God sent Jesus to pay the penalty for our sin (Romans 6:23). Those who believe in Jesus and accept what he did for them will be saved (Romans 10:9-10). When you do that, you become a part of God's family (John 1:12).

Have you ever asked God to forgive you for your sins and told him that you believe what Jesus did for you? If you don't understand what it means to have Jesus as your Savior, talk to a pastor or Sunday school teacher.

Mrs. Noah: God Saves

God loved the world so much that he gave his one and only Son, so that everyone who believes in him will not perish but have eternal life.

JOHN 3:16

God created a perfect world. He wanted to walk and talk with the people he made. But sadly it didn't stay that way. The problems started with Adam and Eve eating the fruit in the Garden. From then on every person was born with the desire to sin and disobey God. By Noah's time things had gotten so bad that God decided to destroy everything and everyone but the Noah family and start over.

Noah was saved from the Flood by acting in faith—trusting that God would take care of him as he had promised. God provided a way for Noah and his family to be saved from the Flood when Noah built the ark.

In the same way, God offers us a way to be saved from our sins. God wants us to live with him in heaven, but since no sin is allowed in heaven, no one would qualify for eternal residence with God. So God chose to make a way for us to live with him there. And that way is his Son, Jesus.

Jesus became a man on earth and lived a sinless life. Then he died on the cross as a sacrifice for sin. From the time Adam and Eve first sinned until the day Jesus died, people had to offer animals as sacrifices. When Jesus died on the cross, the need for sacrifices was gone. He became the final sacrifice. And then he overcame death by coming back to life three days later.

Now instead of offering an animal as payment for sin, we simply need to believe that Jesus died for our sins and rose from the dead.

Just as Mrs. Noah and her family boarded the ark and were saved, you can claim Jesus' payment for your sins and ask God's forgiveness, and you will be saved from sin and be assured of eternity with God in heaven.

Quiz Time

On January 19, we learned how our actions can shine brightly for God. How bright is your light? Take the quiz below to find out. Circle the answer that best describes what you would do in each situation. Be honest!

1. You are tired of riding your old bike around the neighborhood and are saving for a new one. During your church's mission conference, they announce that a special offering will be taken to build a school in a poor country. You
   A. give a little bit of your money. You understand that they need the school, but you need the bike too.
   B. give all the money. You can mow lawns during the summer to earn money for the new bike.
   C. keep your money. You already put some of it in the offering plate at church, so why feel you need to give more?

2. You are on your way into school when you see the class bully fall. His backpack is open, and stuff goes everywhere. An apple rolls down the sidewalk and lands at your feet. You
   A. hand him his apple and continue on to class.
   B. stop and help him gather his belongings.
   C. think it serves him right and continue on without another thought.

3. You finish your math work early. The teacher suggests you help a struggling student. The same student called you names at lunch. You
   A. help her with one problem and then get a book to read until class is over.
   B. explain to her how to do the problems and watch that she does them correctly.
   C. say, "No thanks." She really embarrassed you at lunch.

Count how many you have of each letter.

A's _____

B's _____

C's _____

If you have mostly A's, your light is fading. You know what you should do but only do it halfheartedly. Ask God to give you a good attitude about shining for him.

If you have mostly B's, your light is bright. You are giving to others unselfishly and letting the love of Jesus flow through you. Ask God to show you more ways to shine your light.

If you have mostly C's, your light is dim. You aren't letting God's love shine through you. But God wants to do amazing things through you, if you let him use you. Ask God to help you unselfishly reach out and give to others.

thinking it through

Changes aren't always easy. Sarah had to leave a bustling city for Nowhere-ville, yet the Bible doesn't mention her complaining about the changes.

Are you known as a complainer? Or do others know you as someone who handles changes and challenges well? The next change you face, remind yourself to be a "bright light" for God by not complaining (Philippians 2:13-15). Instead, ask God to help you trust him to take care of you no matter what changes come.

Sarah: Dealing with Changes

One day Terah took his son Abram, his daughter-in-law Sarai (his son Abram's wife), and his grandson Lot (his son Haran's child) and moved away from Ur of the Chaldeans. He was headed for the land of Canaan, but they stopped at Haran and settled there.

GENESIS 11:31

Abraham and Sarah, then called Abram and Sarai, lived in Ur of the Chaldeans along the Euphrates River in what is now southern Iraq. This was an important city in the ancient world. If you picture the people of this time as uneducated and living as cavemen, think again. Ur was a flourishing city. It was the center of culture, power, and wealth. It was at its peak of power in Abraham's day. Abraham was probably a very educated man, and Sarah most likely had all the luxuries of life.

Abraham's father, Terah, decided to move the whole family from the thriving town of Ur to the land of Canaan—a land very different from Ur. The family packed up and said good-bye to their home and all they knew. Then they set out. But for some reason, Terah stopped halfway to Canaan in the village of Haran in what is now southern Turkey, and the family remained there.

Sarah's life took a dramatic turn when she left behind the art, culture, and thriving businesses of Ur to follow her family. The Bible doesn't say much about this move, but we can guess that it was hard for Sarah to leave her life in Ur to become a traveler and then reside in Haran. Yet she accepted it, and the family stayed there until Terah's death.

Sarah: A Journey of Faith

The LORD had said to Abram, "Leave your native country, your relatives, and your father's family, and go to the land that I will show you."

GENESIS 12:1

Sarah made the move from Ur, the New York City of the ancient world, to Haran. She settled there with her family for many years. The whole family remained in Haran until her father-in-law, Terah, died. After Terah's death, God called Abraham to finish the journey Terah had started.

This move was truly a journey of faith and obedience. God didn't tell them where they would be going when they set out, but they trusted him to take care of them. Once again Sarah had to pack up and leave all she knew to follow God's leading. The family journeyed another six hundred miles into the area that is now modern Israel. In exchange for their trust and obedience, God made a promise to Abraham and Sarah. He promised them that they would become a great nation and would be famous—not famous in the way that a movie star or sports figure is famous, but they would always be remembered—and blessed. This was God's covenant, or agreement, with Abraham: "Follow me and I will bless you."

Abraham did follow God and finished the journey to Canaan with Sarah at his side. Abraham and Sarah were the father and mother of the Israelite nation. King David, one of the most famous rulers of Israel (yep, the same one who defeated the giant Goliath), was part of their family tree. So was Jesus, who was born to save us all from sin and death. If Abraham and Sarah hadn't trusted in God and obeyed him, God wouldn't have poured his blessings out on their family for generations to come. Sometimes making the right decision and obeying God doesn't just affect one person here and now, but it can make a difference for future family members too.

thinking it through

Why did Abraham and Sarah obey God even when they had no idea where they were going? Because they trusted that God knew what was best for them. God wants you to obey him too. No, you don't have to journey by camel 1,200 miles, but there are things you can do now:

Obey your parents (Ephesians 6:1).
Be kind to others (Ephesians 4:32).
Think about things that are true, pure, and excellent (Philippians 4:8).
Forgive anyone who is unkind or offends you (Colossians 3:13).
Can you think of anything else?

thinking it through

Here are just a few of God's promises. Look up each Scripture given to read the promise right from the Bible.

God promises eternal life to everyone who believes in Jesus (John 3:16).
God promises to show you a way out of all your temptations (1 Corinthians 10:13).
God promises peace when you pray and take your worries to him (Philippians 4:6-7).
God promises to supply all you need (Philippians 4:19).

Choose one promise from God, then write it down and place it where you'll see it every day.

Sarah: Claiming God's Promises

The LORD took Abram outside and said to him, "Look up into the sky and count the stars if you can. That's how many descendants you will have!"

GENESIS 15:5

God promised Abraham and Sarah that their family would be like the stars in the sky—it would be so big they wouldn't be able to count everyone. The problem with that? They didn't have any children. So there was no chance of grandchildren, let alone future generations.

Do you ever wonder what was going through Sarah's mind? God gave her a promise, but no babies had arrived. Years had gone by, and now she was long past the age of having children. Did she think God had forgotten? Or did she just wonder when and how God would send them a baby?

Sarah knew that God had made a promise to Abraham and to herself. But she didn't know how he would keep it. She knew that this promise was from the same God who created the world, the moon, sun, and stars, all the animals, and people. Certainly the God who did all this could cause Sarah to have a child, even in her old age. But it still seemed impossible.

Do things in your life seem confusing right now? Are there situations that make you wonder if God is listening and if he really cares? The God of Sarah and Abraham is the same God who is watching over you. He has given you his message in his Word, the Bible. He has promises for you in the Bible that are as true today as they were when the Bible was first written. You can claim them for your own and believe them as though they were written just for you.

Sarah: Waiting for God to Work

They that wait upon the LORD shall renew their strength; they shall mount up with wings as eagles; they shall run, and not be weary; and they shall walk, and not faint.

ISAIAH 40:31, KJV

Many years passed between when God first promised to make Abraham and Sarah a great nation and when Sarah actually gave birth to their son, Isaac. During the wait Sarah had a lot of time to worry, doubt, fear, plan, pray, and trust. And she probably did each of those things many times.

Waiting is hard. Maybe you are waiting to hear from a friend who has moved. Maybe you are waiting for spring break because you are going on a special trip. Perhaps you've had to quit your favorite activity because a parent is waiting to hear about a new job. There are lots of different waiting times in your life.

Sometimes Sarah patiently waited for God to keep his promise. Other times she took matters into her own hands. One time Sarah figured God wasn't going to give her a child. She told Abraham to have a baby with her servant, Hagar. She thought maybe that child could be her promised child.

That didn't work out well. After Hagar got pregnant, she bragged to poor Sarah, who had been unable to have a child. And when Sarah finally did have a child herself at age ninety, Hagar's son, Ishmael, made fun of her son, Isaac.

Waiting for God to work isn't always easy, but it's the best thing. Running ahead of God or taking matters into your own hands often makes a mess of things. That doesn't mean God won't give you the wisdom and strength to handle some situations on your own. He will. He promises wisdom to those who ask (James 1:5). He will give you peace in your heart about choices you've made when they are the right ones. If you don't feel peace about a decision, it may not be the best choice or timing. If God says wait, then wait.

thinking it through

Sometimes it can be hard to know when God is telling you to wait—it can seem like he isn't paying any attention. But that's not true! Are you waiting for anything right now? What can give you patience and courage to keep trusting God while you wait? Write some of God's promises on an index card to remind you that God is faithful.

thinking it through

Read Proverbs 27:4 above. Why do you think jealousy is so dangerous?

Is there something that one of your friends has or is able to do that you wish you could have or do? Have you ever been jealous of that friend? Be honest! Now think of something you have or are able to do and thank God for it. Every time you're tempted to feel jealous of someone, stop and thank God for something he's given you. Try to thank him for something different each time.

Sarah: The Cure for Jealousy

Anger is cruel, and wrath is like a flood, but jealousy is even more dangerous.

PROVERBS 27:4

Sarah got tired of waiting for God to keep his promise to give her a baby and took matters into her own hands. She told Abraham to have a baby with her servant. She planned to raise that baby as her own—a custom women in those days followed when they couldn't get pregnant themselves. Yet when Hagar became pregnant and started flaunting it in front of her mistress, Sarah was angry. Then she blamed Abraham for the problem.

Jealousy brings out the worst in people. When someone has talents, possessions, or popularity that another person wants, it can become ugly. Imagine that a less popular girl shows up at school in a really cute outfit and some popular girls make rude comments about how it looks. Why would they do this? Because they don't think the less popular girl deserves that outfit. They should be the ones with those clothes.

Or imagine that one group of girls has been the cheerleading squad for three years straight. Then a new girl tries out and bumps one of them from the squad. Uh-oh. She'd better look out. She now has the position another girl wanted, and having what someone else wants can make that person jealous. The girl whose spot was taken will be tempted to watch for any little flaw in the new girl's performance. The friends might make the new cheerleader feel unwelcome.

There is no reasoning with jealousy. Whether you are jealous like Sarah, or the brunt of the jealousy like Hagar, life is difficult. The only cure for jealousy is to learn to be content with what you already have. Rather than playing the comparison game, be thankful for your own talents, abilities, and possessions.

Sarah: Waiting for Answers

Keep on asking, and you will receive what you ask for. Keep on seeking, and you will find. Keep on knocking, and the door will be opened to you.

MATTHEW 7:7

The years of waiting were over. God had heard Sarah's prayer and answered. Now at ninety years old, Sarah had her long-promised baby. Why didn't God answer Sarah's prayer years earlier and give her a child while she was young? Or even a whole houseful of children? The Bible doesn't give a reason, but it does say God is in control of all things. He could have filled Abraham and Sarah's house with a dozen children right away. For some reason, God chose to make Sarah wait for the desire of her heart.

God hears prayer. He answers prayer. Sometimes he doesn't give us the answer we want or give it to us on our own schedules. You might wonder, "Why pray if God is going to do what he wants anyway?" That's a hard question and one that theologians have debated for years. What we do know is that God wants to have a relationship with us, and communicating with him is part of that relationship.

God sees the whole picture of our lives, while we see only a section at a time. God knew how Abraham's and Sarah's lives would play out, and he decided how many children they would have and when. Perhaps he knew that if they had young children, they wouldn't have been as ready to obey and move. Or maybe God knew that by making Sarah wait so long, Isaac would be an extra-special child.

We don't always know the "whys" of God's answers.

Are there things you have asked God for and not received? Keep praying. God may have you waiting for a very special reason.

thinking it through

Set aside time to pray every day. Here is a good way to remember: Clean out an empty soup can and cut a piece of wrapping paper or colored paper to fit all the way around the can. Glue or tape the paper in place and decorate the can any way you like. Then write your prayer requests on slips of colored paper. Put them in the can. Every time you walk by the can, take out a slip of paper and pray for the request written on it. Once you've prayed for all the requests, put the papers back in the can and start over.

thinking it through

God wants you to daily put aside your own desires for his. Your talents, energy, and possessions should be given over to him to carry out his plan in your life. Giving them *over* to him doesn't mean that he will ask you to give them *up*. Sure, he might do that. But he's the one who gave you those talents in the first place, so he may use the things you are passionate about to carry out his plans. What might it look like for you to give your talents and possessions over to God?

Sarah: Giving It Up for God

Dear brothers and sisters, I plead with you to give your bodies to God because of all he has done for you. Let them be a living and holy sacrifice—the kind he will find acceptable. This is truly the way to worship him.

ROMANS 12:1

Abraham and Sarah received their promised child after a very long wait. They loved their son, Isaac. Then they faced the biggest test of all. God told Abraham, "Take your son, your only son—yes, Isaac, whom you love so much—and go to the land of Moriah. Go and sacrifice him as a burnt offering on one of the mountains, which I will show you" (Genesis 22:2).

Can you imagine how Abraham must have felt? He and Sarah had waited for decades to have this baby. When Sarah couldn't get pregnant, Abraham tried having a child with another woman, but that was not the special child God had promised. Now Abraham and Sarah finally had a child and God wanted them to give him up. Abraham could have argued with God. He could have refused. But Abraham did as God said and took Isaac to Moriah.

The story has a happy ending. God didn't allow Abraham to offer Isaac as a human sacrifice. God just wanted to know that Abraham was willing to do whatever he asked. God provided a ram for Abraham to sacrifice instead.

Where was Sarah when all this was going on? The Bible doesn't say. She may have been in on the decision to obey God, or it may have been Abraham's test alone. But we can assume that Sarah walked in faith and obedience to God just as Abraham did.

God doesn't require animal sacrifices anymore, but he does ask us to sacrifice ourselves to him. We do that by being willing to give up activities and possessions if he asks us to and being willing to give up our own plans for his. He doesn't ask this to make us unhappy but because his plans are better than anything we could plan for ourselves.

Puzzle Page

n January 25, we learned about waiting for God to answer our prayers. What did the psalmist say about waiting? Solve the Balloon Puzzle to find out.

Directions: Each balloon has both a scrambled word and a number in it. There are also numbers next to the blank spots in the verse. Look at the number next to the blank. Find the balloon with the same number. Unscramble the word in that balloon, and write it on the line. Check your answers at the bottom.

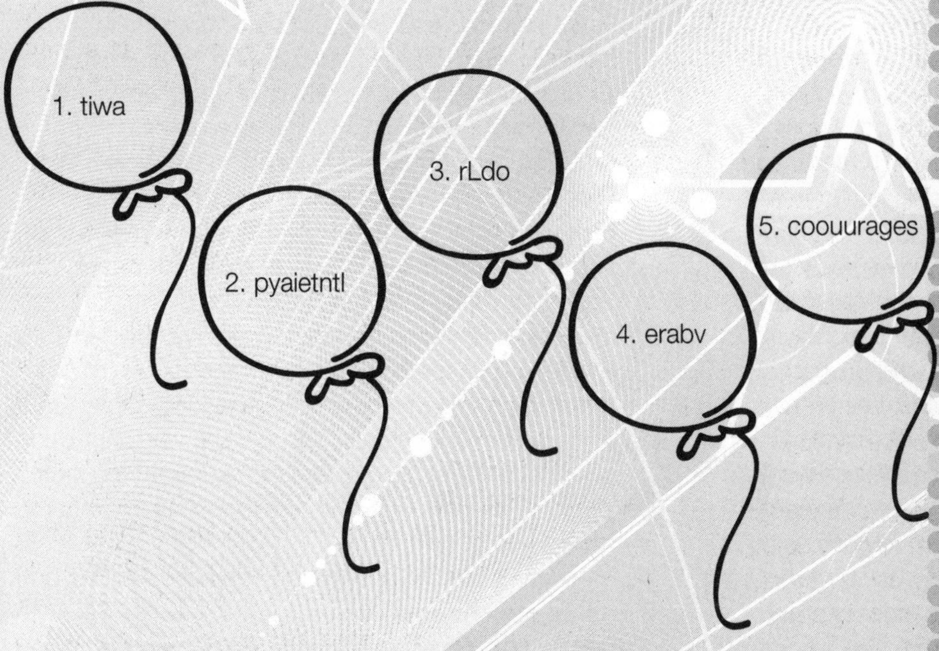

1. tiwa
2. pyaietntl
3. rLdo
4. erabv
5. coouurages

1. ________ 2._________ for the 3._________. Be 4._________ and 5._________. Yes, 1._________ 2._________ for the 3._________.

What two things does this verse tell you to do while you wait? How can you do them?

Answer: Wait patiently for the LORD. Be brave and courageous. Yes, wait patiently for the LORD. (Psalm 27:14)

thinking it through

Can you think of a time when someone got what you wanted? How did you feel?

Has there been a time when you had something (a possession, a talent, an award) someone else wanted? How did that make you feel?

No matter whether you are the one who wants what another has or the one who has what someone else wants, it's important to act graciously and with kindness. Jealousy and pride both lead to hurt.

Hagar: When Someone Gets What You Want

Sarai said to Abram, "This is all your fault! I put my servant into your arms, but now that she's pregnant she treats me with contempt. The LORD will show who's wrong—you or me!"

GENESIS 16:5

Hagar's story is intertwined with Sarah's. If you've been reading this book the last few days, you know God promised that Abraham and Sarah would start a great nation, but years passed, and they still had no children. Sarah came up with her own plan. She told Abraham to have a child with her servant, Hagar. So Abraham did what Sarah asked, and Hagar became pregnant.

Sarah had wanted to have a child for years, but it was Hagar who was pregnant. Since Hagar was pregnant with what was assumed to be the promised child, she began to act like she was more important than Sarah. That was too much for Sarah.

Sarah was strong in faith, but she was human. She had the same emotions you have when you see someone else getting what you want, especially if they flaunt it in your face. Sarah was jealous, she was angry, and she took it out on Hagar. She blamed Abraham for the situation, even though it was her own idea for Hagar to have a son for him.

Hagar teased Sarah. Sarah became jealous and angry. No one was winning. Abraham told Sarah to handle it however she wanted, and Sarah mistreated Hagar. The situation was so bad that Hagar fled to the desert to escape Sarah.

As the problems between Hagar and Sarah show, jealousy and teasing do not lead to good relationships.

Hagar: When You Get What Someone Else Wants

Because of the privilege and authority God has given me, I give each of you this warning: Don't think you are better than you really are. Be honest in your evaluation of yourselves, measuring yourselves by the faith God has given us.

ROMANS 12:3

Jealousy can eat away at you, make you angry, and leave you wanting to get even with others. But what about when you are on the other side? When you are the one someone else is jealous of? That was the case with Hagar.

God blessed Hagar. He gave her a son. Hagar knew how badly her mistress, Sarah, wanted a son. She may have been with the family during many of those long years they waited to have children. She watched as time went by and Sarah didn't get the desire of her heart. Hagar showed off. She had what Sarah so desperately wanted. And she flaunted it. Sarah was constantly aware that it was Hagar who was pregnant, not she herself.

Has God blessed you with many talents? Are you the one who gets chosen to sing the solo? The one who always makes the team and starts every game? Are you often chosen for academic honors, or do you always get on the honor roll? Do you have more clothes or shoes than those around you? Perhaps you have all the latest electronic gadgets—the newest and best of everything.

There is nothing wrong with having talents and possessions. But flaunting them or trying to make others feel less important or left out is wrong. Whatever talents you have, God gave them to you. The things you own, he allowed you to have. What you do with those things is what really matters. Do you use them to make yourself look good or to show how great God is?

thinking it through

You can't control other people's reactions to you, but you can make sure you have the right attitude about what you have. Try one of these ideas:

- Admit that all good things come from God.
- Share with others who have less.
- Use your talents to help others.
- Let others praise your talents—don't praise them yourself.
- Remind yourself that you are just the guardian of what God has given you.

thinking it through

Are there any problems you wish you could run away from? First John 5:14 says, "We are confident that he hears us whenever we ask for anything that pleases him." Talk to God about your problems. You can be confident that he will hear you and help you work them out.

Hagar: God Hears

The angel of the LORD found Hagar beside a spring of water in the wilderness, along the road to Shur.

GENESIS 16:7

Things had gotten so bad between Hagar and her mistress, Sarah, that Hagar fled into the desert. She was probably lonely, frightened, and not sure what would happen to her. Without Abraham and Sarah she didn't have a home or food.

An angel came to her in the desert and told her to return to Sarah and submit to her. God promised her that he would work it out. Thankfully God is a God who can work out problems. And in this case the problems were caused by the actions of

- Sarah, who got tired of waiting for God to give her a child and decided Hagar should have a child for her;
- Abraham, who went along with Sarah's plan; and
- Hagar, who ran away from the problems she had with Sarah.

None of these things were part of God's plan, but neither did they catch him by surprise. He knew ahead of time which actions each person would take. The angel told Hagar she would have a son and that she should call him Ishmael, which means "God hears."

If you are facing difficulties today, God does hear your prayers for help. He will work out your problems just as he worked out Hagar's. God didn't leave Hagar alone in her despair, and he doesn't leave you alone either. If you are facing difficulties today, take time to talk to the God who hears.

Hagar: Handling It When Someone Treats You Wrongly

When people's lives please the LORD, even their enemies are at peace with them.

PROVERBS 16:7

Like Hagar, you may find yourself on someone's bad side. What do you do? Hagar ran away into the desert to avoid the mistreatment from Sarah. Not an option for you. You can't hide out in the school restrooms trying to avoid the person all day. You can't stay home sick until the school year is over.

So what do you do when you are the target of someone's teasing, rudeness, or bullying? First, look for the reason you are a target or are being teased. For Hagar, it was a combination of her flaunting her pregnancy and Sarah's jealousy. For you, it may be something you have done, such as making fun of someone or showing off. Or it may be something you can't control, like being the smallest one in the class or not having as much money as someone else.

Is there anything you can change about your actions or attitude to fix the problem? Maybe you need to have a one-on-one talk with a classmate to apologize for the way you've treated her or to fix a problem that happened earlier in the school year. Maybe you can adjust your attitude toward someone else. Or perhaps there isn't an obvious answer.

If there isn't an easy solution, don't try to just tough it out. Talk to someone who can help—a parent or guidance counselor. You might feel like it will just make the problem worse, but you shouldn't have to put up with meanness or physical abuse. Ask an adult you trust for advice on how to handle the problem. It may even be a problem an adult needs to handle.

Know that God is with you. He met Hagar in the desert, and he'll be with you in the classroom, at home, or wherever you go. You don't have to face the tough times alone.

thinking it through

Are you the target of someone's anger or teasing? What do you think caused the problem? Is there anything you can do to fix it? Think of three trusted adults you could talk to about the problem (parent, teacher, counselor, youth leader, coach). Talk to one of them today if someone is mistreating you. Read Proverbs 16:7 above. Ask God to help you live in a way that pleases him, and trust him to take care of you.

thinking it through

You don't need to be a victim of bullies. Try these things when you're the target:

- Talk to your parents. Encourage them to contact the school about starting a zero-tolerance program for bullies.
- Don't react. If you don't react, it won't be as fun for them.
- Talk to the school guidance counselor. Be specific. Keep track of everything the bully does to hurt you.

Remember that God's love is unfailing. When you ask him to help you, he will.

Hagar: Girl Bullies

Help me, O LORD my God! Save me because of your unfailing love.

PSALM 109:26

Sarah mistreated Hagar. We aren't given the details, but we know that it was serious enough for Hagar to flee into the desert.

If you've ever been the target of a girl bully, you know how Hagar felt. You may think of a bully as being the big, dumb boy who has failed a grade or two and has few or no real friends, except maybe a trusted sidekick. This isn't true of a girl bully. Girl bullies tend to be

- pretty;
- dressed in the latest fashions;
- smart;
- involved in at least one school activity such as cheerleading, choir, or drama; and
- part of a clique with at least two other girls.

Girl bullies don't usually fight with their fists; they fight by saying mean things, spreading rumors, forcing girls to do what they want, and leaving girls out—ignoring girls and maybe even getting others in the class to ignore or make fun of them. On some occasions girl bullies may physically attack another girl, but for the purpose of humiliating her rather than actually hurting her body.

Girl bullies may not leave you with cuts and bruises—at least not ones you can see. They wound your heart and shred your self-esteem.

The sad thing is that girl bullies often get away with it. They may look like innocent bystanders when really they are being quietly hateful. When there's no violence or physical acting out, teachers may not notice or may choose to ignore it.

If you are the target of one or more girl bullies, you are in a lonely place. You probably feel alone in your hurt, and it may seem like there is no hope. But there is! No one needs to put up with being bullied—with punches or words.

Hagar: Take Action

I can do everything through Christ, who gives me strength.

PHILIPPIANS 4:13

Sarah chose Hagar to have a baby in her place. Then Hagar teased Sarah because she could have a baby and Sarah couldn't. Sarah became angry and treated Hagar badly. Hagar ran away to the desert. After Hagar fled to the desert to escape Sarah, God told her to return to Sarah, and she did as he asked. Years passed. Finally Sarah's promised child, Isaac, was born. After this, things went bad again. Hagar's son, Ishmael, made fun of his young half brother, Isaac. This angered Sarah, and she sent Hagar and Ishmael away.

Hagar and Ishmael went into the desert with food and water provided by Abraham. When the food and water were gone, Hagar began to weep. She was sure she and Ishmael were going to die. There was nothing to eat or drink, and they were all alone.

God came to Hagar and gave her two commands. First he told her not to be afraid. Then he told her to get up and take Ishmael by the hand, and God led her to a well of water. God provided for Hagar and Ishmael.

God will always guide you when you ask. There are times when you may need to pray and wait for an answer. But there are other times when you can provide part of the answer yourself. God has given you the knowledge and ability to do many things for yourself, and if you listen to him, he will give you the wisdom to know what to do. If Hagar had continued just to sit and wait, she and Ishmael would have died of thirst in the desert. But God told her to get up and take action. And she did.

Doing nothing about a problem will make you feel discouraged and defeated. Instead, ask God for wisdom on how to deal with your problems, and then take action.

thinking it through

If you've been letting a problem get you down, it's time to take action. God told Hagar, "Lift the boy up and take him by the hand" (Genesis 21:18, NIV). Sitting in the desert feeling sorry for herself wasn't solving Hagar's problem—the need for food and water. What is your biggest problem or need today? What resources has God given you to help you with that problem? (Intelligence, people you can ask for help or advice.) Ask God to lead you to the perfect solution.

thinking it through

If you ever feel alone or like you are an outcast, be honest with God about it. You can tell him how you feel and ask for his help. He promises never to abandon you.

This week look for someone who might need a friend. Is anyone eating lunch by herself? Is someone all alone during recess? Take a simple step toward friendship, like giving the person a smile or a compliment, and see what happens.

Hagar: No Outcasts with God

I will never fail you. I will never abandon you.

HEBREWS 13:5

After she was sent from Abraham and Sarah's home, Hagar felt alone. She was an outcast. She was sure she and her son were doomed.

Perhaps you feel like an outcast in your family, school, or church. It may seem people ignore or snub you. You might feel like you don't have many friends. Your days are spent doing homework in your room or watching TV by yourself.

The good thing is, there are no outcasts with God. He told Hagar to get up and take care of her son, Ishmael, because he was going to make a great nation from him. Isaac, Abraham and Sarah's son, became the father of the Jewish people. Ishmael became the father of the Arab people.

No, you won't be the founder of a nation like Isaac or Ishmael, but God does have an awesome plan for you. Today is just one small piece of the whole puzzle. The rest is yet to come. Like Hagar, don't accept being an outcast. Ask God for wisdom in how to make needed changes in your life. Look for his plan for you each day. The plan doesn't start when you are eighteen or twenty-one. It starts now.

Quiz Time

Are you living as an outcast? Take the quiz below to find out.

1. How hard are you on yourself?
   A. I know I make mistakes. Doesn't everyone?
   B. I have a large L for loser on my forehead.
   C. I'm almost always right, and I'm the best in all I do.

2. How do you feel about who you are?
   A. God created me in his image. I'm excited about the possibilities.
   B. God goofed.
   C. I have plenty of talents and abilities, not to mention a winning personality.

3. How often do you spend time with others socially?
   A. I'm in one or more clubs or activities.
   B. Does Facebook count?
   C. I run the school.

4. What do you do when you see someone alone?
   A. I make it a point to smile and say, "Hi."
   B. I show her my loser sign.
   C. I ignore her. I have enough peeps.

Give yourself 3 points for each A, 1 point for each B, and 5 points for each C.

Total __________

4-9 points: You might be spending too much time alone. Even if you enjoy a lot of time by yourself, you still need other people. Reach out to family and friends more. Consider joining a club, team, or other activity. There are a lot of ways you can make a difference in your corner of the world.

10-15 points: You understand that God created you and has a plan for you. You aren't perfect, and don't feel you need to be. You do things that make life better for others and make a difference in your school and home.

16-20 points: You seem to have forgotten that all your talents, looks, and personality are gifts from God. He created you in a unique and wonderful way in order to fulfill his plan, not your own. Take a few minutes to think about what his plan for you might include.

thinking it through

Have you been reluctant to follow God because you're afraid you'd have to give up the fun stuff you do now? Matthew 19:29 says, "Everyone who has given up houses or brothers or sisters or father or mother or children or property, for my sake, will receive a hundred times as much in return and will inherit eternal life." Why is it worth it to give things up for God? Pray and ask God for the courage to leave behind anything that distracts you from following him.

Mrs. Lot: Don't Look Back

Lot's wife looked back as she was following behind him, and she turned into a pillar of salt.

GENESIS 19:26

Lot and his family lived in Sodom. The city was filled with people living in very ungodly ways. The people were so wicked that God was going to destroy the city along with the city of Gomorrah.

Abraham begged God to save his nephew Lot and Lot's family. God sent angels to warn Lot that the city would be destroyed. He and his family needed to leave. Lot led his wife and his two daughters reluctantly out of the city. Even though the city was going to be destroyed, Lot's family didn't want to leave. They owned many things, and it was hard to leave them behind. But they believed God would destroy the city.

The first time he'd promised to destroy the wicked, God sent a flood. This time God rained down burning sulfur from heaven on Sodom and Gomorrah.

The angels had told Lot and his family to hurry, not to stop until they got to the next village, and not to look back. But Mrs. Lot didn't want to leave her old life behind. She loved the pleasures and lifestyle of the wicked city more than she loved God. Mrs. Lot made a big mistake. She looked back, and God turned her into a pillar of salt.

Jesus uses Lot's wife as an illustration to warn people about the end times: "Remember what happened to Lot's wife! If you cling to your life, you will lose it, and if you let your life go, you will save it" (Luke 17:32-33). Jesus warns people to leave their old sinful ways behind while there is still time.

It's important to decide now to follow Jesus. Once you do, look ahead. Don't be like Lot's wife, who looked back and longed for all she'd left behind.

Rebekah: Rebekah's Kindness

Before he had finished praying, he saw a young woman named Rebekah coming out with her water jug on her shoulder. She was the daughter of Bethuel, who was the son of Abraham's brother Nahor and his wife, Milcah.

GENESIS 24:15

Sarah had died. Isaac, Abraham and Sarah's promised child, had grown up but had not yet married. The Canaanite women around them didn't worship God. So how would Abraham find a wife for the son who would fulfill God's promise to make Abraham a great nation?

Abraham called his most trusted servant, Eliezer, to him. He told Eliezer to go back to their homeland and get a wife for Isaac. Eliezer loaded ten camels with gifts and supplies for the long journey. He was a man of faith, and once he'd reached his destination, he turned to God for wisdom in choosing the right woman. He set up a signal with God. Eliezer would wait by the well. This was the source of water for the whole village. When a woman came to the well, Eliezer would ask for a drink of water. If the woman not only offered him water but also offered to draw water for his camels, that would be the right woman to marry Isaac.

Before Eliezer finished talking to God, Rebekah came to the well to get water for her family. The conversation happened just as Eliezer had asked God. Eliezer asked for a drink. Rebekah drew water from the well for him and then offered to water his camels, too. Eliezer knew he had found the right wife for Isaac.

Drawing water from the well was no easy job, yet Rebekah gave water not only to Eliezer but also to his ten camels. Rebekah did this for a stranger, not knowing there was any special significance behind it. You never know what your kindness may mean to someone else. The things you do for others show your true character.

thinking it through

What if Rebekah had ignored Eliezer's request? Think about the last time your brother, sister, or parent asked you to do something, such as getting a drink or handing over something. What did you say? "Get it yourself." "Are your legs broken?" Try to do one act of kindness for someone each day for the next week. Play the yes game: every time someone asks you to help with something, say yes right away. Watch what happens as a result of your kindness.

Rebekah: It's Okay to Wait

Live clean, innocent lives as children of God, shining like bright lights in a world full of crooked and perverse people.

PHILIPPIANS 2:15

Most of what we know about Rebekah we learn from reading about the things she did and the way she acted. One of the few descriptions we have of her is given in Genesis 24:16: "Rebekah was very beautiful and old enough to be married, but she was still a virgin." Rebekah was both beautiful and pure.

All around you girls your age are already focusing on guys. They giggle when a cute guy walks by or hang around where the guys are sure to notice them. Some girls may pair off with guys before and after school, and some of them may have gone way beyond flirting and are already hugging, kissing, or more.

God planned for guys and girls to be attracted to each other. That is good and healthy. But he also wants you to keep yourself pure (Ephesians 5:3). Set your standards high. You don't need to kiss every boy you like, and they shouldn't expect you to. Boyfriends can change quickly in middle school and even high school. If you kiss each one, you may have kissed ten to twenty boys before you even graduate. It's better to wait and save those kisses for someone who is really special.

Why not focus on getting to know guys as friends rather than as boyfriends? Find out their hobbies and interests. Spend time talking. Sometimes middle school boys aren't big talkers, but if you hit on the right topic, they'll talk.

It's okay not to date or have a boyfriend in middle school. You may feel left out, but there's so much you can do with the time you might spend on the phone with or texting a guy. Use that time to make friendships that will last. Focus on following God and trust him to bring a special guy into your life when the time is right.

thinking it through

Don't get caught up in the girl-guy thing. There is a lot of time for that later. Instead, focus on the other relationships you have now. Pick three friends or family members and do one thing to make each of them feel special this week.

Rebekah: Go the Extra Mile

If a soldier demands that you carry his gear for a mile, carry it two miles. Give to those who ask, and don't turn away from those who want to borrow.

MATTHEW 5:41-42

Have you heard the expression "Go the extra mile"? Going the extra mile means you do a little more than is expected or required. Most people probably don't realize that the expression is actually based on a verse from Jesus' Sermon on the Mount, found in Matthew 5.

Jesus also told the story of the Good Samaritan, someone who literally went the extra mile. Not only did he stop and patch up a wounded stranger, he took him to an inn and even paid for his care. Sometimes it's easier to look the other way when someone needs help. That's what the others did in the story of the Good Samaritan. But it was the Samaritan who made the best choice when he not only stopped to help but also went the extra mile.

Rebekah went the extra mile too. She granted Eliezer's request for a drink, and then she also watered his camels. This isn't like giving a dog water, where you pour a couple of cups of water in the bowl twice a day and you're done. A camel can drink up to twenty-five gallons of water after a long journey, and Eliezer's ten camels had just made a five-hundred-mile trek. That meant Rebekah lifted pitcher after heavy pitcher of water out of the well. She didn't know Eliezer, and the camels weren't her family's camels, but she went the extra mile to do what she felt she should do.

Sometimes it's easier to look the other way or just do what's required, but it's much better to be like Rebekah and go the extra mile.

thinking it through

If a friend asked to borrow fifty cents for lunch, would you give it to her? Would your answer change if the person asking for money was someone you never talked to? What if the person asking for money was someone who made fun of you? Read Matthew 5:41-42 above. What does Jesus say about those who ask to borrow from you? Rebekah gave water to a stranger's camels. The Good Samaritan took care of his enemy. Ask God to show you how you can go the extra mile today—no matter who asks.

Rebekah: Be a Hard Worker

She is energetic and strong, a hard worker. . . . She is clothed with strength and dignity, and she laughs without fear of the future.

PROVERBS 31:17, 25

The above verses are from Proverbs 31, which describes what people often call the "virtuous woman" or the "wife of noble character." The chapter talks about the woman who has it all together. It describes Rebekah in many ways.

Remember the ten camels that may have drunk up to twenty-five gallons of water each? The milk jug in your refrigerator is probably one gallon. Imagine twenty-five of those each for ten camels—250 gallons. Now imagine Rebekah with a heavy clay pitcher lifting out that water and carrying it to the trough for the camels pitcher by pitcher. That was a lot of work.

Rebekah wasn't getting paid for the work. She didn't know Eliezer and had no idea his request for water was a test to find a wife for Isaac. Rebekah was just energetic and a hard and unselfish worker. She probably made the trip to the well for water for her family twice a day. She willingly multiplied that work many times over. God knew she would be the perfect wife for Isaac.

Do you rise to the challenge like Rebekah when there is hard work involved? Do you gladly take on extra jobs, or do you hope someone else will step forward? Sometimes when there is work to be done, everyone seems to disappear. You may take part in the choir concert, but do you help stack chairs and clean up afterward? You might enjoy a party, but do you help collect trash and put things back in place afterward? If you do those things, the words from Proverbs 31 will apply to you, too: "She is energetic and strong, a hard worker."

thinking it through

You probably have jobs you do to help at home, like washing dishes or taking out the trash. Do you tackle each job with a good attitude and plenty of energy? Make a chart with the days of the week written across the top and your normal chores down the side. Each day you do your jobs energetically and with a good attitude, put a smiley face in the right box. Think of Rebekah as you do these jobs each day. At least you are not drawing water for ten stinky camels!

Rebekah: Practice Hospitality

When God's people are in need, be ready to help them. Always be eager to practice hospitality.

ROMANS 12:13

After his camels were cared for, Eliezer asked Rebekah whose daughter she was. She identified herself to him. Eliezer asked her if there was room for him at her house. She responded that they not only had room for him, but they had straw and fodder for the camels, too. Rebekah showed hospitality to Eliezer. She welcomed him into her family's home.

What exactly is hospitality? The dictionary defines it as kindness in welcoming guests and strangers. Sometimes hospitality is hard to find today. People tend to look out for themselves. They are busy with their own needs, fulfilling their dreams and pursuing their goals. There is little time to invite someone over, cook a meal for extra people, or offer a place to sleep to a traveler. Hospitality is a lost art.

Sometimes people don't welcome others into their homes or go out of their way for others because their house isn't as big or fancy as some of their friends' homes or they are afraid of how their families might act in front of visitors. Maybe they fear that someone is just pretending to be in need in order to get something for free. These things can happen, but when we worry about it or assume the worst of others, we miss out on showing hospitality to those who really need help.

You don't own your own home, so you can't just invite others over, but perhaps that is something you can do as a family. Or maybe your family already occasionally invites a missionary family, a single military member, or the pastor and his family over. If so, make sure to take part by helping with preparations. Or maybe you can invite a friend from school or your neighborhood for dinner or invite the new girl at church to spend Saturday afternoon at your house. What you choose to do doesn't have to be fancy to be meaningful; it just needs to be from the heart.

thinking it through

Hospitality is simply kindness in welcoming a guest. We often think of it as having someone into our homes for a meal, and that is certainly one way of showing hospitality. But there are other ways too. You can show hospitality in welcoming others into God's house—your church. Or you can welcome new families to your neighborhood. Romans 12:13 says we should always be eager to practice hospitality. What is one way you can show hospitality this week?

thinking it through

Second Corinthians 5:7 says, "We live by believing and not by seeing." What is one thing you believe without seeing? Is there anything you have trouble believing without seeing? Ask God to help you step out in faith, like Rebekah did.

Rebekah: Stepping Out in Faith

"Well," they said, "we'll call Rebekah and ask her what she thinks." So they called Rebekah. "Are you willing to go with this man?" they asked her. And she replied, "Yes, I will go."

GENESIS 24:57-58

Eliezer went to Rebekah's home. He told her family that he had come to find a wife for Isaac, and he gave gifts to the family members. It was agreed that Rebekah would become Isaac's wife. Eliezer spent the night with the family, and the next day he was anxious to begin the long journey back home.

Rebekah's family asked that he give the family ten days before he took Rebekah home to marry Isaac, but Eliezer wanted to leave immediately. The family said it was up to Rebekah. They called her in and asked her if she would go with Eliezer right away.

Rebekah said, "I will go." She packed up and began a journey of faith to see the man she was going to marry—a man she had never met.

Her family had decided that her marriage to Isaac was a good plan, but Rebekah had to agree. She agreed not only to marry Isaac but also to leave the very next morning on a long trip through the desert. She took only her nurse, Deborah, with her. Rebekah packed and bid farewell to her family, knowing she would probably never see them again. Then she went with Eliezer.

It may have been scary for Rebekah to leave everything behind for a man she'd never met, but she trusted that this was the path God had for her. If Rebekah had not been willing to step out in faith, she would have missed all God had planned for her.

Puzzle Page

We've been learning a lot about Rebekah this past week, and we just learned about her faith in God. What does the Bible say about faith? Use the Box Code below to help you decode the verse.

Is this verse true about Rebekah? Why or why not? How can this verse apply to you?

Answer: We live by faith, not by sight. (2 Corinthians 5:7, NIV)

thinking it through

Do you know someone who perseveres during difficult times? Describe that person. What other character traits do you see in him or her? Can you think of a time when you persevered, even though you felt like giving up? Philippians 3:14 tells us to "press on," so let's keep going even when we feel like giving up.

Rebekah: Perseverance

I press on to reach the end of the race and receive the heavenly prize for which God, through Christ Jesus, is calling us.

PHILIPPIANS 3:14

Rebekah demonstrated perseverance. Perseverance means working hard and not giving up, even when you feel as if you want to quit. Maybe you know some girls or adults who persevere. These people know what they want to achieve, and they head for that goal—no matter what obstacles stand in their way. These are the people who are the achievers at your school, at your church, or in your family.

Rebekah may or may not have had goals for herself, but she certainly persevered. She accomplished her tasks, even if she may have been tired. She went to the well to get water for her family when they needed it. She drew water for Eliezer and then for his camels. After that, she invited Eliezer to stay with her family, which meant more work for her, as she probably cooked and did her other chores as well as helping Eliezer feel welcome during his visit.

A person who shows perseverance stands out from the crowd. The girl who perseveres will be the last one cleaning up after an event when everyone else has left. She's the girl who will clean up her room before watching her favorite TV show, even when watching TV would be more fun. She works hard to finish her math homework, not giving up when a math problem seems too difficult to solve.

Rebekah continued to work on her tasks even when she may have felt tired. She did what needed to be done—no matter what. Her perseverance made her stand out among her family and peers. Persevering even when times are tough will do the same for you.

Rebekah: Decision Making

Don't copy the behavior and customs of this world, but let God transform you into a new person by changing the way you think. Then you will learn to know God's will for you, which is good and pleasing and perfect.

ROMANS 12:2

Some people walk through life confidently and with purpose. Others ramble through life taking whatever comes. Rebekah was among the first group. Life did not pass her by while she was caught up in daily chores. Rebekah grasped an opportunity, and her life took on new meaning. She became Isaac's wife, and through their son Jacob, God kept his promise to make Abraham a great nation.

Do you want to go through life confidently and with purpose? Then you need to be able to make wise decisions just as Rebekah did. Not every decision is a major one. Some are as simple as what to wear. Others are a little more complex, such as what to do for your science project. Still others are major life decisions, such as which college to attend or which career to pursue.

Wait on the Lord, but don't just sit around to see what happens. Listen for his voice as you go through life. God promises wisdom when you ask for it. Then you will be able to make good choices.

Want to start making decisions that will lead you on the path God has for you? Let's pretend that it's time to sign up for a new club. Here are some ideas for how to make that decision.

- *Know what you want.* Do you want to do community service? learn new skills?
- *Collect information.* Get a list of the clubs that match you with what you want.
- *Write down the possibilities.* Look at the pros and cons of each.
- *Ask God for wisdom.*
- *Make your decision.*
- *Evaluate it.* After a few meetings, think about whether you made the best choice. Don't be afraid to change if it doesn't work.

thinking it through

Rebekah's choice took her five hundred miles from home and made her a part of Bible history. Where will your choices take you? What choices do you need to make this week?

thinking it through

You don't need to be overly concerned about your future, but it's never too early to start learning skills that you will use the rest of your life. What skills are you learning now that will help you when you move out on your own? (Cooking, cleaning, organizing, managing your money.)

Rebekah: Preparing for the Future

As the Scriptures say, "A man leaves his father and mother and is joined to his wife, and the two are united into one."

EPHESIANS 5:31

One of the first commands God gave was the command to leave our parents and be united with a husband or wife (Genesis 2:24). Adam and Eve had no problem obeying because both were created by God as adults and neither had parents.

Rebekah not only obeyed the command to leave her parents and live with her husband, but she traveled five hundred miles from home to be married to a man she'd never met. She left knowing she would probably never see her family again.

Right now marriage may seem far away. You probably haven't even gone out on an official date yet. You might still be hoping the cute boy at church will say hi to you in youth group or that the middle school basketball star will give you a valentine today. But the time will go faster than you think, and one day you will be old enough to walk down the aisle as someone's bride.

When the time came for her, Rebekah was ready to go. There wasn't a long engagement, and there was no wedding to plan. One day she was going about her daily life drawing water from the well of Nahor, and the next she was being asked to leave everything she knew to travel to another country and be married. She was ready and she went.

Rebekah was ready to be married because she'd already learned the important things at home. She'd been taught to love and obey God. She knew how to cook and take care of the house. She had probably been doing these things at a much younger age than you are now.

Fun times are important. But it's also important to think ahead and begin learning the skills you need so that, like Rebekah, you are ready for what the future holds—marriage, the military, college, Christian service, a career in sales, or anything else that's in your future.

Rebekah: Waiting Time

For everything there is a season, a time for every activity under heaven.

ECCLESIASTES 3:1

God promised Abraham that he would be the father of the Israelite nation, but many years passed before Sarah had baby Isaac. Isaac married Rebecca, and his offspring would carry on Abraham's line. But just like with Sarah, years passed, and no babies came for Isaac and Rebekah.

In Sarah and Rebekah's day, having children was a sign of God's blessing, and being barren (unable to have children) was a shame. In today's world if someone can't have a baby it is equally heartbreaking, but there are some medical options available to help them. They can go to a doctor who can perform tests and make a treatment plan. Sometimes it works and a baby is born, and other times it doesn't work.

But Sarah and Rebekah's only hope was that God would miraculously enable them to have children. They both gave birth, but it was in God's time. Why did God make both of them wait so long? We don't know. Maybe it was so their children would mean much more to them. Sometimes people value things more when they wait for them. Or perhaps God wanted to teach them to depend on him and grow in faith. Or maybe it was so that when a child did come, they would know he was from the Lord.

Waiting time is never easy for any of us, but things happen on God's schedule, not ours. We want to know the plan from the beginning, but God doesn't always choose to share it with us.

Maybe there is something you want. God might grant your request right away. He may deny it. Or he may ask you to wait. Waiting is hard, but it is never without purpose. Like Sarah and Rebekah, use waiting time to get to know God better, spend more time in prayer, and value the answer more when it comes.

thinking it through

God may not tell you his reason for asking you to wait, but you can be assured that there is a reason. Isaiah 55:8-9 tells us that God's ways are higher than our ways. Is that frustrating or encouraging for you? Why? Ask God to help you trust that his ways are always best.

thinking it through

Is prayer part of your daily life? Try one of these ideas:

- Set your watch to beep on the hour. Each time it beeps, pray for a different person.
- Each time the bell rings at the beginning or end of class, pray for the person nearest to you.
- Pick someone different to pray for each day of the week. On Monday pray for a teacher or coach. On Tuesday pray for a family member. On Wednesday pray for a friend, and so on.

Rebekah: Pray Every Day

Don't worry about anything; instead, pray about everything. Tell God what you need, and thank him for all he has done. Then you will experience God's peace, which exceeds anything we can understand. His peace will guard your hearts and minds as you live in Christ Jesus.

PHILIPPIANS 4:6-7

Prayer played a remarkable part in Rebekah's life. First, Eliezer prayed when he was sent to find a wife for Isaac. He asked that God would give him success that day. Then he spelled out for God the sign that would show him the right woman. Rebekah was prayed for even before Eliezer knew who she was.

After Rebekah was unable to have children for many years, Isaac prayed to the Lord for her. We don't know how often he talked to God about the problem or when he first began to plead with God, but the Bible tells us that Isaac prayed and God answered. Rebekah had not only one child, but twins!

There were probably many more prayers said both by Rebekah and for Rebekah than are recorded, but these are the two we read about in the book of Genesis. Prayer played a big part in the two most important events in Rebekah's life—her marriage and the birth of her children.

God wants you to pray about the big events in your life. It's not too early to start praying about the young man who might someday be your husband. Pray that God will help him keep his thoughts and his body pure. Pray for his physical safety and his spiritual growth. Pray that he is becoming a man who follows God more and more each day.

Pray about everyday things too—your class schedule, the piano teacher you can't please, your best friend, and your worst enemy. God cares about all of it.

Rebekah: Don't Play Favorites

Yes indeed, it is good when you obey the royal law as found in the Scriptures: "Love your neighbor as yourself." But if you favor some people over others, you are committing a sin. You are guilty of breaking the law.

JAMES 2:8-9

Rebekah gave birth to the first known twins, Jacob and Esau. Esau was born first and was hairy and red. Then came Jacob. He was grasping Esau's foot. As they grew up, their personalities were very different, just like some siblings today. Esau loved the outdoors, and he became a hunter. Jacob preferred to stay at home. Their father, Isaac, who enjoyed eating wild game, loved Esau best, but Rebekah loved her stay-at-home boy, Jacob, best. And that's where the problems began.

You may feel like your parents have a favorite child, but most of the time when it seems that way, they don't really have a favorite. They may just be giving your little brother more attention at the time. Or if your older sister is better behaved and gets more privileges, it may seem like your parents like her best.

But in the case of Jacob and Esau, each parent had a favorite. Isaac was drawn to the child who loved the outdoors and was often out on adventures. Rebekah favored the one who stayed at home. She probably spent more time with him since Esau was often out in the fields hunting.

You may tell yourself that you won't play favorites when you are a parent, but you may already be showing favoritism in other ways. When you choose to sit with one friend and ignore the others, that is favoritism. When you choose to hang out with the cool kids and ignore the shy or lonely kids, that is favoritism. The truth is, most people don't treat everyone the same. Don't think that's true? Be a people observer today and watch for signs of favoritism in your own life and in those around you.

thinking it through

In James 2:8-9, the reminder to love others as you love yourself is followed by a warning against favoritism. You show favoritism when you

- treat someone better because she is wearing cute or popular clothing;
- choose your friends based on their looks or possessions; or
- act friendlier when the people you want to impress are around.

It's not wrong to have friends you feel closer to than others, but don't treat people unkindly because of their looks or possessions. Today, ask God to help you love *everyone* as you love yourself.

thinking it through

Do you take initiative like Rebekah, or do you wait to act until asked?

Sometimes it's hard to know when to act yourself and when to wait on God. Always wait if

- the thing you are considering goes against any of God's laws (don't lie, don't steal, obey your parents).
- trusted adults advise you to wait or not to do it at all.
- you don't feel peace in your heart or a clear conscience about what you are going to do.

Stop, pray, and ask for advice from a godly, trusted adult if you are not sure about a decision.

Rebekah: Letting God Work

The LORD told her, "The sons in your womb will become two nations. From the very beginning, the two nations will be rivals. One nation will be stronger than the other; and your older son will serve your younger son."

GENESIS 25:23

In Rebecca's lifetime, the firstborn son got most of the privileges, land, and money. But God told her that the younger son would be honored.

Rebekah must have wondered why God chose to do that. She didn't mind, because her favorite son was the younger one. In fact, she took it upon herself to help God along. In this case, that was not a good thing.

Esau had already given Jacob his birthright in exchange for food. (The birthright gave special privileges to the firstborn son, such as authority and a bigger portion of the money and land.) It was time for the official blessing to take place. This is when Isaac would speak special words over Esau. Isaac was old, and he couldn't see very well. He called his oldest son to him. He told Esau to hunt some wild game and prepare it for him. Then he would give Esau his blessing.

Rebekah overheard this. She knew God had said the blessing would go to the younger son. Rebekah decided to help God out. She told Jacob to bring her two goats. She used them to make a stew that would taste like the wild game stew that Esau often made for Isaac.

Rebekah covered Jacob's arms, hands, and neck with the goatskins so he would feel hairy like Esau. She gave him Esau's clothes and sent him in to Isaac. Jacob fooled Isaac and received the blessing meant for Esau.

God's plan to have Jacob rule over Esau was now a reality, but it was done with deceit. Because Jacob lied, Esau hated Jacob and promised to kill him after their father died. Jacob fled from his home.

How would God have accomplished his plan if Rebekah hadn't stepped in and deceived Isaac? We don't know. But God is all-powerful, and the things he told Rebekah would have come true in his own timing.

Puzzle Page

Decode the verses in the puzzle below to read what Isaiah said about God's plans.

Directions: The words in the word bank fit into the blanks below. A number after a word means it is used that many times in the puzzle. The best way to solve the puzzle is to start with the longest words first. Then if you have many short words with the same number of letters left, you can fill them in by what words make sense in each blank spot. Give it a try.

anything	ways (3)	beyond	imagine	higher (3)	
far	could	heavens	thoughts (2)	just	earth

My ___ ___ ___ ___ are ___ ___ ___   ___ ___ ___ ___ ___ ___   ___ ___ ___

___ ___ ___ ___ ___ you ___ ___ ___ ___ ___   ___ ___ ___ ___ ___ ___ ___.

For ___ ___ ___ ___ as the ___ ___ ___ ___ ___ ___ ___ are ___ ___ ___ ___

___ ___ than the ___ ___ ___ ___ ___, so my ___ ___ ___ ___ are

___ ___ ___ ___ ___ ___ than your ___ ___ ___ ___ and my

___ ___ ___ ___ ___ ___ ___ ___ ___   ___ ___ ___ ___ ___ ___ than your

___ ___ ___ ___ ___ ___ ___ ___.

Answer: My ways are far beyond anything you could imagine. For just as the heavens are higher than the earth, so my ways are higher than your ways and my thoughts higher than your thoughts. (Isaiah 55:8-9)

thinking it through

Do you know anyone with a nickname or a reputation that came out of one mistake he or she made? Maybe you've never been able to live down the time you cut in line in the cafeteria or yelled at someone during youth group. Look at Isaiah 43:25 above. Ask God to forgive your sins, and then take joy in the fact that he chooses to forget them.

Rebekah: Everyone Makes Mistakes

I—yes, I alone—will blot out your sins for my own sake and will never think of them again.

ISAIAH 43:25

God made a promise to Rebekah that her son Jacob would become the family leader and serve as the firstborn even though he was the younger twin. Rebekah tried to help God along by deceiving her husband, Isaac. As a result, Jacob fled for his life while Rebekah remained with Esau and Isaac—who both knew about her lies and her favoritism toward Jacob.

Why did God allow Rebekah's plan to succeed? Because God can take our messes and mistakes and work them out for his good. Deceiving Isaac could not have been God's plan for carrying out his promise, because God's own Word says that lying and deceit are wrong. Yet he let it happen. In the end Jacob got the blessing meant for the firstborn, but no one won. Jacob had to leave home, Esau was bitter and angry, and Isaac probably felt betrayed by both Rebekah and Jacob.

Obviously it would have been better to wait and see how God was going to work, but sometimes in the middle of a situation we do things that are easy for us to justify. Rebekah may have thought she was helping God out.

Our mistakes and sins don't catch God by surprise. He can work through them. So if you make a wrong choice or fail in an attempt to do right, don't despair. Talk to God about it and then let him work. Rebekah was a godly woman with a human nature that allowed her to do wrong, but she was still a big part of God's plan to send his Son, Jesus, into the world in a human family so that he could live a perfect life and then die for our sins. Rebekah was part of Jesus' family tree.

Deborah: Helpers in Our Lives

They said good-bye to Rebekah and sent her away with Abraham's servant and his men. The woman who had been Rebekah's childhood nurse went along with her.

GENESIS 24:59

When Rebekah agreed not only to be Isaac's wife but to leave the very next day to make the five-hundred-mile journey to a new land, this decision didn't affect just Rebekah. Rebekah's nurse, Deborah, went with her.

We aren't told much about Deborah (we learn her name in Genesis 35:8), but we can assume she remained at Rebekah's side for most of Rebekah's life, including the twenty years that Rebekah longed for a child. She would have been present when Jacob and Esau were born and would have helped with their care.

As an adult, Jacob left and went to the land that Rebekah had called home years earlier. He stayed there for many years before returning to his homeland. Although we aren't told when Deborah joined him, she is with him on the return trip, so it is likely that she was sent to be with him and help care for his wives and their children.

Deborah was loyal to the family she served. She cared for Rebekah and Rebekah's children and grandchildren. When she died, the family mourned her death. Even though she was a servant, she was loved as though she were part of the family because of her many years of service to them.

Sometimes we overlook the "servants" in our lives. These are the helpers we would be lost without. They don't live with us through the years like Deborah did for Rebekah, but they do make our lives better.

Who are they? They are the maintenance crews who keep things clean and running. They are lunch ladies, bus drivers, and crossing guards. They are librarians and nurses. And many more. Pay attention to those who serve you and be sure to thank them.

thinking it through

How many of the people who help you do you greet by name each day? If you don't, make it a challenge to learn the names of the people who serve you and thank them for the difference they make each day. Every day this week, talk to a different helper in your life. It could be as simple as saying hello or thank you.

thinking it through

Jacob was looking forward to marrying Rachel so much that seven years of work seemed like only a few days to him. When there's a reward to look forward to, hard work is worth it and even goes by faster.

Are you dreading any hard work? Create a reward for yourself, like watching your favorite TV show only after you do your math homework. It will make the time go by faster too!

Rachel: Making Time Go Faster

Jacob worked seven years to pay for Rachel. But his love for her was so strong that it seemed to him but a few days.

GENESIS 29:20

Jacob and Rachel's story is a true love story. Jacob stole the blessing his father was going to give his brother, Esau, because he was the oldest. Esau was very angry because Jacob had taken not only the rights he had as firstborn, but now his special blessing, too. Esau said he would kill Jacob after their father died, so Jacob ran away to his mother's family. At the end of his long trip to his uncle Laban's home, Jacob stopped to ask some shepherds if they knew Laban.

"Yes," they said. "And here comes his daughter Rachel with the sheep."

Then Jacob saw Rachel for the first time. Jacob rolled the stone away from the mouth of the well and gave her sheep water. Then Rachel ran and told her father that Jacob had come. He stayed with the family, and after he had worked for Laban for a month, Laban asked him what wages he wanted.

Jacob wanted to marry Rachel. In those days a man would give gifts to the family of the girl he wanted to marry. Since Jacob had nothing to give, he said he would work seven years for Laban in order to marry Rachel.

Jacob worked the seven years, and the Bible tells us that they seemed like only a few days to him because of his love for Rachel. What a lesson that is for us today. Jacob worked for many years in order to marry the girl he loved, but it wasn't that difficult because his love for her was so great.

If you feel pressured to go out with a boy at your school or church, look at the story of Jacob and Rachel. Jacob was willing to wait seven years for Rachel, and he didn't even complain.

Rachel: God Works in Spite of Our Mistakes

We know that God causes everything to work together for the good of those who love God and are called according to his purpose for them.

ROMANS 8:28

God's promise to Abraham continues in Rachel. As we follow Abraham's family story, one thing is obvious: God works in spite of people's mistakes. Sarah made a mistake when she used her servant, Hagar, to have a baby in her place. Then Sarah got angry with Hagar, and Hagar and her son became outcasts. God still blessed and used Sarah.

Rebekah and Isaac made the mistake of each favoring one son over the other. As a result, Jacob had to leave home and go to his mother's family hundreds of miles away. Even then God was working, and he led Jacob to Laban's house. Laban was Rebekah's brother, Jacob's uncle.

Jacob met Laban's daughter Rachel and fell in love with her. He wanted to marry her. Laban didn't play fair, though. He substituted brides, and Jacob married Rachel's sister, Leah, when he thought he was marrying Rachel. He was allowed to marry Rachel when his wedding week with Leah was completed, but he had to work another seven years for Rachel.

Where we live today, it is illegal to have two wives, but that wasn't the case then.

Both sisters being married to the same man caused a lot of heartache and jealousy. Even then God was working. He chose one of Leah's sons, Judah, to carry on the line that would give birth to Boaz, Jesse, David, and eventually, Jesus. And Rachel gave birth to Joseph, who played a big part in the history of the Israelites.

When situations seem mixed up and hopelessly muddled, God still works. The lives of these Bible women prove it.

thinking it through

Do you share any of the same feelings the women you've read about had (jealousy, anger, favoritism, impatience)? Pray the following prayer, filling in the blanks as you go:

Dear God, I am having a real problem with _______ (feeling). Sometimes it causes me to make wrong choices like _______. I want you to work in my life like you did in the lives of Sarah, Hagar, and Rebekah. Take the bad situations and feelings in my life and use them for good. Amen.

thinking it through

You can trust God to bring good things your way when you are faithful in the small things. Do your schoolwork and housework, enjoy time with your friends and family, and ask God to show you his plans for you at just the right time. Does going about your daily life seem boring? See if you can remember a time when something good happened unexpectedly. Then thank God and look forward to the next surprise he has in store for you.

Rachel: A Job Well Done

Look, here comes his daughter Rachel with the flock now.

GENESIS 29:6

Rachel and Rebekah had one thing in common: When they met or heard about their future husbands, both of them were faithfully going about their work, not knowing that their lives were going to change. Rebekah was getting water for her family when she offered water to a stranger and his camels. Rachel was taking her father's sheep for water at the well the shepherds used when Jacob noticed her.

Certainly Rebekah and Rachel had thought about marriage. They both probably wondered what kind of man they would marry. Would he be handsome? kind? a farmer? a shepherd? But neither of them sat around waiting for Mr. Perfect to show up. They were busy with their daily work, doing what they were supposed to be doing when God brought them his choices for their mates.

What would Rebekah and Rachel be doing if they lived in our time? Would they gossip about boys on their cell phones? Would they text guys? Would they plan where to sit to get the right guy to notice them? Probably not.

If Rebekah and Rachel lived in our time, they would go about their work just as they did then. They would turn their homework in on time, do projects to the best of their abilities, and study diligently for tests. They would help at home and do their daily jobs without complaining or having to be reminded. They would trust God to bring the right guys to them at the right time. And those are things that you can be doing too.

Rachel: Comparing Sisters

When Jacob woke up in the morning—it was Leah! "What have you done to me?" Jacob raged at Laban. "I worked seven years for Rachel! Why have you tricked me?"

GENESIS 29:25

Getting married is one of the greatest events in life. Plans start months ahead with picking out a wedding gown, choosing colors, ordering flowers, selecting bridesmaids and their dresses, and planning a reception and honeymoon.

Jacob and Rachel's wedding didn't involve all that, but it included a seven-year wait. Finally Jacob told Laban he was tired of waiting for the wedding.

Laban prepared a wedding feast. The bride was probably dressed in flowing clothes with a headdress and veil. She was dressed this way when Jacob took her into their home to spend their first night together. How excited he must have been to be married. But when morning came, he saw he had married the wrong sister! Laban had substituted Leah.

Laban's excuse was that it was the custom for the oldest daughter to get married first. Laban said Jacob could marry Rachel after his wedding week with Leah, but he must work another seven years after that for her.

Where was Rachel when all this happened? We don't know, but we can guess that she was not happy with the turn of events. The man she loved and who had worked seven years for her was now married to her older sister. She was allowed to marry him, but Leah was his first wife. What problems this must have caused between the sisters!

The Bible doesn't tell us about the relationship between Leah and Rachel before Jacob came along. It does say, "Leah had weak eyes, but Rachel was lovely in form, and beautiful" (Genesis 29:17, NIV). It's possible that Leah was often overlooked, but Rachel turned heads as she went about her shepherdess duties. Comparing siblings can lead to a lot of problems, including jealousy, hurt feelings, and low self-esteem. If you have a sibling, you might know what that feels like.

thinking it through

Sisters often are best friends. But sometimes they can be rivals, too. If you have a sister (or a brother), how are you alike? How are you different? Do people compare you? Whether or not you have a sibling, remember these things:

- God created you in his own image with your own personality.
- God gave you your own set of talents and abilities.
- You are the only one who can carry out the plan God has for you. No one else can do it, not even your brother or sister.

thinking it through

If you are waiting for a special day or for something to happen, don't waste time sitting around daydreaming. Use the time well. Look at the ideas at the bottom of the page and put a check mark by the ones that interest you.

Ask God to show you the best ways to use your time, so you can do things for him *and* make the time go fast as you wait for the special day to arrive.

Rachel: Use Your Time

For everything there is a season. . . . A time to cry and a time to laugh. A time to grieve and a time to dance.
ECCLESIASTES 3:1, 4

Ecclesiastes says that there is a time for everything. Jacob and Rachel certainly found this to be true. They waited seven years for the big wedding—only to have the brides swapped. Instead of marrying Rachel, Jacob discovered that her father had tricked him into marrying Rachel's sister, Leah. So Jacob and Rachel waited until Jacob's wedding week with Leah was finished before they were married.

Someone once said, "Good things come to those who wait." That may not be true all the time, but in this case it was correct. Jacob and Rachel were united after a long wait.

Waiting is difficult. Just think about those last few days before Christmas. Endless. Or the week before your birthday. Can time go any slower? Or what about the countdown to summer vacation? Time drags as you wait for your family vacation or summer camp.

Are you waiting for something special? If time seems to be dragging, follow Jacob's lead and keep busy so you aren't focused on the length of time. The days seemed to fly by for Jacob because he was busy, and he had his eye on the end goal. Time will seem to go faster for you, too, if you use the time well and keep focused on the finish line. Here are some ideas for spending your time in waiting:

Keep a journal—either on the computer or in a special notebook.

Organize your special pictures, tickets, and other keepsakes into a scrapbook.

Join a sports team. Even if you don't think you are athletic, it'll still be fun to try and to make new friends on your team.

Try a dance or gymnastics class.

Volunteer at your local humane society, or volunteer with your family at your local soup kitchen.

Volunteer to help with younger children at church.

Quiz Time

re you like Rebekah and Rachel? Are you careful to do your work faithfully? Take the quiz below to find out. Choose the answer that sounds the most like what you would do in each situation.

1. Your grandmother is coming for a visit. Your mom needs extra help cleaning the house, getting the guest room ready, and preparing meals while your grandmother is here. You
   A. complete your regular jobs, then ask what else you can do to help.
   B. complete your jobs quickly so you can still have time to spend with friends.
   C. wish your grandmother had picked another time to visit. You are really busy right now.

2. The teachers are piling on the work. You
   A. do what you can and don't worry about the rest.
   B. get up a little earlier so you can get some of the extra work out of the way before school and have time to finish after school.
   C. use your regular study time but work a little harder in hopes of getting it all done.

3. Your piano recital is coming up. Your piano teacher is counting on you to perform first. You
   A. do your regular piano practice every day.
   B. put in some extra practice time so you perform your piece with excellence.
   C. relax. You already know your piece. No need to work on it anymore.

Score yourself:

1. A—5 points, B—3 points, C—1 point
2. A—1 point, B—5 points, C—3 points
3. A—3 points, B—5 points, C—1 point

Total ______

3-5 points: You do what you can get by with. You often leave things undone and hope someone else will pick up the slack. Put more effort in your jobs, and do work that you can be proud of.

7-10 points: You do what is expected at home. You turn your work in on time at school. Put a little extra into your work and make it stand out.

11-15 points: You take pride in your work. You give a little extra in everything you do, and that makes your work stand out. You are like Rebekah and Rachel.

thinking it through

Jealousy leads to bitterness. When your heart is full of bitterness, it's hard to keep your thoughts focused on following God. How do you get rid of jealousy? Philippians 2:3-4 tells us to be humble, thinking of others as better than ourselves. One idea for getting rid of jealousy is to try praying for the person you feel jealous of. When you honestly pray for someone else, you begin to see that person more like God sees him or her, and it's harder to feel jealous of the person.

Rachel: Jealous of a Sister

When Rachel saw that she wasn't having any children for Jacob, she became jealous of her sister. She pleaded with Jacob, "Give me children, or I'll die!"

GENESIS 30:1

Three women of God—Sarah, Rebekah, and Rachel—all with one thing in common: none of them were able to have children until God intervened and allowed them to do so. All three waited. Two felt terrible jealousy against others in their lives who were able to have children.

Why was it so important? Because having children was a sign of favor. If a woman didn't have children, people wondered what she had done wrong to be infertile. Sarah tried to solve the problem by giving her maid to Abraham to have a son for her. This was often done in those times. In fact, Rachel did the same thing.

Leah was able to have children and had four sons named Reuben, Simeon, Levi, and Judah. Rachel wasn't able to have children, so she gave her maid, Bilhah, to Jacob to have children for her. Bilhah had a son whom Rachel named Dan. Then Bilhah had another son, Naphtali.

Leah hadn't had any more children, so she, too, gave her maid to Jacob to bear children for her. Leah's maid, Zilpah, had two sons, Gad and Asher. Then Leah began having children again and gave birth to Issachar, Zebulun, and a girl named Dinah.

This was too much for Rachel. She pleaded with God for a son. The Bible says that God heard Rachel and remembered her and gave her a son. When Rachel gave birth, she said, "God has removed my disgrace." Until she was able to have a child, she felt shamed. She named her son Joseph. He is the most well known of all Jacob's sons.

Rachel's years of marriage to Jacob were good years, but they were also hard years because of the rivalry with her sister, Leah, and the jealousy they felt for each other, much of which had to do with giving birth to sons for Jacob.

Rachel: Sharing Her Family's Faith

Potiphar . . . realized that the LORD was with Joseph, giving him success in everything he did. This pleased Potiphar, so he soon made Joseph his personal attendant. He put him in charge of his entire household and everything he owned.

GENESIS 39:3-4

Rachel's firstborn son brought great joy to her and to his father, Jacob. To Rachel, Joseph was the sign of God's favor toward her. Together Rachel and Jacob planted the seeds of faith in young Joseph's life. They probably told him stories of the great things God had done for Noah, Abraham, and Isaac. They taught him to love and serve God.

When Joseph was still young, Jacob decided to leave his father-in-law, Laban, and move his family back to his original home. Rachel was pregnant with her second son at this time. Sadly, she died giving birth on this trip. Before she died, Rachel named the child Ben-Oni, meaning "son of my sorrow," but Jacob renamed him Benjamin, meaning "son of my right hand."

What a tragedy that Rachel died before Joseph became a great leader. Sold by his brothers into slavery, Joseph worked in Potiphar's house and God blessed him in all he did. Even Potiphar saw that Joseph's God blessed him and made him successful, so Potiphar put him in charge of his household. Because of this, Joseph was in the right place to help store up food so that people would not starve in the coming famine. He was able to be reunited with his brothers and to save his family.

Even though it seems that Rachel's life ended too soon, she passed a great heritage of faith on to her son Joseph. Jacob and Rachel loved and worshiped God, and that was nurtured in Joseph. He knew everything that happened to him was part of the plan God had for him. He did the things he knew were right and avoided the things that were against God's laws. Even in the most trying of circumstances, Joseph clung to the faith his parents had taught him.

thinking it through

Are your parents or other relatives passing on a heritage of faith to you? How?

Write a letter to your future children or to the next generation of your church. Tell them about your life right now and what you are learning about following God. You can begin creating a heritage of faith today.

thinking it through

The Bible says that God made each of us by hand, the way a potter makes something out of clay. He paid great attention to detail when he made you and each person in your family, and he doesn't make mistakes. If you're tempted to compare yourself to a sibling or anyone else you know, think of one thing that is unique about you and thank God for it.

Leah: Rivalry between Sisters

O LORD, you are our Father. We are the clay, and you are the potter. We all are formed by your hand.

ISAIAH 64:8

Genesis 29 introduces us to Leah with these words: "Leah had weak eyes, but Rachel was lovely in form, and beautiful" (verse 17, NIV). We aren't given a lot of information about either sister's physical appearance; instead we are given a comparison. Leah's "weak eyes" may mean that she had an eye problem, or it may just mean they had no sparkle; they were dull.

The problem with comparisons is that someone always comes out the loser. In this case it was Leah. Rachel was the beautiful one, and Jacob loved her. That wouldn't have been a problem if it weren't for Laban. He tricked Jacob into marrying Leah. So not only was Leah compared to Rachel, but they also ended up married to the same man.

Comparisons often lead to rivalry, and this was the case with the sisters. In Rachel and Leah's day, having children was desirable, especially if they were sons. Sons would help protect the family and land. They would carry on the family line. The rivalry between Leah and Rachel centered on having children. Leah had several sons while Rachel had none. Rachel was the wife Jacob loved best, but she was unable to have children for a long time. Leah was the unloved wife, yet she was able to give Jacob many sons.

How different this story might have been if Laban had not resorted to trickery to get Leah a husband! If Leah had her own husband who loved her, the two sisters might have been the best of friends, helping each other plan their weddings and sharing in all the good times. But as it was, their adult years were spent as rivals for Jacob's affection.

Leah: The Problem with Comparisons

Acknowledge that the LORD is God! He made us, and we are his. We are his people, the sheep of his pasture.

PSALM 100:3

Comparisons go as far back as Leah and Rachel—Rachel was beautiful, Leah had weak eyes—and comparisons are everywhere today. Just look at all the pageants that take place each year, everything from the competition at the local fair to the nationwide Miss America Pageant. These pageants are based on comparisons: Who looks best in a swimsuit? Who is the most talented? Who can give the best answer to an interview question? Just a few extra pounds or a bit of acne, and you are no longer in the running.

Weeks or even months before the pageants, young women are preparing. They diet, and some go as far as starving themselves. They get manicures and pedicures and walk around with bleach strips on their teeth. They practice the perfect smile and the perfect answers to practice questions. Why? So they will compare favorably with others.

There is nothing wrong with wanting to be your best. But there is something wrong with comparing yourself to others. In order to be your best, you take a look at your own talents, looks, and personality and decide how you can improve. But in the comparison game, you try to figure out how to be better than others. If you fail, your self-esteem suffers a blow.

God made you who you are. He gave you your looks, talents, and personality, and he wants you to do your best with them. It's not wrong to compete, but it gets out of hand when people compare themselves to others and do whatever they can to come out on top.

thinking it through

You are custom designed by God for a purpose. When you compare yourself with others, you aren't looking at the purpose God has for you alone. Instead of trying to be better than someone else, try competing with yourself. Can you run the mile faster than you did last month? Can you sing more enthusiastically in choir than you used to?

thinking it through

The book of Galatians says, "Let us not become conceited, or provoke one another, or be jealous of one another" (Galatians 5:26). That tells us what not to do. The verses before this one tell us that we should live the way the Holy Spirit leads us. When we do that, there will be evidence of God in our lives. Look up Galatians 5:22-23 and write down the characteristics you have in your life when you listen to God.

Leah: Avoid the Comparison Game

Oh, don't worry; we wouldn't dare say that we are as wonderful as these other men who tell you how important they are! But they are only comparing themselves with each other, using themselves as the standard of measurement. How ignorant!

2 CORINTHIANS 10:12

Can you imagine the conversations that must have gone on between Leah and Rachel?

"He loves me more."

"I gave him a child to inherit his land."

"I'm more beautiful."

"I'm the mother of six sons."

And on and on it might have gone. Or if it wasn't said aloud, you can be sure the thoughts were there.

In the verse above, Paul is telling the people of Corinth how ridiculous comparisons can be.

Playing the comparison game is wrong because of what it does to you—and to those you compare yourself with. By comparing yourself to someone who weighs more, is less attractive, or is less talented, you build yourself up. Pat yourself on the back too often and you might develop a pride problem. You may find yourself looking down on others you think are inferior.

If you are the one who is built like a pear, with wider hips when other girls look like straws, the one who has pimples while your friends have clear complexions, the one who can't carry a tune when your best friend gets the lead in the musical, then the comparison game is going to leave you feeling worse about yourself. You may resent those who come out on top.

One of the most important things you can do is to accept yourself as God made you. Be your own personal best, and don't compare yourself to others. God has an individual plan for you, tailor-made to fit you just the way you are.

Leah: Ignoring Comparisons

The LORD your God is living among you. He is a mighty savior. He will take delight in you with gladness. With his love, he will calm all your fears. He will rejoice over you with joyful songs.

ZEPHANIAH 3:17

It's good to realize that the comparison game is wrong and that your self-worth doesn't come from being considered better than others. But just because you know that, it doesn't mean everyone around you will come to the same conclusion. Rachel and Leah suffered from comparisons much of their lives, and the same thing continues today. In fact, people will still be comparing themselves to others and comparing friends against friends long after you are gone.

Girls especially have a tendency to compare. I went to school with a girl who would walk into the restroom where most of us gathered right before our first class of the day. She'd pause just inside the doorway and look each girl over. She'd note what clothes we had on and how our hair and make-up were done. She never said anything aloud, but we could all see that she was mentally comparing us and coming to her own conclusions. A few times one of us would ask, "Do I pass inspection?"

There will always be someone who picks up on your "flaws" and points them out for everyone to see. You can't control what others think or say about you, but you can control how it affects you. Does a nasty comment from a rude or stuck-up classmate ruin your day? It doesn't have to. Don't react, and some of the fun is gone for her. Others can say things about you, but they can't control your reactions to them. Only you can do that. Be confident in who you are, and let the unkind words and comparisons go right on by.

thinking it through

Sometimes there are things you can do to keep girls from criticizing your appearance. Before you leave the house, it's a good idea to make sure you are clean, your hair is brushed, and your clothes aren't wrinkled. But remember, even if you change your clothes or hairstyle, it doesn't change who you are on the inside. That's the real you.

Look at Zephaniah 3:17. God takes delight in you—no matter what other people say. Ask God to calm your fears about what others think and to give you courage to be yourself.

thinking it through

Are you feeling like Leah? Look up the verses below, and claim one as your own special message from God. Write it on a note card and put it on your mirror or in your locker where you will see it often. You might even want to memorize it so you can remind yourself of it often.

- Psalm 139:13-14
- Jeremiah 29:11-13
- Jeremiah 31:3
- John 15:9

Leah: God Cares

She soon became pregnant again and gave birth to another son. She named him Simeon, for she said, "The LORD heard that I was unloved and has given me another son."

GENESIS 29:33

Leah knew that Jacob loved Rachel. He had married Leah only because he was tricked into it. What did Leah do? She poured her heart out to God. Leah gave birth to a son and named him Reuben, meaning "Look, a son!" She knew God had heard her cries and had sent her the gift of a child.

Leah gave birth to a second son. She named him Simeon, meaning "one who hears" because God had heard her. Her third son was named Levi, meaning "being attached" or "feeling affection." Leah was hoping Jacob would feel bonded to her because of the children she gave birth to, but that didn't happen.

The fourth son was named Judah, meaning "praise." Leah said, "Now I will praise the Lord." After this Leah's servant gave Jacob two sons in Leah's place, and then Leah had two more sons and a daughter herself.

Leah was a victim of her father's deceitful plan to marry her to Jacob. She was unloved by her husband and the object of her sister's envy, but she learned to call out to God and receive all she needed from him. For Leah, God's answers came in the form of giving birth to children. This was a sign to her of God's love and care.

If you are feeling unloved or inferior, ask God to give you your own sign of his care, and be sure to thank him for the things he has already blessed you with.

Awesome Activity

We've been learning about the rocky relationship between Rachel and Leah, but sisters can be best friends. There are lots of things you can do together, including making matching purses.

Here is an easy way to make matching purses. If you don't have a sister, find a friend who can make a purse with you.

You need:
Back pocket cut from old jeans. You need both layers of the pocket.
Ribbon
Scissors
No-Sew glue. This comes in several brands and takes the place of sewing. You can find it in the sewing section of a store.

Do this:
Cut a piece of ribbon the same width as the pocket.
Glue the ribbon along the top of the pocket.
Cut another piece of ribbon long enough to be the handle.
Glue one end of the ribbon to each side of the pocket at the top.
Your purse is ready to use!

thinking it through

The writer of Psalm 27 says the thing he seeks most is to spend time in the house of the Lord, delighting in God's perfections. How could focusing on God's perfections affect the way you think about yourself? What is one thing you can do to focus your energy and thoughts on God and listen to him this week?

Leah: Handling Disappointment

The one thing I ask of the LORD—the thing I seek most—is to live in the house of the LORD all the days of my life, delighting in the LORD's perfections and meditating in his Temple.

PSALM 27:4

Because Leah was considered less beautiful than Rachel, she learned to depend on God for her self-worth. She poured her heart out to God and listened for his answers. She was able to praise God because he blessed her with children, a sign of his favor.

When you feel unloved or rejected, you can do one of two things. You can let the rejection and unkind words make you bitter, or you can let them turn you to God.

How do you turn toward God? Make room in your heart and life for him. In Mark 12:29-30 Jesus shared the most important commandment: "Hear, O Israel, the Lord our God, the Lord is one. Love the Lord your God with all your heart and with all your soul and with all your mind and with all your strength"(NIV).

Focus your energy and thoughts on what God wants for you. Listen for him to speak to your heart. Read his Word, the Bible, daily, and look for ways to apply it to your life. As you focus on God, the things happening around you will lose their importance. Sure, the cruel words will still hurt, but they don't change who you are. The teasing is unpleasant, but it doesn't change the plan God has for your life.

Take a lesson from Leah and don't let life's disappointments turn you bitter; let them turn you toward God.

Women of the Bible: Overcoming Obstacles

No, despite all these things, overwhelming victory is ours through Christ, who loved us.

ROMANS 8:37

As you read about Bible women, are you noticing some common themes? One thing that stands out is that all the women had problems, some of them heartbreaking or with no obvious solution. But each woman overcame her obstacles with God's help. Many times God intervened directly to solve the problem.

Often waiting time was part of the woman's life. Sarah waited years to have a child. She was ninety by the time it happened. Rebekah and Rachel also waited, disappointed year after year when no child came. Mrs. Noah waited out the Flood on the ark. Many of the women faced changes. Eve left her familiar garden home. Sarah moved twice. Rebekah traveled five hundred miles to be married. Rachel and Leah made the same five-hundred-mile journey to go with their husband, Jacob.

Whether the situation involved an inability to have children, a long journey, a new world, jealousy and bitterness, or being unloved, God worked through it. We remember the women for the problems they overcame with God's help.

You may be facing problems in your life. Perhaps your parents are getting divorced, or one of them is getting remarried and adding stepsiblings to the family. Maybe you have a disease your friends don't understand. Maybe school is hard for you, or maybe you are dealing with a bully. Maybe your sister is mean to you, or your best friend just decided she wanted to be best friends with someone else. These things are part of your life for now, but the ending is not yet written.

Stay close to God and ask him to give you solutions and help just as he did for the women of the Bible. He knows and cares about you just as much as he did those women.

thinking it through

Write God a letter about a problem you are facing right now:

Dear God,

Right now I'm having a hard time with __________. Help me to have patience like Sarah, courage like Rebekah, and strength like Leah. Thank you for loving me and helping me overcome any problem.

Your child,

____

Make this your prayer to God today. He will hear and answer. The answer may not be immediate or even the answer that seems best to you, but know God is with you and is working in your life.

thinking it through

It's easy to admit that we shouldn't behave like Potiphar's wife, but it's harder to follow Joseph's example—he did the right thing and was punished anyway, when Mrs. Potiphar lied to her husband. Have you ever been punished or teased for doing the right thing? Even if someone else lies, God knows the truth, and he will reward you. Ask God for courage to follow him—no matter what.

Mrs. Potiphar: Wanting Her Own Way

No one here has more authority than I do. He has held back nothing from me except you, because you are his wife. How could I do such a wicked thing? It would be a great sin against God.

GENESIS 39:9

Joseph was young and handsome, and he was one of Potiphar's most important men. Everything he did he accomplished through God's power, so he was successful in all he tried. Potiphar's wife noticed how handsome and successful Joseph was. She wanted to have a relationship with Joseph.

Joseph was quick to say no each time. Potiphar trusted Joseph and gave him more responsibilities and privileges than his other workers. Potiphar's wife was spoiled and selfish. She was used to getting what she wanted. She didn't know much about Joseph's God or Joseph's high standards. She was upset that Joseph would turn her down.

Potiphar was one of the pharaoh's important officials, so he was probably gone on business a lot. During those times, Joseph was in charge. One day when Potiphar was gone and no one else was around, Mrs. Potiphar again tried to flirt with Joseph. He told her no. She grabbed his cloak, and he ran away from her, leaving it behind.

Unable to accept that Joseph didn't want anything to do with her, she told her husband that Joseph had attacked her. We don't hear any more about Potiphar's wife after this, but we do hear a lot more about Joseph. He continued to honor God even in prison, and God continued to give him success. Eventually he became the second most important person in the land.

Potiphar's wife was all the things that followers of God shouldn't be. She was spoiled and selfish. She wanted her own way. She lied and tried to ruin Joseph's life when she didn't get what she wanted. Because Mrs. Potiphar had many bad character traits, she can remind us of what *not* to do as followers of God.

Shiphrah and Puah: Ignoring Orders

Pharaoh, the king of Egypt, gave this order to the Hebrew midwives, Shiphrah and Puah: "When you help the Hebrew women as they give birth, watch as they deliver. If the baby is a boy, kill him; if it is a girl, let her live."

EXODUS 1:15-16

You may not know Shiphrah and Puah by name, but you might know the story they are part of. Rachel's son, Joseph, ended up in Egypt, where God warned him of a coming famine, and the pharaoh, or king, put him in charge of storing up food ahead of time.

Many years passed. Joseph and all his brothers were dead. His family, known as the Israelites, had grown immensely. Now there were so many Israelites in Egypt that the new pharaoh, who didn't know Joseph's story, was afraid the Israelites would fight against them and take over the land.

To keep this from happening, he made the Israelites slaves. That didn't keep them from becoming greater in number, though. So Pharaoh ordered the midwives (women who helped deliver babies) to kill all the baby boys born to the Hebrew (Israelite) women.

Shiphrah and Puah were two midwives who knew they couldn't follow that order. There might have been other midwives who didn't follow the order, but these are the only two mentioned by name.

Shiphrah and Puah feared Pharaoh, but they feared God more. (We'll talk more about what it means to fear God tomorrow.) When Pharaoh called them in to ask why they hadn't followed his orders, they told him that the Hebrew women had their babies so fast that the babies were already born by the time Shiphrah and Puah got there to help. The midwives lied to Pharaoh because they knew they could not take innocent lives. That might not have been the best way to answer, but they did it with sincere hearts trying to honor God, and God blessed them for it. He kept them safe from Pharaoh, and he gave them families of their own.

thinking it through

What gave Shiphrah and Puah the courage to disobey Pharaoh's order? What do you think you would do if you were ordered to do something that went against your beliefs?

thinking it through

Read the verses below. What does each say about fearing God?

How joyful are those who fear the LORD—all who follow his ways! (Psalm 128:1)

He grants the desires of those who fear him; he hears their cries for help and rescues them. (Psalm 145:19)

No, the LORD's delight is in those who fear him, those who put their hope in his unfailing love. (Psalm 147:11)

Fear of the LORD is the foundation of wisdom. Knowledge of the Holy One results in good judgment. (Proverbs 9:10)

Shiphrah and Puah: Fear the Lord

Because the midwives feared God, they refused to obey the king's orders. They allowed the boys to live, too.

EXODUS 1:17

Shiphrah and Puah feared God. Does this mean they lived in terror of him? Some people say that to "fear the Lord" means to have a deep reverence for him. Others believe that when the Bible says to "fear the Lord," it means to have terror or real fear. The Bible uses more than one word for fear. The word used in the verse about the midwives is translated both "fear" and "revere."

God is to be feared because he hates sin, and he punishes those who disobey him. In the Old Testament he used some fearful punishments such as the ground opening up and swallowing people or fire coming from heaven to consume people. God is just and fearful, but he is also loving and was willing to sacrifice his own Son to save everyone from the punishment of their sins.

The midwives probably feared God's judgment if they killed innocent children, and they also had a deep respect for God. It showed in the decisions they made.

People don't talk about fearing, or respecting, God much anymore. His name is often used as a swear word, and few people acknowledge him as Lord. People who fear or respect the Lord stand out because they want to please God. They recognize that God is holy, and that he wants them to be holy too. They worship him and obey his commands.

You will probably never face a decision like Shiphrah and Puah faced, but you do make choices every day. If you choose to respect God, you will stand tall above the others. You'll be confident in your place as God's child. It's important to make choices that please God each day, and to ask him for help doing that. Choose to follow God and obey his Word above all else and you will be a truly exceptional person.

Shiphrah and Puah: Choosing to Do Right

Humility and the fear of the LORD bring wealth and honor and life.

PROVERBS 22:4, NIV

Shiphrah and Puah appear in only a few verses of the Bible, but they are remembered for honoring God. Even though most people don't recognize their names, history would not have been the same if they had obeyed Pharaoh and killed the Hebrew baby boys. Many of the children they spared grew up to love and worship God.

The midwives made a choice to honor God even though it could have meant serious consequences for themselves. You probably won't face being put to death for respecting God in your choices. But choosing to revere and fear God in all you do may lead to some criticism and unkind comments. Sometimes doing the right thing isn't popular.

There are probably students around you who swear, cheat, bully others, and act up in class. Yet they may be the ones who are popular. You might find yourself doing what is right but being alone. Maybe there is no one else to take a stand with you. It might be easy to join in what everyone else is doing to be popular, but you will know in your heart that you are making wrong choices.

Jesus was put down for doing right. People turned on him, and many even rejected him. What did Jesus do when this happened?

- He showed love and compassion.
- He was patient and kind.
- He forgave, even though the people didn't want his forgiveness.
- He was humble and a servant to all.
- He took time away to think and pray.
- He kept his eyes on the end goal.

It's hard to do these things when others hurt you, but you can make decisions that honor God, and you can respond to others in the same way Jesus did.

thinking it through

Have you ever made a decision or acted in a way you knew was right but others criticized you or didn't understand? How did you respond to them? Was it easy or hard?

Look around for Christian friends who will take a stand for right with you. If you don't know any, see if your school has any Christian clubs you can join. Try to find at least one Christian friend. If you already have some, thank God for them.

thinking it through

If you were to live by the four principles each day, what kind of difference would it make: in the clothes you wear? in the TV shows you watch? in the music you listen to? in the way you treat your siblings? in what you talk about with your friends? in your attitude toward your parents? in the way you spend your free time?

Shiphrah and Puah: Four Principles to Live By

Now, Israel, what does the LORD your God require of you? He requires only that you fear the LORD your God, and live in a way that pleases him, and love him and serve him with all your heart and soul.

DEUTERONOMY 10:12

When Shiphrah and Puah were working as midwives in Egypt, God had not yet given his people the laws that are recorded in the book of Deuteronomy. But they knew God and feared him. Today's verse pretty much sums up how they lived and how we should live:

- Fear God.
- Live in a way that pleases him.
- Love him.
- Serve him—not just outwardly but with our hearts and souls.

Can you imagine what a difference it would make if everyone lived by these four principles every day? Hatred would stop. Racism would cease. Terrorism would be a thing of the past. Wars would end. The poor would be given clothing and shelter. The hungry would be fed. Orphans would be given homes.

How about at your school? Everyone would be welcome to sit at any lunch table. No one would throw food or call people names. No one would cheat. Bullies wouldn't exist.

These things aren't likely to happen because not everyone acknowledges God. Even people who do believe in God aren't able to live by the four principles above at all times. But every time someone does choose to fear God, live in a way that pleases him, love him, and serve him, it makes a difference both in that person's life and to the people closest to him or her.

It might be hard to think of all four things all day, but make it a point to watch for chances to live out the four principles each day. What kind of difference would that make in your life?

Puzzle Page

Sometimes we let life's problems and disappointments get us down. What should we do instead? Solve the Balloon Puzzle below to find out.

Directions: Each balloon has both a scrambled word and a number in it. There are also numbers next to the blank spots in the verse. Look at the number next to the blank. Find the balloon with the same number. Unscramble the word in that balloon, and write it on the line. Check your answers at the bottom.

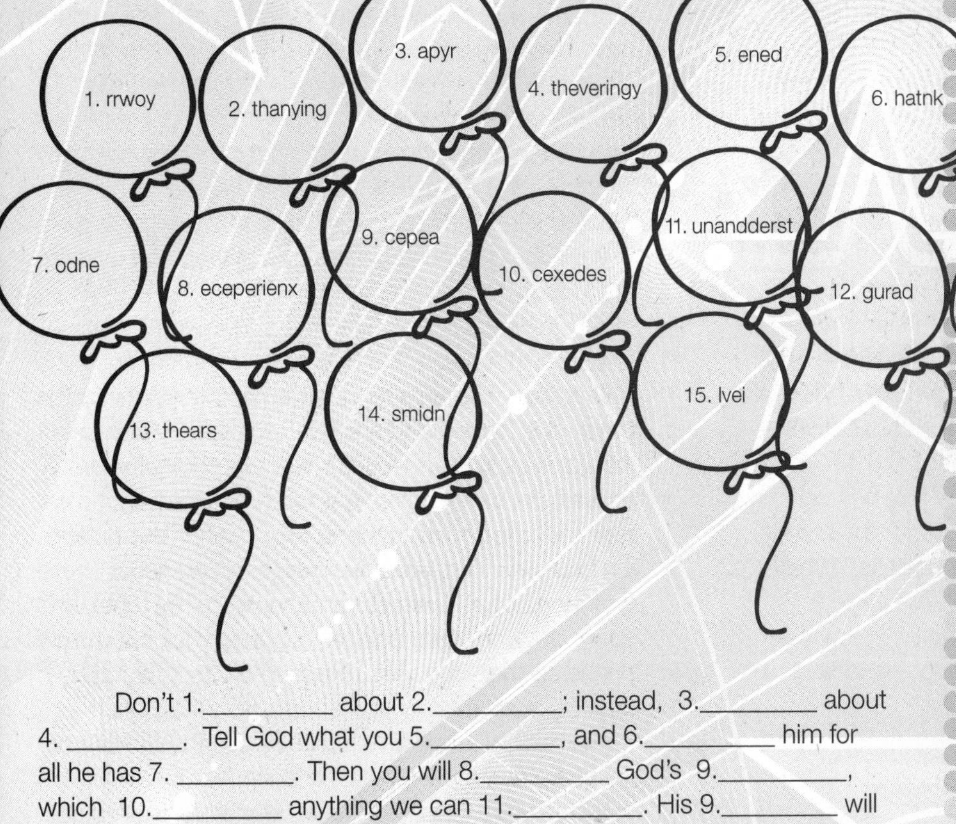

Don't 1.__________ about 2.__________; instead, 3.__________ about 4. _________. Tell God what you 5.__________, and 6.__________ him for all he has 7. _________. Then you will 8.__________ God's 9.__________, which 10.__________ anything we can 11.__________. His 9.__________ will 12.__________ your 13.__________ and 14.______ as you 15.__________ in Christ Jesus.

What can you do today when problems get you down?

Answer: Don't worry about anything; instead, pray about everything. Tell God what you need, and thank him for all he has done. Then you will experience God's peace, which exceeds anything we can understand. His peace will guard your hearts and minds as you live in Christ Jesus. (Philippians 4:6-7)

thinking it through

Shiphrah and Puah stood firm in their determination to do what was right. By sparing the Hebrew baby boys, they were serving God, and it made a difference. It's just as important for you to be busy doing what is good. 1 Corinthians 15:58 says, "Be strong and immovable. Always work enthusiastically for the Lord, for you know that nothing you do for the Lord is ever useless." What does this verse tell you to do? How can you do this today?

Shiphrah and Puah: Standing Firm in Your Choices

The LORD's plans stand firm forever; his intentions can never be shaken.

PSALM 33:11

Shiphrah and Puah had a choice to make: Kill the baby boys or honor life. Obey God or obey Pharaoh. The obvious choice was to spare the innocent baby boys. But that meant disobeying Pharaoh and facing severe punishment. They might have been killed for not obeying if they were caught.

You will face many choices in life. Some are easy; some aren't. And sometimes the choice comes down to whether you will do what's right or take the easy way out. You may think you will always choose right, but sometimes the choice is difficult. You might feel like you are the only one trying to please God and trying to stand firm.

Gayla was a sophomore in a public high school. All through ninth grade she had been lonely because she didn't fit in. Her values made it hard to relate to the other girls. When she started tenth grade, she didn't think she could handle the loneliness another year.

Gayla began to share her faith with Jenna, who sat next to her in computer class. Soon Jenna was attending church with her and decided to follow Jesus. Those two then began talking to another girl in the class, and soon all three were attending church, studying, and spending their free time together. Gayla now had two friends to talk to at school and to sit with at lunch.

It's hard to stand firm alone. Look around for other girls who share your beliefs and values. If you go to a public school, find out if there are any Christian clubs, such as Fellowship of Christian Athletes or Young Life, that meet at school. Try to find one other person who will stand up for what's right with you.

Shiphrah and Puah: Standing Firm against Life's Difficulties

Above all, you must live as citizens of heaven, conducting yourselves in a manner worthy of the Good News about Christ. Then, whether I come and see you again or only hear about you, I will know that you are standing together with one spirit and one purpose, fighting together for the faith, which is the Good News.

PHILIPPIANS 1:27

Shiphrah and Puah knew how to stand firm. Standing firm takes many forms. When my daughter Jasmine was a toddler, she would make her way to the edge of the ocean and then stand there as the waves came. A wave would wash into shore, and the power of it would knock her over. This happened again and again. She didn't have the strength and balance to withstand the waves. But as weeks passed, she learned to plant her feet and stand firm against the waves.

Just as standing firm kept Jasmine from being knocked over by the force of the ocean, standing firm can keep you from getting knocked over by the problems of life. Isaiah 7:9 says, "If you do not stand firm in your faith, you will not stand at all" (NIV).

Jesus also gave an illustration of standing firm. He said, "Therefore everyone who hears these words of mine and puts them into practice is like a wise man who built his house on the rock. The rain came down, the streams rose, and the winds blew and beat against that house; yet it did not fall, because it had its foundation on the rock" (Matthew 7:24-25, NIV).

If your life is built on Jesus' words and you are growing daily in your faith—learning more about how God wants you to live and acting on it—you will have a much easier time standing firm when the winds and waves of life come.

thinking it through

Sometimes the wind and waves in life can be pretty rough. They might take the form of feeling pressured to do something you know is wrong, getting left out, or being made fun of. What can you do to stand firm? When you have a relationship with God, he will give you strength to stand firm when the tough times come.

thinking it through

How can the armor of God help you stand firm like Shiphrah and Puah did? Which piece of armor can you put on today to help you?

Shiphrah and Puah: The Armor of God

Put on every piece of God's armor so you will be able to resist the enemy in the time of evil. Then after the battle you will still be standing firm.
EPHESIANS 6:13

How can you be ready to stand firm like Shiphrah and Puah did? Think of yourself as a soldier in God's army. Soldiers prepare for battle. They learn how to use their weapons, how to engage the enemy, and how to keep themselves safe. The same is needed for the battles in your life. When you struggle to do right, you can use the weapons God has provided.

What are they? Ephesians 6 lists them. God offers you

the belt of truth—Jesus is the source of all truth.
the body armor of God's righteousness—live in a godly way so sin can't sneak into your life.
for shoes, the peace that comes from the Good News—be ready to share the Good News about Jesus wherever you go.
the shield of faith to stop the fiery arrows of the devil—put your faith in God, and let him be in control of your life.
salvation as your helmet—God provided us salvation when Jesus died for our sins.
the sword of the Spirit, which is the Word of God—we can use Scripture to defeat temptation.

God gives you these weapons to help you live right and fight evil, but they'll do you no good if you don't use them. In Bible times, the Roman guards always wore their armor. The same is true for you. God equips you for battle—not a real battle but a spiritual battle. A spiritual battle goes on when you are tempted to sin, when those who are evil are in control, and when Satan and his demons are around.

Whether you are standing against the ungodly things around you or are engaged in a tough spiritual battle, the armor of God equips you so you can be the victor.

Jochebed: Faith in Action

It was by faith that Moses' parents hid him for three months when he was born. They saw that God had given them an unusual child, and they were not afraid to disobey the king's command.

HEBREWS 11:23

Jochebed was a woman with a problem. Her son was in danger, and she needed to do something about it.

It really all began when Joseph moved his family to Egypt to escape a famine, and the family stayed there for 430 years. As the years passed, the family grew in number—into the thousands and beyond. The pharaoh was afraid they would take over Egypt, so he made them slaves.

Still worried about the growing number of Israelites, the pharaoh told the midwives to kill all the Hebrew baby boys. When that didn't work, he said all the newborn baby boys should be thrown into the river.

During this time, Jochebed gave birth to Moses. She knew from the beginning that he was a special child and was destined to do great things. She hid him for three months, but then it became too difficult to hide him. If you have a baby sibling or you babysit, you understand this. Babies don't like to lie quietly doing nothing. So Jochebed made a special basket for Moses, waterproofed it, and placed it in the reeds along the edge of the Nile River.

You might know what happened next. The pharaoh's own daughter found Baby Moses and realized he was a Hebrew baby. She wanted to raise him as her own but needed someone to care for him until he was old enough to live at the palace. Moses' sister, Miriam, who was watching nearby, offered to get her mother to help. So Moses ended up staying with his own family during his earliest years.

Jochebed didn't know what would happen when she put Moses in the river, but she had faith that God was in control of all things. It was that faith that allowed her to keep Moses safe even if it meant giving him up.

thinking it through

What do you think of when someone says the word *faith*? Hebrews 11:1 says that "faith is the confidence that what we hope for will actually happen."

Jochebed knew she couldn't save Moses by herself. She needed God's help. Her faith in God helped her act. Has there been a time in your life when you did something with the faith that God would work things out?

thinking it through

We need to have faith that God will work out our problems, but that doesn't mean we should sit around and do nothing while waiting for God to work. What can you do to come up with a solution for a problem you're facing?

Jochebed: Plan B

When she could no longer hide him, she got a basket made of papyrus reeds and waterproofed it with tar and pitch. She put the baby in the basket and laid it among the reeds along the bank of the Nile River.
EXODUS 2:3

Jochebed had faith in God that caused her to act. The first thing Jochebed did was think of a plan. How could she save her baby boy? If he was discovered, he would be killed.

At first Jochebed hid him. She might have been hiding him in a stable or among the clay jars where she stored food, but wherever she had him hidden, it was no longer working. It was time for plan B.

We don't know how Jochebed thought of putting Moses in a basket in the river. Did she and her husband, Amram, sit around at night brainstorming ideas? Did God reveal it to her? Pharaoh ordered the baby boys to be thrown into the river. Maybe that is what made her think of putting him in a basket in the river.

Sometimes the best ideas are thought of in times of trouble. When there is a need for action, planning takes place. Ideas are created. Some are discarded; some are put into practice. This was true for Jochebed, and it's still true today.

Do you have a problem? Have faith that God is going to work it out, and then take action just as Jochebed did. Use the good mind God has given you to think through the problem and brainstorm a plan B, C, D, and E if necessary. Talk to the people God has put in your life who can give you advice. Then pray and ask God for wisdom. You'll want to tell him about the issues you face, and he'll help you come up with the solution.

Jochebed: Creative Solutions

They couldn't reach him because of the crowd. So they went up to the roof and took off some tiles. Then they lowered the sick man on his mat down into the crowd, right in front of Jesus.

LUKE 5:19

Jochebed's faith in God helped her come up with a good plan to save Baby Moses. Her trust in God led to creativity. Jochebed wove by hand a mini-ark for Moses made of long, flexible papyrus stems. She waterproofed it with pitch. After it had dried, she placed Moses in it and set it afloat.

Jochebed wasn't the only one whose faith led to a creative solution. One day as Jesus was teaching, people came from every village of Galilee and from Judea and Jerusalem. The house where they met was packed full of people listening to Jesus speak and watching him heal the sick.

A group of friends brought a man on a mat. He couldn't walk. The friends tried to get him into the house so that Jesus could heal him, but it was no use. The house was too crowded. The men knew Jesus could heal their friend if only they could get him to Jesus. Their faith led them to a creative solution. They went up on the roof, made a hole in it, and lowered the man down into the house right in front of Jesus. When Jesus saw their faith, he healed the man.

How's your faith? Does your trust in God help you make good plans? Does it help you think outside the box for solutions to problems? No matter what you are dealing with, whether big or small, take a lesson from Jochebed and the friends of the paralyzed man and put your faith in action.

thinking it through

Do you have a problem that needs a creative solution? Can you think of solutions you haven't tried? If not, ask a friend to help you. Make a list of ideas and pray about them together.

If you aren't facing any problems that need creative solutions right now, there are other ways to put your creativity to work. You might express your abilities by creating a new dessert, jazzing up an old pair of jeans with decals, writing a prayer to God, or making a greeting card for a friend. Think of one creative thing to do this week.

thinking it through

Psalm 56:3 says, "When I am afraid, I will put my trust in you." What should you do when you are afraid? The answer is simple, but it takes faith. Ask God to calm your fears and to help you trust him.

Jochebed: Courage to Take Action

Be strong and courageous! Do not be afraid and do not panic. . . . For the LORD your God will personally go ahead of you. He will neither fail you nor abandon you.

DEUTERONOMY 31:6

What scares you? Spiders? Bees? Thunder? Giving an oral report at school? Going to the dentist? If any of those things scare you, you are not alone. Those are some common fears people have.

If you could ask Jochebed what she feared, she might say it was having her newborn son killed by Pharaoh. Wow. That's one we don't have to worry about. But then again, maybe Jochebed wasn't afraid. Hebrews 11:23 says she wasn't afraid to disobey the king's command; she wasn't scared of what Pharaoh said he was going to do.

Why wasn't she afraid? Because of her great faith in God. She trusted God with her baby's life.

When I was in college, I had an assignment to work with a partner on an unusual project. One partner was blindfolded. The other partner led the blindfolded partner around the campus. The blindfolded partner had to try to tell where he or she was by touch and sound. This was to help us realize what it would be like to be blind.

It felt strange not knowing where I was. In fact, if I hadn't had a partner I trusted leading me, I might have been worried. Especially if I didn't know I could just take the blindfold off and see again.

Jochebed might have felt a little bit like I did with a blindfold on. She didn't know exactly where she was going, but she knew God was in charge. That gave her the courage to take action to save her baby boy. Trusting God can give you courage to face the hard things in your life too.

Quiz Time

e've been learning how Jochebed dealt with her big problem. How well are you dealing with a problem in your life? Take the quiz below to find out.

1. Your best friend isn't talking to you. You see her look at you and then whisper to another girl. You
   A. have another friend ask her what is going on.
   B. ignore her. Whatever happened will blow over in a few days.
   C. call her after school and ask her if you did something to upset her.

2. Tryouts for the Easter musical are next week. You don't think you sing well enough to get a good role, but your grandma is coming for Easter and assumes you will be in the program. You don't want to disappoint her. You
   A. have your mom tell her that you aren't going to be in it.
   B. pretend to be sick the day of tryouts. Then you have an excuse for not being in the program.
   C. give it a try. Even if you don't get one of the big roles, you may get a small part, and you can do your best with it.

3. It's the night before science projects are due, and your real-life erupting volcano blows up! You
   A. have your dad write a note to the teacher explaining what happened.
   B. don't turn in a project. There's not enough time to redo it.
   C. take in your report and display board complete with pictures of the aftermath of the eruption. The volcano worked!

How did you do?

Mostly A's: You have other people solve your problems for you. It's okay to get assistance, but with God's help, you can work through the problem yourself.

Mostly B's: Avoiding problems doesn't make them go away. Sometimes it even makes them worse. Ask someone to brainstorm possible solutions with you and then choose the best one and act on it.

Mostly C's: You try to solve your problems by seeing what needs to be done and doing it. You realize that things don't always turn out like you want, but it's still important to step out in faith and give it a try.

thinking it through

The book of Proverbs has a lot to say about the wisdom of being a hard worker. Read the following verses. How might they motivate you to work hard this week?

Lazy people are soon poor; hard workers get rich. A wise youth harvests in the summer, but one who sleeps during harvest is a disgrace. (Proverbs 10:4-5)

A hard worker has plenty of food, but a person who chases fantasies has no sense. (Proverbs 12:11)

Work hard and become a leader; be lazy and become a slave. (Proverbs 12:24)

Jochebed: Willingness to Work Hard

She is energetic and strong, a hard worker.

PROVERBS 31:17

We aren't given many details in the story of Jochebed preparing a basket for Baby Moses and getting him safely to the river. How long did it take her and her family to gather the papyrus? How long did it take her to weave the basket? What was she thinking during that time?

The story may not give us details, but it does show us that Jochebed was not only creative and strong in her faith, but she was hardworking as well. When she needed to act, she didn't shy away from the work. She went about doing her daily tasks of feeding and caring for her family and then put her plan for Moses into place on top of everything else.

Many Bible women shared a willingness to work hard. Mrs. Noah helped Noah gather food and animals for the ark. Rebekah went to the well for water for her family. Rachel took the family flock of sheep to water. Shiphrah and Puah helped women in childbirth.

Being willing to work hard is a good quality to have. It will help you at home as you do your share of the work, and it will help you later as you go to high school and college, get a job, and maybe get married someday. Some people are known for their laziness. They disappear when work needs to be done or leave the work for others. Other people are known for their hard work, such as Rebekah, Rachel, and Bible women you'll read about in weeks to come. Which group are you a part of?

Jochebed: Sacrificing for God's Plan

Later, when the boy was older, his mother brought him back to Pharaoh's daughter, who adopted him as her own son. The princess named him Moses, for she explained, "I lifted him out of the water."
EXODUS 2:10

Only a strong faith in God would allow Jochebed to give up her child not once but twice. First Jochebed gave Moses up when she placed him in the floating basket in the river, trusting that God would look out for him and keep him safe. She sent Miriam, Moses' older sister, to keep watch and see how God would work.

Moses was given back to Jochebed for her to raise him until he was old enough to live at the palace. Jochebed used these years to teach Moses about God and instill her strong faith in him. Then Jochebed gave her son up a second time when he went to live in Pharaoh's palace.

How could Jochebed give up her son? She knew he was a child of destiny. When she released him, she realized she was giving him over to God's work. Jochebed didn't know what God's plan was for Moses, but she believed God had a plan and that everything that was happening was part of it.

It's never easy to make sacrifices, especially when we aren't sure of the outcome, but this is exactly what Jochebed did. Her faith in God was strong enough for her to surrender her son to God's work.

God may ask you to sacrifice something in order to fulfill his plans for you. Maybe there is a friend he wants you to give up. Or perhaps he has a different college in mind from the one you choose down the road. He might want you to give up your dream career for a different one. The important thing to remember is that when God asks you to give something up, he always has something much better in mind for you.

thinking it through

Have you ever felt God was asking you to give something up or to do something hard? How did you respond? How does a strong faith in God and knowing that God has a plan for your life affect your decisions?

thinking it through

Each act of kindness you do touches someone. Go outside and find three stones. With a marker, write on each stone one small thing you can do to make a difference in someone's life. Keep the stones in your room to remind you to perform your small acts of kindness this week. At the end of the week, find a pond, stream, or puddle you can drop the stones into. Watch the ripples they create. That's the effect your kindness will have on others!

Jochebed: Ripples

The way you live will always honor and please the Lord, and your lives will produce every kind of good fruit. All the while, you will grow as you learn to know God better and better.

COLOSSIANS 1:10

Have you ever thrown a pebble in a pond? What did it do? It sent out ripples that moved farther and farther from the place the pebble landed. And that's how it was with Jochebed's influence.

Even though we don't know much about Jochebed herself, we do know about her three children. Miriam was the firstborn. She watched over Moses when he was in the river. Her quick thinking and actions resulted in Moses' being cared for by his own mother. Miriam was also helpful during the years the Israelites wandered in the wilderness after they left Egypt. She was a musician and led the women in a song of victory after God delivered the Israelites from Pharaoh's army. (We'll talk more about Miriam in a few days.)

Aaron was the second born. He became the first high priest of Israel. Aaron went with Moses as spokesman to ask the pharaoh to free the Israelite slaves. He was Moses' right-hand man during the years of wandering in the wilderness.

Moses, the youngest, was God's choice for leading the Israelites out of slavery. Even though he lived in Pharaoh's palace, he didn't join in worshiping false gods and living as a pagan. He stayed true to God, as he was taught in his earliest years. Jochebed's influence stayed with him all his life, even though he spent most of his youth in the palace.

Jochebed had a strong influence on her children, and that influence extended throughout history because of the things her children accomplished. You may not feel like you are accomplishing much right now, but you never know what kind of difference you may make in a person's life. That simple act of kindness, friendship, or a helping hand may start a ripple effect in someone's life.

Pharaoh's Daughter: Acting out of Compassion

When the princess opened [the basket], she saw the baby. The little boy was crying, and she felt sorry for him. "This must be one of the Hebrew children," she said.

EXODUS 2:6

The pharaoh's daughter was walking along the riverbank when she spotted something in the water. It was a tiny floating basket. When she looked into it, she realized she was looking at a Hebrew baby boy—a child who, according to her father, should be thrown into the river and drowned. The princess felt compassion for the baby and decided to keep him.

The pharaoh's daughter certainly didn't have to show compassion for Moses. She could have followed her father's wishes and had the Hebrew boy killed. But she didn't. Not only did she spare his life, but she took him home to raise as her own son. She lived in the palace with her father, who had ordered the babies killed, which meant Moses would grow up in the house of the man who had ordered Moses' own death. Can you imagine how the pharaoh reacted to the news that his daughter was going to raise a Hebrew child?

The princess's compassion led her to act in kindness as she delivered Moses from the river, and in courage as she took into the palace one of the children her father had ordered to be killed. What does your compassion lead you to do?

Here are some ideas:

Donate nice outgrown clothing to a homeless shelter.
Buy a baby item for a pregnancy center.
Collect canned food from your neighbors for a local food bank.
Ask your parents for ways you can raise money and sponsor a child through World Vision, Compassion International, or another program.
Invite a new student or one who is often alone to sit with you at lunch or to come over after school.

thinking it through

The princess's compassion led her to rescue Moses and take care of him. She met his immediate needs by getting someone to care for him until he was old enough to live at the palace. Then she raised him as her own. What could your compassion lead you to do? Look at the list of ideas, and choose one of them to try this week.

thinking it through

How can you be courageous, obedient, patient, and responsible in your life? Ask God to show you how you can follow Miriam's example.

Miriam: Four Good Character Traits

The baby's sister then stood at a distance, watching to see what would happen to him.

EXODUS 2:4

When we first meet Miriam, it is in the role of big sister. In an attempt to keep three-month-old Moses safe, his mother, Jochebed, placed him in a waterproof basket at the edge of the Nile River. Miriam hid nearby to see what would happen to her brother. Most Bible scholars believe that Miriam was between seven and twelve years old at this time, although a few say she was younger and a few say she was much older.

However old Miriam was, she was quick thinking. When the pharaoh's daughter found Moses, Miriam approached her and offered to find someone to nurse the baby for her. Then she went and got her own mother.

Even though this is all we are told about Miriam's childhood, it gives us clues to who Miriam was.

- She was *courageous* to stay and watch Moses and then to approach the princess.
- She was *obedient* in watching over Moses.
- She was *patient*. The Bible doesn't tell us how long Moses was in the river before the princess came along, but Miriam was content to wait and watch.
- She was *responsible*. She knew it was her job to wait and watch, and that is exactly what she did.

Miriam: Being Responsible

Am I my brother's keeper?

GENESIS 4:9, NIV

"Am I my brother's keeper?" These words were spoken by Cain to God when God asked Cain where Abel was. The truth was, Cain had killed Abel. God knew it, but he asked Cain anyway.

The answer to the question "Am I my brother's keeper" is often *yes*. Miriam was definitely her brother's keeper. She stood watch over him to see how God would work and protect her baby brother.

If you have younger siblings, there may be times when you need to watch them while your mom prepares dinner, or you might be the one to help your sister with her math homework. Maybe your brother bugs you constantly to play a game with him or help him with the computer. Although you might find these things annoying at the time, they give you the chance to have a positive influence on a younger brother's or sister's life.

Helping with younger siblings also gives you the chance to develop and demonstrate responsibility just as Miriam did. Each time you do a task without being told, do a job to the best of your ability, or follow through on a commitment, you show those around you that you can be trusted.

If you show you are responsible in the little tasks, you will find people trust you with bigger things. And if people trust you, you will probably have more privileges along with more responsibility.

thinking it through

Which of the tasks below do you do that show you are responsible?

- I turn in my completed homework every day.
- I follow the rules even if the teacher steps out of the room for a minute.
- I do my jobs at home every day.
- I can be counted on to do what I say.
- I can be counted on by my parents to help out.

Do all of the sentences above describe you? If not, pick one to work on this week.

thinking it through

Aren't sure God really has a plan for you? Does it sometimes seem like nothing is going right? Psalm 138:8 says that God will work out his plans for your life. How can Psalm 138:8 encourage you today?

Miriam: Families Are God's Idea

Father to the fatherless, defender of widows—this is God, whose dwelling is holy. God places the lonely in families.

PSALM 68:5-6

Families are God's idea. He put Miriam, Aaron, and Moses in the exact family they needed to be in, in order to be safe during a hard time in Jewish history. God knew which parents and siblings needed to be together.

Jochebed was the mom Moses needed to think of a plan for his safety. She was the one who taught Miriam to be brave and responsible in her early years. Jochebed raised three children who were leaders and made a mark on the Israelite nation.

God placed Amram, Jochebed, Miriam, Aaron, and Moses together in what was the best family for each of them. The same is true for your family too. God chose the parents, brothers, and sisters he wanted you to have.

You might look at your family and feel that God made a mistake. How could this be the best family for you when your parents argue about how the other person spent money or who was supposed to buy the milk? Does God understand that you and your siblings fight over who chooses the TV show, walks the dog, or does the dishes? He does. There are no perfect families. Each family has strengths and weaknesses.

Your family is where you learn what you need to know to be a successful adult. The experiences you have are what make you who you are. Even if it seems your family has more than its share of problems, remember that this is only the beginning of your life. The end is not yet written. God holds the plan for you. He knows all about you and your family, and he will work out his plan for you.

Puzzle Page

God has good plans for our lives! Decode the Telephone Puzzle below to read what the psalmist wrote about God's plan for his life.

Directions: This puzzle has two numbers under each line. The first number is for the phone button. Only button numbers 2-9 have letters on them. The second number tells which letter on the button to use. All the buttons except 7 and 9 have three letters on them. Numbers 7 and 9 have four letters. Look under the first line. You see 8.1. That means button #8. Then choose the first letter on that button. That is T. Write it on the line. Finish the puzzle, and check your answer below.

1
2 ABC
3 DEF
4 GHI
5 JKL
6 MNO
7 PQRS
8 TUV
9 WXYZ
*
0 OPER
#

____ ____ ____ LORD ____ ____ ____ ____ ____ ____ ____ ____
8.1 4.2 3.2 9.1 4.3 5.3 5.3 9.1 6.3 7.3 5.2

____ ____ ____ his ____ ____ ____ ____ ____ ____ ____ ____
6.3 8.2 8.1 7.1 5.3 2.1 6.2 7.4 3.3 6.3 7.3

my ____ ____ ____ ____—for ____ ____ ____ ____
5.3 4.3 3.3 3.2 9.3 6.3 8.2 7.3

____ ____ ____ ____ ____ ____ ____ ____ ____ ____ ____ ____,
3.3 2.1 4.3 8.1 4.2 3.3 8.2 5.3 5.3 6.3 8.3 3.2

____ LORD, ____ ____ ____ ____ ____ ____ ____ forever. Don't
6.3 3.2 6.2 3.1 8.2 7.3 3.2 7.4

____ ____ ____ ____ ____ ____ ____ ____ ____, ____ ____ ____
2.1 2.2 2.1 6.2 3.1 6.3 6.2 6.1 3.2 3.3 6.3 7.3

____ ____ ____ ____ ____ ____ ____ ____ ____.
9.3 6.3 8.2 6.1 2.1 3.1 3.2 6.1 3.2

Answer: The LORD will work out his plans for my life—for your faithful love, O LORD, endures forever. Don't abandon me, for you made me. (Psalm 138:8)

Miriam: Birth Order

Always be humble and gentle. Be patient with each other, making allowance for each other's faults because of your love. Make every effort to keep yourselves united in the Spirit, binding yourselves together with peace.

EPHESIANS 4:2-3

Miriam watched over Moses because she was the older sister. Birth order plays an important part in family life. Birth order is pretty easy to figure out if there are only two or three children in the family. You are either the oldest, middle, or youngest child. It's more complicated if there are stepchildren or adopted children, an oldest child with special needs, a large age gap between children, or twins or triplets.

While there is no set way in which all oldest, middle, or youngest children act, there are some general characteristics, advantages, and disadvantages that are shared by birth position.

As the firstborn, you had your parents to yourself, at least for a short time. You may get more privileges and responsibilities. Since you were the first, your parents didn't have experience in parenting. They may overprotect you or have unrealistic expectations for you. You may be responsible, goal oriented, and motivated.

As the middle child, you don't get to be the first to do things. You have to share your parents' attention with the older child. Your parents are more realistic about what to expect. You might try to be completely different from your older sibling and create ways to stand out in your family. You may be easygoing and spontaneous.

If you're the youngest child, your parents are more relaxed in their parenting. You have less parental attention, but you have older siblings to copy and who can help you out. If you feel you are living in your siblings' shadows, you might find ways to get attention, such as being charming or clowning around. Youngest children might be accepting, easygoing, and attention seeking.

Each birth order position has its own good and bad points. The important thing is to do your best whether you are the first, middle, or youngest child.

thinking it through

How many children are in your family? What number are you? Do you fit the descriptions to the right? Why or why not?

Look at Ephesians 4:2-3. No matter where you fall in the birth order (or if you're an only child), there are challenges about being you. Family members need to overlook your faults as much as you need to overlook theirs. Think about this verse as you interact with your family members this week. Try to be humble and gentle, and show them love.

Miriam: Sibling Squabbles

Since God chose you to be the holy people he loves, you must clothe yourselves with tenderhearted mercy, kindness, humility, gentleness, and patience. Make allowance for each other's faults, and forgive anyone who offends you. Remember, the Lord forgave you, so you must forgive others.

COLOSSIANS 3:12-13

We aren't told much about Miriam, Aaron, and Moses as children. Until Moses went to live at the palace, they were probably pretty much like any other siblings. They knew their family was special because God had kept Moses safe, but they were also normal children and probably had their share of sibling squabbles. Perhaps Miriam was a little too bossy at times. Or maybe Aaron ran off to play without doing his share of the chores.

All siblings have squabbles, even Bible siblings. The fights are caused by a lot of things:

- Too much togetherness—you share a room and have to listen to your sister on the phone with all her friends, or you have to pick up her clothes from your side of the room.
- Territorial rights—your sibling invades your space or privacy or takes your things.
- Attention seeking—you and your siblings all want your parents' attention.
- Competition—one sibling gets a privilege or reward the others don't; one seems to be treated better than the others or has more friends or talents.
- Anger or bad moods—if things go wrong at school, it's easy to take them out on your family. An F on a math test can cause you to pick a fight later.
- Hunger or tiredness—if you come home hungry and tired from a sports practice or you're burned out from school, you are more likely to fight. That's why many fights take place right before supper.

Sibling squabbles are normal, but it's good to avoid them when you can.

thinking it through

Do any of the things listed at the lower left lead to arguments or fights between you and your siblings? If you don't have siblings, then between you and your closest friends? Which one causes most of the fights? What are some things you could do to help solve fights?

thinking it through

Memorize Romans 12:18 and say it to yourself every day so that when you encounter an argument, you'll be reminded to look for the peaceful way out. The next time a squabble starts, try some of the ideas to the right, and look for the best way to end disagreements so that everyone wins.

Miriam: Keeping Fights Fair

Do all that you can to live in peace with everyone.
ROMANS 12:18

We can learn a lot about families by reading about Bible characters such as Miriam and her siblings. There is more ahead about how they got along as adults.

Yesterday you looked at some things that might cause problems between you and your siblings (or close friends if you don't have siblings). Hopefully you thought about a way to avoid some of the squabbles that happen. But you probably won't avoid them all. The important thing is to fight fair when you do end up in a disagreement. Fair fighting keeps people from getting hurt.

Here are some rules for a fair fight.

- Be respectful. Don't call the other person names or use cut downs. Slamming each other with words won't lead to a positive solution.
- Be safe. Don't kick, hit, bite, or pull hair. If you get angry, walk away. Go shoot baskets and then come back to the problem.
- Attack the problem, not the person. The goal is to find a solution, not tear down the other person.
- Listen to the other side of the story. Make sure you both understand each other's point of view.
- Resolve the problem by bedtime. Don't let things carry over to the next day.
- Forgive and forget. Once the fight is over, it's over. Let go of it.
- Make peace your goal. Sure, arguments among brothers and sisters are normal, but try to have more peaceful times than not.

Friends come and go, but your family is for life. One day your siblings may be your best friends.

Miriam: Family Together Time

Love each other with genuine affection, and take delight in honoring each other.

ROMANS 12:10

Miriam, Aaron, and Moses lived long before there were cars or electricity. There was no TV to watch or video games to play. But that doesn't mean they sat around doing nothing. Bible children made up their own games, and they had plenty of work to do to help take care of the family.

Families spent a lot more time together since there were no trips to the mall or nights out at the bowling alley. Oftentimes several generations of family lived together or near each other. This meant a lot of time spent with cousins, aunts, uncles, and grandparents. Family members were involved in each other's daily life and stuck together.

If you can't imagine spending that much time with your family, maybe it's time to look for things you have in common rather than things that are different. Then plan some together times. You might plan a movie night where everyone votes on a DVD, or if there is enough time, watch each person's favorite. Perhaps your family is more athletic, and a trip to the park allows you to play tennis, shoot baskets, inline skate, skateboard, or jog. It doesn't matter so much what you do together as it does just being together.

With today's busy schedules, time together will take effort and planning. And it takes everyone's cooperation. Before you discard the idea of together time, try talking to family members, and see if they would be willing to set aside one evening or weekend afternoon to spend together.

Families have changed a lot over the years, but God still wants families to spend time together and support each other in good times and bad.

thinking it through

Romans 12:10 says to love and honor each other. How can you love and honor your family members?

Do you spend much time together as a family? Why or why not? What are your family's favorite activities? If you don't have any activities you do together, you might want to try some of these. Pick a couple and then talk to your parents about doing them.

- Watch a DVD and make popcorn.
- Play board games—Monopoly, Life, Uno, and all your favorites.
- Bowl.
- Skate (roller or ice).
- Have a make-your-own sundae night.
- Swim at the indoor pool.
- Go to a play or concert.

thinking it through

When you were little, you may have gone for walks and noticed all the trees, bugs under rocks, and flowers. You looked at the clouds and the changing leaves. Now that you're older, they may not hold the same fascination. But they should.

You can also see God's work in your own life and the lives of those around you.

In what ways do you see God's power every day? As you walk to the bus stop or go outside today, notice all that God has made and done.

Miriam: God's Power on Display

Moses and the people of Israel sang this song to the LORD: "I will sing to the LORD, for he has triumphed gloriously; he has hurled both horse and rider into the sea."

EXODUS 15:1

In her youth, Miriam was a devoted sister to Moses. In her adult years, Miriam took part in leading the people of Israel out of slavery alongside her brothers, Moses and Aaron. Miriam had already seen God work. First she witnessed God's care of Moses when the pharaoh's daughter found Baby Moses and spared his life. Although she didn't see it, she knew that God spoke to Moses from a burning bush and told Moses he was chosen to lead God's people out of slavery.

Next Miriam heard of God's power when Aaron's staff turned to a snake in front of Pharaoh. This was followed by ten plagues sent by God to convince the pharaoh to let the Israelites go. Miriam watched the river turn to blood, frogs invade the land, dust turn to gnats, and flies swarm the region. She saw all the Egyptian livestock die, boils break out on the people, hail kill the slaves and animals left unprotected, locusts devour the crops, darkness cover the land for three days, and finally, the firstborn children and animals die. Many of these things happened only to the Egyptians, not to the Hebrews.

Miriam witnessed God's miraculous power over and over. She realized that everything she was seeing was God at work. When the pharaoh agreed to free the slaves, Miriam was ready to step in and help her brothers lead the Israelites to the Promised Land.

We don't often get to witness miraculous acts of God like those Miriam saw. But we can see God work in many little ways around us. The book of Romans says that nature points to God (Romans 1:20). Think of the change of seasons: the heat of the sun, the falling leaves, and the arrival of snow show God's power. Look for God's power all around you today.

Miriam: How God Leads

The LORD went ahead of them. He guided them during the day with a pillar of cloud, and he provided light at night with a pillar of fire. This allowed them to travel by day or by night.

EXODUS 13:21

After the Passover, when the firstborn Egyptian males and animals died, Pharaoh summoned Moses and told him to take all the Israelites and leave. The Egyptians were eager to see them leave before God sent more horrible punishments, and they gave the Israelites silver, gold, and clothing for the trip.

Moses was the leader for the Israelites, but Miriam and Aaron both helped lead also. All three of them knew that since God had called them to be in charge, he would guide them.

God used a cloud to lead them during the day and a pillar of fire to lead them at night. If the cloud moved, the people moved. If it stopped, the people stopped. This was God's sign to them.

Do you want to be a leader among your friends and classmates? Look to God for guidance. He probably won't use a cloud or fire, but he will help you make decisions and know what to do. How does he do that? He may speak to you directly through his Word. (That's why it's important to read at least a few verses of the Bible every day.) He may lead you through a sermon you hear, a Sunday school lesson, or a youth rally. He may speak to you through a missionary, a song on the radio, the words of a Christian friend, or a book you're reading. Or he may speak to you in the stillness of your heart.

thinking it through

It's important for leaders to look to God for guidance. It's also important to pray for those in leadership positions. What leaders should you pray for? Write down the names of the leaders of your

- country;
- state;
- city;
- school;
- church; and
- family.

Take time to pray for one or two of these leaders every day this week.

thinking it through

Joy is a big part of the Christian life. How can being joyful make you a better leader? Look back at the list of leaders from March 31. Are any of those leaders more joyful than others? Think about what they do that you could imitate.

Miriam: Be Joyful

Miriam the prophet, Aaron's sister, took a tambourine and led all the women as they played their tambourines and danced.

EXODUS 15:20

There are a lot of books in print that tell how to be a good leader. You can find shelves filled with them at your public library or local bookstore. These books list things effective leaders must do—communicate with peers, come up with ideas, plan, work hard, get others to help out, and so on. These are all true. What about adding one more? One that isn't likely to be on any list you'll find in a book. This is it: be joyful!

After God miraculously parted the Red Sea so the Israelites could cross on dry land, he let the waters fall back on the pursuing Egyptian army. The enemies were washed away. When Miriam saw how God had delivered them, she grabbed her tambourine and led the women in dancing to express praise to God.

Did you ever wonder if God might have a leadership role for you now among your friends, church youth group, classmates, or even siblings? Leadership comes with lots of responsibility and decisions, but be like Miriam and be joyful in your leadership. True joy comes from the heart and is a response to what God has done for you. You will have more joy as you develop a closer relationship with God. Look for chances to praise God and lead others in doing the same. Find joy in the journey.

Quiz Time

re you a peacemaker? Take the quiz below to find out. Circle the answer that best describes what you would do in each situation.

1. It's your turn to pick the television show, but there is a show your brother really wants to watch. You
   A. let him watch it. You don't really care.
   B. agree to swap days. You pick tomorrow.
   C. watch your show. A deal is a deal.

2. Your younger brothers are fighting over the last piece of pizza. You
   A. give one of them your piece so they both have an extra piece.
   B. cut it in half and give each of them half.
   C. eat it yourself. Problem solved.

3. Game night turns into a brawl because no one can agree on what game to play. You
   A. agree to whatever the others want to do.
   B. suggest that you make popcorn and everyone bring their pillows into the living room and watch a movie.
   C. go to a friend's house where it is quieter.

How did you do?

Mostly A's: You are giving in, not being a peacemaker. Don't let people use you as a doormat. That doesn't solve problems.

Mostly B's: You try to solve the problem using compromise, sharing, and planning. Good for you.

Mostly C's: It's all about you, and that doesn't help solve problems. Look for positive solutions to problems that are fair to everyone.

Miriam: The Credit Goes to God

Miriam sang this song: "Sing to the LORD, for he has triumphed gloriously; he has hurled both horse and rider into the sea."

EXODUS 15:21

Miriam and her brothers were good leaders. They loved God and listened to what he told them to do. God gave them success, and they were careful to acknowledge God's hand in the good things that happened.

When God parted the Red Sea for them to cross and then destroyed the Egyptian army with a torrent of water, Moses and Miriam didn't claim any part of the victory. They didn't point out that they had led the masses across the dry seabed successfully. They didn't claim extraordinary leadership skills or any superpowers. They both burst into song, giving God the credit for the victory. They knew God alone deserved the glory for the miracles he worked on their behalf and for the way he protected and delivered them.

Sometimes when people accomplish something grand, they take all the credit for it. Sure, they may have worked hard for their achievements. But God gives people the strength, wisdom, talents, and abilities to work hard and to succeed. That's why it's always nice to hear a famous athlete give God the credit for his or her talent or to hear a movie or TV star say that God is more important than the acting he or she is doing. They are acknowledging the talents and success God has given them.

True leaders and role models give credit where credit is due, and in the case of Miriam—and the rest of us—the credit goes to God. Listen to authority figures and celebrities and see if they acknowledge those who have given them help—including God.

thinking it through

Do the people you look up to give God the credit for accomplishments, talents, and abilities? Can you think about a time when someone on TV thanked God for something? When was it? Make it a practice to give God credit for the good things he does in your life each day. Someday it might be you in front of the television cameras!

Miriam: Leadership through Service

Make me truly happy by agreeing wholeheartedly with each other, loving one another, and working together with one mind and purpose. Don't be selfish; don't try to impress others. Be humble, thinking of others as better than yourselves. Don't look out only for your own interests, but take an interest in others, too.

PHILIPPIANS 2:2-4

Over the last few days you've read about some things that made Moses, Aaron, and Miriam true leaders. They were joyful, they followed God's leading, and they gave God credit for their successes. Another thing that set Miriam, Moses, and Aaron apart as leaders is that they served the people rather than expected people to serve them. The trio journeyed among the people they were leading. They took part in the work and never asked others to do what they themselves weren't willing to do. They were hard workers. You wouldn't find them lounging in their tents while others waited on them. Serving others is a true mark of a leader but one you don't see often.

Jesus is our ultimate example of a leader who served others. He didn't come to earth as a king on a throne. He didn't demand special treatment because he is the Son of God. He worked alongside his earthly father in a carpenter shop. He traveled among the poor and the sick. He didn't live in a mansion or have riches. He traveled with only the clothes on his back. He took on himself the lowly task of washing his disciples' feet to illustrate that the person who wants to be great must be a servant to others.

Being able to give a speech to a large crowd isn't a mark of a true leader, and neither is making a grand entrance. Having a large group of followers doesn't make one a great leader nor does being dressed better or owning more things than others.

Moses and Jesus are models for true leaders. If you want to be a great leader, follow their examples. And look for leaders today who lead by serving others.

thinking it through

Read Philippians 2:1-4 again. List as many traits of a leader as you can find. Pick one of these traits and work on it this week.

thinking it through

What are your strong points? Do you feel these help you to be a leader or a support person? Why? It can take courage to be a leader—even Moses was afraid of public speaking! It can also be challenging to let others shine while you work hard behind the scenes. Ask God for the strength to accept the role he has for you, and work at it for his glory.

Miriam: Leader or behind the Scenes

I brought you up out of Egypt and redeemed you from the land of slavery. I sent Moses to lead you, also Aaron and Miriam.

MICAH 6:4, NIV

Not everyone is called to be a leader. God chose Moses, Aaron, and Miriam to lead the Israelites out of Egypt. He selected them because they had the qualities needed to get the job done. Moses was reluctant at first, and God had to reassure him he was the right one for the task. Then Moses proved himself capable, as did Miriam and Aaron.

Sometimes people want to be in a leadership position for their own benefit. They might want to see certain things happen. They may want to write new rules. Or it might seem like a good way to get attention.

Sometimes leaders today are surrounded by important people. They get the best hotel room, the nicest table at a restaurant, and a special car and driver for transportation. They get their faces on the front of important news magazines. But these things don't make a person a great leader.

The truth is, being a leader is hard work. And as we saw from Miriam's life, being in charge means listening to God, giving God credit, and being a servant. It's not always glamorous. The best leaders are the ones digging a trench right next to their men or serving food at the homeless shelter. They don't worry about getting their pictures on the front of a magazine or being interviewed on TV.

Maybe you feel called to be a leader. That's good, but not everyone is designed by God to be a leader.

The important thing is to do what God has for you, whether it's being a leader or a behind-the-scenes support person. God gave you certain characteristics and talents in order to live out his plan for you.

Miriam: Leaders Make Mistakes

Miriam was kept outside the camp for seven days, and the people waited until she was brought back before they traveled again.

NUMBERS 12:15

Miriam's life wasn't all about victory and praise. She had jealous and bitter moments like other Bible women. Miriam began to complain about Moses' Cushite wife. She was upset that this foreigner had a place among them. Miriam, along with Aaron, also questioned Moses' leadership by asking, "Has the LORD spoken only through Moses? Hasn't he spoken through us, too?" (Numbers 12:2). God heard them and answered them by saying he had spoken to them through dreams and visions, but he had spoken to Moses personally.

God punished Miriam by giving her leprosy, a skin disease that required her to live apart from the others. Aaron repented. Moses, a loving brother, pleaded with God to heal Miriam. God did, but he also said she had to be confined outside camp for seven days.

All the people loved Miriam, so they decided to wait to continue their journey until she could go with them. Once the seven days were up, they again continued on toward the Promised Land.

It's good to have godly leaders and role models. Look up to them, but remember that they are not without sin. They are humans too. It's important to look to Jesus above all others because he is the only sinless leader.

If you are feeling defeated by a past mistake or failure, don't let it get you down. Admit it, fix it, and go on. Even godly men and women make mistakes. Adam and Eve sinned in the Garden, Sarah treated Hagar poorly, and Rachel showed favoritism and deceived Isaac. None of the Bible women you are reading about in this book were without weaknesses and faults, but God is faithful to forgive. Miriam died before the Israelites reached the Promised Land, but the memory of her leadership, joy, and courage went with them.

thinking it through

Even though Miriam had her down moments and her weaknesses, the people loved her. They recognized her as a leader and someone through whom God worked. That's why they were willing to wait while she was confined for seven days. Why do you think the people loved Miriam so much? What characteristics drew them to her? How can you develop those characteristics in your own life?

thinking it through

Which of the following traits do you think your teacher will remember about you after you have left his or her class? If you are homeschooled, you can do this for your Sunday school, soccer team, or other group.

Enthusiastic
Loyal Caring
Courageous
Unselfish Reliable
Respectful
Ambitious
Thoughtful
Honest Friendly
Hardworking
Responsible
Courteous Focused
Cooperative

Pick one trait and work to develop it in your life throughout the following week. Ask God to help you leave a legacy of following him.

Zipporah: Leave a Legacy Behind

The priest of Midian had seven daughters who came as usual to draw water and fill the water troughs for their father's flocks. But some other shepherds came and chased them away. So Moses jumped up and rescued the girls from the shepherds. Then he drew water for their flocks.

EXODUS 2:16-17

One day, before God had called Moses to lead the Israelites out of Egypt, Moses saw an Egyptian beating an Israelite slave. Moses killed the Egyptian. Word got back to Pharaoh, and Moses fled to Midian. Exhausted, he sat down by a well, where he came to the rescue of seven sisters and watered their sheep.

The sisters told their father, Jethro, what had happened, and he instructed them to bring Moses to the house for a meal. Jethro gave Zipporah to Moses to be his wife. Moses was now living in a foreign land with a foreign wife. But it was here that God called Moses to lead the Israelite slaves out of bondage.

Zipporah is an undistinguished wife in the Bible. The Bible doesn't indicate she shared Moses' faith or practiced his religious customs. Her father was a Midianite priest. They had their own gods. Although the Midianites didn't worship the true God, it appears Jethro came to believe in God after hearing about all God did for Moses and the Israelites (Exodus 18:11), but little is said about Zipporah.

Was Zipporah brave and kind? Did she stay loyal to her pagan gods or put her faith in the true God? We don't know. How sad to be married to a great leader but not leave a legacy behind. Unlike Miriam, there are no brave deeds mentioned, no words of wisdom recorded, no acts of kindness known.

How will others remember you? Will your influence carry on after you leave your school? Will your coaches remember you for the good things you did? the positive influence you had on your peers? Live so your life makes a difference to those around you.

Rahab: God Chooses Unlikely People

Joshua secretly sent out two spies from the Israelite camp at Acacia Grove. He instructed them, "Scout out the land on the other side of the Jordan River, especially around Jericho." So the two men set out and came to the house of a prostitute named Rahab and stayed there that night.

JOSHUA 2:1

Joshua and the people of Israel are on the doorstep to the Promised Land when we first meet Rahab in the Bible. Joshua sent two spies to check out the land of Jericho. The Israelites would have to conquer it to claim the Promised Land.

The spies went to Rahab's house. She lived in a house on the wall surrounding Jericho. The wall was wide enough on top for buildings and a road. Because Rahab entertained all sorts of men at her house, two unknown spies wouldn't be noticeable there. People were used to seeing men come and go. Rahab's house would give the spies a chance to look over the city and also study the walls, which they would have to get through to conquer Jericho.

Jericho was part of the Amorite kingdom. The people there were violent and sinful. Have you ever been arguing with siblings or parents and heard one of your parents say, "I've had enough"? This is how God felt about the people in Jericho. He had no patience left for their sinfulness. God ordered the Israelites to wipe them from the face of the earth.

Rahab had a sinful lifestyle too. She had wrong relationships with men, and she didn't know the true God. She would have been destroyed along with the wicked city if God hadn't sent the spies to her house. Rahab was an unlikely person to be chosen to help God's people, but God knew what he was doing. Rahab not only welcomed the spies, but she was the one God used to save their lives.

God doesn't always choose the people we think he should or would. But he knows people's hearts and how they will respond to his call.

thinking it through

First Corinthians 1:26-31 says that God has chosen foolish and powerless people to do his work so that "no one can ever boast in the presence of God" (verse 29).

Write down verse 31 and put it in a place where you'll see it: "If you want to boast, boast only about the LORD." God may use unlikely people so that they will give credit to him.

thinking it through

Rahab seems like an unlikely person to be saved from destruction, but we are all sinners in need of God's forgiveness and salvation. How are we all saved? Why is God's salvation a gift?

Rahab: Acting in Faith

No wonder our hearts have melted in fear! No one has the courage to fight after hearing such things. For the LORD your God is the supreme God of the heavens above and the earth below.

JOSHUA 2:11

Some men who lived in Jericho found out the Israelite spies were at Rahab's house and went to capture them. The men asked Rahab to turn the spies over to them. Rahab told them the spies had already left, and she urged them to hurry so they could catch up with the spies.

Many people debate whether Rahab should have lied. Some say it was okay because she was protecting the Israelites. Others say it was wrong, but God used her anyway. God does not like lying. He tells his people to be honest, but Rahab didn't know anything about God. Lying was part of her culture, and it came naturally to her. It would be unrealistic to expect her to know God's rules.

The important thing was that Rahab risked her life to save the spies. She hid them under flax on her rooftop. If they had been found, she would have been punished, possibly by death.

Rahab made a faith choice. She told the spies that her people had heard what God did years before in parting the Red Sea and how the Israelites had defeated many nations. She declared that the Lord is God in heaven above and on earth below. Rahab chose the God of the Israelites over her pagan gods.

The spies promised to save Rahab as long as she left the scarlet cord hanging from the window through which they escaped. They told her that her family must also be in the house to be saved.

Rahab placed her faith in God and trusted the spies to keep their word. She did what they said, and when the walls of Jericho fell, she and her family were saved. God spared her because he had things for her to do, and this was only the beginning.

Puzzle Page

Decode the Thermometer Puzzle below to read a verse that applies to each of us concerning God's grace.

Directions: Look at the thermometer. Each temperature has a corresponding letter. Look at the temperatures under the lines below. Above each line, write the letter that goes with each temperature. Check your answer below.

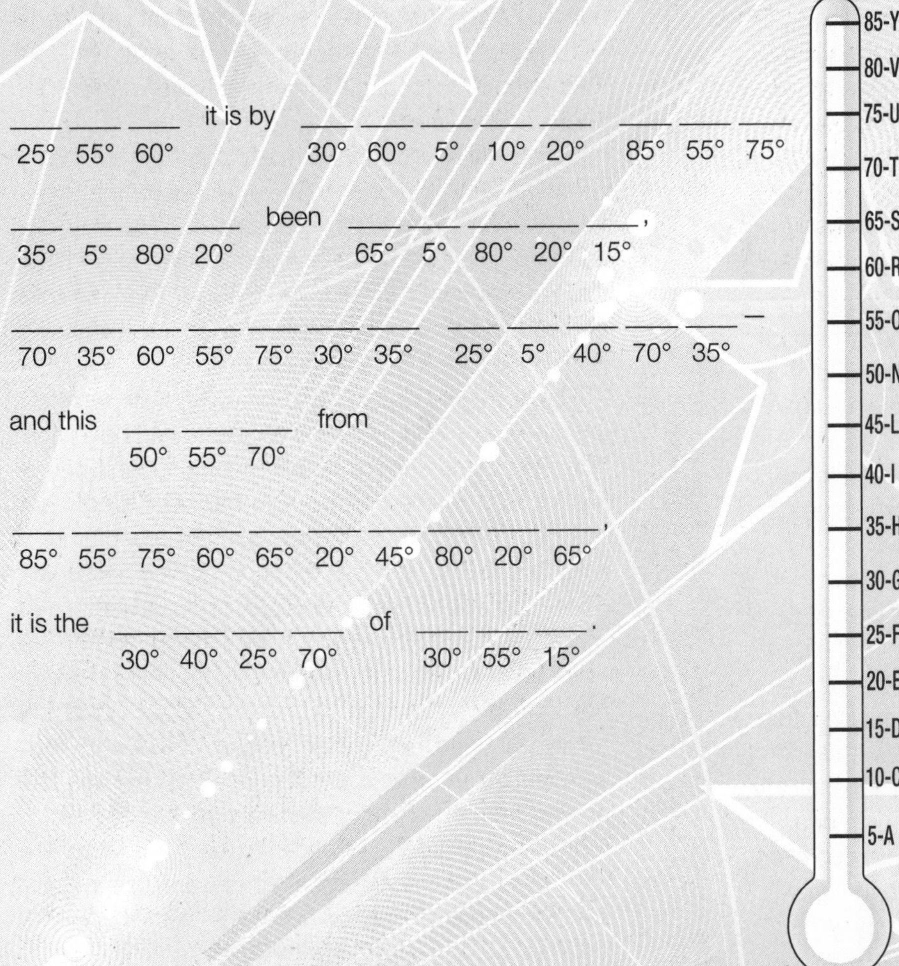

Answer: For it is by grace you have been saved, through faith—and this not from yourselves, it is the gift of God. (Ephesians 2:8, NIV)

Rahab: God Changes People

He is so rich in kindness and grace that he purchased our freedom with the blood of his Son and forgave our sins.

EPHESIANS 1:7

God led the Israelites to the Promised Land. The Israelites waited outside the city while the spies went in. Rahab was going about her daily life, not realizing the changes that were about to take place when the spies showed up at her door. This encounter changed her whole life, career, and future.

When Rahab got up that morning, she had no clue what was in store for her. She was Rahab the prostitute. Her whole existence was one of sinfulness, and she lived in bondage to her wrongdoing in a culture that was going to be destroyed by God. Then the spies showed up, and this one event changed everything. Rahab became a believer in God.

Rahab's story doesn't end here. Her faith was real, and she was a changed woman. God used her in spite of her past, and she played an important role in Jewish history. She married an Israelite named Salmon, and she gave birth to Boaz. Boaz was the grandfather of King David. This is the line through which Jesus was born. That means Rahab was part of Jesus' family tree.

Rahab wasn't brought up in a godly home. She was raised in a wicked, pagan culture, but she wasn't beyond God's salvation. When God saved Rahab, he totally changed her. Rahab began to live out God's wonderful plan tailored just for her. God changes anyone who turns to him for salvation, not just Rahab.

If someone around you seems beyond God's grace, remind yourself that God can redeem and use that person just as he did Rahab.

thinking it through

Are there people around you who seem to be living a totally ungodly lifestyle? They are not beyond God's grace. You may hesitate to share your faith with them because it doesn't seem possible they would be interested. But God may be working in their hearts.

Which of these things could you do this week?

- Tell a peer one thing God has done for you.
- Share a Scripture verse with a friend.
- Invite a classmate to church or a youth group event.
- Share the gospel story with someone.

Rahab: Believing

He saved us, not because of the righteous things we had done, but because of his mercy. He washed away our sins, giving us a new birth and new life through the Holy Spirit.

TITUS 3:5

Rahab lived in a city that was destined to be destroyed by God. In faith, Rahab hung a scarlet cord out her window as the Israelite spies instructed her. That act of faith saved her and all her family who were in the house with her.

The scarlet cord may have been symbolic of the blood of Christ that was shed when he died on the cross for each of us. Just as Rahab was doomed until she took a step of faith, all of us are lost until we reach out to Jesus in faith.

It isn't enough just to believe. It takes a commitment. Rahab knew that the God the spies served was real. She believed he would destroy the city. Rahab was saved from destruction only when she asked the spies to spare her, and because she hung the cord out the window as they said.

It's good to believe Jesus died on the cross to save everyone from his or her sins, but that alone doesn't save a person. Each person has to personally ask Jesus to forgive her sins and be her Savior. The words that are used don't matter. Believing Jesus is God and accepting him as Savior are what count. Just as Rahab was saved by her faith in God, so we are each saved by our faith in Jesus. Praise God for his gift of salvation today!

thinking it through

If you have never put your faith in Jesus, why not do it today? If you have, why not share that with someone today?

First Peter 3:15 says, "You must worship Christ as Lord of your life. And if someone asks about your Christian hope, always be ready to explain it." That means you should be ready to share with those around you the hope you have in Jesus. Write a pretend letter to a friend, telling her how Jesus has changed your life.

thinking it through

What signs of new life have you seen so far this spring? Look out the window right now and see what you notice. Say a prayer thanking God for the new life he creates each year and for the new life he gives us in Christ.

Rahab: A New Creation

This means that anyone who belongs to Christ has become a new person. The old life is gone; a new life has begun!

2 CORINTHIANS 5:17

Rahab lived in Old Testament times long before Jesus came to earth. Her life was changed by her encounter with God. Now lives are changed by believing in Jesus.

In springtime it's easy to see signs of new life and new birth. Just look around you. Bulbs are starting to poke through the soil. Flowers bloom, adding color where everything was previously bleak and dead during winter. Trees are getting new leaves. Snow and slush are gone, and grass is turning green again. That fuzzy caterpillar is getting ready to transform into a beautiful butterfly.

That's what happened in Rahab's life when she placed her faith in God. The darkness and slush of a sinful life were transformed into something new and beautiful. Her heart became pure and clean. This doesn't mean she never sinned again. Sure she did, but she knew God's way was the right way, and that he alone offered forgiveness for her sin.

God transforms lives. Rahab is one example of a changed person. Paul in the New Testament is another. Once known as Saul, he persecuted Christians. Not only didn't he believe in Jesus, but he tortured and even killed those who did. Then Jesus shone a bright light right into his face to get his attention, and he spoke to him. Paul was a changed person. He became a great missionary and preacher, and many people turned to Jesus because of him.

Perhaps you have been a believer since you were very young. You might not feel like your life changed dramatically like Rahab's or Paul's. That's because they were both adults and living sinful lifestyles when they met Jesus. Praise God you have avoided those things and are growing up in your faith. It doesn't make your salvation any less important. What a great testimony it is to be able to say you have followed Jesus all your life.

Rahab: No Turning Back

Joshua spared Rahab the prostitute and her relatives who were with her in the house, because she had hidden the spies Joshua sent to Jericho. And she lives among the Israelites to this day.

JOSHUA 6:25

Rahab made several choices, and once she did, there was no turning back. First she chose to let the men into her house. She knew they weren't from Jericho. They dressed and talked differently from the men she saw every day. Then she chose to hide them and send those looking for them another way.

Rahab chose to believe God sent these men, and that God was going to destroy her city. And finally Rahab made a decision that she wouldn't be destroyed along with the others. She made the spies promise to spare her. Then she acted on faith and did exactly what they told her to do. She hung a red cord out her window and gathered her family so they would be spared too.

Once Rahab did these things, there was no turning back. In fact, there was nowhere to turn back to. Her city was gone. How different Rahab was from Mrs. Lot, who didn't want to leave her home even though it was going to be destroyed. (You can read more about Mrs. Lot on February 5.) Mrs. Lot looked back and longed for all she had left behind. Not Rahab. She took the escape route the spies provided and lived among the Israelites from that time on. Mrs. Lot was one of a handful of godly people in all of Sodom, yet she turned back and longed for what she'd left behind, and she is remembered for her tragic choice. Rahab had lived a sinful lifestyle before she met the Israelite spies, yet she chose to honor God and help his people, and she is known as a hero of faith.

Once Rahab made her decision, there was no turning back. Do you share that same desire? Will you follow Jesus wholeheartedly?

thinking it through

No matter what you have done in the past, you can be known for the choices you make today. If you haven't done so already, commit to following God right now. If you've been following God for a while, don't give up. Ask God to help you make choices that honor him today and in the future.

Rahab: Family Too

Those who won't care for their relatives, especially those in their own household, have denied the true faith. Such people are worse than unbelievers.

1 TIMOTHY 5:8

When Rahab turned to God, she turned her back on her old way of life, her city, and everything she knew except for her family. Rahab asked the spies to spare her family as well as her. And they granted her request as long as her family members were in her house when the time came.

Can you imagine Rahab going to visit her family members and explaining what had happened to her? They must have known she led a sinful life. Then she showed up on their doorsteps, telling them the Israelite God was the true God and he was going to destroy their city. It sounds a bit like Mrs. Noah's story. But the difference is that no one believed Mr. and Mrs. Noah. Rahab's family did believe her and were saved along with her.

If your family shares your faith, you are blessed. You probably attend church together and might have family devotions each morning or evening. Rahab didn't have the advantage of serving the true God while she was growing up, just as many of the girls around you may not be learning about Jesus or attending church either.

Perhaps your parents don't share your faith. If that's true, good for you for being faithful in reading your devotions and praying each day. It's hard to do it alone. Hopefully there is someone in your life who will encourage you in your Christian walk, and maybe your family will one day share your faith just as Rahab's family came to believe in God too.

thinking it through

Does your family share your faith? If so, how do you live out your faith together? (Attend church or Bible studies, have devotions.) Can you think of a project your family could do together to share your faith with others? (Serve at a soup kitchen, sponsor a child in a poor country, volunteer at a shelter.)

If your parents don't share your faith, is there someone who encourages you in your Christian walk? Who? If not, pray God will bring someone into your life.

Five Sisters: How to Make a Request

Moses brought their case before the LORD. And the LORD replied to Moses, "The claim of the daughters of Zelophehad is legitimate. You must give them a grant of land along with their father's relatives. Assign them the property that would have been given to their father."
NUMBERS 27:5-7

Zelophehad was a man who had five daughters but no sons. His daughters were Mahlah, Noah, Hoglah, Milcah, and Tirzah. They lived during the forty years the Israelites were wandering the wilderness. During this time, Zelophehad died.

When the Israelites reached the Promised Land, the men would be given land. The five sisters wanted the land that would have been given to their father. It would have automatically been given to a son, but Zelophehad didn't have one. So there would be no land in their father's name.

The sisters approached Moses and asked that the land be given to them so their father's family name wouldn't be lost. Moses took their request directly to God, and God granted it. The sisters would be given land among the tribe of Manasseh.

If you've ever wanted to ask your parents for something, you know that there are good ways to go about it and bad ways. For instance, it might not be a good idea to ask your parents for a special request when they are tired or angry, or right after giving them a poor report card. You also know that if you whine or complain, you'll have less of a chance of getting what you want.

If you want to get a positive response from your parents, you wait until they are in a good mood. Then you approach them calmly and maturely and present your request.

This is what the sisters did. They waited until a good time. They were also well informed about the law. Then they approached Moses and presented their request in a polite and direct manner. Moses took the request to God, and the answer was yes.

thinking it through

Pretend you want to go on a mission trip this summer. Act out what you would say to your parents. If you really want a yes, then it's best to approach your parents at a relaxed moment and to be knowledgeable about the trip dates, costs, training, and requirements.

Use this approach each time you want to get a positive answer to a request. You might not get a yes every time, but your chances are much better if you approach your parents this way.

thinking it through

You can count on your heavenly Father to give you what you need. Matthew 7:7 says, "Keep on asking, and you will receive what you ask for. Keep on seeking, and you will find. Keep on knocking, and the door will be opened to you."

What three things does verse 7 tell you to do, and what three things will happen as a result? What one thing will you ask God for today?

Acsah: Ask for What You Need

She said, "Give me another gift. You have already given me land in the Negev; now please give me springs of water, too." So Caleb gave her the upper and lower springs.

JOSHUA 15:19

Caleb was a brave Israelite. He and Joshua were among the original spies sent into the Promised Land to see what kind of land it was. Ten spies said it would be impossible to conquer the land. Joshua and Caleb said that with God's help they could take the land. The people sided with the ten spies, and because of the Israelites' unbelief, they had to wander in the wilderness for forty years.

Time passed, and Caleb had a daughter who was now old enough to get married. Caleb said the man who captured Kiriath-sepher could marry his daughter. Othniel, a warrior, captured it and was allowed to marry Acsah. Caleb gave them land.

Acsah looked around and realized they had land but no water. She approached her father and asked to be given water, too. Caleb gave her two springs of water, so now the new couple had all they needed for a happy life together.

This is the only story we have about Acsah, but it tells us two things about her. The first is that she had a good relationship with her father. She could make a request of him and be sure it would be granted. The second is that she knew what she wanted and how to ask for it. She acknowledged the gift her father had already given her, and then she asked specifically for what she wanted. She didn't play games with him, hint at what she wanted, complain, or beg. She asked for exactly what she needed.

Acsah wasn't afraid to ask her father for what she wanted. Hopefully you have a good relationship with your father or mother in order to do the same. Even more important is that you have a relationship with your heavenly Father that allows you to ask for what you need, knowing God will hear and answer.

Quiz Time

Rahab followed God just like most of the Bible women you've read about so far. But some weren't followers of God. Do you remember who is who? Take the quiz below to see how well you remember the Bible women so far.

Eve **Hagar** **Nurse Deborah** **Mrs. Potiphar** **Mrs. Noah**
Mrs. Lot **Rachel** **Shiphrah and Puah** **Sarah** **Rebekah** **Leah**
Jochebed **Pharaoh's daughter** **Miriam** **Zipporah** **Rahab**

Choose the correct answer from above.

1. Although married to Moses, she didn't leave a legacy of faith behind. __________
2. She lived on a floating zoo while God destroyed the world with a flood. __________
3. Although not Abraham's wife, she gave birth to his first son. __________
4. She hung a red cord from her window in order to save her and her family. __________
5. She listened to the serpent rather than God and had to leave her garden home. __________
6. She had compassion on the Hebrew child she found floating in the river. __________
7. She had her first and only child at the age of ninety. __________
8. She made the long journey with Rebekah to Isaac's homeland. __________
9. She was used to having her own way. When she couldn't have Joseph, she made up a lie about him. __________
10. She didn't want to leave her home. She looked back and was turned into salt. __________
11. These brave women refused to kill the Hebrew baby boys. __________
12. She traveled five hundred miles to marry someone she had never met. __________
13. When she could no longer keep her infant son safe, she set him afloat in the river. __________
14. She was the more beautiful sister and Jacob's true love. __________
15. She was a dutiful older sister watching over her brother in the river. __________
16. She was Jacob's first wife but not his first choice. __________

Answers: 1. Zipporah 2. Mrs. Noah 3. Hagar 4. Rahab 5. Eve 6. Pharaoh's daughter 7. Sarah 8. Nurse Deborah 9. Mrs. Potiphar 10. Mrs. Lot 11. Shiphrah and Puah 12. Rebekah 13. Jochebed 14. Rachel 15. Miriam 16. Leah

thinking it through

Which of Deborah's character traits do you think is most important? Why?

Why do you think God allowed the Israelites to be captured over and over again? Do you think God ever allows problems in our lives so we will turn to him?

Deborah: God Raises Up a Rescuer

Deborah, the wife of Lappidoth, was a prophet who was judging Israel at that time.

JUDGES 4:4

The book of Judges is full of stories of courage. It is also a sad book because of the Israelites' failure to obey God and trust him. When the Israelites went in and took the Promised Land, they didn't drive out all the enemies as God had said.

Sometimes these enemies rose up and dominated the Israelites until God sent a leader—called a judge—to deliver them. Then there would be peace in the land, and the people would obey God.

After a while the people would start doing whatever they wanted and disobeying God again—and another nation would conquer them. They would again turn to God, and he would raise up another leader to deliver them. This happened over and over. It seemed the Israelites would never learn.

When we meet Deborah, the Israelites had been in captivity to the Canaanites for twenty years. The Canaanite king, Jabin, had a commander in chief named Sisera. Sisera had nine hundred chariots of iron, and the Israelites were afraid to go against him in battle.

Out of this darkness and oppression, God raised up Deborah, a remarkable woman who shared many character traits with the other women you've read about in this book. She had faith like Sarah's. She had initiative just as Rebekah did. She was a hard worker like Rachel. She had spiritual insight like Leah. She had courage as Shiphrah and Puah did. She was creative like Jochebed. She had leadership abilities like Miriam.

In fact, Deborah had everything God needed to rescue his people from the Canaanites—wisdom, courage, initiative, strength, and spiritual insight. Beyond that, Deborah had faith that God would give her the victory, and she didn't waver.

We can learn much from Deborah, who lived her life courageously and passionately as she charged headfirst into all God had planned for her.

Deborah: Recognizing Good Advice

She would sit under the Palm of Deborah, between Ramah and Bethel in the hill country of Ephraim, and the Israelites would go to her for judgment.

JUDGES 4:5

Deborah was an exceptional woman who was blessed by God with many talents and abilities. For one thing, Deborah was skilled as a mediator, adviser, and counselor. This was because she had a good relationship with God. She loved him and followed his commandments, and she was able to tell what God wanted the people to do. She sat under a palm tree, and the Israelites would come and talk to her when they had problems. They knew Deborah would give them good advice.

People could trust Deborah's counsel because God led Deborah in what she said to others. There are a lot of people who give advice—there are self-help columns in magazines and newspapers. There are talk shows where the host or hostess gives advice. There are counselors trained to offer help and suggestions. The problem is, not all of these people give good advice. Deborah's counsel lined up with what God wanted. Much of the advice given today is totally opposite from what the Bible teaches.

How can you know if advice is good? You can tell by whether it follows God's standards, but you will know this only if you are familiar with God's Word and the things it instructs you to do. Anytime someone tells you it's okay to do something against God's Word, he or she is giving you wrong advice. There are no exceptions or special circumstances.

Deborah never claimed to be wise by herself. She knew God was the source of her wisdom, and that is why her counsel was sound. If you are in need of advice, find someone with a heart like Deborah's who will point you in the right direction.

thinking it through

Proverbs 4:11 says, "I will teach you wisdom's ways and lead you in straight paths." Who gives you the wisdom you need each day? Is there a situation you need wisdom to figure out? Ask God for wisdom, and he will give it to you.

thinking it through

Deborah gave good counsel based on God's desires. You have the Bible to help you know how God wants you to live. It might seem like a big task to try to read and remember the whole Bible—especially if you haven't read much of it before. But if you read just a little bit each day and ask God to direct you, you'll be on your way to learning good advice. Why not start today, with the story of Deborah in Judges 4–5?

Deborah: Counsel from God's Word

If you need wisdom, ask our generous God, and he will give it to you. He will not rebuke you for asking.

JAMES 1:5

Deborah was a wise lady, and she was able to use her understanding to help others. Why was she such a good counselor for the Israelites? Because she was in touch with God. She knew what he wanted.

God has a plan for each one of us, and he has given us a guide to follow along the way. Choosing the right path and making the right choices in life only happen when we follow that guide—his Word. The Bible teaches us what is right and wrong, and through the Bible we gain understanding and knowledge.

Deborah didn't have the benefit of the complete Word of God like we have today, but she talked to God and tried to find out what pleased him. God had called her to do this work, so of course he blessed her in it.

You may have friends who ask your advice about things, just as people came to Deborah for advice. Their questions may be different, but the answers come from God just the same. Your friend may want to know: Should I be friends with Popular Girl? Should I talk to Cute Boy? What should I do about my parents, who constantly fight?

The best thing to do is give advice based on God's Word. Assure your friend that God has a plan for her, and he already knows about the things that are happening in her life. Point her toward God. Proverbs 8:17 says, "I love those who love me, and those who seek me find me" (NIV).

Deborah could give good counsel because she was in touch with the very God who created her and those around her. Who better to know how to solve their problems? Are you in touch with your Creator so that you can offer good advice to those who need it? If not, start spending time each day getting to know God better.

Deborah: Wise Words

Wise words are like deep waters; wisdom flows from the wise like a bubbling brook.
PROVERBS 18:4

Do you ever stop to consider what effect your words have on the lives of those around you? Or do words come rushing out of your mouth before you stop and think? Deborah's words changed lives both when she counseled the Israelites and when she gave the order to go into battle. She spoke words from the Lord that were full of godly counsel.

Proverbs 18 says wise words are like deep waters. Think about a time when you were really thirsty. Perhaps you ran out of water at soccer practice or forgot to take a water bottle along to basketball practice. Or maybe you'd been riding for a long time in the car and needed a drink. Or you were at the park or beach and it was hot. When you finally got water, it refreshed you. You may have even felt like you had more energy than before.

Wise words are the same. They refresh. They energize. They may even be life changing—Deborah's were. Her words set people on the right path. They encouraged action and change. Her words turned the people back to God.

How about you? What do your words accomplish? Do they build up or tear down? Do they encourage or discourage? Do they motivate people to take godly action? Think before you speak today, and pray these words written in the Psalms: "May the words of my mouth and the meditation of my heart be pleasing to you, O LORD, my rock and my redeemer" (Psalm 19:14).

thinking it through

Are your words like deep waters, refreshing others? Write down Psalm 19:14 on an index card, and put it on your bathroom mirror or in your locker at school. Let that verse guide your words today—and every day.

thinking it through

Deborah did something totally remarkable when she courageously accompanied Barak into battle. When is the last time you did something exceptional with God's help?

If you can't think of something you've done, ask God to work in your heart and prepare you to do something remarkable just as Deborah did; then step out, trusting him to guide you. God may not lead you into a military battle, but he may lead you into new and unexpected opportunities to serve him.

Deborah: A Courageous Woman

"Very well," she replied, "I will go with you. But you will receive no honor in this venture, for the Lord's victory over Sisera will be at the hands of a woman." So Deborah went with Barak to Kedesh.

JUDGES 4:9

While Deborah was sitting under her palm tree counseling others, she sent for Barak. Deborah told him God wanted him to go into battle against Sisera and his nine hundred chariots of iron. She even told him how God was going to give him the victory.

How did Barak, the army general, respond? "I won't go unless you go with me." This might not have been such a strange request except that Barak was talking to a woman. In Bible times women were not in the military. Yet Barak wasn't willing to go into battle without Deborah. He felt her presence would ensure their victory.

What did Deborah do? She agreed to go. No sitting under her tree counseling others while Barak went to fight. She would be right in the midst of the battle. Deborah wasn't afraid. She knew God was with her, and the victory was already sure. But because Barak wasn't willing to trust God and go into battle without her, Deborah prophesied that Sisera would fall to a woman. (She wasn't prophesying about herself, but about Jael. You will read about her on April 30.)

Deborah had total faith in God, and that faith gave her courage. The Israelites didn't have chariots or fancy swords and shields, but they had the power of God. Can you imagine Deborah as she went into battle, the lone woman among ten thousand men? A courageous woman posted among the men in the woods on the mountainside, watching as God gave them the victory he had promised?

No wonder Deborah tells the story in song afterward. She had done something other women hadn't done. She'd displayed more courage than mighty Barak, and she'd done it by faith alone.

Deborah: Facing Life Courageously

This is my command—be strong and courageous! Do not be afraid or discouraged. For the LORD your God is with you wherever you go.
JOSHUA 1:9

When Deborah went into battle with Barak, she was part of an army hiding in the woods and armed with short swords as Sisera's mighty army approached in iron chariots. The Canaanite general made a mistake, though. He positioned his chariots along the river Kishon. A sudden downpour turned the river into a torrent. The valley floor became muddy, and Sisera's chariots were stuck. He'd lost the advantage.

The Israelites, with Deborah in the midst encouraging them and reminding them of God's promises, charged down the mountainside and slaughtered the enemy. Sisera fled on foot, but God had plans for him. (You'll read about that when you read about Jael on April 30.)

Can you imagine what it would have been like for Deborah to be part of this victory? She was not a warrior, but she was God's chosen deliverer for his people. God gave her all she would need to do the job he'd called her to do.

God has given you all the talents, abilities, and personality to do the work he has for you, too. If you aren't seeing God use you to make a difference in the lives of those around you, perhaps you aren't seeking out all he has for you. Deborah was ready. She was prepared to face courageously whatever she was called to do. Are you?

thinking it through

Are you courageous when it comes to doing things for God? How true are the sentences below?

- When the youth leader announces a ministry project, I am one of the first to sign up.
- When I see someone treated wrongly at school, I come to her defense.
- When I see someone who needs to hear about Jesus, I share my faith.
- When it comes to trying new things, I jump right in.

Are any of those sentences areas where you could be more courageous? You don't have to be a daredevil for Jesus; just live with courage.

Deborah: I'm on It

Barak told her, "I will go, but only if you go with me."
JUDGES 4:8

Deborah called for Barak. She told him it was time for him to take the troops into battle against the Canaanites. She told him exactly where to take the troops and how to defeat the enemy.

How interesting that a woman needed to call in a military leader and tell him to go into battle. And how sad that he wasn't willing to act even when she laid out the plan for him.

In a television show I enjoy watching, a team of people solves crimes. Many times one of the team members is already checking out clues before the boss even tells him or her to do so. If not, the immediate response is "I'm on it, Boss" or "On my way." There is never any hesitation, questioning, or arguing.

Deborah was an "I'm on it" kind of person, but Barak wasn't. That's why he is remembered for refusing to go into battle unless Deborah went with him. Barak could have been known as a great military leader or a brave general who trusted God above all else, but he chose not to act in faith. He was a "You go first" person rather than an "I'm on it" person.

Which kind of person are you? No one can do it all, but do you step out and take the initiative when it's within your power to do so? Do you say, "I'm on it," when your parents or teachers mention that something needs to be done? Do you answer, "I'm on it," when God speaks to your heart, asking you to do something? If not, try answering that way this week, and you may be surprised at all God can accomplish through you.

thinking it through

Choose two things you can do this week either without being asked or by answering, "I'm on it," when asked to do them.

Do an extra job at home to lighten someone else's load.
Prepare or clean up after a meal.
Take care of a pet.
Help a teacher clean up the classroom.
Turn in a project early.
Practice for music lessons or band.
Learn a Bible verse or study a lesson for Sunday school or your church class.

Quiz Time

Are your words like deep waters refreshing others? Read each sentence below. Pick A for always, S for sometimes, or N for never.

1. If someone asks me a question, I stop to think of the best answer.

   A S N

2. When a friend asks for advice, I base my answer on what I know is true from the Bible.

   A S N

3. I make sure things are true before I share them.

   A S N

4. When I am angry, I take time to calm down so I don't say something I regret.

   A S N

How did you do?

Mostly A's: Your words are spoken with care. You give the best answer you can using God's Word as a guide. People can count on you to say the right thing.

Mostly S's: You need to pause before you speak. Ask yourself if what you are about to say is the best thing. Ask God to give you a clear answer to help others.

Mostly N's: Take time to memorize Psalm 19:14 (see the April 19 devo). Let that verse guide your words today—and every day.

thinking it through

Is there something you have been putting off that you need to do? How will you accomplish it?

What does it mean to be active in seeking God's plan for you today? How can you do this?

Deborah: Actively Seek God's Plan

Turn from evil and do good; seek peace and pursue it.

PSALM 34:14, NIV

Deborah counseled from under a tree, but she wasn't just there relaxing. She was actively involved in helping others. When there was a battle to be fought, she fought it. Deborah knew when it was time to sit and when it was time to get up and fight. Whether she was sitting or fighting, Deborah was doing what God wanted her to do.

Deborah displayed initiative by seeking out God and his plan for her. Sometimes this meant being a wife; sometimes it involved being a prophetess. Other times it led her to offer words of wisdom to one or more of the Israelites, and it led her into battle with Barak, who wouldn't go alone.

What would showing initiative in seeking out God's plan mean for you day by day? You can't sit under a tree and offer advice, and you're too young to go into battle. But you certainly are not too young to take steps in following God's plan.

Perhaps for you, showing initiative means being the first to do what's right when in class and when dealing with other students. Maybe it means doing something today—right now—that you've been putting off, such as starting a report or doing a job your mom has asked you to do. Maybe it means actively looking for ways to help others. Perhaps it means responding quickly to avoid a bad situation, such as leading yourself and friends away from a group of students who are displaying poor behavior.

Deborah didn't know God's plan for her in advance, but she listened to God and followed his leading. Then she was ready to do his will without delay. Determine that you will have that same readiness to follow God's direction.

Deborah: Fit for Battle

At Kedesh, Barak called together the tribes of Zebulun and Naphtali, and 10,000 warriors went up with him. Deborah also went with him.

JUDGES 4:10

Deborah was extraordinary—from palm-tree counselor to soldier sidekick, from wife to wisdom giver. We don't know anything of Deborah's childhood years, her family life, or how she came to do all she did. But to accomplish the things she did, she had to have been a strong woman. Not strong in the sense that she was pushy or forceful, because there is no sign she was either of those things. Rather, she was strong in body and mind.

It couldn't have been an easy task following Barak around while assembling the troops and then walking to the battlefield. This was definitely a no-frills operation. It required valor, stamina, endurance, and strength.

Deborah lived in the days before air-conditioned gyms, aerobics classes, weight training, or PE class. Yet we know she was fit, because she kept up with the army as they went into battle.

Maybe you wonder if it's really important to be in shape. After all, isn't God more interested in what's in your heart than how fit you are? That's true. But that doesn't mean it's not important to take care of your body. After all, your body is the temple of God, and he deserves the best (1 Corinthians 6:19-20). Besides, being fit will give you more energy to accomplish God's plan for you. It's hard to be passionate and ready for action when you are feeling tired or sluggish.

You don't have to be a superjock or into extreme sports to be fit. You can accomplish it by working exercise into your daily life. Give it a try. When God leads you to do something, you want to be full of energy and ready to go like Deborah.

thinking it through

You can make fitness part of your everyday life. Choose two of these to try this week.

Start your day with ten minutes of walking or jogging in place.

Ride your bike to school instead of taking the bus.

Go bowling with your friends instead of sitting around.

Shoot baskets or play catch with your younger siblings.

When you need a break from homework, walk up and down the stairs three times or jump rope for ten minutes.

Walk the dog.

thinking it through

The preteen and early teen years are ones of physical and emotional change. Peer pressure increases, schoolwork increases, and so does stress. It's easy to become overwhelmed with it all. But you can be victorious through Jesus.

What enemies are you battling today? Stop and claim Philippians 4:13 as your own message from God: "I can do everything through Christ, who gives me strength."

Deborah: Trusting God for Victory

The LORD is my strength and shield. I trust him with all my heart. He helps me, and my heart is filled with joy. I burst out in songs of thanksgiving.

PSALM 28:7

Before God called Deborah, life for the Israelites was nearly unbearable. Trade had ceased. Farming was risky because farmers could be the target of a surprise attack or raid. The streets were deserted. Hope was gone. Children didn't know what freedom was. King Jabin dominated the land.

But the real problem wasn't King Jabin. It was the Israelites. God had delivered them over and over, yet they had turned from him and back to their sinful ways each time. They didn't need to live in fear of Jabin and his army. They just needed to call out to God to be rescued.

Deborah was their one hope because she had faith in God. She knew he was more powerful than Jabin and Sisera and his chariots. Did Deborah have any secret fears or doubts about going into battle? No. In fact, she said to Barak, "Get ready! This is the day the LORD will give you victory over Sisera, for the LORD is marching ahead of you" (Judges 4:14). Deborah knew God so well that she had total faith he would go before them and defeat their enemies.

What kind of enemies are you facing today? You aren't battling the Canaanites or Philistines, but how about the enemies of fear, doubt, ridicule, low self-esteem, neglect, abuse, illness, loneliness, eating disorders, or depression? These enemies aren't visible, but they are just as dangerous as the ones that are, because they destroy you from the inside out. Yet just like the Israelites, you can claim the victory from these enemies through God. Don't let them control you any longer.

Deborah: Valor

Down from Tabor marched the few against the nobles. The people of the LORD marched down against mighty warriors.

JUDGES 5:13

Deborah was a woman of valor. We don't use the word *valor* much anymore, but it's a good word to describe this unique woman. Valor is that character trait that allows a person to encounter danger up close and personal. It's more than just bravery. Valor requires strength of mind as well as strength of body. It requires integrity, the spirit that allows someone to do what's right even when it's hard.

How did Deborah show those things?

By giving people wise counsel even if it wasn't what they wanted to hear.
By commanding Barak to gather the troops.
By agreeing to go with him.
By assuring the people God had already given them the victory.
By accompanying the troops into the battle.
By living a no-fear lifestyle, knowing God was in control.

Can you imagine the changes that would take place in our homes, churches, schools, and country if we had more men, women, and young people of valor? They would face problems with the courage to change them—even if it was hard—just because it was the right thing to do. They would stand up for leaders and laws that were moral and good. They would speak out against injustice and take part in changing it. They would help rid the world of hatred and poverty.

You can't do all those things alone, but you can be a person of valor in your own home, school, and community. Start by making a difference right where you are.

thinking it through

Wonder whether you can make a difference in your corner of the world? You can. What effect would it have on your life if you continually sought after God?

How can you be a young woman of valor in your home? in your school? in your church? in your community? Ask God to give you the strength to stand up for things that please him.

thinking it through

Are you part of any group activities? If not, consider choosing one or two and getting involved wholeheartedly. But be careful not to get into projects that take up a lot of time but don't accomplish much. Make sure the activities and organizations you are involved in are accomplishing good things.

Be passionate about God. Be passionate about his plan for you. Be passionate in helping others. You will be amazed at the good you can do.

Deborah: Live with Passion

Deborah said to Barak, "Get ready! This is the day the LORD will give you victory over Sisera, for the LORD is marching ahead of you." So Barak led his 10,000 warriors down the slopes of Mount Tabor into battle.
JUDGES 4:14

Deborah's thoughts and heart were fixed on God, and she was ready to go. She didn't say, "Well, I guess we may as well do this." No, she said, "Get ready! This is the day the LORD will give you victory over Sisera."

You can sense a real passion for the project in Deborah's words. She was involved wholeheartedly and was enthusiastic about what God was going to do for the Israelites. No doing things halfway with Deborah. She claimed the victory before the battle started and went into it knowing the Israelites would be successful in defeating the Canaanites and restoring peace to their land.

Do you throw yourself wholeheartedly into your plans and projects? Is there something you feel passionately enough about to do that? Maybe you are involved in a school club that is making a difference in your community. Perhaps you are a mentor for another student. Maybe you are involved in a ministry with your youth group. You might be a volunteer, team member, or cast member. What in your life makes you jump out of bed ready to get going in the morning?

If you aren't passionate about anything you are doing, seek out ways to be involved in making a difference around you. Living day after day on the fringe without getting involved isn't really living. It's existing. Don't settle for that. Find something you are enthusiastic about and live with passion.

Deborah: Be Willing

Remember, dear brothers and sisters, that few of you were wise in the world's eyes or powerful or wealthy when God called you. Instead, God chose things the world considers foolish in order to shame those who think they are wise. And he chose things that are powerless to shame those who are powerful.

1 CORINTHIANS 1:26-27

Today the people who most stand out are the athletes, politicians, musicians, and movie stars who grace the covers of magazines and dominate the news. Deborah didn't have the kind of talent or beauty that would draw attention today.

Thankfully God doesn't judge success or usefulness by our income, looks, talents, intelligence, or any of the other things people consider important. In fact, he chooses those who aren't likely heroes. Why? Because they know they have to depend on God for their strength and help.

Look at Deborah. She is described as the wife of Lappidoth. No great credentials, wealth, education, or power. Yet God chose her to be a prophetess, judge, counselor, and even a warrior. A great leader and soldier might claim the victory for himself. By choosing someone with no power of her own, God would shine through the events that followed.

Deborah's qualification to be used by God was that she was willing. She had a firm faith in God, listened to him, and allowed him to use her in many ways. That is the same thing God wants from you today—willingness.

Not a great student? That's okay. Not model material? That's fine. Broke until next week's allowance? No problem. Willing? That's all God asks!

thinking it through

Are you willing to be used by God today? You don't have to be popular, athletic, or rich. You don't have to have good grades, hold a class office, or be on a sports team. God can use you just as you are. If you are willing, write God a note and let him know!

Deborah: Acknowledge Your Abilities

There were few people left in the villages of Israel—until Deborah arose as a mother for Israel.
JUDGES 5:7

After God gave Deborah and Barak the victory, Deborah wrote a song telling of the battle. In the song, Deborah is not proud, but she acknowledges that God called her to deliver the Israelites from the Canaanite oppression.

Sometimes after great accomplishments, people are quick to grab glory for themselves. A volleyball player may claim she's the most valuable player because she won the most points with her serves. A student who received an A on a group project may boast that her hard work was the reason for her group's good grade. They have talents and abilities, but they are claiming for themselves something that was a team victory. They also fail to acknowledge God as the source of their talents.

Did God bless you with musical ability? Then use that talent, acknowledge your gift, and be sure to give God credit for putting the ability within you. Are you the math whiz? Great. Be a tutor. Win the math competition for your school or city. Be proud of your ability, but never forget that it came from God.

Tim Tebow, who has become a top name in football, is an example of good pride. He realizes his playing puts him in the limelight and plans to use that for good. When he cited John 3:16 in a championship game, it was Google's number one searched-for item that day.

The difference between good pride and wrong pride is whether you acknowledge God as your creator and the one who blessed you with your talents and abilities. Are you careful to thank God for your musical or athletic ability? Do you thank him that you can draw or act? Do you give God credit for making the honor roll, winning the science fair, or getting a lead role in the play? Yes, you used your talents to accomplish those things, but God gifted you to do them. Take pride in your accomplishments, but be careful to give God the glory.

thinking it through

Can you think of a time you saw someone display good pride in his or her talents on television or in real life? Can you think of an example of someone showing wrong pride in himself or herself? What was the difference between the two? Thank God for the abilities he's given you, and ask him how you can use those abilities to honor his name.

Puzzle Page

We've been learning how Deborah went to God for direction. Decode the Thermometer Puzzle below to find out what the Bible says about asking God for help.

Look at the thermometer. Each temperature has a corresponding letter. Look at the temperatures under the lines below. Above each line, write the letter that goes with the temperature. Check your answer below.

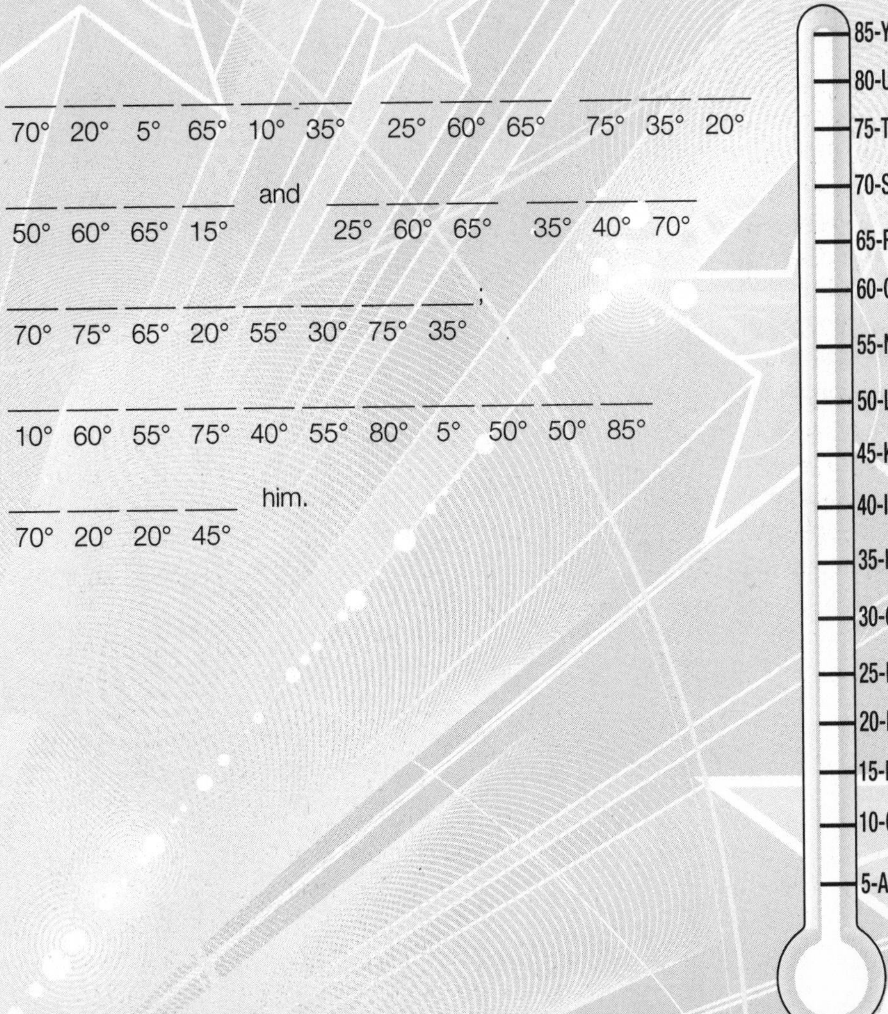

Answer: Search for the LORD and for his strength; continually seek him. (Psalm 105:4)

thinking it through

Look around the room. What items are nearby? List the first ten or so items you see. Can you use any of them to meet a need? Be creative.

The Israelites won the battle in part because Jael seized the opportunity she had. Ask God to point out opportunities where you can influence a situation for good. Be on the lookout for chances to honor God in your life this week.

Jael: Seizing the Opportunity

When Sisera fell asleep from exhaustion, Jael quietly crept up to him with a hammer and tent peg in her hand. Then she drove the tent peg through his temple and into the ground, and so he died.

JUDGES 4:21

When it became obvious his army wasn't going to be victorious, Sisera fled on foot to Jael's tent, where he thought he would be safe. Was he ever wrong! Sure, Jael gave him a drink and covered him with a blanket. She watched over him until he fell into a deep sleep. Then, wham! She drove a tent peg through his temple clear into the ground.

Wow! Jael is not a typical Bible woman, yet she is praised in Deborah's song in Judges 5:24: "Most blessed among women is Jael, the wife of Heber the Kenite. May she be blessed above all women who live in tents." This doesn't mean God likes violence, but this incident was during a time of war. God sent his people to defeat the Canaanites. Jael, not an Israelite, was praised for aiding God's people, using what she had.

Jael didn't possess any great talent that allowed her to defeat Sisera. Jael seized the opportunity to act, using what was at hand—a tent peg. Since she lived in a tent, Jael was probably very familiar with tent pegs and quite capable of hammering one into the ground. She was just doing what she knew how to do to accomplish God's purpose.

When an opportunity arises for you to act, do you reach for what is at hand to meet the need? You won't need a tent peg, but how about a cookie sheet to bake cookies to encourage someone, or a calculator to help your brother with his math homework? Perhaps you have a sewing machine and can help repair clothes, or you know how to knit and can make a baby blanket for the local pregnancy center.

Like Jael, you don't have to have any special talent to serve God. Whenever you have the chance, seize the opportunity to act using what is at hand.

Jephthah's Daughter: An Honorable Daughter

She said, "Father, if you have made a vow to the LORD, you must do to me what you have vowed, for the LORD has given you a great victory over your enemies, the Ammonites."

JUDGES 11:36

We don't know much about Jephthah's daughter, but we know Jephthah was a great commander and a believer in God. The Israelites asked him to be their leader against the Ammonites.

Jephthah gathered his army and prepared to go to battle. But before he did, he made a foolish vow. He promised if God gave him the victory, he would offer as a sacrifice whatever came out of his house first to greet him. Maybe he thought it would be the family pooch. He surely didn't expect it to be his only daughter.

Jephthah was distraught when he faced his daughter and told her what he had promised. She told her father he must keep his promise to the Lord but asked for two months to mourn first. She would not let him go back on his promise. I'm not sure I could be as honorable as she was. I fear I would have protested it wasn't fair for my father to make that kind of decision without consulting me. Or I would have tried to talk him into substituting Fido in my place.

Did Jephthah literally sacrifice his daughter as a burnt offering, or did he sacrifice her to be a servant in the Temple so she could never marry and have children? No one knows for sure, but since God forbids human sacrifice, it seems unrealistic Jephthah would risk angering God by offering his daughter as a literal sacrifice.

If only Jephthah had displayed the faith of Deborah, instead of making a rash vow to God, life might have been very different for his only child.

thinking it through

James 5:12 says, "Never take an oath, by heaven or earth or anything else. Just say a simple yes or no, so that you will not sin and be condemned." Why do you think James warns us about making vows? Why do you think Jephthah made the promise to God? Have you ever made a foolish promise in a time of trouble? Did you keep the promise afterward? Would it have been better not to have made the promise?

thinking it through

Can you think of a time when it was hard to make the right choice? What happened?

Though we don't have to grow our hair long or follow the special rules of the Nazirites, God does call us to be set apart today. Ask God to help you make choices today that will show others his goodness.

Samson's Mother: Choosing to Do What's Right

When her son was born, she named him Samson. And the LORD blessed him as he grew up.

JUDGES 13:24

Samson's mom is one of the unnamed women of the Bible, yet her son is well known. Samson's parents had been unable to have children. Then an angel appeared to Samson's mom and told her she would have a son, but she would have to follow some special rules. She couldn't drink wine or other fermented drink, and she couldn't eat anything considered unclean according to Jewish law. The angel told her no razor should be used on her son's hair because he would be set apart as a Nazirite—a group of people chosen to do special work for God. These people had certain rules to follow besides not cutting their hair. God said he would use Samson to deliver the Israelites from the Philistines.

Samson's mom never doubted the angel's message. God said her son would be a deliverer, and she believed him. When the baby was born, he was named Samson and raised as a Nazirite, set apart for God's work just as the angel had instructed.

Samson's mom was a woman who believed in God and obeyed his law. She taught Samson about God and God's mission for him, yet Samson made wrong choices, especially when it came to women. He chose to have relationships with women who did not love and honor God, and this often got him into trouble.

I'm sure Samson's mom was sad about the decisions he made, but she had done her part in teaching him God's laws. Each time he faced a decision, he could either make the right choice or do things his own way.

Each day you face decisions too. You have to decide whether you will do things God's way or your own way. Hopefully you are so in tune with God that your choices are his choices. Then doing what's right will feel natural, and that's the best way to live.

Delilah: The Wrong Kind of Girl

Some time later Samson fell in love with a woman named Delilah, who lived in the valley of Sorek. The rulers of the Philistines went to her and said, "Entice Samson to tell you what makes him so strong and how he can be overpowered and tied up securely. Then each of us will give you 1,100 pieces of silver."

JUDGES 16:4-5

What kind of woman would you pick for one of God's chosen deliverers? Certainly not an unfaithful Philistine wife, a prostitute, or someone who would betray him. Yet those are the women Samson chose.

First Samson married a Philistine, one of the enemy, who did not worship the true God. Then he visited a prostitute. His enemies planned to catch him leaving her house and kill him, but he left sooner than they expected. Later, when he started seeing Delilah, they offered her a great amount of money to find out the secret of Samson's strength and tell them.

Samson was physically very strong but spiritually and morally weak. He didn't keep the Nazirite rules. He chose the wrong women. He was someone who truly didn't live up to his potential for God.

Four times Delilah asked Samson what made him so strong. The first three times he lied to her. So when she tied him up and called his enemies, he easily broke free.

Once more Delilah begged him to tell her the real secret of his strength. The smart thing would have been to get rid of this woman who had tried to betray him three times already, but this time he told her the truth. He had power because his hair had never been cut. It wasn't that his hair actually gave him his strength, but that his long hair symbolized his special relationship with God. His enemies shaved his head, and Samson was now powerless. Delilah collected her money, and Samson was led away and blinded by his enemies.

thinking it through

Have you ever told someone a secret and regretted it later? Why? Are there some secrets that should not be kept? Could it ever be okay to tell someone else's secret? When?

Ask God to help you be a trustworthy friend and to give you wisdom to know when to keep your mouth closed.

thinking it through

What does the Bible say we should seek first? Read Matthew 6:33: "Seek the Kingdom of God above all else, and live righteously, and he will give you everything you need." How does Jesus say we should live? What will God give us if we live this way?

Delilah: Not a Storybook Romance

Three things will last forever—faith, hope, and love—and the greatest of these is love.

1 CORINTHIANS 13:13

Think of your perfect storybook romance. Is it Cinderella and Prince Charming? Beauty (Belle) and the Beast? Princess Tiana and Prince Naveen? All of these stories include a fight between good and evil, characters overcoming obstacles to be together, and a happy ending. How about Samson and Delilah?

Good and evil are found in Samson and Delilah's story—God's call on Samson's life was good; Delilah and the men who paid her to find out the secret of Samson's strength were evil.

How about obstacles? Well, there weren't any dragons to slay or wicked stepmothers to outwit. But Samson was set apart for God's work and had to keep his Nazirite vows, while Delilah did not believe in or worship God. Samson chose to compromise his faith in order to be with Delilah. That never leads to a happy ending.

There is certainly no happily-ever-after to this love story. It ends dramatically, but not joyfully.

Here's the ending: Samson's captors shaved his head and gouged out his eyes. Time passed, and the Philistine rulers and a large number of guests gathered together. They brought Samson out so they could make fun of him. The rulers didn't think about the fact that Samson's hair had grown back in the time he'd been their prisoner.

Samson asked a servant to lead him to the central pillars that held up the temple. He told the servant he wanted to lean on them. And lean on them he did! Samson asked God to give him strength one last time. Then he put a hand on each pillar and pushed. The temple collapsed on the rulers and guests. Samson killed more people in his death than while he lived.

This is not a storybook romance, but a sad story of love that didn't honor God and seek him first.

Delilah: A Friend Is Loyal

A friend is always loyal, and a brother is born to help in time of need.

PROVERBS 17:17

What do you look for in a friend? A sense of humor? A fun personality? Common interests? A listening ear? How about loyalty? That's a big one. Who wants a friend who talks about her behind her back or runs at the first sign of trouble? Not me, and probably not you.

But that's the kind of friend Delilah was. Disloyal, unfaithful, untrustworthy. The opposite of what most of us want in a friend. Yet that's who Samson picked. She asked him the secret of his strength four times. Three times he gave her false answers. She passed these answers on to his enemies, and they tried to capture him.

A smart person would have learned the lesson the first time. "I gave you an answer, and you used it to betray me. Get out of my life." Not Samson, though. He welcomed Delilah into his life and finally told her a secret he should have kept. She told his enemies and watched as they led him away. Did she have any regrets? Probably not. She was well paid for obtaining that secret.

If you're thinking this story happened long ago in Old Testament days, you're right, but that's not to say the same kind of disloyal behavior couldn't happen today. That's why it's important to be careful in choosing friends. Friends do betray friends and leave invisible hurts on their hearts. Sometimes these wounds never heal. Be loyal to your friends, and expect the same from them.

thinking it through

Do you have a friend you can count on? Write her a letter, telling her how much she means to you. It could make her day! Memorize Proverbs 17:17 to remind yourself what type of friend you should look for—and be.

Delilah: Light and Darkness

Don't team up with those who are unbelievers. How can righteousness be a partner with wickedness? How can light live with darkness?

2 CORINTHIANS 6:14

Oil and water don't mix. That's a well-known scientific fact. Believers and unbelievers don't mix either. That's a well-known biblical fact. The story of Samson and Delilah is a good example of why it doesn't work. Samson believed in God; Delilah worshiped idols. Samson had a God-given mission; Delilah was paid to destroy Samson.

Does this verse mean Christians and non-Christians shouldn't hang out at all? Not necessarily, but there are advantages to having peers who are trying to live for Jesus as your best friends. The Bible says, "As iron sharpens iron, so a friend sharpens a friend" (Proverbs 27:17). Just as one piece of iron can make another piece sharp by rubbing against it, two Christian friends can have the same positive effect on each other. Christian friends can encourage each other to read the Bible and pray; they can share what they learn about God; they can encourage each other to take a stand for God at school; and they can be involved in worthwhile activities together.

The same principle applies once you begin dating. Christians need to date other Christians. Even more than that, it's important to date Christians who are actively living out their faith. Many people will tell you they attend church or believe in God, but this doesn't mean they are really serious about living the way God wants them to live.

Avoid the heartache Samson faced when he associated with those who didn't believe in God. Be sure your closest friends and the boys you may date love and honor God the way you do.

thinking it through

Does your best friend love the Lord and encourage you in your Christian walk? If not, is there a way to encourage her to be more interested in God and living for him? If you answered no to both questions, it might be time to rethink the friendship. You don't have to abandon your friend who isn't as interested in God, but your closest friend should be one who shares your heart for God.

What about you? Do you encourage your friends in their Christian walk? Ask God to help you honor him with your friendships.

Quiz Time

elilah was not a loyal friend to Samson. Are you a loyal friend? Read each sentence below, and then circle A for always, S for sometimes, or N for never.

1. I keep my friend's secrets (unless it's a secret about something that is going to hurt her).

   A S N

2. If I say I will do something with or for my friend, I follow through.

   A S N

3. When my friend and I disagree about something, we come to a compromise.

   A S N

4. I stand by my friend if others say unfair things about her.

   A S N

5. I am happy for my friend when good things happen to her.

   A S N

How did you do? Give yourself 2 points for every A, 1 point for every S, and 0 points for every N.

7-10 points: You are a loyal friend. No one will ever accuse you of being like Delilah. You want the best for your friend, and you stand by her when times are tough.

4-6 points: You are sometimes a loyal friend, but you may not stand by your friend when a better deal or tough times come. Reevaluate your faithfulness to your friends.

0-3 points: Are you related to Delilah? Work on being a loyal friend. Stand by your friends and desire the best for them. Start placing their needs before yours, and see what happens.

thinking it through

When is it hardest for you to be totally honest?

- when you forget to do a job at home
- when you forget to do homework
- when you lose something
- when you break something
- when you don't want to hurt a family member's or friend's feelings
- when you don't want to admit a mistake

Are there any others you can think of? Ask God to help you be totally honest all the time, especially the times you identified above.

Delilah: Streaks of Deception

Honesty guides good people; dishonesty destroys treacherous people.

PROVERBS 11:3

Deception is a relationship killer, and in the story of Samson and Delilah, the streaks of deception ran deep. Delilah was deceptive down to the bone. She may originally have felt some attraction for this man who was stronger and more powerful than anyone around. But her motive for the relationship quickly turned to finding out the secret of Samson's strength to receive a large amount of money.

Samson was also deceptive when he made up stories about the secret of his strength. The honest thing to do would have been to tell Delilah he wasn't going to share that secret with her because it was between him and God.

Samson and Delilah had a relationship built on deceit. Most of us will never be involved in such a dishonest relationship as theirs, but we all have streaks of deception running through our lives. It might be something small like telling a "little white lie" to keep from getting into trouble over the homework you forgot to do: "I know I did that math worksheet. I must have left it in my dad's car." Or it may be pretending to be someone or something you are not: "I'm a really good swimmer. I get the award at camp each year." Or even lying to avoid hurting someone's feelings: "No, really, that haircut looks great." These things don't have deadly consequences like Delilah's deceit, but they aren't honest, either.

The best way not to fall into a pattern of dishonesty is to purge it totally from your life. Be a young lady of integrity. Admit mistakes, set the record straight, and value honesty.

Delilah: How to Be a Good Friend, Part 1

Many will say they are loyal friends, but who can find one who is truly reliable?

PROVERBS 20:6

Delilah was everything you don't want in a friend. She was manipulative and deceptive. She was looking out for herself and using people for her own gain. These are not the marks of a good friend. Would you want a friend who would betray you? Of course you don't want a friend like that.

What should you look for in a friend? Glad you asked. Here are four things to look for in a friend. We'll look at four more tomorrow.

Someone who listens. A true friend wants to know how you feel. She cares about the things that are bugging you. She will listen as you talk about the fight you had with your older brother. If you try to talk to your friend about a problem and she jumps in, trying to top your story with how much worse her problems are, she's not being a good listener.

Someone who keeps the things you share confidential. The last thing you want is to have your friend share with the whole volleyball team something you told her in secret. If she "just couldn't resist" telling your secret to one or two other girls, she's not being a good friend.

Someone who is honest. A friend needs to be up front with you, even about the little things. If she doesn't want to spend the night, she should just tell you rather than make up excuses. It might be hard to hear the truth sometimes. Who likes to hear they are in the wrong, are wearing inappropriate clothes, or need to try harder? But a real friend needs to feel free to share those sorts of things in a kind way.

Someone who keeps her word. A true friend will do what she says when she says she'll do it. Dependable, reliable, responsible—roll all these things together for a friend who keeps her promises. If your friend doesn't call when she says she will, is always late for the movie, or doesn't show up to study together as planned, she isn't someone you can depend on.

thinking it through

Just as the four things on the left are important in your friends, it's important you do these things too. Then you will be a good friend to someone else. Which of the four things on the left is easiest for you to do? Which is the hardest? Why? How can you improve in that area today?

thinking it through

We've looked at eight things that are important in a friendship. But there are many more things that are important too. What do you think are the ten most important character traits to look for in a friend? Write out your top ten list. Now ask a close friend how well those traits apply to you. Ask God to help you work on any that are a struggle.

Delilah: How to Be a Good Friend, Part 2

There are "friends" who destroy each other, but a real friend sticks closer than a brother.

PROVERBS 18:24

I hope you've spent some time this week thinking about marks of a good friend and traits that don't make for a loyal friend. Samson would have done well to do the same. But sometimes when you are in a relationship, it's hard to think clearly, so it's good to know what you want in a friend or boyfriend ahead of time.

Yesterday you read four things that are true of a good friend. Here are four more things to look for in a friend.

Someone who is an encourager. You don't need someone to point out how badly you messed up at play tryouts. You already know that. You've relived the moment over and over. You need someone who will tell you to practice and try again. It's easy to find someone who will criticize you, so look for someone who will be an encourager even on the toughest days.

Someone who shares interests with you. You don't have to share every hobby, but if there isn't anything you enjoy doing together, then you aren't going to have much fun. The best friends are those you look forward to spending time with, doing something you both like. Learn a hobby or play a sport together.

Someone who shares your faith. Samson and Delilah weren't a good pair because light and darkness don't mix. He was chosen by God, and she didn't believe in God. God has a mission for you, too, and a true friend will help you find and carry out that plan. You can do the same for her.

Someone who can accept your differences. You may be short and your friend tall. Or you may be shy while your friend is outgoing. That's okay. Differences are fine as long as they aren't differences about your values or lifestyles. Your being short and her tall won't keep you from having fun together, but if she lies and swears and you don't, that won't work out. Friends accept each other, differences and all.

Naomi: A Difficult Choice

In the days when the judges ruled in Israel, a severe famine came upon the land. So a man from Bethlehem in Judah left his home and went to live in the country of Moab, taking his wife and two sons with him.

RUTH 1:1

Naomi and her husband, Elimelech, lived in Bethlehem. They were well known and highly respected in this small Jewish town. Life was going well. Naomi gave birth to two boys, and the whole family loved and served God.

Then things fell apart. There was a famine, food was scarce, and Elimelech feared his family would die. He made the choice to move his family to Moab, where there was food. The problem was that Moab was a pagan country, and the Moabites and Israelites despised each other. So moving to Moab meant leaving a culture that believed in God for one that didn't, and leaving people who knew and loved them for a land where they were strangers.

Why did Elimelech choose to move his family to a pagan land rather than trust God to care for him in his own land? We don't know. It may have seemed like the logical choice for his family at the time, but sometimes the logical choice may not be the path God wants his people to take.

There will always be problems in our world. There are major tragedies like earthquakes, hurricanes, and droughts, and worldwide problems like hunger, homelessness, and abuse. There are more personal problems like families falling apart, friendships that end, homework that seems too hard, and teachers who are demanding or unreasonable. God knows about all these things, and he will be with you through whatever difficulties you face. Look to God for solutions, but don't be quick to take the easiest or most logical way out. Trust God to show you the path he has for you.

thinking it through

Jesus knew we would have problems here on earth, but John 16:33 says that he has overcome the world. How does knowing that help you to "take heart"?

Naomi: When Everything Is Gone

The two sons married Moabite women. One married a woman named Orpah, and the other a woman named Ruth. But about ten years later, both Mahlon and Kilion died. This left Naomi alone, without her two sons or her husband.

RUTH 1:4-5

When famine hit Bethlehem, the hometown of prominent citizens Elimelech and Naomi, Elimelech moved his family to Moab. He did this so his family would have plenty to eat and wouldn't face death in a land without food.

Unfortunately, Elimelech didn't accomplish what he wanted to with this move. First Elimelech himself died. Next Elimelech and Naomi's two sons, Mahlon and Kilion, married Moabite women. This was not a good idea since the Moabites worshiped idols instead of God.

Sometime after this, both sons died. Again, we don't know how or why or even if they died at the same time. All the Bible tells us is that they died, and neither had a child.

Naomi, once well loved and surrounded by friends and family in her own land, was now alone in a foreign country except for two Moabite daughters-in-law, grieving the loss of her husband and two sons. She didn't have any friends who shared her faith or worshiped her God. In fact, Naomi felt God himself had forsaken her.

Naomi was filled with grief and despair. Everything was gone. How she must have regretted the day her family left Bethlehem for Moab. But thankfully, this wasn't the end of the story for Naomi as you'll see later when you read about Ruth. With God there is always hope.

Sometimes we, too, wish we could go back and undo a situation or decision that seemed right at the time but ended in heartbreak. We can't do things over, but we can ask God to take control and work through the situation to accomplish his plan.

thinking it through

Has there ever been a time you felt like Naomi? How did you get over the feelings? Or, if you still feel that way, what might help you deal with the feelings?

Sometimes when tragedy happens, it can leave us feeling like there was something we could have done differently to prevent it. A lot of the time it isn't truly our fault. But God promises to care for us no matter what happened in the past.

Naomi: Returning Home Empty

"Don't call me Naomi," she responded. "Instead, call me Mara, for the Almighty has made life very bitter for me. I went away full, but the LORD has brought me home empty. Why call me Naomi when the LORD has caused me to suffer and the Almighty has sent such tragedy upon me?"

RUTH 1:20-21

Naomi left Bethlehem with a husband, two sons, and a heart filled with hope. Within ten years all her hopes were dashed and her family gone. She had only her two Moabite daughters-in-law left. Naomi heard God had blessed Judah (the region Bethlehem was in) with good crops again, and she realized it was time to leave the foreign, idol-worshiping Moab and return to her homeland. One daughter-in-law, Ruth, decided to go with her.

When Naomi reached Bethlehem in Judah, the people recognized her even though she had aged. "Is it really Naomi?" her longtime friends asked each other. It had been ten years since they'd seen her, and they couldn't believe she'd returned.

"Don't call me Naomi," she said. "Call me Mara." The name *Naomi* means "pleasant," but Mara was a name that meant "bitter," and Naomi felt bitter because of all that had happened. She told her friends and family in Bethlehem that she'd gone away full but had come home empty. Naomi had lost not one, but three close family members through death.

Coping with the death of someone close is hard. A flood of emotions hits you—denial, grief, guilt, bitterness, and maybe even relief, if the death follows a long illness. It can take years to work through those feelings.

The move back home was a good one for Naomi. Now she could receive the love and support of family and longtime friends. Ruth, her daughter-in-law, was at her side experiencing life in a God-worshiping country for the first time. Naomi's emptiness could now be filled with the love of those who truly cared about her.

thinking it through

How do you think Naomi felt as she entered the country she'd left ten years before? Why do you think it was important for Naomi to be surrounded by people who cared about her?

thinking it through

You or a friend may be hurting and not getting the help you need. Are you or your friend experiencing any of these problems?

- trouble sleeping
- eating much more or less than before
- low self-esteem
- lower grades
- not caring about once-favorite activities
- deteriorating relationships with family or friends

If one or more of these are true about your friend, the best thing you can do is encourage her to talk to a school counselor, pastor, or other trusted adult. Talk to a trusted adult if any of these are present in your own life.

Naomi: When Grief Becomes Unhealthy

"O death, where is your victory? O death, where is your sting?" For sin is the sting that results in death, and the law gives sin its power. But thank God! He gives us victory over sin and death through our Lord Jesus Christ.

1 CORINTHIANS 15:55-57

Naomi dealt with the loss of her husband and her two sons. Her two daughters-in-law dealt with the loss of their husbands. This was a lot of pain for one family. Sometimes grief can tear a family apart, or maybe one family member grieves alone.

Naomi and her daughters-in-law grieved the loss of a mate. That's not an experience that relates to you right now, but you may have faced other losses that left you feeling very sad. You may have

had a pet die;
had a grandparent become seriously ill, unable to visit anymore, or die;
had a close friend move away;
had a parent move out; or
had to move to a new location and leave your friends, school, and church behind.

Even though these situations are different from the ones faced by Naomi's family, they can still leave you with a broken heart and feelings of sadness that don't feel like they'll ever go away.

If you allow yourself to get stuck in that sad place, it can become unhealthy. It's hard to move on because it feels like there's nothing left for you. But there is.

Naomi and Ruth were able to go on and have satisfying lives because they realized that God still had more planned for them. Life was different, and perhaps there were still times of sadness, but they made new lives for themselves as they followed God's leading for their futures.

Puzzle Page

We will face hard times in our lives, just as Naomi did, but Jesus has comforting words for us. Fill in the puzzle to read Jesus' words.

Directions: The words in the word bank fit into the boxes below. The best way to solve these puzzles is to start with the longest words first. Then if you have many short words with the same number of letters left, you can fill them in by what words make sense in each box. Give it a try.

trials	earth	overcome	have	will
many	take	Here	you	heart
sorrows	because	have	world	

__ __ __ __ on __ __ __ __ __   __ __ __   __ __ __ __

__ __ __ __   __ __ __ __   __ __ __ __ __ __ and

__ __ __ __ __ __ __. But __ __ __ __

__ __ __ __ __, __ __ __ __ __ __ __ I __ __ __ __

__ __ __ __ __ __ __ __ the __ __ __ __ __.

Answer: Here on earth you will have many trials and sorrows. But take heart, because I have overcome the world. (John 16:33)

Naomi: How to Grieve

I will never forget this awful time, as I grieve over my loss. Yet I still dare to hope when I remember this: The faithful love of the LORD never ends! His mercies never cease.

LAMENTATIONS 3:20-22

Naomi and her daughters-in-law, Ruth and Orpah, all faced loss. They had each other's support in their time of sorrow, yet we are told nothing about how they dealt with their grief. Grieving, which is an emotional, physical, or spiritual reaction to death or loss, is normal, but no two people grieve their losses exactly the same. One person may vent and act out in pain while another suffers in silence.

Girls just like you are experiencing loss right now. They may have lost a grandparent after a long illness or a parent to a heart attack. Even the loss of a parent through divorce or a friend moving away can cause feelings of sorrow and emptiness. Maybe you've had a loss like that.

Grieving is personal, and how you grieve depends on your personality, the support you have, how the loss took place, your previous life experiences, and more. Your grief may change as time passes. There is no timeline for grief.

Some things that have helped others deal with grief are taking part in funerals or memorial services; being with close friends and family; talking about it; expressing themselves through writing, art, or music; creating a memorial such as a scrapbook for someone they've lost; and joining a support group.

Today is the anniversary of my dad's funeral, which took place many years ago. He'd suffered the effects of several strokes for many years, so in a way I had lost him years earlier, but today was the day I said my final good-byes. It was a beautiful and sunny day, and I remember thinking the day seemed too pretty for a funeral. I was sad, but at the same time I rejoiced because he was in heaven, no longer paralyzed by the strokes and no longer unable to talk. Death never wins; Jesus always wins.

thinking it through

It's important to keep memories of your lost loved ones alive. I wrote letters to my dad in a journal for a year after his death. No, he'd never read them, but it helped me work through my feelings and feel connected.

If you are hurting today, take time to grieve. It's okay to feel sad. But don't let the sadness overwhelm you, because there is hope in Jesus. Write out or memorize Lamentations 3:20-22 and read or say it to yourself whenever you start to feel hopeless.

Naomi: Moving On

For everything there is a season, a time for every activity under heaven. . . . A time to cry and a time to laugh. A time to grieve and a time to dance.

ECCLESIASTES 3:1, 4

Naomi had a long season of grief mixed with happiness. First Naomi's husband died, causing her great sorrow. Then there was a time of happiness again when her two sons married. Naomi hoped the young couples would have many children, and the family name would be passed on. She would have her sons to care for her in her old age and grandchildren to fill the house with laughter.

These hopes were dashed when both of her sons died, and neither had fathered any children. The family name would not be passed on, and there would be no sons or grandsons to care for her. Now all hope was gone. Naomi was too old to remarry or have more children. Her future seemed empty. She was alone in a pagan land with only the company of her two Moabite daughters-in-law.

Then one day Naomi decided it was time to leave this country, the land where she had lost all she held dear. She knew in her heart it was time to return home, to the land where God was known and worshiped. It was a land where she'd had happy times with her husband and sons and had been a prominent citizen.

Naomi was welcomed home by friends who remembered her. Her words to them in Ruth 1:21, "The LORD has caused me to suffer and the Almighty has sent such tragedy upon me," showed she clearly wasn't over her grief, but going home was a step toward healing. In the coming months she began experiencing joy again through the things God did for her through her daughter-in-law Ruth, who had left her family and land behind to journey to Bethlehem with Naomi.

There is a season for sorrow, but also a season for joy, and God journeys with his children through both.

thinking it through

Have you ever been through a season of sorrow? What did it feel like? Maybe you are in a place right now where it seems the sadness will never end. If so, it may help to talk to a pastor or trained counselor.

Naomi: When Sorrow Turns to Joy

The neighbor women said, "Now at last Naomi has a son again!" And they named him Obed. He became the father of Jesse and the grandfather of David.

RUTH 4:17

Naomi would never forget her husband and sons. She had years of happy memories. But her husband and sons were gone, and life had continued. Ruth, her daughter-in-law, made the journey back to Bethlehem with Naomi and helped care for her.

It would have been easy for Naomi and Ruth to wallow in self-pity, but the more important thing was to find a way to live. It was harvest time when the two women arrived in Bethlehem, and Ruth went into the fields and gathered fallen grain after the men had harvested. God was working out his plans for the two women when Ruth went to a field owned by Boaz to gather grain.

Ruth later married Boaz, and they had a son whom they named Obed. When Obed was born, he carried the name of Ruth's first husband according to the law at that time. Aging and grief had previously filled Naomi with despair, but Ruth's new baby filled her with hope. The baby continued her husband's line and was someone to love after losing her own sons. Naomi delighted in helping to care for this new child.

Naomi probably still had moments of sadness as she thought about all she had lost, but now she had joy to fill up the empty places in her heart as she cared for this new baby, a baby who was in the family line that Christ—the hope of the world—would someday be born into.

thinking it through

Sorrow and grief come, but with God, you can once again find joy. Psalm 30:5 tells us, "Weeping may last through the night, but joy comes with the morning." How can knowing God give you joy?

Orpah: The One Who Went Home

Again they wept together, and Orpah kissed her mother-in-law good-bye. But Ruth clung tightly to Naomi. "Look," Naomi said to her, "your sister-in-law has gone back to her people and to her gods. You should do the same."

RUTH 1:14-15

Orpah was married to one of Naomi's sons, and just like Naomi and Ruth, she lost her husband. When Naomi decided to return to her homeland, both Ruth and Orpah started out with her. Naomi thanked them for the love they had shown her and her sons, and she encouraged the young women to go home to their families.

According to the law at this time, if a woman's husband died and the couple had no sons, a brother of the husband was to marry the widow. Naomi pointed out to Ruth and Orpah that she didn't have any other sons for them to marry, and she was too old to have a son. Naomi encouraged them to find someone else to marry.

Here the young women parted ways. Orpah turned back and went home to her family, while Ruth went on to Bethlehem with Naomi. Orpah is never mentioned in the Bible again after this point. We are left to wonder:

- Did she marry again?
- Did she have children?
- Did she ever wish she'd gone with Naomi and Ruth?
- How would her life have been different if she hadn't turned back?

Whatever happened to Orpah, it was a result of her choice to go back to Moab.

You face many decisions in the coming years. You will have to choose whether to go to college, join the military, start a full-time job, or take another path after high school graduation. Each decision you make affects your future. Seek God as you make the best choices for yourself.

thinking it through

What choices do you need to make right now? What choices are in your future? How can you make the best choices for yourself? God will help you make the best choices if you ask him.

thinking it through

If you've messed up and feel like God can't use you, you're wrong. If God used only perfect people, then no one would qualify. God will give you the wisdom to change the things in your life that need changing and will help you stay on the path he has planned for you.

Talk to God about anything in your life that is keeping you from serving him.

Ruth: God Can Work through Mistakes

The two sons married Moabite women. One married a woman named Orpah, and the other a woman named Ruth.

RUTH 1:4

Ruth has been mentioned in the previous devotions about Naomi because much of their stories overlaps. Naomi and her family moved to Moab to escape the famine in Bethlehem. Ruth lived in Moab, a land inhabited by Lot's descendants, on the other side of the Dead Sea from Judah.

Although Elimelech and Naomi raised their sons, Mahlon and Kilion, to believe in and worship the true God, both sons married Moabite women. This was against God's laws, yet if it weren't for these marriages, a piece of Bible history would be missing, and we wouldn't have the book of Ruth, which is one of the best love stories ever written. Even though Mahlon married someone from an idol-worshiping culture, God worked in that situation. Ruth embraced Mahlon's God and followed her mother-in-law to a country that was foreign to her.

Elimelech may seem to have made a wrong choice to move to Moab. His sons may appear to have made wrong choices in choosing wives from an idol-worshiping country. But God is greater than these mistakes, and he chose to work in the situation to bring good out of it. We all make wrong decisions and do things that God doesn't want us to, but God doesn't give up on us when this happens.

We see only a small part of God's plan for us, but he sees the whole thing. Our mistakes don't catch God by surprise and leave him wondering what to do next. He created us and knows each of us better than anyone else does. He knows how to take our messes and fix them. That doesn't mean we won't suffer any consequences. But God still has a plan for us and still wants the very best for us.

Ruth: A Life-Changing Journey

Naomi heard in Moab that the LORD had blessed his people in Judah by giving them good crops again. So Naomi and her daughters-in-law got ready to leave Moab to return to her homeland.

RUTH 1:6

The book of Ruth is set during the dark times of the judges. These were the years when the Israelites would fall into sin, be oppressed by another nation, and need a deliverer. During this time God's people did what they wanted rather than what God wanted. Some Bible scholars suggest the famine that took place in Bethlehem was a punishment from God for the Israelites' sin. Yet even in dark times, there are some who are faithful to God. Naomi, Ruth, and Boaz were among these.

When the book of Ruth begins, Ruth is a young widow with an uncertain future. Naomi and Orpah are in the same situation. Being a widow in Bible times was hard. Widows were often ignored or taken advantage of. They lived in poverty unless there was someone to care for them. Under God's law it was the responsibility of the dead husband's closest male relative to care for the widow, but in this case, the three widows were alone in Moab. Naomi had no other sons to marry her daughters-in-law, Ruth and Orpah. There were no male relatives to provide for the women.

Even in these desperate circumstances, we don't see any self-pity or bitterness in Ruth. Her concern is for her aging mother-in-law. Naomi wanted to return home to Bethlehem, where there was once again food and where some of her relatives perhaps were still alive. Orpah went back to her family in Moab, but Ruth and Naomi set out for Bethlehem. It was a long and hard journey for two women on their own, but Ruth was determined to go with Naomi.

This trek was the beginning of a life-changing journey for Ruth as she left behind everything she knew and ventured toward a new beginning.

thinking it through

How do you think Ruth felt as she prepared to leave her old life behind and make the journey to Bethlehem with Naomi? Are you facing any new beginnings or unknown circumstances today? Maybe you'll be going to a new school next year—perhaps even starting middle school or high school. Or maybe you're going to a new camp or on a mission trip this summer to a place you've never been before. Ask God for the courage of Ruth each time you face something new in your life.

Ruth: Loyalty

Ruth replied, "Don't ask me to leave you and turn back. Wherever you go, I will go; wherever you live, I will live. Your people will be my people, and your God will be my God."

RUTH 1:16

Naomi had packed her few belongings and started her journey home. Ruth and Orpah began with her, but Orpah turned back at Naomi's urging. Not Ruth. She was determined to stay with Naomi. Ruth said, "Don't ask me to leave you and turn back. Wherever you go, I will go; wherever you live, I will live. Your people will be my people, and your God will be my God."

The words Ruth spoke to Naomi are often used in wedding ceremonies as couples pledge to live together from that day onward. But for Ruth, they were spoken to the mother of her dead husband. These few words were life changing for Ruth. They were her pledge to leave behind her country—she would go where Naomi went and live where Naomi lived. She also promised to leave behind family and the religious practices she had been raised with. She would accept Naomi's country, family, and God as her own.

Ruth didn't know what to expect when she left her own home behind and made the long trek with Naomi to her land. There were new sights and places to see, the customs were different, and the Israelites worshiped the true God, not idols. Ruth embraced this new land with its customs and people as her own.

In a way, that's what you do when you start your faith journey. You turn from your own way, believe in Jesus, and become part of his family. Your old, sinful ways are behind you, and you start out on a new journey following Jesus. Everything is new. Second Corinthians 5:17 says, "Anyone who belongs to Christ has become a new person. The old life is gone; a new life has begun!"

This was true for Ruth as she embraced Naomi's country, customs, and religious practices, and it's still true today for those who place their faith in Jesus.

thinking it through

What changes took place in Ruth's life when she left her hometown? What changes take place when a person believes in Jesus? Where are you in your journey with Jesus? Have you taken steps toward following him? If not, what is holding you back? Read more about how to begin your faith journey in the January 21 devo.

Puzzle Page

Ruth and Naomi were sad when their husbands died, but God turned their sadness into joy. Solve the Speedometer Puzzle below to see what the Bible says about sad times.

Directions: Each blank line has a number under it. Those numbers correspond to a letter on the speedometer. Look at the number under the first line. It is 90. Look at the speedometer. The letter with 90 is W. Write W on the line. Finish decoding the words and check your answer below.

___ ___ ___ ___ ___ ___ ___   ___ ___ ___   ___ ___ ___ ___
90 20 20 65 35 55 25   50 5 95   45 5 75 80

___ ___ ___ ___ ___ ___ ___ the ___ ___ ___ ___ ___,
80 30 70 60 85 25 30   55 35 25 30 80

___ ___ ___   ___ ___ ___   ___ ___ ___ ___ ___
10 85 80   40 60 95   15 60 50 20 75

with the ___ ___ ___ ___ ___ ___ ___.
50 60 70 55 35 55 25

Answer: Weeping may last through the night, but joy comes with the morning. (Psalm 30:5)

thinking it through

Take a tour of your house right now. What do you see that needs to be cleaned, fixed, or put away? Is there anything you can spend half an hour working on that would help a parent or sibling? Try it and see what happens!

Proverbs 12:11 says, "A hard worker has plenty of food." You probably don't have to work for your food, but how can this verse apply to your life right now?

Ruth: A Hard Worker

Ruth worked alongside the women in Boaz's fields and gathered grain with them until the end of the barley harvest. Then she continued working with them through the wheat harvest in early summer. And all the while she lived with her mother-in-law.

RUTH 2:23

Ruth and Naomi were two women alone without a way to care for themselves. Naomi was too old to work, so Ruth needed to find a way to provide for them. The Jewish law said grain dropped by the harvesters as they gathered crops should be left for poor people to pick up. This was the perfect solution for Ruth.

One day Ruth went to Boaz's fields to collect grain. She worked hard under the hot sun, gathering a small pile of grain, which grew larger as the day went on. She was determined to provide for both herself and Naomi and worked diligently to have a large supply of food.

The work was tiring and the grain got heavy, but there is no record that Ruth complained. Like Rebekah, who watered Eliezer's camels, and Rachel, who watered the family sheep, Ruth was a hard worker. She determined to do the job, and she did. Because of her diligence, Ruth and Naomi had what they needed to live. Her hard work also caught the attention of the landowner. You'll read about that in tomorrow's devo.

How are you when it comes to hard work? When Dad says it's time to mow the lawn, do you grab the mower and take the first turn, or do you disappear into your air-conditioned room? Are you the first in line to help tidy the garage or clean up after the pets? Make it a point to be a diligent worker this week. Surprise your parents by being the first to tackle the tough jobs.

Ruth: Hard Work Is Noticed

She bowed down with her face to the ground. She exclaimed, "Why have I found such favor in your eyes that you notice me—a foreigner?"

RUTH 2:10, NIV

Ruth's hard work in gathering grain was quickly noticed by the landowner, Boaz. He arrived at his fields, saw Ruth, and asked his workers who she was. They told him she was the woman from Moab who had come to Bethlehem with Naomi.

Boaz approached Ruth and spoke to her: "My daughter, listen to me. Don't go and glean in another field and don't go away from here. Stay here with my servant girls. Watch the field where the men are harvesting, and follow along after the girls. I have told the men not to touch you. And whenever you are thirsty, go and get a drink from the water jars the men have filled" (Ruth 2:8-9, NIV).

The conversation continued with Ruth asking Boaz why he was showing her this kindness, and he replied he had heard of all she'd done for her mother-in-law and how she'd left her own land and journeyed with Naomi to a new country.

Ruth answered very graciously. "May I continue to find favor in your eyes, my lord," she said. "You have given me comfort and have spoken kindly to your servant—though I do not have the standing of one of your servant girls" (Ruth 2:13, NIV). At this answer, Boaz invited Ruth to join him for food and drink.

This scenario is very different from the way things are done today. Ruth was not seeking attention, nor did she flirt or do anything to gain Boaz's favor. Boaz noticed her hard work, knew of her reputation, and singled her out for his attention. He made sure she was taken care of.

Ruth made an impression on Boaz through her hard work, loyalty to her mother-in-law, and her gracious manners. Soon Ruth was known throughout the town as a hard worker and loyal family member. And this was the start of a perfect storybook romance.

thinking it through

When have you noticed someone else's hard work? Did you compliment him or her on it? When has someone noticed your hard work and complimented you for it?

Ruth wasn't working hard to show off, but her actions were noticed anyway. Colossians 3:23-24 says, "Work willingly at whatever you do, as though you were working for the Lord rather than for people. Remember that the Lord will give you an inheritance as your reward." The next task you are given, work hard, but do it for God's glory. And if no one notices, you can still be content to know that God will reward you.

thinking it through

In what ways did Samson and Delilah differ from Ruth and Boaz? How were their relationships different?

Are you known as an unselfish and loyal friend? Do you try games and activities that others want to do first, or do you insist on deciding what the group will do? Do you pay attention to others' feelings, or do you talk about your own feelings first? This week, pay attention to the way you treat your friends. Ask God to help you put others first.

Ruth: A Storybook Romance

"Who are you?" he asked. "I am your servant Ruth," she replied. "Spread the corner of your covering over me, for you are my family redeemer."

RUTH 3:9

When Ruth arrived home at the end of the day and told Naomi about how kind Boaz had been to her, Naomi told Ruth that Boaz was related to her late husband, Elimelech. Ruth continued to pick up grain in Boaz's field until the end of the harvest season. Naomi saw this as an opportunity to make sure Ruth would be well taken care of in the future.

Naomi gave Ruth instructions for following an ancient Jewish custom, where a widow would ask a male relative to take her as his wife. Naomi said, "Now do as I tell you—take a bath and put on perfume and dress in your nicest clothes. Then go to the threshing floor, but don't let Boaz see you until he has finished eating and drinking. Be sure to notice where he lies down; then go and uncover his feet and lie down there. He will tell you what to do" (Ruth 3:3-4).

Ruth did as Naomi said, slipping into the dark of night and making her way to Boaz's land. Boaz woke up in the night and found Ruth at his feet. Boaz was honored that Ruth had chosen him. But he told her that there was another closer relative who should be the first choice for Ruth to marry. He promised Ruth he would talk to the other relative and make sure the man didn't want to marry her.

Boaz kept his word and found the other relative, who declined the offer to marry Ruth. So Ruth soon found herself married to a wealthy landowner who was also a kind and compassionate man, willing to care not only for her but also for Naomi.

Do you remember the story of Samson and Delilah? (See May 4.) Boaz and Ruth's story stands in stark contrast to it. Samson and Delilah's relationship was one of deceit and greed between two people who did not share the same faith. Boaz and Ruth both loved God and were unselfish and willing to care for others. What a difference these things made in the endings of these stories.

Ruth: What Makes a Strong Relationship?

Who can find a virtuous and capable wife? She is more precious than rubies.

PROVERBS 31:10

Why did Ruth and Boaz's relationship endure and remain an example for us today while Samson and Delilah's ended tragically? It was because of the character traits demonstrated by both Ruth and Boaz.

Take a quick look at the comparisons between the two couples.

Samson and Delilah	**Boaz and Ruth**
Deceitful	Honest
Lustful	Pure
Greedy	Generous
Lazy	Hardworking
Selfish	Selfless
Unfaithful to God's laws	Faithful to God's laws

Just looking at this list should give you an idea of why one relationship thrived while the other failed. One couple was focused on God; they were giving and hardworking while the other was unfaithful to God, greedy, and living for their own pleasure and gain.

What does this have to do with you? Everything! The choices you make today determine what kind of person you will be tomorrow. You can choose to be honest or dishonest. If you practice dishonesty today, it will be harder for you to be honest tomorrow, and you won't blossom into a person of integrity in the future. You have to choose honesty each time you face the temptation to lie.

You can choose whether to keep yourself pure. If you determine to save your affection for your husband, you will always be known for purity. The same is true for the other character traits. You can choose greediness or generosity, laziness or hard work, selfishness or selflessness, unfaithfulness or faithfulness to God. Remember that each choice you make is important and is part of who you are becoming.

thinking it through

Are you more like Samson and Delilah or Boaz and Ruth? Look at the list of traits each couple displayed. Rate yourself in each area on a scale of 1 to 10 (1 being Samson and Delilah, and 10 being Boaz and Ruth). Did you score any 1s? How about 5s? Even if you scored 9s, you can work on your character—and you don't have to do it alone. Ask God to help you replace the negative character traits with godly ones.

thinking it through

Are you developing good character? Make a list of some character traits Ruth showed (selflessness, patience, responsibility, etc.). Look through the book of Ruth in your Bible if you need some help. Can you work on any of these traits this week? Pray right now and ask God to help you develop into a woman of good character.

Ruth: Character Counts

Boaz took Ruth into his home, and she became his wife. When he slept with her, the LORD enabled her to become pregnant, and she gave birth to a son.
RUTH 4:13

Ruth and Boaz are two well-loved Bible characters, and their story is one of the best romantic tales there is. Poor girl meets rich boy; they marry and live happily ever after. The thing that makes their story so powerful and so tender at the same time is their character, not where they came from or who they were related to.

Sometimes people spend too much time focused on *who* someone is—his or her family background or connections—rather than *what* the person is like inside. Poor behavior may be overlooked in someone because of his or her family connections. For Ruth and Boaz, their family backgrounds were overlooked because of their good behavior.

Ruth was a Moabite. The Jews despised her people. The Moabites had refused to help the Israelites years earlier when they had left Egypt for the Promised Land. Deuteronomy 23:3-4 says, "No Ammonite or Moabite or any of their descendants for ten generations may be admitted to the assembly of the LORD. These nations did not welcome you with food and water when you came out of Egypt."

What about Boaz's family? Matthew 1:5 gives us his family connections: "Salmon was the father of Boaz (whose mother was Rahab). Boaz was the father of Obed (whose mother was Ruth). Obed was the father of Jesse." Boaz's family tree includes Rahab, once a well-known prostitute, who chose to join the Israelites when Jericho was destroyed.

Despite their family backgrounds, God chose to make Ruth and Boaz a part of Jesus' family tree. They gave birth to Obed, who was the grandfather of King David, and Jesus was from David's line.

God looks at character, not background. No one gets to choose the family into which she is born, but everyone can decide what kind of person she will become. And that is what matters to God.

Ruth: Devoted to Family

Her children stand and bless her. Her husband praises her: "There are many virtuous and capable women in the world, but you surpass them all!"

PROVERBS 31:28-29

Families are God's idea. He started with one man and one woman, then told them to have many children to populate the world. Before God created Eve, Adam had only the animals to keep him company. Psalm 68:6 says, "God places the lonely in families." God knew Adam would be lonely without a companion, because people get lonely by themselves.

God placed Ruth in a birth family. Then she married into Elimelech's family, where she had a mother-in-law (Naomi), husband (Mahlon), brother-in-law (Kilion), and sister-in-law (Orpah). Then the two brothers died, and it was just the three women on their own. Orpah went back to her birth family, and Ruth and Naomi became a family of two.

Ruth could have abandoned Naomi and gone back home in hopes of finding a new husband to provide for her, but she didn't. Ruth knew if she did, Naomi would have no one at all. So Ruth remained loyal to Naomi, leaving her own homeland for Naomi's.

God didn't leave the two women alone. He led Ruth to Boaz's field. God knew Boaz would be the perfect husband for her. Boaz had already heard how Ruth had cared for Naomi and was impressed by it. He said, "May the LORD, the God of Israel, under whose wings you have come to take refuge, reward you fully for what you have done" (Ruth 2:12).

Sometimes it's difficult to put the needs, or even wants, of family members above our own. What happens when your pesky younger brother has a dental appointment at the same time you have a soccer game or when your sister needs to be driven to gymnastics when you need a ride to the mall to meet your friends? How easy is it to put their needs first? Maybe not all that easy, but practice looking out for their needs as much as your own.

thinking it through

Think of three situations in which you can put a family member's needs above your own. When you encounter a conflict like the ones described at the end of today's devo, ask God to help you make the selfless choice.

thinking it through

Romans 12:11 says, "Never be lazy, but work hard and serve the Lord enthusiastically." What could make you "enthusiastic" about hard work? Let that be your motivation this week.

Ruth: A Wise Worker

She is energetic and strong, a hard worker. She makes sure her dealings are profitable; her lamp burns late into the night.

PROVERBS 31:17-18

Proverbs 31 talks about the wife who is virtuous and capable. This woman has her act together, and others look up to her. She doesn't just sit at home and think noble thoughts. She is a hard worker, up early in the morning to get things done, and she invests her money to make more. She doesn't waste her money on things that don't pay off, because she wants to take care of her family. She is clothed in strength and dignity.

Ruth was the same way. She was up early and off to the fields where she gathered grain all day. Even though Boaz provided extra for her and she had enough to last for a while, she still went to the field each day.

Today many people are taken in by get-rich-quick schemes. This is because people are eager to get something for nothing. They'd rather have things handed to them than work for them. You wouldn't find these people out gathering grain to provide for an aging mother-in-law. In fact, you wouldn't find them doing any manual labor at all. These are the people who fall for e-mail scams, such as, "You have been chosen to inherit a million dollars from Mr. Bigbucks in Iraq. Simply send five hundred dollars to begin the process of claiming your inheritance." If people didn't fall for such a silly scheme, there wouldn't be so many of those e-mails circulating.

The problem is, some people would rather have money handed to them than work for it, so it's easy to fool them, but there is always something hidden or downright phony in get-rich-quick schemes. This results in people losing all their money rather than gaining any. The Proverbs 31 woman had the right idea. She would make money and then invest it wisely so she'd have more money to care for her family.

Take a lesson from Ruth, and don't shy away from work. Be like the Proverbs 31 woman and work hard, and then use your money wisely.

Quiz Time

What kind of worker are you? Rate yourself by reading each sentence and circling N for never, S for sometimes, or A for always.

1. I do my work without complaining.

   A S N

2. I am the first to volunteer when a job needs to be done.

   A S N

3. When I do a job, I give it my best.

   A S N

4. My parents and teachers would describe me as a hard worker.

   A S N

5. I am proud of the jobs I complete.

   A S N

How did you do? Give yourself 2 points for every A, 1 point for every S, and 0 points for every N.

Total _____

8-10 points: You are industrious like Ruth. You are hardworking and not afraid to tackle the tough jobs. You complete your tasks well and can be proud of your work. Be sure not to try and do it all yourself, though. Everyone needs help or a break at times.

5-7 points: You help out, but sometimes you slack off or leave the worst jobs for someone else. When you do your best, you can be proud of the work you do.

0-4 points: Too often you leave the work for someone else. You'd rather have fun than labor. Ask God to give you the desire to work hard and do your part. Give each job your best effort so you can be proud of the work, and others will notice too.

If you didn't score well, do your best with work this week and try the quiz again.

Ruth: Devoted to God

Charm is deceptive, and beauty does not last; but a woman who fears the LORD will be greatly praised.
PROVERBS 31:30

Ruth had not been raised to believe in God. She had not heard stories passed down about the parting of the Red Sea or the fall of Jericho's walls. She hadn't watched her parents go to the Temple or offer sacrifices to God. Ruth grew up in a pagan society.

Ruth must have learned about God while married to Naomi's son, and while living with Naomi. She declares her faith to Naomi in Ruth 1:16: "Ruth replied, 'Don't ask me to leave you and turn back. Wherever you go, I will go; wherever you live, I will live. Your people will be my people, and your God will be my God.'" Ruth tells Naomi that not only will she leave her country to go to Naomi's country, but also she'll leave her religion behind and accept Naomi's God. Ruth may have already believed in God from watching Naomi's family, or she may have just declared it for the first time here. Either way, Ruth chose to follow God, and she never looked back.

Boaz, also a believer in God, became Ruth's kinsman-redeemer. A kinsman-redeemer was a close male relative of the dead husband. A kinsman-redeemer could avenge deaths, claim inheritance for poor family members, and marry the widow of his relative. Basically he was someone who helped or rescued another person in his family. In Ruth's case, Boaz would marry and provide for her. He could buy back any land Elimelech had leased or sold when the family left for Moab. Under law, their first son would be counted as an heir of Ruth's first husband, so Elimelech's family line would continue.

Jesus acts as our kinsman-redeemer when he saves us from our sins and makes us part of his family. Ephesians 1:7-8 says, "He is so rich in kindness and grace that he purchased our freedom with the blood of his Son and forgave our sins. He has showered his kindness on us, along with all wisdom and understanding." Boaz showered Ruth with kindness and shared all he had with her. Jesus has done the same for us.

thinking it through

Ruth learned about the true God from her husband's family. Could someone learn anything about God from watching your family? How does your life reflect God's love to others? Think of one way you can shower someone with kindness this week.

Ruth: Pure

Ruth lay at Boaz's feet until the morning, but she got up before it was light enough for people to recognize each other. For Boaz had said, "No one must know that a woman was here at the threshing floor."

RUTH 3:14

Naomi was concerned about Ruth's future. When Naomi saw that Ruth admired Boaz, Naomi came up with a plan. Ruth would marry Boaz, and he would be a kinsman-redeemer to her. (You can learn about a kinsman-redeemer in yesterday's devo.) Naomi told Ruth how to let Boaz know she wanted to marry him.

Workers often slept near the grain during the harvest season. Naomi told Ruth to go where Boaz was sleeping and to lie down at his feet. Ruth did this, and when Boaz awoke in the night, she told him why she was there. Following a Jewish custom, he quickly agreed to marry her, and then he told her to sleep until morning, when he sent her home before light so no one would know she was there.

Some people try to make this into something dirty, saying Ruth was seducing Boaz, but this is absolutely not true. She lay down at his feet, not his side, and Boaz referred to her as a virtuous woman (Ruth 3:11). Ruth was pure, and Boaz guarded that purity.

The Bible doesn't talk about Ruth's or Boaz's appearance, only their reputations. Ruth won the approval of everyone who knew her even though she was a Moabite. Boaz praised her for her family loyalty and her virtue. Boaz was hardworking and compassionate. Ruth and Boaz's relationship was based first on their admiration for each other's character, then on their commitment to each other and their love, rather than on physical attraction and passion.

Many of your peers are already in girlfriend-boyfriend relationships. Listen as they talk about those relationships. What is most important to them? Are they more concerned about his looks or his character? About his popularity or his behavior?

Naomi, Ruth, and Boaz are all reminders that godly character does count and is rewarded.

thinking it through

What do you think are the top things girls look for in guys? What things *should* they look for? List the five things you think are most important. We will look at some of Boaz's characteristics in the next two devotions. See how those traits match your list.

thinking it through

Take a look at the guys around you. Which of them are friendly and kind to others? What actions tell you they think of others as equal to themselves? How do they treat the new kid or the kid who dresses or acts differently from everyone else?

How about you? Do you treat everyone equally, no matter where they come from or what they wear? Pay attention to your attitudes this week, and ask God to help you treat others the way Boaz would have.

Ruth: Traits of a Godly Man, Part 1

While she was there, Boaz arrived from Bethlehem and greeted the harvesters. "The LORD be with you!" he said. "The LORD bless you!" the harvesters replied.

RUTH 2:4

You've been reading about Ruth, but her story wouldn't be complete without a look at Boaz. He had many good qualities. We meet Boaz at the beginning of Ruth 2. It says, "Now there was a wealthy and influential man in Bethlehem named Boaz, who was a relative of Naomi's husband, Elimelech."

This verse tells us only who he is, not what kind of person he is. Boaz had money and power. There are many men today who have both money and power. Some men use it to help people. Others use it to accumulate cars and houses. Others use it to hurt people.

The first clue to what kind of man Boaz is comes a few verses later when he arrives at his field and greets his workers. He says, "The LORD be with you!" to which they reply, "The LORD bless you!" Then Boaz asks who Ruth is. When they tell him, he goes to talk to her. Boaz tells her to stay in his fields and to share his water. He invites her to eat with him and his workers.

Boaz's words and actions show he is a kind man. He doesn't think of himself as better than others even though he owns the land. He greets his workers and Ruth graciously and values them as equals.

If you attend a public school, there are all kinds of students around you. Some of your peers have parents who own their own businesses, while others have parents who depend on food stamps. Some of the parents may be on the city council, where they make decisions that affect others, while some parents work the night shift at a restaurant. But none of those things make any student more or less important. Who your parents are or who your peers' parents are should not affect how you treat those around you.

When you begin dating, look at how your date treats you and others. Does he treat everyone fairly? Is he kind? If not, it's time to look elsewhere.

Ruth: Traits of a Godly Man, Part 2

At mealtime Boaz called to her, "Come over here, and help yourself to some food. You can dip your bread in the sour wine." So she sat with his harvesters, and Boaz gave her some roasted grain to eat. She ate all she wanted and still had some left over.

RUTH 2:14

Even though Boaz was wealthy and influential, he put others ahead of himself. He showed this by the way he was generous and encouraging to others and faithful in meeting their needs. Boaz could have just sat and supervised his workers and ignored Ruth's need. But he didn't. Boaz mingled with his workers. He ate with them and even invited Ruth to join them for the meal.

When Ruth approached him to request he marry her, he sent her home with extra grain. Then he kept his word to her that he would talk to the other man who was a closer relative than he was to Elimelech. He would see if that man wanted to marry Ruth, which was the custom. When the other man declined, Boaz married Ruth.

Some people think of themselves first. They want their needs met. Instead of looking for what they can do for others, they look for what others can do for them. Boaz was not one of these men, and that is one reason why Ruth and Boaz had a marriage blessed by God. Not only was their relationship blessed, but God also gave them a son named Obed, who was the grandfather of King David and an ancestor of Jesus.

Decide now while you are young that you won't settle for less than God's best when it comes to marriage. Look for a man who has some of the same characteristics as Boaz. He was first of all a worshiper of the true God, and from that sprang his friendliness, kindness, generosity, and faithfulness.

thinking it through

Want to be like Ruth and Boaz? God can give you the wisdom to live the kind of life Ruth and Boaz had.

James 3:17 says, "The wisdom from above is first of all pure. It is also peace loving, gentle at all times, and willing to yield to others. It is full of mercy and good deeds. It shows no favoritism and is always sincere."

What things in the verse above describe Ruth or Boaz? Which one will you work on developing in your life this week?

Hannah: Something's Missing

Elkanah had two wives, Hannah and Peninnah. Peninnah had children, but Hannah did not.

1 SAMUEL 1:2

We are introduced to Hannah at the beginning of 1 Samuel with the words "Peninnah had children, but Hannah did not." During Hannah's time, the Philistines oppressed the Israelites, but Hannah didn't worry about that. She was concerned with the fact that she didn't have any children, and what was worse, her husband's other wife did.

Does this sound familiar? It should. Hannah is the fourth woman in the Bible who couldn't have children but desperately wanted them. First there was Sarah. After years passed and Sarah still didn't have children, she told Abraham to have children by her servant Hagar. This resulted in a lot of problems between the two women.

Then there was Rebekah. She didn't face ridicule or rivalry from other women for being childless the way Hannah, Sarah, and Rachel did, but she still longed for a baby. Rachel was the third Bible woman to want a child. And like Hannah, she shared her husband with another wife who was able to have children. What was worse was that the other wife was Rachel's older sister. Rachel's and Hannah's stories are also similar because it was the favorite wife who was unable to have children.

All four of these women grieved over their inability to have children. They felt their lives were missing something. At one time or another, all of us feel our lives are missing something. At your age, it isn't a baby you long for, but perhaps you wish for a best friend or for a guy to like you. Maybe your parents are divorced, and you wish they were together. Or one parent is seldom home because of frequent business trips.

No matter what is missing in your life, talk to God about it. That's what Hannah did. God doesn't always answer our prayers the way we want, but he does answer them in the best way for each of us.

thinking it through

Do you feel like anything is missing in your life? Write a prayer to God asking him to fill up the empty place caused by what's missing.

If you feel content about the way things are in your life right now, that's great! Write a prayer of thanks for all God's given you.

Hannah: Desires of the Heart

Hannah was in deep anguish, crying bitterly as she prayed to the LORD. . . . "Oh no, sir!" she replied. "I haven't been drinking wine or anything stronger. But I am very discouraged, and I was pouring out my heart to the LORD."

1 SAMUEL 1:10, 15

Hannah desperately wanted a son, and she knew what to do. Every year the family made a trip to the Tabernacle to worship and offer sacrifices. Hannah was deeply troubled by her failure to have any children, so she went into the Tabernacle alone to pour out her despair to God.

Eli, the priest, saw Hannah praying. She was praying with such passion that her lips were moving, but no sound was coming out, so Eli assumed she had come to the Tabernacle drunk! He told her to get rid of her wine.

Can you imagine how Hannah felt to be praying with such passion and to have the priest assume she was drunk? Hannah graciously explained that she was praying out of extreme sadness.

"In that case," Eli said, "go in peace! May the God of Israel grant the request you have asked of him" (1 Samuel 1:17).

Once Eli realized how wrongly he had judged Hannah, he quickly blessed her and asked God to grant her petition. The blessing of the high priest was considered to be prophetic, so Hannah may have already assumed her prayer had been answered.

Even though Hannah desperately wanted a son, the Scripture doesn't show her complaining to her husband or being bitter against God. In fact, her desire for a child turned her to God as she went and prayed alone in the Tabernacle.

Where do you turn when you want something? Do you share the desires of your heart with your friends or with God? It's okay to talk to your close friends about the important things in your life, but take a tip from Hannah and find a place where you can talk to God alone.

thinking it through

When you delight in the Lord, you want the same things for yourself God wants for you. To delight in someone means you have pleasure from being in his or her company. This happens when you are close to that person and know him or her well. How can you get to know God better this week?

thinking it through

What are you asking God for today? Why do you want God to answer that prayer? Why do you think motives matter to God?

Hannah: Right Motives

She made this vow: "O LORD of Heaven's Armies, if you will look upon my sorrow and answer my prayer and give me a son, then I will give him back to you. He will be yours for his entire lifetime, and as a sign that he has been dedicated to the LORD, his hair will never be cut."

1 SAMUEL 1:11

Hannah's promise to God is one of the most well-known promises in the Bible. Sometimes people use this verse to say it's okay to bargain with God—if you do this for me, I'll do that for you. But this wasn't what Hannah was doing.

When a person tries to strike a bargain with God, she is usually doing it for selfish reasons or to get out of a difficult situation. Hannah wanted what God wanted for her. She loved God so much she was willing to give him what she wanted most, a son. If God blessed her with a son, Hannah was willing to sacrifice him to the Lord's work. Hannah prayed with the right motives.

When we pray, we may be able to fool others about our motives. Sometimes we can even fool ourselves. But we can never fool God. He sees our hearts. When our motives are right, he is more likely to grant our prayers. Hannah could have prayed that God would give her a child so her husband's other wife would stop teasing her. She could have prayed for a child so she would be just like everyone else. But Hannah prayed for a child so she could dedicate him to the Lord's service.

When you pray, stop and ask yourself what your motives are. Are you praying that you'll be voted class president so you can be more popular or so you will be in a better position to share your faith? Are you praying to get a part in the play to show off for others or so you can bring honor to God through your talents? No matter what you are praying for, motives matter. Make sure your motives are in line with God's plans for you.

Puzzle Page

Use the Box Code below to help you decode the verse and see what God says about our desires.

in	Take	desires	give	heart's
delight	Lord	will	you	
the	and	he	your	

______ ______ ______ ______ ______,

______ ______ ______ ______ ______

______ ______ ______.

Answer: Take delight in the LORD, and he will give you your heart's desires. (Psalm 37:4)

thinking it through

How do your prayers compare to Hannah's? How can you pray with purpose? Ask one person to join you in praying with purpose this week.

Hannah: Praying with Purpose

Rejoice in our confident hope. Be patient in trouble, and keep on praying.

ROMANS 12:12

Hannah was driven to prayer by her despair over not having a child. First Samuel 1 shows Hannah pouring out her heart to God in the Tabernacle, but this certainly isn't the only time that she prayed for a child.

Crystal was a woman similar to Hannah. She had been married seven years but had been unable to have children. During those years she asked God to send her a baby, but she still wasn't able to get pregnant. Crystal wondered if she'd done something to make God angry at her.

Finally Crystal decided to pray not for a child but for God to make his plan for her life clear and fulfill her longing to be a mother. Crystal's prayers had changed, but she was still praying with purpose—that somehow she would be able to be a mother.

The beginning of the answer to that prayer happened later that week when she started a conversation with a mother of three young children standing behind her in line at the grocery store. She found out that the mom had adopted the three children. The mother shared about the need for homes for children without parents and gave Crystal the phone number of a social worker.

Crystal talked to her husband about the possibility of adoption. He agreed, and they began the paperwork. Ten months later, they were the parents of a thirteen-month-old girl.

Crystal prayed that she would be a mother, and God answered her prayer by bringing a needy, motherless child into her life.

Sometimes when we pray, we pray random, general prayers—bless this day, be with the missionaries, be with me at school, and so on. God wants us to pour out our hearts before him just as Hannah did. He wants us to ask for the true desires of our hearts. Then we are praying with purpose.

Hannah: Power in Prayer

Confess your sins to each other and pray for each other so that you may be healed. The earnest prayer of a righteous person has great power and produces wonderful results.

JAMES 5:16

Does prayer really accomplish anything? God already knew Hannah wanted a baby, so why did she have to keep praying? Couldn't God have just given her the desire of her heart without her asking? He could have, but unlike your earthly father, your heavenly Father doesn't mind if you ask him for the same thing over and over. In fact, he loves when his children pour out their hearts to him as Hannah did.

Maybe it seems like your problems are so big that your prayers won't make a difference. You're not alone if you feel your prayers lack power to change anything, but it's God's power, not yours, that makes the difference. Tap into his power by talking to him regularly.

Your life may be packed full of friends, activities, and responsibilities at home. It's easy to forget to pray, yet prayer will make the things in your life fall into place. It will keep you focused on God and his plan for you. When you get close to God through prayer, you will desire the things he wants for you, and you will sense him guiding you on the path he's chosen for you.

Becoming a young woman of prayer doesn't mean you won't have any more problems, but it does mean that God will guide you through them or will give you the power to overcome them. You will draw comfort and wisdom through talking to God about the hard things in your life.

Sarah, Rachel, Hannah, and many others discovered the power of prayer in their lives, and you will too as you begin to spend time in conversation with God.

thinking it through

When could you spend a few minutes praying each day? Right after you wake up? After lunch? When you get home from school or camp? Just before bed? Set aside a few minutes each day this week to pour out your heart to God as Hannah did. You may be surprised at how God works in your life.

thinking it through

Choose three people for whom you will stand in the gap this week. Ask them if there is something you can pray about for them. Write down their names and requests. Then make sure to pray each day.

Hannah: Standing in the Gap

You want what you don't have, so you scheme and kill to get it. You are jealous of what others have, but you can't get it, so you fight and wage war to take it away from them. Yet you don't have what you want because you don't ask God for it.

JAMES 4:2

God wants you to pray for your needs just as Hannah did. Praying for your needs is not a selfish thing to do. But it's also important to pray for the needs of others. When you pray for another's needs, it is called intercessory prayer. That means you are asking God to act on someone else's behalf. One example of this in the Bible is when Abraham asked God to spare Sodom. Abraham was standing in the gap between the wicked people and God. Since there were no righteous people in Sodom, God did not spare the city, but he did listen to Abraham's prayer and answer him by saving Lot's family.

There are many people in your life who could use your prayers. You might pray for

- your parents;
- your siblings;
- other relatives;
- your friends;
- your local police officers and firefighters;
- your pastor; or
- your youth leaders or Sunday school teacher.

Each of these people has needs you may know nothing about, but God does. One may be sick; another may need a better job or more money. One may have family or marriage problems or a child who is making bad decisions. One may be facing a big decision or a change in his or her life.

Ask God to meet the needs of those around you. Your prayers will make a difference.

Hannah: When and Where to Pray

Keep on asking, and you will receive what you ask for. Keep on seeking, and you will find. Keep on knocking, and the door will be opened to you.

MATTHEW 7:7

It's easy to spend too much time worrying about when and where to pray and not enough time actually praying. Hannah prayed in the Tabernacle. That is like you praying at church, but you don't have to be at church to pray. Throughout the Bible, people talked to God in a lot of different places, at different times.

Adam and Eve walked and talked with God in a garden (Genesis 3).

Daniel prayed to God by his window—and later he undoubtedly prayed in the lions' den (Daniel 6:10, 19-23).

Elijah talked to God in a cave (1 Kings 19:8-18).

Moses met God on the mountaintop (Exodus 19).

Samson made one last request of God in the Philistine temple (Judges 16:23-31).

Jesus prayed in many places, including a garden and a mountaintop (Matthew 26:36; Luke 6:12).

Stephen prayed at his stoning (Acts 7:59-60).

Paul and Silas sang and prayed in jail (Acts 16:16-31).

It's good to have a set time and place to pray, such as first thing in the morning in your room, but that's not a requirement for prayer. The important thing is that you spend time talking to God each day. You can pray silently for upcoming classes and tests while on the bus to school. You can talk to God about someone in your neighborhood when you pass him or her on the street. You can send up a silent prayer when you hear someone is sick or injured. There is no limit to when or where you can pray.

Try choosing a time when you can be alone in your room to pray for things you've written down on a prayer list, but also send up short prayers throughout the day as things come to mind you want to mention to God.

thinking it through

Make yourself a prayer card with the following information. Then pray every day!

This week I will pray at:

Time

____

Place

____

Five things I will thank God for:

Five things I will pray about for others:

Five things I will pray about for myself:

thinking it through

Are you careful to thank God for his answers to prayer and for the things he does for you? Sometimes we don't even notice God's work in our lives. As you go through the day today, look for God's blessings and his answers to prayer in your life. Try to notice at least three. Then write a prayer of thanks for one of them.

Hannah: Thanking God

Hannah prayed: "My heart rejoices in the LORD! The LORD has made me strong. Now I have an answer for my enemies; I rejoice because you rescued me."

1 SAMUEL 2:1

The Bible records two of Hannah's prayers. The first prayer is one of despair as she silently cries out to God to give her a son and promises to give him back to the Lord to do God's work. That prayer came from a sad and burdened heart. Hannah's second prayer is one of joy from a heart full of gladness as she praises God for his answer to her prayer.

Hannah knew God was in control of all that happened in her life and that each event in her life was part of God's overall plan for her. She prayed for a son, and God granted that prayer. He blessed her by giving her the desire of her heart. Hannah acknowledged God's blessings in her second prayer. Sometimes we ask God for something, but then when the answer comes we forget to acknowledge God's part in it or to thank him.

Do you know the story in the New Testament of the ten men who had leprosy? Leprosy is a skin disease that is contagious, and people who had it during that time were rejected by others. They had to keep their distance from other people. As Jesus walked by, these men called out to him to heal them. Jesus told them to go and show themselves to the priest. Only the priest could declare that a leper was healed and could be around other people again. The men started on their way to the priest, and as they went, they were healed.

When one of the lepers saw he was healed, he turned back, threw himself at Jesus' feet, and thanked him for healing him. Jesus asked, "Didn't I heal ten men? Where are the other nine?" (Luke 17:17).

God wants us to pray and ask him for things, but he also wants us to be like Hannah and the one leper. They thanked him for what he'd done. Let's not be like the nine lepers who went on their way without thanking Jesus for their healing.

Hannah: Let God Even the Score

Stop acting so proud and haughty! Don't speak with such arrogance! For the LORD is a God who knows what you have done; he will judge your actions.
1 SAMUEL 2:3

When Hannah prayed these words, she was probably thinking of Peninnah, Elkanah's other wife. Peninnah was proud and hateful. Whenever the family made the trip to the Tabernacle, Peninnah would taunt Hannah for not having any children. During these times, Hannah acted graciously. She knew that all things were in God's hands and trusted him to work it out.

God gave Hannah a very special child, who went on to be influential in Jewish history. Samuel, her son, became the last judge, a priest, a prophet, and the one who anointed Israel's first two kings, Saul and David. Not only was Hannah blessed with this very special son, but God also gave her five more children.

Taunting and ridicule were around back in Hannah's day and unfortunately still continue today. Kelsey was a middle school girl who was deaf. She had many friends among the other students, but there were some who made fun of her both openly and behind her back. Kelsey accepted that being deaf was part of God's plan for her, and because of that, she was able to ignore the ridicule she faced at school. Kelsey was an A student, often far surpassing the grades of those who made fun of her, yet she never said an unkind word to any of them. She was gracious to her tormentors just as Hannah was, and Kelsey was able to accomplish many things for God later in her life.

It's easy to be hateful to someone who is hateful to you or to seek revenge when someone constantly taunts you. Most of us have been made fun of like Hannah or Kelsey for some "flaw" in our lives. We would understand if Hannah had pointed out that she was the favorite wife each time Peninnah reminded her that Hannah didn't have children. But Hannah didn't. She simply thanked God for giving her a child of her own.

thinking it through

It's easy to admit that Hannah had the right attitude toward her tormentor. But when someone makes fun of you, it really hurts, and it's hard not to want to get back at the person. What can you do? Write the first few verses of Hannah's prayer, 1 Samuel 2:1-3, on a note card. Carry it around with you, and the next time someone makes fun of you, take it out and pray Hannah's words. They will help you talk to God about what you're feeling and think through the way you should respond.

thinking it through

What do you think of when you hear the word *worship*? What are some ways you can acknowledge who God is? Try one of them right now.

Hannah: Worship

The entire family got up early the next morning and went to worship the LORD once more.

1 SAMUEL 1:19

Elkanah and Hannah worshiped in the Tabernacle more than once during their trip to Shiloh. Sometimes when the word *worship* is used in the Bible, it is talking about the work done in the Tabernacle, or ministering there. Other times it means acknowledging God for who he is. While we no longer have Old Testament priests who serve in a Tabernacle, we can all express gratitude and praise to God.

Many times when we talk about worship, we think of song time at church, when we praise God through music. But worship isn't just about singing, repetition, ritual, or even prayer or Bible reading. Worship is about God. It's acknowledging and exalting God and expressing love and awe at who he is.

Music is certainly one way to do that, but how many times have you found yourself singing along in church without really thinking about the words or what they mean? Sometimes you may sing because everyone else is singing, and you find it more interesting than listening to the sermon.

Worship is a condition of the heart, a willingness to lift God up as Creator and Lord. How you express that is individual and personal. You might worship God through singing, playing an instrument, or dancing for him. You may do it by reading the Psalms or praying aloud. You might worship God through service to others.

We know some of the ways Hannah worshiped God: she took her cares to him through prayer, and she prayed a prayer of thanksgiving after he gave her Samuel. In that prayer she acknowledged that God rescued her, is holy and strong, judges actions, controls people's fates, and protects his children. Hannah knew who God was and spent time in worshiping him.

Quiz Time

Are you like Hannah? Do you handle your tormentors with dignity and grace? Take the quiz below to find out. Read each situation and choose what you would most likely do. Be honest!

1. It's tryout day for summer swim team. You fall off the start block, and the star two hundred individual medley swimmer snickers and makes a rude comment. You
   A. hope she does worse than you.
   B. plan to hide her clothes while she's in the pool.
   C. ignore her, and determine to do your best if you make the team.

2. You see a group of popular girls at the beach. They have on skimpy two-piece suits, and when you walk by in your modest one-piece, they laugh and ask if you borrowed your mom's swimsuit. You
   A. hope all their exposed skin gets sunburned.
   B. consider kicking sand on them "accidentally."
   C. remind yourself that God is honored when you dress modestly.

3. Your family is on a canoe trip, and you lose a paddle in the water. Your brother laughs and takes a video on his cell phone. You
   A. hope he drops the phone in the water.
   B. plan to tip the canoe over once you are closer to shore so he loses the phone.
   C. remind yourself that this is a fun family outing, not the Olympic tryouts, and enjoy your day.

How did you do? It should have been obvious that C was the best answer, but if you thought about circling a different answer, you are normal. It's only natural to want to say something rude or do something mean to those who make fun of you. But take a tip from Hannah, and pray about the things that bother you. Then leave them in God's hands.

thinking it through

What do you think is the biggest benefit of attending church?

Do you go to church? If so, what is the best part of church for you? What part could you work on appreciating more? Ask God to help you get the most out of your time in his house. If you don't go to church, ask if one of your parents could take you this week or if you could go with a friend.

Hannah: Why Go to Church, Part 1

Where two or three gather together as my followers, I am there among them.

MATTHEW 18:20

The Tabernacle Hannah visited was not like our modern churches. There wasn't a morning service, youth group, or choir practice. A band didn't play on Sunday mornings, and a pastor didn't stand and preach. Instead, people went to the Tabernacle to offer sacrifices for sin or to demonstrate thanksgiving to God. Sometimes there were special holy days or feasts when people visited the Tabernacle.

We are fortunate to live in a time when there are churches right in our own cities where we can meet together for singing, sermons, prayer, youth meetings, missionary conferences, revivals, and more.

If you go to church, why do you go? Is it to worship God? to learn things from the Bible that will help you in your daily life? to spend time with your friends? to take part in youth events? All of these are good reasons.

Some Christians don't go to church, but God doesn't want his children to try to live the Christian life alone. Just as you wouldn't do very well trying to live without a family, God's children don't do well living the Christian life apart from a church family.

In the New Testament, Paul would travel to different cities. As people began to believe in Jesus, he would form a church where they could gather and worship. Acts 20:7 (NIV) says, "On the first day of the week we came together to break bread. Paul spoke to the people and, because he intended to leave the next day, kept on talking until midnight." Until midnight? Yes! Paul often preached well into the night. This verse is from a story about a young man named Eutychus, who fell asleep in an upstairs window during Paul's sermon. He fell and died, but Paul raised him from the dead.

Church attendance is important. Next time you're tempted to complain about how long a service is, just think of poor Eutychus and be thankful the sermon doesn't last until midnight!

Hannah: Why Go to Church, Part 2

Let us not neglect our meeting together, as some people do, but encourage one another, especially now that the day of his return is drawing near.
HEBREWS 10:25

Elkanah and Hannah had a long journey to the Tabernacle each time they went to worship and sacrifice. Most of us live just minutes from a church, but many people fail to attend.

The Bible gives us a lot of reasons why we should attend church. Here are a few:

- *To use our spiritual gifts.* First Corinthians 12:7 says, "A spiritual gift is given to each of us so we can help each other." God gave each of us a gift so we can all work together to build each other up.
- *To be cared for spiritually.* First Peter 5:2 says to pastors, "Care for the flock that God has entrusted to you. Watch over it willingly, not grudgingly—not for what you will get out of it, but because you are eager to serve God." Pastors are people God has called to be in charge of teaching and guiding those in the church.
- *To acknowledge our relationship with God.* God wants those who believe in Jesus to let others know about it (Matthew 10:32-33). Attending church is one way of identifying yourself as a Christian.
- *To be with other Christians.* The verse at the top of this devotion says not to neglect getting together with other believers but to encourage each other. You can do that in Sunday school, church, or youth meetings.

It's important to attend church, but your heart attitude about going is even more important. God wants you to desire to be in church, not to go because your parents make you. If you are not enjoying church, perhaps you can talk to your parents or youth leader about ways to change that. They may have some ideas.

thinking it through

Maybe you go to church, but you don't get much out of it. How can you make it more meaningful for yourself? Here are some ideas.

- Participate in all parts of the service—singing, praying, and the sermon.
- Have a special notebook where you jot down at least one meaningful verse and one thought you can apply to your life in the coming week.
- Ask how you can help at church. Perhaps you can help in children's church.
- Be involved with the youth events in your church.

thinking it through

How can you give of your time, talents, and money? Write down three ways you can give your time. Then write down three ways you can give your talents. Finally, write down three Christian organizations to give your money to. Choose one of these to give to this week.

Hannah: Giving Back to God

"I asked the LORD to give me this boy, and he has granted my request. Now I am giving him to the LORD, and he will belong to the LORD his whole life." And they worshiped the LORD there.

1 SAMUEL 1:27-28

Hannah promised God that if he gave her a son, she would give her child back to the Lord to do God's work. When Samuel was just a young child, she kept that promise and took him to live at the Tabernacle with Eli, the priest.

It was probably difficult for Hannah to leave Samuel with the priest. Eli was elderly, and his sons were wicked. First Samuel 2 describes them as "scoundrels who had no respect for the LORD or for their duties as priests" (verses 12-13). Yet Hannah left her son because she knew Samuel was really in God's care. Hannah gave her firstborn son to God not out of duty, but out of joy because of her love for God and her gratitude for his answer to her prayer.

What do you have that you could give to God? You don't have children to dedicate to God, but how about your time? Could you set aside some time to help an elderly neighbor mow her lawn as an act of service to God? Or could you play with your younger sibling for an hour to give your parents a break out of love for God? Maybe you could use your time on Saturday morning to help clean the church or trim the grass.

How about your talents? Are there things you are good at that you could give back to God? If you're musical, perhaps you could help with children's choir or sing in the youth choir. If you're good with children, maybe you could be a teacher's assistant for Vacation Bible School.

Perhaps you babysit or have some sort of part-time summer job. You can give some of your money to God's work.

Hannah gave her son to the Lord's work. What can you give to God?

Hannah: Samuel

The boy Samuel continued to grow in stature and in favor with the LORD and with men.

1 SAMUEL 2:26, NIV

A look at Hannah's life wouldn't be complete without taking a look at her son, through whom God was working in big ways.

Samuel was just a young child when Hannah first took him to the Tabernacle and left him with Eli. Samuel observed Eli and did small tasks and errands. Samuel did so well at his work that he was allowed to wear an ephod, a long, sleeveless vest made of plain linen.

During the time Samuel served under Eli, God didn't speak much to the people or appear to them in visions. Many people did whatever they wanted and ignored God's rules. Eli's sons were among the worst. They abused their positions in the Tabernacle by taking advantage of those who came to worship and sacrifice.

One night as Samuel was lying down he heard a voice call his name. He ran to Eli and said, "Here I am." Eli told him he hadn't called him, and sent him to lie back down. This happened a second time and a third. Finally Eli realized it must be God who was calling Samuel. Eli told Samuel that, if the voice called again, he should say, "Speak, LORD, your servant is listening" (1 Samuel 3:9).

Samuel heard the voice again and did as Eli had said. God told Samuel he was going to judge Eli's family because of the sins of Eli's sons and Eli's failure in disciplining them. Samuel didn't want to tell Eli what God had said, but Eli called him and asked what the message was, so Samuel told him.

Samuel was faithful in the small things God gave him to do, so God used him in greater ways throughout his life. Samuel was the last, but best judge in Israel. He was used by God to give messages to God's people.

Hannah prayed for a baby and gave him back to the Lord's work. God accepted Hannah's gift of her son and used him in great ways.

thinking it through

How faithful are you in the things God has given you to do? Luke 16:10 says, "If you are faithful in little things, you will be faithful in large ones." What can you expect if you serve God in small ways now? Ask him to show you how you can serve him and to help you to be faithful in what he has called you to do.

thinking it through

This week, do all you can to be the opposite of Peninnah. Spend time with the neighbor girl no one else wants to hang out with. Compliment the girl at the pool who laughed at you—even if she makes fun of you again. And the next time you're tempted to tease someone, think of something kind to say instead.

Peninnah: The Provoker

Because the LORD had closed her womb, her rival kept provoking her in order to irritate her.

1 SAMUEL 1:6, NIV

We don't know much about Peninnah other than that she was Elkanah's second wife. Elkanah loved Hannah more than Peninnah, but Peninnah was able to have children and Hannah wasn't.

Peninnah probably felt she was the better wife to Elkanah because she was able to give him children, and that was very important in that time. But Elkanah loved Hannah and was even kinder to her because she desired children but wasn't able to have any, a fact Peninnah teased and ridiculed Hannah for.

Peninnah would be the type of girl who hangs around in the school hallway, just waiting for the shy or awkward girl to walk by so she can make fun of her hair, clothes, looks, lack of friends, or behavior. She would be the one who reacts in jealousy when someone has something she doesn't have, wins a coveted part in the play or musical, or wins an award.

Do you know any Peninnahs? The Peninnahs of the world suck the joy out of life. They put down and poke fun at people. They are discouragers rather than encouragers, and they don't care who they hurt. Maybe you've experienced a Peninnah's kind of taunting. Or maybe you've seen her making fun of someone else. Maybe you've even made some Peninnah-like comments yourself.

It's not always easy to be an encourager, especially when it might make you a target for teasing, but God will give you courage to take a stand. And eventually people will respect you for it. How much better it is to be an encourager rather than a provoker and discourager like Peninnah.

Ichabod's Mother: A Woman without Hope

She named the child Ichabod (which means "Where is the glory?"), for she said, "Israel's glory is gone." She named him this because the Ark of God had been captured and because her father-in-law and husband were dead.

1 SAMUEL 4:21

Ichabod's mother was a woman without hope. She was married to Eli's wicked son Phinehas. During this time, Israel was at war with the Philistines. Some of the people decided to take the Ark of the Covenant, the sacred box that held the Ten Commandments, into war as a good-luck charm. Eli's sons, Hophni and Phinehas, were among the people with the Ark.

Things didn't turn out the way the Israelites had planned. Instead of Israel winning, thirty thousand Israelite soldiers, including Hophni and Phinehas, were killed, and the Philistines captured the Ark of the Covenant. When Eli heard his sons were dead and the Ark was captured, he fell from his chair and died too.

During all this, Phinehas's wife gave birth to a baby boy, whom she named Ichabod, which means "Where is the glory?" because the glory was gone from Israel. Then she died. Now baby Ichabod's grandfather, father, uncle, and mother were all dead. We don't know what kind of life he lived or who raised him, but it is sad that Ichabod's mother didn't turn to God in her time of need and died in despair.

Eli was a good priest, but he failed to discipline his wicked sons. Phinehas's wife must have heard about the way her husband behaved in the Tabernacle and knew he was not serving God. She herself may not have had faith in God, at least not enough to get her through the hard times. Because of this, the only mention of her in the Bible is that she died after giving birth to a son.

Hard times come, and bad things happen. You can give up, or you can hang on to God and trust him to get you through the difficult times.

thinking it through

Ichabod's mother didn't turn to God for strength when she needed it the most.

Is there something worrying you? Turn to God for help; he will listen to you and take care of you.

thinking it through

Do you feel jealous of anyone in your family? Maybe you are part of a blended family, and you feel jealous of the attention your stepsibling is getting from your parent. Or maybe you resent your cousin because he got to go on vacation with your grandparents and you didn't. Instead of trying to sabotage someone's future like Saul did, treat the one you are jealous of with *extra* kindness. What can you do to build bridges today so you can avoid resentment tomorrow?

Michal: Michal Loves David

In the meantime, Saul's daughter Michal had fallen in love with David, and Saul was delighted when he heard about it. "Here's another chance to see him killed by the Philistines!" Saul said to himself. But to David he said, "Today you have a second chance to become my son-in-law!"

1 SAMUEL 18:20-21

David was a prize catch for any young woman, but it was King Saul's daughter Michal who had her eye on him. David was her brother Jonathan's best friend, so he was probably around Michal a lot too. David was not only strong and tan from his time as a shepherd, but he was a national hero because he had been the one to conquer the giant Goliath. All this, not David's love for God, was what caught Michal's attention.

King Saul, Michal's father, was intensely jealous of David's popularity. As Saul's hatred of David grew, so did Michal's love for David. When Saul realized Michal and David cared for each other, he saw it as a chance to get rid of David.

King Saul told David the price to marry Michal was a hundred dead Philistines. He figured David would get killed trying to fulfill that price, and he'd be rid of the young man who was everyone's favorite. It didn't work that way, though. David killed not just one hundred but two hundred Philistines. Now he was Michal's hero more than before, and Saul had no choice but to let Michal marry David. Saul's worst enemy was now part of his own family.

Can you see how some of these things might lead to problems between Saul, Michal, and David? Saul was bitterly jealous of David to the point of wanting him dead. Michal loved both her father and David. David was determined to serve God above all else, but he married a woman who didn't serve God wholeheartedly.

Even though Michal loved David, the differences in their faith and outlook on life were too much, and this led to problems in future years.

Puzzle Page

God has told us the way to deal with our worries. Solve the Thermometer Puzzle to find out what the Bible says we should do when we're afraid.

Directions: Look at the thermometer. Each temperature has a corresponding letter. Look at the temperature under the lines below. On each line, write the letter that goes with the temperature. Check your answer below.

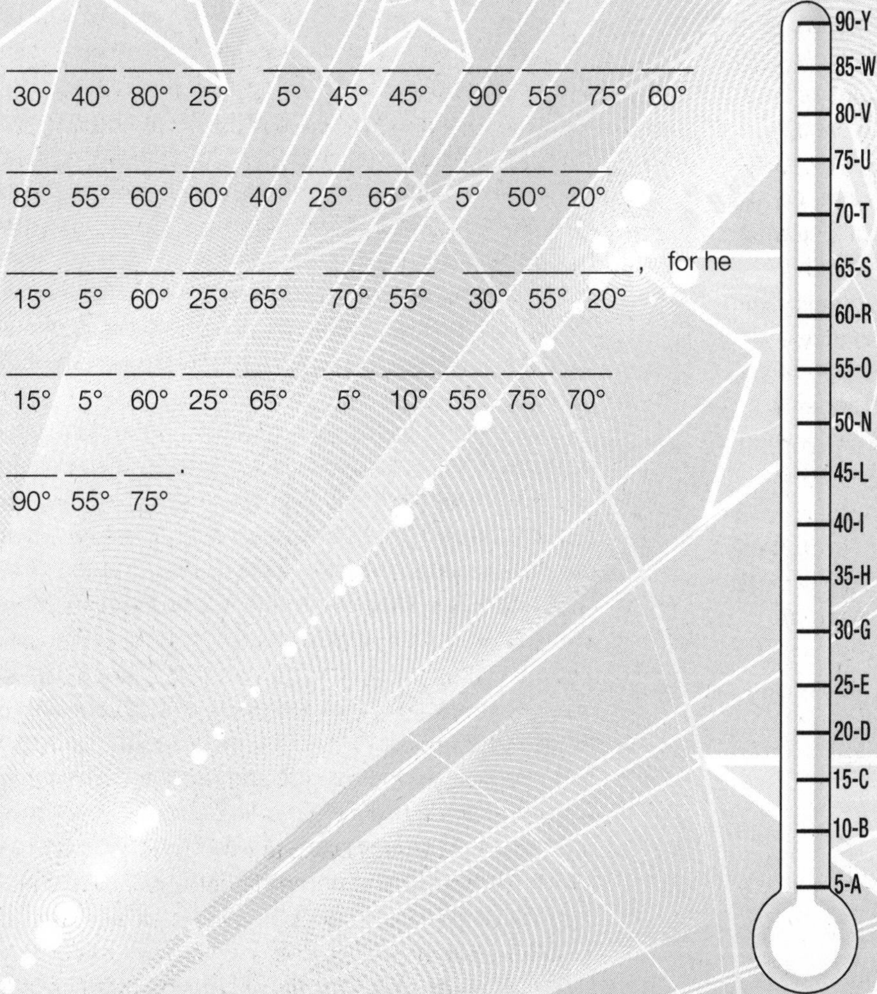

Answer: Give all your worries and cares to God, for he cares about you. (1 Peter 5:7)

thinking it through

By having idols in the house, Michal disobeyed a basic command of God's—in fact, it's one of the Ten Commandments. Deuteronomy 13:4 says, "Serve only the LORD your God and fear him alone. Obey his commands, listen to his voice, and cling to him." How did Michal disobey this command? How can you obey it?

Michal: Michal Saves David

Saul sent troops to watch David's house. They were told to kill David when he came out the next morning. But Michal, David's wife, warned him, "If you don't escape tonight, you will be dead by morning." So she helped him climb out through a window, and he fled and escaped. Then she took an idol and put it in his bed, covered it with blankets, and put a cushion of goat's hair at its head.

1 SAMUEL 19:11-13

At one time Michal's father, King Saul, welcomed David into his house. When Saul was troubled, David played soothing music on his harp for the king. Then came the day David slew Goliath with only a sling and a stone. King Saul made David a commander in his army.

One day when the army returned victorious from battle, the people sang and danced. They called out, "Saul has killed his thousands, and David his ten thousands" (1 Samuel 18:7). This made Saul angry and jealous.

Saul tried to kill David repeatedly. One night Saul positioned his men around David's house with orders to kill David in the morning. Michal learned of her father's plot and helped David escape through a window. She put an idol in his bed and dressed it up to look like David. She said David was sick. When the men came in to kill him in his bed, they found an idol.

Saul asked Michal why she had helped David escape, and she told her father David had threatened to kill her if she didn't. Michal was caught between two warriors—her father and her husband. She loved David, but she loved her father, too, and she never gave up her idols in order to serve David's God. She had an idol in the house that she used to trick the men into thinking David was in his bed.

Even though Michal didn't understand or share David's love for God, she loved David enough to defy her own father and help him escape.

Michal: Gone and Back

Saul, meanwhile, had given his daughter Michal, David's wife, to a man from Gallim named Palti son of Laish.

1 SAMUEL 25:44

Michal rescued David by warning him Saul was going to kill him. She helped David escape through a window and covered him. David had to hide from Saul for a long time. During this time it doesn't appear David made any attempt to go back for Michal. While David was gone, Saul declared Michal's marriage to David over and gave her to a man named Palti.

Michal's days with her strong, handsome hero were over, and she became the wife of another man. We don't know how Michal felt about this, but she wasn't given a choice. Although it seems unfair and even cruel, her father could give her to any man he chose. Meanwhile, David married two more women. This was common back then but was not God's plan.

Many more years passed and David became king. He demanded Michal be returned to him as his rightful wife. The Bible doesn't say how Michal felt about leaving her husband of many years for her former husband, but it says her husband Palti walked behind her weeping. Then Abner, a general in Saul's army, sent him away (2 Samuel 3:16).

Michal was given to David to be his wife in exchange for one hundred dead Philistines; she was taken from David and given to another husband for many years and then torn from her second husband and returned to David. Michal must have felt that she had no control over her own life. The two powerful men in her life—Saul and David—made the decisions for her.

Does it seem like other people make all your decisions too? You really want to go to a friend's house, but your mom says you have to watch your little sister at home. There's a volleyball camp you're desperate to attend, but your parents don't want to pay for it. Even when it seems like other people are controlling your life, God is always in charge, and he has a plan for you.

thinking it through

How do you think Michal felt about being married to David, then Palti, and then David again? Are you frustrated by the way other people make decisions for you sometimes? Talk to God about it. Ask him to help you trust his plan for your life.

thinking it through

Do you feel resentment toward anyone for past hurts or wrong treatment? What are some positive ways you can deal with those feelings? Talk to God about your feelings. Ask him to heal your hurt and take away your bitterness. You might want to talk with a friend, parent, or trusted adult as well and ask for his or her advice on dealing with the resentment.

Michal: Michal Despises David

As the Ark of the LORD entered the City of David, Michal, the daughter of Saul, looked down from her window. When she saw King David leaping and dancing before the LORD, she was filled with contempt for him.

2 SAMUEL 6:16

The Ark of the Covenant, a religious box that was normally kept in the Tabernacle, had been in Abinadab's house for twenty years. It had been there ever since it was returned by the Philistines after Eli's sons took it into war as a good luck object and lost it to them. David wanted the Ark of the Covenant to be in Jerusalem, where it belonged, and arranged for it to be moved.

There was a great celebration with singing and dancing when the Ark arrived. David was so caught up in the celebration that he took off his kingly robes and danced in a linen ephod that wasn't meant for outer clothing.

As Michal looked down at David from an upper window, she didn't see a man full of love for God dancing in celebration. All she saw was her husband, the king, dancing enthusiastically among the commoners in an immodest garment. She looked on with disgust.

It may have been more than David's dance before God that set Michal off. He'd deserted her, married other wives, reclaimed her years later, and married yet more wives. Michal had been the first wife, and now she was sharing him with other women. On top of that, she didn't understand his devotion to God.

Michal may have felt hurt, abandoned, and used. She certainly had a right to feel resentment. But letting resentment fester and burst out in anger is not a good idea for anyone. Everyone experiences hard times, some people more than others. But blaming one's circumstances is rarely helpful. In fact, it usually keeps that person from dealing with the hurt in productive ways and from turning the hurt over to the Lord.

If you feel bitter feelings toward someone today, it's better to talk it out than let it negatively affect your life.

Michal: Unhappily Ever After

When David returned home to bless his own family, Michal, the daughter of Saul, came out to meet him. She said in disgust, "How distinguished the king of Israel looked today, shamelessly exposing himself to the servant girls like any vulgar person might do!"
2 SAMUEL 6:20

Can you imagine Michal watching David with disgust from her upper window? She was filled with anger—so much so that she couldn't wait to tell him off. When David returned home to share his joy with his family, she went out to meet him and confronted him in anger, telling him he was undignified.

David answered her, "I was dancing before the LORD, who chose me above your father and all his family! He appointed me as the leader of Israel, the people of the LORD, so I celebrate before the LORD. Yes, and I am willing to look even more foolish than this!" (2 Samuel 6:21-22). David was saying he would worship God in whatever way expressed his praise to God.

Not everyone worships or praises God in the same way. Some people may do it in a quiet, reserved way, such as praying silently or writing a psalm to God. Others praise God in more open and exuberant ways. Either way is okay as long as the worship and praise are genuine and motivated by love for God.

Michal disapproved of David's dance and reacted to him in anger rather than understanding this was his way of worshiping. Perhaps if she'd waited and listened to David's explanation, things might have been different.

The last thing the Bible says about Michal is that she died without having any children. Some people believe this is because God kept her from having children as punishment for her treatment of David. Others say this is a sign she no longer lived as David's wife, so they didn't have children. Either way, to die with no children was a disgrace in Michal's time.

Michal was married to a man whom God called "a man after my own heart" (Acts 13:22), yet Michal herself never embraced God. It's hard not to feel sorry for Michal, who let her resentment keep her from having a full life with David.

thinking it through

Michal reacted in anger to David's dance. Read James 1:19: "You must all be quick to listen, slow to speak, and slow to get angry." What three things does James caution us to do? How well do you follow those instructions? Practice being quick to listen and slow to speak each time you interact with someone today. Do you think it will be easy or hard? How might it help you be slow to get angry?

thinking it through

How might Michal's life have been different if she'd trusted God to help her overcome her circumstances? Are you going through tough times today? How can you trust God to work out the situation? Spend a few minutes praying—and listening—right now.

Michal: When Life Hands You Lemons . . .

If God cares so wonderfully for wildflowers that are here today and thrown into the fire tomorrow, he will certainly care for you. Why do you have so little faith?

MATTHEW 6:30

Michal didn't have an easy life. She was torn between the man she loved as a young woman and her powerful father. She was passed between husbands with no thought given to her desires or happiness. She was the daughter of a king, and then married to a king, but life as a princess and queen wasn't as glamorous as it seemed.

You've probably heard the expression "When life hands you lemons, make lemonade." The point is that you don't always have control over what happens to you, but you can control how you react to it.

Some girls grow up in homes with parents who love them and each other. Other girls grow up in homes filled with anger. Some are separated from their parents and grow up in foster homes. Some girls grow up in luxury, while others grow up in poverty-filled countries, wondering where their next meal is coming from. Some girls have parents who teach them about God and encourage them in their faith, while others have parents who don't know God or have chosen not to follow him.

The good news is, no matter what kind of family you grow up in, God has a plan just for you. It may be hard to see his plan when you are in the middle of hard times. You may wish God would just deliver you from your circumstances. And you might find it hard to understand why he'd let some girls be hungry or abused while others are pampered. I don't think we'll really understand why these things happen until we see God face-to-face in heaven. In the meantime God wants us to trust him to work out all the circumstances in our lives and follow his leading—unlike Michal. The story of your life has begun, but only God knows the ending. Listen to him, and do your best to follow his leading each day.

Michal: The Importance of Marrying a Believer

We can tell who are children of God and who are children of the devil. Anyone who does not live righteously and does not love other believers does not belong to God.

1 JOHN 3:10

David loved and served God, but it doesn't appear Michal ever truly believed in God. She had idols in the house, and she didn't share David's enthusiasm when the Ark of the Covenant was returned to its rightful place. She didn't understand his devotion to God or why he danced joyfully in front of the people when the Ark was returned. When one person is devoted to God and the other is not, heartbreak usually follows.

Now is the time to decide you will date only someone who shares your faith. Does this mean you can't be friends with a boy who isn't a Christian? No. But sometimes you may start out as friends, and it turns into more. Once your heart gets involved and you're emotionally attached, it's harder to think clearly about things. It may seem he is nicer than the Christian boys you know, and he doesn't mind it when you talk about God. In fact, maybe he even believes in God. Many people believe in God but don't accept Jesus as their Savior. They know in their heads there is a God who created them, but he's not Lord of their lives.

Many girls do what is called "missionary dating." The girl dates someone with the belief she will be able to share her faith with him and he will eventually come to know Jesus. It sounds good, but in reality it rarely works. Better to invite him to church and be his friend, but wait to date until he does share your faith—for real, not just to get you to go out with him.

The best thing to do is decide before you ever begin dating that you will date only a guy who is a genuine Christian and seeks to honor God by the way he lives. That will help you avoid conflicts over values, beliefs, and lifestyle, and it will give you the common ground of wanting to please Jesus in your dating relationship.

thinking it through

When you have a crush on a guy, it's easy to overlook things about him that don't make him a good match for you. Decide what's important right now, so it will be easier for you to make the right choice if you fall for the wrong guy. What problems might a girl have if she dates someone who doesn't believe in Jesus? Why do you think missionary dating might not work? Ask God to help you make wise choices in your relationships. You can even begin praying for your future relationships today.

Abigail: Wisdom in Action

This man's name was Nabal, and his wife, Abigail, was a sensible and beautiful woman. But Nabal, a descendant of Caleb, was crude and mean in all his dealings.

1 SAMUEL 25:3

Abigail moved quickly as she gathered food. Time was critical. David, deeply offended by her fool of a husband, planned to kill all the men in her household by morning. She needed to deliver enough food for six hundred hungry men in time to prevent David from carrying out his threat.

This is what Abigail is most known for—her quick thinking that saved her foolish, drunken husband and all the men who were part of the household. Abigail had the wisdom to know what to do and to do it quickly.

While David was an outlaw from King Saul, he gathered six hundred men. He and his men camped near where Nabal's shepherds kept his sheep. David and his men not only didn't raid the flocks for food, but they helped protect the flocks against roaming thieves.

Nabal was one of the richest men around, with three thousand sheep and one thousand goats. During sheep-shearing time, Nabal provided food and drink for his shearers. It was during this time that David sent a messenger asking for food for his men since they had helped guard the sheep. Nabal refused and sent the messenger away empty handed. When word got back to David, he was deeply offended and vowed to kill Nabal and all the other men in the household.

One of Nabal's servants found Abigail and told her what had happened. He confirmed that David and his men had treated them well and protected the sheep.

Abigail sprang into action. She quickly gathered two hundred loaves of bread, five sheep that had been slaughtered, nearly a bushel of roasted grain, one hundred clusters of raisins, and two hundred fig cakes. She loaded the food on donkeys, then hopped on her donkey and went to save the day.

Abigail kept a clear head in a time of crisis. Her quick thinking saved many people that day.

thinking it through

How would this story have ended if Abigail hadn't quickly gathered food for David and his men? Do you keep a clear head or panic in times of crisis? How can you prepare yourself to respond quickly and intelligently when emergencies arise?

Quiz Time

The Bible cautions us to be quick to listen, slow to speak, and slow to get angry (James 1:19). How well do you follow that advice? Take the quiz below to find out. Circle the answer that sounds most like what you would do.

1. You hear that another girl made a rude comment behind your back about your history presentation. You
   A. ignore it. You don't know if it's true, and anyway, it doesn't really matter because you got an A.
   B. find the girl and demand to know if she made the comment.
   C. verbally trash her history project too.

2. Your brother broke the mug your best friend brought you from Disney World. You
   A. go outside and shoot baskets until you calm down.
   B. hit him.
   C. snap his favorite DVD in half.

3. Your best friend just abandoned you at lunch to sit with the guy she knows you like. You
   A. vow never to tell her anything again.
   B. start a rumor about her.
   C. ask her later why she sat with him.

Best answers: 1: A, 2: A, 3: C

It's pretty easy to pick out the right thing to do in each situation above, but in real life things aren't so easy. There are a lot of things that can trigger your anger and an equal amount of ways to deal with it. The important thing is not to react in your anger but to wait until you've cooled down and thought things through before you act.

thinking it through

Are you good at deflecting anger? Or do you tend to make tempers flare? The next time someone gets upset at you or even threatens you, ask God to give you wise and gentle words to speak.

Abigail: Wisdom in Words

Now, my lord, as surely as the LORD lives and you yourself live, since the LORD has kept you from murdering and taking vengeance into your own hands, let all your enemies and those who try to harm you be as cursed as Nabal is.

1 SAMUEL 25:26

Abigail's wisdom and quick thinking in gathering food for David and his six hundred men not only saved her household from harm, but it kept David from committing a terrible sin. David had vowed to kill Nabal and all the men in the household. This was not the same as when David killed men in battle. This time David was going to murder men for revenge. This would have been a sin against God, and since David was going to be the king, it would have been a black mark on his record. Things might have turned out very differently for the king if he had slaughtered all the males in Nabal's household.

Abigail showed wisdom in her actions and in her words to David. She didn't scold David for threatening to kill the men, but she appealed to his reason. First, Abigail got off her donkey and bowed before David. She knew who he was and had heard of his conquests in battle. She apologized for her husband's actions and assured David she wasn't there when his messenger was turned away. Then Abigail begged David to accept the food she had brought.

Abigail went on to remind David of how God had protected him from those who wanted to kill him. She pointed out that David shouldn't have the guilt of murder on his conscience when he became king. Abigail knew David was the one God planned to be king.

Abigail approached David with such wisdom in her words that he listened to her and changed his mind about killing the men in Nabal's household. God gave Abigail wisdom to say what David needed to hear to stop him from committing murder. Many conflicts could be avoided if people took a lesson from Abigail and spoke wisely in times of crisis.

Abigail: Wisdom to Live above Circumstances

I know how to live on almost nothing or with everything. I have learned the secret of living in every situation, whether it is with a full stomach or empty, with plenty or little. For I can do everything through Christ, who gives me strength.

PHILIPPIANS 4:12-13

Some people are hard to get along with. Do you know a person like that? A dark cloud hangs over her head. If you say hello, she will grunt in reply, if she answers at all. If you do need to ask a question, you brace yourself for an unkind reply. Life is better on the days you don't have to deal with her at all.

Abigail had someone like that in her life. In fact, she was married to him. The Bible describes Abigail as sensible and beautiful. It describes her husband, Nabal—whose name means "fool"—as "crude and mean in all his dealings" (1 Samuel 25:3). When Abigail reasoned with David she said, "I know Nabal is a wicked and ill-tempered man; please don't pay any attention to him. He is a fool, just as his name suggests" (verse 25).

No one had anything good to say about Nabal. He was wicked, mean, and impossible to get along with. He was often drunk, and that just made him worse. He was not the type of man who deserved a kind, compassionate, wise wife like Abigail. Most likely theirs was an arranged marriage like Michal's and many others' were at the time. Nabal was rich. He probably came from a wealthy family, and Abigail's father thought him a prize catch for his daughter.

Abigail's faith in God is what got her through the years of being married to a wicked man. She knew God was in control of all things and he hadn't forgotten her. She trusted him to work things out.

We can't always control our circumstances, but we can control how we react to them. This was a lesson Michal didn't learn. But Abigail chose to be gracious and kind in spite of her husband's actions. If you can learn to cope graciously with the unkind people in your life now, it will help you the rest of your life.

thinking it through

Look at Philippians 4:12-13. What does Paul say is the secret to living in every situation? How does faith in Jesus give you strength?

thinking it through

What are some bad times to talk to someone about a problem? (Example: when the person is tired.) What are some better times? Do your answers change depending on whom you are talking with?

Fortunately, there is no bad time to talk with God. He is there to give you wisdom any time of the day or night.

Abigail: Wise Timing

When Abigail arrived home, she found that Nabal was throwing a big party and was celebrating like a king. He was very drunk, so she didn't tell him anything about her meeting with David until dawn the next day.

1 SAMUEL 25:36

When Abigail heard that her husband had refused to give food to David and his men, she took action without telling Nabal. She knew he'd say not to give his resources to strangers. He'd claimed David and his men weren't his workers, but Nabal's shepherds told Abigail how David's men had protected the sheep anyway.

Abigail acted quickly and secretly. This was the only way to save Nabal's life and keep David from murdering innocent men.

When Abigail returned home after meeting with David, Nabal was drunk, and Abigail was wise enough not to confront him at this time. She waited until the next morning to tell Nabal that his actions had almost cost all the men in the household their lives.

When Nabal heard everything that had happened, he was struck down. Some Bible versions say his heart stopped, and others say he had a stroke. He was paralyzed and lay on his bed for ten days. Then he died.

Abigail was wise to act without telling her husband. When a husband and wife love the Lord and each other, they can share their feelings and agree on how to do things, but Nabal was disagreeable and impossible to please, so Abigail acted alone. She wisely waited until the effects of his wine had worn off before confronting him. If Abigail had tried to talk to him while he was still drunk, he may have reacted in anger toward her.

Abigail showed wisdom in all she did: gathering the food, meeting with David, and waiting to tell her husband what she'd done. She knew timing was important in talking to both David and Nabal.

Do you need to talk to someone about a problem or confront someone about something he or she did? Ask God to help you know when the timing is right, just as he did for Abigail.

Abigail: Wise Counsel

David replied to Abigail, "Praise the LORD, the God of Israel, who has sent you to meet me today! Thank God for your good sense! Bless you for keeping me from murder and from carrying out vengeance with my own hands."

1 SAMUEL 25:32-33

When Abigail took food to David, she wisely reminded him that he was God's servant. She pointed out that King Saul was trying to kill David, and that if David killed all the males in Nabal's household, he would be no better than Saul, hunting innocent men. Abigail suggested that David wouldn't want the guilt of murder on his conscience when he became king.

David praised God for sending Abigail, who kept him from getting revenge on Nabal. He recognized she was speaking wisdom from God. David sent her back home after he blessed her for coming to him and promised not to kill Nabal.

David was impressed by Abigail's graciousness and her wise words to him. He respected her counsel. When David heard Nabal was dead, he praised God for avenging Nabal's treatment of David's men. David sent messengers to Abigail, asking her to become his wife. Abigail agreed to marry him; she said she would even have been willing to become his servant if he had asked.

David married more wives, but Abigail was by far the wisest. Abigail knew how to think clearly, make good decisions, deal with difficult people, and organize and carry out a plan. David knew her counsel could be trusted and probably counted on her wisdom and insight in dealing with the people he ruled.

David tended to be willful and to act without thinking. Abigail's gentle spirit provided a balance for him. She had a calming influence on him and perhaps helped him learn to think before taking action.

Can other people count on you to give them good advice like Abigail gave David? When you seek God, he will give you his wisdom to deal with any situation.

thinking it through

Are you more like David, who acted quickly without thinking, or Abigail, who acted quickly but wisely? Can others depend on you for godly wisdom? Is there someone you can count on for good advice?

One way you can start learning how to give godly advice is by reading the wisdom books found in God's Word. The book of Proverbs is a great place to start. Begin by reading Proverbs 1:1-7 today.

thinking it through

Here's how to check whether you have godly wisdom: "If you are wise and understand God's ways, prove it by living an honorable life, doing good works with the humility that comes from wisdom" (James 3:13).

Are you known for good behavior or conduct? Do you find yourself often doing good works without trying to take credit for them? Do you trust God to give you the understanding to deal with life's situations?

Abigail: Wisdom from God

The wisdom from above is first of all pure. It is also peace loving, gentle at all times, and willing to yield to others. It is full of mercy and good deeds. It shows no favoritism and is always sincere.

JAMES 3:17

Abigail was full of wisdom, but what does that really mean? Being wise is not the same as being smart. You can memorize the whole periodic table, know every algebraic equation, and name each battle in the Civil War and not be wise. Wisdom can't be learned just by memorizing a bunch of facts.

Wisdom is knowledge in action, or smarts mixed with common sense. It's using your knowledge to come up with the best solution to a problem or the best course of action. We are never told that Abigail was a genius. In fact, in Bible times women rarely received any kind of education outside the home. But we do know she was full of wisdom. She knew what to do, when to do it, and how best to do it.

Sometimes when people talk about wisdom, they are talking about being worldly wise—like making smart business deals and getting the best offer. The wisdom the Bible talks about is practical and godly. Here's how the Bible describes the wisdom that God gifts people with:

- peace loving
- gentle
- merciful
- accepting
- sincere

You will see the traits above in the life of someone who is truly wise. And they describe Abigail perfectly. She sought peace between her family and David's men. She was gentle in her dealings. She showed mercy to her wicked husband. She was accepting of others' strengths and limitations, and she was sincere in her words and actions toward David.

Do you have this kind of wisdom?

Abigail: How to Be Wise

The LORD grants wisdom! From his mouth come knowledge and understanding.

PROVERBS 2:6

Was Abigail born with the wisdom to know how to defuse the situation between Nabal and David? Did she instinctively know to hurry and prepare food? Did the words she spoke to David to prevent him from committing murder just flow from her lips? No, they came from a lifetime of seeking God, following him, and trusting him to work out the circumstances of her life.

Many people try to be wise on their own, but according to James 3:14-16 they are jealous and are trying to get ahead in the world. They boast, lie, and seek all the world has to offer. That kind of wisdom might get them ahead in the business world, but it doesn't score any points with God.

How do you develop the other kind of wisdom? By getting to know God better. You can do this by spending time reading the Bible and praying every day and by listening to the messages at church and in Sunday school.

When you are faced with a decision, pray about what God wants you to do. Look in the Bible to see if you can find any verses that talk about the situation. Talk to other adults who are more mature Christians.

Ask yourself what God would want you to do in each situation, and do it even if it's not the popular thing to do. When you listen for God's leading, you will sense his guidance in your heart, through your conscience. When you consciously ask God to direct you, listen for his leading, and then follow it, you will find wise actions coming naturally to you. It will be easy to know the wise and right thing to do. That is how Abigail was able to quickly take action and save the day for her household, and it will help you, too.

thinking it through

You will gain godly wisdom when you practice walking with God and seeking his direction. Which of these things can you do this week to help you do that?

- Read from the Bible each day.
- Talk with God.
- Spend time with godly friends.
- Listen in church and jot down key points that will help you during the week.
- Ask God to give you the words to say when faced with a difficult situation.
- Ask God to help you know what to do when a decision comes up.

thinking it through

Why do you think God reveals our future to us only one day at a time? Why is it unwise to try and find out our future through other methods?

Imagine a friend wants to read the horoscope page of a magazine with you, or some girls at a party want to use a Ouija board. You don't think it's a good idea, but they say, "It's just for fun." How would you respond?

Medium of Endor: God Knows the Future

Saul then said to his advisers, "Find a woman who is a medium, so I can go and ask her what to do." His advisers replied, "There is a medium at Endor."

1 SAMUEL 28:7

The Philistines had set up their camp near Saul. When he saw the vast army, he panicked. He tried praying but didn't get an answer, and God didn't speak to him through the prophets, either. Samuel had already died, so Saul had no one to ask for advice. He was filled with fear.

Saul disguised himself as a commoner and went to visit a medium in Endor. He had previously made it illegal to consult with mediums and anyone who could contact the dead, but when the medium protested, he assured her no harm would come to her.

Saul asked her to call Samuel from the dead. The medium did so, but Samuel was not happy about it. He gave Saul answers but not the kind Saul wanted. Samuel told Saul that God was his enemy. The Philistines would defeat the Israelite army, and Saul and his sons would be killed.

What Samuel's spirit said came true, and that has caused a lot of debate among Bible scholars. The Bible states that any kind of witchcraft, including talking to the dead, is wrong. The Old Testament law forbade the Israelites from practicing these kinds of customs as some of their pagan neighbors did (Leviticus 19:31; Deuteronomy 18:9-12). In light of that, was it really Samuel who appeared to Saul? Did God work through the medium this once and allow Samuel to give an accurate prophecy about what would happen to Saul? Was God allowing Saul to know of his death in time to get his house in order?

We don't know the answer to those questions, but we can be sure God doesn't want us to consult any kind of fortune-teller or horoscope to determine our future or to make decisions. God alone knows all that our future holds, and he reveals it to us one piece at a time.

Quiz Time

Are you like Abigail, responding graciously to those who are mean, and trusting God to work through unhappy circumstances? Take the quiz below to find out. Read each statement and circle A for always, S for sometimes, or N for never.

1. When someone says something unkind to me, I answer him or her kindly or walk away without answering.

   A S N

2. When someone treats me in a rude manner, I act graciously. I plan to do right whether or not they do.

   A S N

3. If an argument breaks out with my brothers or sisters, I try to be fair and act with dignity. (That means no name-calling, throwing shoes, etc.)

   A S N

4. When someone is in a bad mood, I say something encouraging to the person or give him or her space to work it out.

   A S N

5. When I see someone who is grouchy, I realize that something is causing the person to act that way and say a prayer asking God to bless him or her.

   A S N

Give yourself two points for every A and 1 point for every S. You get 0 points for N.

How did you do?

8-10 points: You are gracious and understanding in your thoughts and actions. You have a rare maturity and insight into what makes people act the way they do. You are a young Abigail.

4-7 points: You make an effort to keep the peace and overlook it when people are rude. You aren't always able to control your urge to tell them off or react to them in anger. Allow God to help you be gracious to those who are not.

0-3 points: Are you sure you aren't related to Nabal? It can be easy to react with anger or impatience with others who have wronged you. Ask God to give you the desire to act in a godly way even when others don't.

Bathsheba: Bathsheba Goes to David

When the period of mourning was over, David sent for her and brought her to the palace, and she became one of his wives. Then she gave birth to a son. But the LORD was displeased with what David had done.
2 SAMUEL 11:27

King David decided to stay home one spring and take it easy while his men went to war without him. One day he went for a walk on his roof and noticed a woman bathing. She wasn't lounging in a tub like you'd picture when you think of a bath but was probably sponging herself off using a basin of water.

Many people think of Bathsheba bathing on her roof, but the Bible says David was the one on the roof. We don't know for sure where Bathsheba was. One version of the Bible says, "A beautiful young woman was down below in her courtyard, bathing as her religion required" (2 Samuel 11:2, CEV). So Bathsheba may have been bathing in her courtyard, having no idea anyone was watching.

Bathsheba was very beautiful, and David wanted her. He sent a messenger to bring her to the palace. Did she come willingly? We don't know. She probably did because when the king sent for someone, that person came. She didn't know what was on his mind, either.

David was overcome with her beauty and slept with her even though she was married to another man. Bathsheba found out later she was pregnant. That was grounds for her to be put to death. She sent a message to David, and he made plans to cover up their sin. He ended up having Bathsheba's husband, Uriah, killed in the front lines of battle. After Bathsheba mourned Uriah's death, she became one of David's many wives.

What David did was wrong. God forgave him, but the child he had with Bathsheba died because of David's sin.

God forgives sin and doesn't give up on the one who sinned. David and Bathsheba sinned but were forgiven and went on to serve the Lord.

thinking it through

God hates sin, but he loves people. He forgives sin and gives second, third, and even hundredth chances.

Psalm 51 is David's prayer of confession. In it, David says, "I recognize my rebellion; it haunts me day and night. Against you, and you alone, have I sinned; I have done what is evil in your sight" (verses 3-4).

Is there anything you need to confess to God today? Use David's words in Psalm 51 to confess and ask God for forgiveness.

Bathsheba: Standing Up for Her Son

The king repeated his vow: "As surely as the LORD lives, who has rescued me from every danger, your son Solomon will be the next king and will sit on my throne this very day, just as I vowed to you before the LORD, the God of Israel."

1 KINGS 1:29-30

We know very little about Bathsheba's story before she met David other than that her father, Eliam, was one of David's heroes, and her first husband, Uriah, was a general in David's army.

After their first son died, David and Bathsheba had four more sons. David promised Bathsheba that their son Solomon would be king after him even though he wasn't David's oldest son. Years passed, and David was very old. His son Adonijah was setting himself up as king. Bathsheba remembered David's promise to her years earlier and went to talk to him. She told him what Adonijah was doing and reminded him of his promise.

David talked to Nathan, the prophet who had confronted him with his sin years earlier. He told Bathsheba that Nathan, along with Zadok the priest, would find Solomon and anoint him as king. First Kings 1:40 tells what happened next: "All the people followed Solomon into Jerusalem, playing flutes and shouting for joy."

Bathsheba was happy her son Solomon was king. She had raised him to love and serve the Lord and knew he would be a godly king. He was faithful in following God's commands and in offering sacrifices. Because of this, God appeared to him in a dream and asked Solomon what he most wanted.

Solomon didn't ask for riches or success but for wisdom in ruling the people. God was pleased with his answer and told Solomon he would give him an understanding heart to rule his people *plus* riches and fame!

Even though David and Bathsheba's relationship got off to a wrong start, God was able to use them and their son Solomon because they loved God and learned to keep his commandments.

thinking it through

It doesn't catch God by surprise when we do things that are wrong. He loves us more than we are able to understand. Jeremiah 31:3 says, "Long ago the LORD said to Israel: 'I have loved you, my people, with an everlasting love. With unfailing love I have drawn you to myself.'" This verse was written to the Jewish people long ago, but it is still true for us today. What do you picture when you think of "everlasting love"? How does it feel to know that God loves you this much?

thinking it through

Do you make the most of your time, abilities, and hobbies? Or do you spend too much time not doing much of anything? During the school year how well do you think you spend your time at school? What about your free time? Pick one thing that the virtuous lady from Proverbs 31 does and see how you can do something similar this week.

Bathsheba: Wise Words from Mom

Who can find a virtuous and capable wife? She is more precious than rubies.

PROVERBS 31:10

Mothers have a chance to instill values and beliefs in their young children. Bathsheba taught Solomon God's laws from his early years. He learned to love God and to obey God's commands.

Some Bible scholars believe that Bathsheba influenced the writing of Proverbs 31. Bathsheba may have given Solomon this advice verbally; he may have written the chapter with his mother's example in mind.

Bathsheba wanted Solomon to know that choosing a good wife was very important. The verse asks, "Who can find a virtuous and capable wife?" In other words, who can find a woman who is full of good principles, strong morals, and godly attitudes? If you are thinking a woman like that would be a boring housewife who sits at home and does nothing other than serve her family, you are wrong.

This lady is smart, ambitious, a businesswoman, a counselor, a seamstress, and more. Here are just a few of the things she does:

- She gets up before dawn to prepare breakfast for her household and plan the day's work (Proverbs 31:15).
- She goes to inspect a field and buys it (Proverbs 31:16).
- She makes belted linen garments and sashes to sell to the merchants (Proverbs 31:24).
- When she speaks, her words are wise (Proverbs 31:26).

This lady is far from the woman who stays at home doing nothing. She is a capable woman who has her act together. How can you be like her someday? Start now. Work hard in school, and use your free time well. Don't sit around texting or daydreaming—accomplish something. Being a young woman for God is far from boring.

Bathsheba: Time Management, Part 1

She gets up before dawn to prepare breakfast for her household and plan the day's work for her servant girls.

PROVERBS 31:15

It makes sense that Bathsheba herself tried to do and be the things she encouraged her son Solomon to look for in a wife. The woman in Proverbs 31 had to be very organized when it came to planning her day. No sleeping in late or sitting around for her.

You have a lot going on in your life—school and homework during the school year, extra family activities during the summer, church, youth group activities, lessons or clubs, sports teams, jobs at home, activities with friends, and so on. Like the woman in Proverbs 31, you may need to get up early and plan your day.

Getting up early is probably not your favorite thing, nor mine. But it is one way to get more done. Now during summer you may not have to get up as early, but sleeping until noon doesn't accomplish anything. It's best to go to bed and get up at the same time each day. Then your body gets used to it and knows what to expect. Get enough sleep so that you wake up feeling rested and ready to accomplish what you need to.

Having trouble getting to sleep? That happens. These things can help:

- If you are upset about something, try to resolve it before bed; then don't dwell on it.
- Have a relaxing bedtime routine. Read a book or your Bible, or listen to calm music.
- Make sure your room is dark and cool.
- Turn off all electronics.
- Don't have caffeine within three hours of bedtime.

Getting enough sleep to wake up rested is important so you can accomplish all you need to and be ready to tackle the things God has for you to do.

thinking it through

How's your sleep? Do you get eight to nine hours of sleep each night? Do you wake up ready to face the day? What things keep you awake? What helps you sleep? Do you do any of the things listed at the lower left to help you sleep well?

Psalm 127:2 says that God wants you to work hard, but not to the point of stressing yourself out; he gives rest to his loved ones. Before you go to bed tonight, thank God for his gift of sleep.

thinking it through

Make a time chart of your daily schedule, either for today or for when you are in school. First, fill in school hours or major time commitments. Then add activities, church events, or jobs. Block out time for homework and chores, too. And make sure to leave time just to have fun and relax.

If your chart looks too empty or too full, pray about what God might want you to change in your schedule. Ask a parent or friend to help you decide what to add or drop.

Bathsheba: Time Management, Part 2

Whatever you do, do well. For when you go to the grave, there will be no work or planning or knowledge or wisdom.

ECCLESIASTES 9:10

If you've read the last couple of devos, you'll remember how much was accomplished by the woman in Proverbs 31—the woman likely modeled on Bathsheba's advice and example. She got up early, made a plan, fed her family, made clothes, bought and sold, managed her household, and gave good advice.

What do you need to accomplish today? If you are on summer vacation, you may not have as much to do as usual, but what will your schedule look like once you go back to school? What do you do each day? Homework? Band practice? Gymnastics class? Church choir? Babysitting your little brother?

If it seems like you have more to do during the day than time to do it, it's time to get organized. Here are some ideas to help you get ready for fall:

- List everything you need to accomplish—school assignments, jobs at home, half-finished projects, and so on. You can write it on paper or program it into an electronic planner if you have one.
- Decide what is most important. Work on that one thing until it is complete, then cross it off the list. Go on to the next item.
- Use your school planner or a calendar. Write down all assignments and when they are due. Write down sports events, church events, and other special events.
- Make a time schedule. Write the days of the week across the top of the paper and the hours down the side. Then fill it in.

These things will help you see what you need to do and when you need to do it. If you have more to do than you have time, it's time to drop an activity or two.

Bathsheba: Money Management

She goes to inspect a field and buys it; with her earnings she plants a vineyard.

PROVERBS 31:16

Is there anything this ideal woman of Proverbs 31, based on Bathsheba, can't do? She gets up early, organizes her day, and manages both her time and the household. She also knows how to buy and sell. She's a good money manager.

You may not have much money. Perhaps you get a weekly allowance or money for helping with certain jobs, such as mowing the lawn, babysitting, or helping a neighbor. It won't be long until you can get a part-time job working in a store or a fast-food restaurant. Getting a paycheck each week is exciting.

There are two basic things you can do with money—spend it or save it. Which is your favorite? Probably spending money, right? But there are so many things to spend your money on that if you aren't careful, it's gone before you know it.

It's important to have a plan for your money. It doesn't have to be elaborate. Write down how much money you have, then how you plan to use it. It's good to set aside some money first to place in the church offering or give to someone in need. Then decide how much to save and how much to spend.

Don't know how much to save? It's good to save at least 10 to 25 percent, but if you are saving for something specific, like a bike or an iPod, you might want to save more so you can get it sooner. You can also save for something in the future, such as a mission trip or college.

The money you set aside to spend can be used on a lot of things. Sometimes you will spend money and have nothing to show for it later—such as when you buy a pizza or go to a movie. Other times you will spend it on things that last a little longer, such as shoes or a birthday gift. Be wise when you make your spending choices so you won't regret them later or have nothing to show for your money.

thinking it through

Try using envelopes to keep track of your money. Put money to give in one envelope, money to spend in another envelope, and money to save in a third envelope. You can take the money in the third envelope to the bank and put it in an account where it will earn interest. Then you'll be less tempted to spend it.

What do you do with most of your money? How can you be wiser in your money management? Ask God for that wisdom right now.

Bathsheba: Helping Others

She extends a helping hand to the poor and opens her arms to the needy.

PROVERBS 31:20

Not only does the woman based on Bathsheba's wisdom, described in Proverbs 31, make and spend money, she uses her money to help the poor and those in need. She has the means to do this because of the wise way in which she has used her money and invested it to make more. And on top of using her resources to help others, she becomes personally involved.

What would this woman be doing if she were here today? She might

- give extra money to her church's mission fund.
- give food to the food bank or homeless shelter.
- serve meals at the homeless shelter.
- sponsor a child in a poor country through a Christian organization.
- adopt an orphan.
- donate toward an organization that builds houses for the poor.
- join a team to help build one of the houses.
- invite someone over for a meal.
- give her own clothing or canned food items to a local mission or someone else who needs them.

Some of these things you can't do, but some you can. If you aren't already involved in helping others, talk to your parents about ways you can give your time and money. Maybe it's something you can do as a family.

Your church or youth group might already have a ministry to the poor you could become involved in, or you might suggest to your youth pastor that the youth create a plan for helping others.

Think about ways you can be involved, and talk to an adult about how to make them a reality.

thinking it through

The woman in Proverbs 31 used her money to help the poor. Giving your money to a good cause is nice, but there are also other ways to help needy people. What one good thing can you do for someone this week?

Puzzle Page

In yesterday's devo, we learned how the woman described in Proverbs 31 helped those who were poor and needy. Solve the Balloon Puzzle below to find out what the Bible says about helping others.

Directions: Each balloon has both a scrambled word and a number in it. There are also numbers next to the blank spots in the verse. Look at the number next to the blank. Find the balloon with the same number. Unscramble the word in that balloon, and write it on the line. Check your answers at the bottom.

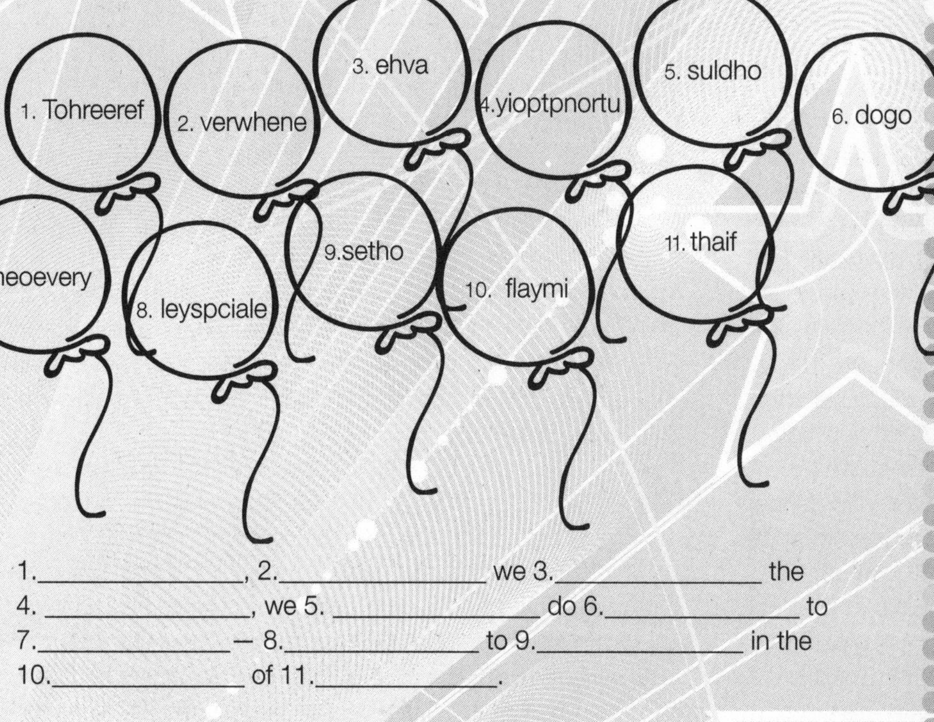

1.________________, 2.________________ we 3.________________ the
4. ________________, we 5. ________________ do 6.________________ to
7.________________ — 8.________________ to 9.________________ in the
10.________________ of 11.________________.

Answer: Therefore, whenever we have the opportunity, we should do good to everyone—especially to those in the family of faith. (Galatians 6:10)

Queen of Sheba: Curiosity Satisfied

She arrived in Jerusalem with a large group of attendants and a great caravan of camels loaded with spices, large quantities of gold, and precious jewels. When she met with Solomon, she talked with him about everything she had on her mind.

1 KINGS 10:2

Far from Jerusalem, in southwest Arabia, the queen of Sheba began to hear rumors of the wise and rich king named Solomon. The queen didn't believe the reports that were trickling in with each passing camel caravan, so she decided to visit King Solomon and see for herself if the reports were true.

Traveling the 1,200 miles or so to Jerusalem was no easy task in a camel caravan with soldiers, servants, gifts, and supplies. It would have taken several months to reach Jerusalem.

This didn't bother the queen of Sheba. She was excited to meet Solomon and satisfy her curiosity about him. It's also possible that the queen of Sheba was interested in business dealings or trade agreements with Solomon.

When the queen of Sheba arrived, she gave Solomon a gift of gold that would be worth over $3 million today. She asked him all her questions, which he was able to answer. The queen was overwhelmed when she realized how wise Solomon was. She admitted to Solomon that she hadn't believed the reports about him, but now she realized he was even greater than others had said.

The queen of Sheba was from a country that worshiped idols. She watched how Solomon worshiped God, and when she left she said, "Praise the LORD your God, who delights in you and has placed you on the throne of Israel" (1 Kings 10:9). This may mean she accepted that Solomon's God was the true God, or at least that she accepted that he had a strong belief in his God.

The queen of Sheba's curiosity and desire for wisdom and knowledge led her on a 1,200-mile trek. Where do your curiosity and desire for wisdom and knowledge lead you?

thinking it through

Are you like the queen of Sheba, wondering about things and wanting answers? Being interested in the things around you is good. It keeps you learning and growing and makes you a more interesting person. And we should always strive to learn more about God.

If you could ask God one question, what would it be? Use a concordance or a Bible encyclopedia to look up what the Bible says about it, or ask a pastor or other Christian adult for his or her thoughts.

Widow of Zarephath: Test of Faith

This is what the LORD, the God of Israel, says: "There will always be flour and olive oil left in your containers until the time when the LORD sends rain and the crops grow again!

1 KINGS 17:14

The widow of Zarephath and her son lived in their own house but had few possessions. She probably had a small barley field and a few olive trees. When the harvest was good, she had enough food to care for herself and her child, but there was a drought, and nothing was growing. She had no way to care for herself and her son.

During this time, the prophet Elijah was on the run. Wicked Queen Jezebel wanted him dead. Elijah went to the widow's town and saw her gathering sticks. He asked her for a drink of water and a bite of bread, but the widow told him that she was down to her last meal before she and her son would die! There was barely enough to feed them, much less Elijah.

Elijah asked the woman to make bread for him first. He told her not to fear because she would never run out of flour or olive oil until the drought was over and crops would grow again.

This woman didn't know Elijah, and she lived in a pagan nation that didn't serve God. She had no way of knowing whether what Elijah said was true. Perhaps she figured she'd take a chance on it since she and her son were going to die of starvation anyway. Or maybe she'd heard stories of what the God of Israel could do. Whichever the reason, she listened to Elijah and made him some bread. Her flour and olive oil were never gone until the drought was over—just as God had promised.

God chose to use a woman in a pagan land to help the prophet Elijah. She had faith in what he said, even though she didn't know his God.

thinking it through

How do you think the widow felt when she realized she was down to only enough food for one last meal? Why do you think the widow did what Elijah asked?

Have you ever felt beyond hope, like the widow of Zarephath? How can her story encourage you?

thinking it through

Can you think of a time when you were rewarded for giving? When might you give and not expect anything in return?

Widow of Zarephath: Give without Expectations

Give, and you will receive. Your gift will return to you in full—pressed down, shaken together to make room for more, running over, and poured into your lap. The amount you give will determine the amount you get back.

LUKE 6:38

The widow of Zarephath was down to her last meal. She must have watched the flour and oil diminishing a little more each day. Perhaps she tried to eat less and less each day so her son could have more of the food. She measured the flour and knew she and her son were about to eat their last meal before they faced starvation. She sadly went out to gather sticks to build a fire so she could cook. While she was gathering the sticks, Elijah saw her and asked her for water. As she was going to get it, Elijah asked for a little bread to go with it.

Can you imagine what went through this woman's mind? She was scrimping together the end of her flour for one last meal, and a stranger asked her for bread. What would you have said? "Are you kidding? I don't even have enough for myself." Or maybe, "Who are you, and why are you asking me for food? Why don't you bring me some food?"

Elijah told her not to be afraid. Then he told her to give him food first. *First?* Why was this man taking advantage of a starving woman?

Elijah assured her she'd have flour and oil until her own crops would grow again. The woman had a decision to make—give the rest of her food to Elijah on faith she'd receive more, or use the rest for herself and her son as she had planned. The widow chose to give all she had left to Elijah in faith.

There are times when we give in hopes of getting something in return, and there are other times when we give, not expecting anything back. When we give to God, we often receive his blessings in return.

Widow of Zarephath: Give What You Can

Whatever you give is acceptable if you give it eagerly. And give according to what you have, not what you don't have.

2 CORINTHIANS 8:12

The widow of Zarephath wasn't out looking for someone to give to; she was collecting sticks to build a fire and cook her last meal. She had nothing extra to give. When Elijah asked her for bread, she gave him all she had left. She couldn't offer him meat or vegetables because she didn't have any. She couldn't give him anything other than water to drink because she didn't have it, but Elijah asked only for what she had, and that was sufficient.

God doesn't ask people to give more than they have. Some people have millions and give only a few dollars to God's work. Others have very little but give generously of what they have. The small amount a poor person gives counts much more to God than a large amount from a rich person. That's because the poor are giving a larger part of what they have.

When I was in elementary school, a man in our church donated a million dollars to start a Christian school. That is a lot of money now, but it went even further back then. Although he remained anonymous, people talked for years about how that generous gift allowed a school to be built. At the same time, a few of the older church members gave very generously toward the school out of their meager retirement money. Yet no one talked about that—or even knew about it—although their gifts were actually more sacrificial because they didn't have extra to give; they gave of their daily living money.

People notice the bigger, grander gifts, but that isn't true of God. He looks at the willingness of the giver and the attitude of the heart. A generous heart is much more important to God than the amount a person is able to give.

thinking it through

If you get an allowance or have a babysitting job, do you give some of the money to God? If not, start this week. Challenge yourself to set aside some money to give right away, before you spend any of it.

thinking it through

Paul had some instructions he wanted Timothy to pass on to his church. They are good instructions for us, too. 1 Timothy 6:18 says, "Tell them to use their money to do good. They should be rich in good works and generous to those in need, always being ready to share with others." What are two ways you can do this today?

Widow of Zarephath: Give Yourself

They even did more than we had hoped, for their first action was to give themselves to the Lord and to us, just as God wanted them to do.

2 CORINTHIANS 8:5

The widow of Zarephath gave the last of her food to Elijah, but she did more than that. She built the fire and cooked the food for him. God instructed Elijah to stay with the widow and her son, and during that time the widow prepared his meals along with her own. She gave of her time and her energy to help Elijah, although she was not even a worshiper of the true God when she first met Elijah.

God wants us to give our whole selves to him, not just our things. When we give ourselves to him first, we are giving him all that we are and all that we have. We want to use whatever we have for him, whether it is money, time, or talents. God doesn't need our acts of service or our money. He owns the universe. But when we put him first, giving back to him is a natural part of life.

How can you give yourself to the Lord? You might remember a time when you went forward at church during an invitation to accept Jesus as your Savior. Or perhaps you made a promise to live for God while at summer camp. Those things are good, but giving yourself to God is a daily thing. Each morning when you get up, tell God you are willing to be used by him that day. Ask him to give you the words to say to people around you and to guide you in what he wants you to do. Try to listen to him with your heart throughout the day, and follow that still, small voice you hear in your heart.

Giving your money to God's work is important, but giving yourself to God is more important. If you don't have money to give, he can use you anyway. He wants your surrender to his plans more than any resources you might have to give.

Widow of Zarephath: Why Give? Part 1

Wherever your treasure is, there the desires of your heart will also be.

MATTHEW 6:21

We don't know the widow of Zarephath's motivation for giving. It might have been that God spoke to her heart and led her to give the rest of her food to Elijah. Or she may have given in hopes that what he said about her flour and oil not running out would come true.

Why do some give generously to God's work and some do not? It all depends on their hearts and their motivation. There are many good reasons for giving to God's work. Here are some of them:

1. God wants us to give. Malachi 3:10 says, "Bring all the tithes into the storehouse so there will be enough food in my Temple." A tithe was the amount the Israelites were required to give under God's law: 10 percent. Some would point out that we are no longer required to follow that law. God's desire for us to give hasn't changed, though.
2. God wants to bless us. The second part of Malachi 3:10 says, "I will pour out a blessing so great you won't have enough room to take it in! Try it! Put me to the test!" God's blessings aren't always money or things. Sometimes they are in the form of peace and assurance of God's presence or courage in the face of difficulty.
3. Giving back to God keeps us from becoming selfish with our money. The blessing is in giving, not in hoarding what we have or just using it for ourselves. Acts 20:35 reminds us of the words of Jesus: "It is more blessed to give than to receive."

The amount of money you have to give doesn't matter; the motivation for giving does. God looks at the heart, not the income. Give because God wants you to give, and he wants to bless you. Your giving will be an encouragement to others.

thinking it through

What is your motive for giving? Why does motive matter?

Widow of Zarephath: Why Give? Part 2

Honor the LORD with your wealth and with the best part of everything you produce.
PROVERBS 3:9

Yesterday we looked at three reasons for giving: God wants us to give, God wants to bless us, and giving keeps us from becoming selfish with our money. Here are a few more reasons we should give:

1. We honor God when we give of what we have. Look at today's verse. According to God's law in the Old Testament, people gave of the crops they grew as well as of their money. We can give our "stuff" as well as our money.
2. Giving to God helps us keep our priorities straight. We aren't just here on earth to see how much we can accumulate; we are here to fulfill God's plan for us. Matthew 6:21 says, "Wherever your treasure is, there the desires of your heart will also be." When we give to God's work, we are storing up treasure in heaven rather than here on earth.
3. Giving back to God reminds us he is the true owner of all we have. First Timothy 6:17 says, "Teach those who are rich in this world not to be proud and not to trust in their money, which is so unreliable. Their trust should be in God, who richly gives us all we need for our enjoyment." Believing that God is the owner of all we have means trusting him, not ourselves, to provide what we need.
4. The money we give helps support churches and Christian ministries. Whether you give to your church or you give in some other way, like sponsoring a child through a Christian organization, God's Word is shared and lives are changed. Paul says, "Tell them to use their money to do good." (1 Timothy 6:18).

The widow gave what little she had. God will use what you give just as he used what the widow gave to Elijah.

thinking it through

Don't think the little bit of money you have will make a difference? It will. You can

1. give it to a special mission offering.
2. send it to a Christian organization for a special need.
3. buy a bag of diapers for a Christian pregnancy center.
4. buy a can of corn or a case of vegetables for the local mission.
5. ask your parents if they will sponsor a child with you.

What one thing can you do this week?

Quiz Time

What kind of giver are you? Take the quiz below to find out. Read each sentence and circle A for always, S for sometimes, or N for never. If the situation has never come up, make your best guess as to what you would do.

1. When I get my allowance, the first thing I do is set some money aside for the church offering.

   A S N

2. When I get some unexpected money (like birthday money), I find myself thinking about how I could use part of it to accomplish something good for someone else.

   A S N

3. I give what I can happily, not just because I feel like I should.

   A S N

4. I try to act as a good manager of the money I receive, because everything I have is really from God.

   A S N

5. I give even if I won't get anything in return.

   A S N

How did you do?

If you circled mostly A's, good for you. You know what it means to be a manager of the money God allows you to have, and you do your best to manage God's money wisely.

If you circled mostly S's, try to be more generous in your giving, and make sure you do it happily, not under pressure from your parents or because you think something bad will happen if you don't. Give out of love for God.

If you circled mostly N's, it's time to take a hard look at your attitude toward your money. God gives us the ability to earn money. Everything really belongs to him, but he lets us use it. When we give back to him, we are only really giving him what is his in the first place. Step out in faith like the widow, and give what you have to help someone else.

thinking it through

Why do you think God chose the widow to help Elijah? Why does God choose some people and not others?

Widow of Zarephath: God Uses Unlikely People

The woman told Elijah, "Now I know for sure that you are a man of God, and that the LORD truly speaks through you."

1 KINGS 17:24

After the widow fed Elijah, she always found enough flour and oil to feed herself, her son, and Elijah. This continued while the drought remained.

Then one day the woman's son became ill and died. The woman was distraught. She thought that Elijah's staying with her had revealed some sin to God, and God had decided to kill her son as judgment. She cried out to Elijah, who took the child to his room. Elijah prayed and stretched himself out over the child three times. The child's life returned to him! The woman proclaimed that Elijah was truly a messenger of God.

There are a lot of places God could have sent Elijah for help. He could have chosen to send Elijah to a rich home where food was abundant, but he chose to send him to a poor widow who had nothing. God also allowed the woman's son to die, but then be brought back to life. Why did God do these things? Perhaps to show that he alone was providing for Elijah and the widow. A rich man would have no need of God's intervention, but the widow knew the food she ate each day was from God. She knew that having her son brought back to life was a gift from God too.

Sometimes God chooses to use the poor, the lonely, and the less important people so that his glory shines through. The rich and powerful may think they have no need of God because they can supply their own needs. They fail to recognize that God created them and gave them the ability to earn money. They don't acknowledge his work, but the ones who have little, like the widow, are better at recognizing God at work in their lives.

We can be encouraged that we don't need to be someone important or rich for God to use us; he is simply looking for those who are willing.

Jezebel: The Queen of Mean

As though it were not enough to follow the example of Jeroboam, [Ahab] married Jezebel, the daughter of King Ethbaal of the Sidonians, and he began to bow down in worship of Baal.

1 KINGS 16:31

Jezebel was the worst queen there ever was. Worse than any of the wicked queens you've read about in fairy tales. How did this wicked Phoenician princess get to be queen of Israel? It goes back to King Solomon's reign.

When he took the throne, Solomon loved and served God just as his father, David, had. He was a good king for many years, but he kept marrying more and more foreign wives, who brought all sorts of idol worship into the kingdom. Because Solomon allowed this to happen, God divided the kingdom. Solomon's son Rehoboam ruled over the southern two tribes of Israel, which became known as Judah. Jeroboam, son of one of the members of Solomon's court, ruled over the ten northern tribes of Israel, which kept the name Israel.

Jeroboam introduced calf worship to Israel. He was only one of the many kings who turned away from God. The worst time in Israel's history was when Ahab was king. Ahab, the seventh king of Israel, married Jezebel, the daughter of Ethbaal, king of Sidon. It may be that Omri, Ahab's father, arranged the marriage with Ethbaal to strengthen ties between their countries, but whatever the reason they married, it was not a match made in heaven. In fact, God was not happy at all that a king of Israel married a foreign idol worshiper.

Jezebel, the queen of mean, tried to kill all of God's prophets and spread Baal worship to God's chosen people. This was a dark time for Israel, but as always, God was—and still is—in control of all things. Even when it looks like evil is winning, God reigns. He may allow evil for a while, but he always wins in the end.

thinking it through

God was displeased by Solomon and Ahab, as well as other kings who allowed idolatry in their kingdoms. We don't have wooden or metal idols sitting in our houses, but we may have things that become more important to us than God. These things are like idols. What are some things people may put above God? Is there anything in your life that you are tempted to put above God? What should you do about it?

thinking it through

Jezebel wasn't the type of person you want to be. She was strong willed, forceful, critical, pushy, a control freak, stubborn, and demanding. But some of Jezebel's character traits have a positive side. Being stubborn could become being determined—to do right, stand against peer pressure, and succeed in school. What are the positive and negative sides of some of your character traits? Ask God to help you make the most of the way he's made you.

Jezebel: Queen with an Attitude

Once when Jezebel had tried to kill all the LORD's prophets, Obadiah had hidden 100 of them in two caves. He put fifty prophets in each cave and supplied them with food and water.

1 KINGS 18:4

Jezebel was a queen with an attitude—a very bad attitude. The sad thing is that Jezebel was gifted, courageous, bright, and a true leader. But she used those character traits for evil.

King Ahab was in a position to turn the people's hearts back to God after the evil and idolatry previous kings had allowed. Instead, Ahab was weak. He allowed Jezebel to bring the worship of Baal and Asherah to Israel, and rid Israel of all the prophets of the true God.

Jezebel built temples to her false gods and cared for their prophets. But God had his own prophet, Elijah, whom he sent to Ahab to say that there would be no dew or rain for the next few years.

In the third year of drought, Elijah challenged the false prophets to a showdown on Mount Carmel. The false prophets were to kill a bull, put it on wood on an altar, and call on their god to set fire to it, and Elijah would do the same. Whichever god answered was the true God.

The prophets of Baal spent hours calling on their god while Elijah stood by and mocked them. Then Elijah flooded his altar with water and prayed to God, and "immediately the fire of the LORD flashed down from heaven and burned up the young bull, the wood, the stones, and the dust. It even licked up all the water in the trench!" (1 Kings 18:38).

Elijah had all the prophets of Baal killed; then the drought ended with a rainstorm. But that storm was nothing compared to the fury of Jezebel when she heard Elijah had killed her prophets.

Jezebel had the opportunity to influence a nation for good and for God, but she chose to use her influence for evil.

Jezebel: A Bright Mind

"Are you the king of Israel or not?" Jezebel demanded. "Get up and eat something, and don't worry about it. I'll get you Naboth's vineyard!"

1 KINGS 21:7

Jezebel was bad to the bone, but she wasn't stupid. In fact, she had a bright mind and could make detailed plans, find solutions to problems, and outthink most people around her. The problem was that she used this gift for evil.

One day Jezebel found her husband, Ahab, sulking. There was a vineyard adjoining his property, and he wanted it, but the owner, Naboth, wouldn't sell, even when Ahab offered him a better piece of land in exchange. The property was Naboth's inheritance, and Jewish law forbade him from selling it.

King Ahab became the king of sulking. He went to bed and lay with his face to the wall, refusing to eat. If you try this, you will probably not get very good results from your parents, but Ahab got results from Jezebel. She assured him she would get the vineyard for him.

Then Jezebel devised a plan. She publicly accused Naboth of cursing God and the king. She even had two false witnesses say it was true. So Naboth was taken outside the city gate and stoned. When Jezebel sent word that Naboth was dead, Ahab immediately went to claim Naboth's vineyard for himself.

Jezebel had a sharp mind and could have used it to make plans to turn the people back to God, or devised ways to help the poor. But she chose to use it for evil.

Has God blessed you with a sharp mind? Can you easily find solutions to problems or create plans? Use that in your home, school, and church to help others. You could volunteer to plan the vacation route for your family trip or organize a campaign for a class office in the fall. You might think of a way to reorganize the overcrowded youth room at church or plan a community outreach program for your Sunday school class. Jezebel used her bright mind to devise evil plans; use yours for good.

thinking it through

Are you quick to figure things out? If you are, think of ways to use that for good. Even if you aren't the first to come up with ideas, you can still use your abilities to serve others by supporting those who do make the plans.

Look around you for problems that need creative solutions this week. Pick one of the problems and make a plan for solving it.

thinking it through

Are you a young woman of courage? Look around for something that needs to be changed or someone who needs a friend to stick up for her, and don't be afraid to step up and make a difference. Ask God to give you the courage to face life head-on. You can accomplish much for God with his help.

Jezebel: Courage Used for Good

Jezebel sent this message to Elijah: "May the gods strike me and even kill me if by this time tomorrow I have not killed you just as you killed them."

1 KINGS 19:2

Jezebel was courageous. No one would accuse her of cowardice. The problem was, her courage usually had a murderous twist to it!

Jezebel brought her idols and false prophets into Israel and tried to turn God's chosen people into Baal worshipers. She tried to get rid of God's prophets. Jezebel made threats against Elijah, one of God's special prophets, and vowed to end his life. Jezebel wanted to secure land for Ahab, so she plotted and carried out Naboth's death.

Jezebel didn't fear any man or even God. Her strength and courage were in herself. There was no wickedness she wouldn't try, no man she wouldn't murder.

Courage is noble when used for good and right. Brave women through the years have accomplished much. Harriet Tubman, former slave, became a conductor on the Underground Railroad and saved over three hundred slaves. Clara Barton, founder of the Red Cross, was known as "Angel of the Battlefield" for her work helping injured soldiers in the Civil War. Rosa Parks refused to give up her seat on a public bus in 1955, sparking the Montgomery Bus Boycott, the first major effort in the civil rights movement. Elizabeth Blackwell, the first American woman to receive an MD, founded the New York Infirmary for Women and Children and the Women's Medical College. She paved the way for women in medicine. These are just a few examples of women of courage who used their bravery for good.

Courage is a powerful force. It can accomplish much good or much evil. Use your bravery to make a positive change in your corner of the world.

Jezebel: Things God Hates

There are six things the LORD hates—no, seven things he detests: haughty eyes, a lying tongue, hands that kill the innocent, a heart that plots evil, feet that race to do wrong, a false witness who pours out lies, a person who sows discord in a family.

PROVERBS 6:16-19

Jezebel had an aggressive personality that drove her to get her own way. Being strong willed or assertive is not bad. In fact, those things can help someone push for what is good and pure and right. Jezebel, however, chose to use her strong personality to do wrong.

In Proverbs chapter 6 God lists seven things he hates. It's safe to say Jezebel was guilty of most, if not all, of them:

Haughty eyes—she was proud of herself and her looks, fixing herself up even as she was facing death.

A lying tongue—she falsely accused Naboth of cursing God and the king.

Hands that kill the innocent—she had as many prophets of God killed as could be found and also had Naboth killed.

A heart that plots evil—whatever Jezebel wanted, she plotted to get. She plotted to get Naboth's land and to kill the prophets, and she was constantly plotting to kill Elijah.

Feet that race to do wrong—can you just see Jezebel scurrying around, making her wicked plots to kill God's prophets and planning the temples she would build for her false gods?

A false witness who pours out lies—again, think Naboth. Jezebel had false witnesses in place to accuse Naboth of something he didn't do.

A person who sows discord in a family—Jezebel married one of God's chosen people and turned him to idol worship. She raised her sons to worship her false gods.

Having a strong personality isn't bad or wrong; it's how you use it that matters. If you are assertive and aggressive, use it to make changes for the better and to influence those around you to do right.

thinking it through

Jezebel was one wicked queen. The list of things God hates could have been written about her. On the other hand, Philippians 4:8 gives us a list of the kinds of things we should think about.

Each day this week, before you get up in the morning or go to bed at night, pick a different word from Philippians 4:8 to focus on, and think about things that word describes. How does it influence your thoughts throughout the week?

thinking it through

Why do you think Proverbs 11:14 says it is safe to have many advisers? If you are a leader, who do you look to for advice? How can you support the leaders in your life?

Jezebel: Wise Leadership

Without wise leadership, a nation falls; there is safety in having many advisers.

PROVERBS 11:14

Jezebel was a gifted leader, but she abused that gift. She used it to turn people away from God, get rid of the righteous, and install her own false gods. How different she was from Miriam, who was also a gifted leader. Miriam led people in praise after God delivered them from the Egyptians. She took her place by Moses' side as they led God's chosen people to the Promised Land.

Some people are born leaders. There is something that makes them stand out, take the reins, and lead. Others follow them. Jezebel had the charisma to lead, but she led people from God rather than to God. Married to a weak king, she was the force behind the throne. Once Ahab died, she ruled through her two sons.

Leaders have influence. They can either accomplish much good or do much harm. If you are someone others look to for leadership, make sure you are using your abilities for God. Make good choices and encourage others to do the same.

If you are a follower rather than a leader, make sure the peers and adults you look to for leadership are the kind you should be following. Don't give your attention or allegiance to someone who rebels against authority, denies God, or lives contrary to the Bible. A true leader will lead others toward God and his ways, like Miriam did, rather than away from God, like Jezebel. Use wisdom and good judgment as you lead and choose whom to follow.

Puzzle Page

Jezebel had many gifts she could have used for good but instead used for evil. God has given you gifts in order to serve others and accomplish good. Solve this Telephone Puzzle to see what the Bible says about your gifts.

Directions: This puzzle has two numbers under each line. The first number is for the phone button. Only button numbers 2-9 have letters on them. The second number tells which letter on the button to use. All the buttons except 7 and 9 have three letters on them. Numbers 7 and 9 have four letters. Look under the first line. You see 9.3. That means button #9. Then choose the third letter on that button. That is Y. Write it on the line. Finish the puzzle, and check your answer below.

1	2 ABC	3 DEF
4 GHI	5 JKL	6 MNO
7 PQRS	8 TUV	9 WXYZ
*	0 OPER	#

If ____ ____ ____ ____ ____ ____ ____ ____ is to
9.3 6.3 8.2 7.3 4.1 4.3 3.3 8.1

____ ____ ____ ____ ____ ____ ____ ____ ____
3.2 6.2 2.3 6.3 8.2 7.3 2.1 4.1 3.2

____ ____ ____ ____ ____ ____, be
6.3 8.1 4.2 3.2 7.3 7.4

____ ____ ____ ____ ____ ____ ____ ____ ____ ____ ____.
3.2 6.2 2.3 6.3 8.2 7.3 2.1 4.1 4.3 6.2 4.1

If it is ____ ____ ____ ____ ____ ____, ____ ____ ____ ____
4.1 4.3 8.3 4.3 6.2 4.1 4.1 4.3 8.3 3.2

____ ____ ____ ____ ____ ____ ____ ____ ____ ____. If ____ ____ ____
4.1 3.2 6.2 3.2 7.3 6.3 8.2 7.4 5.3 9.3 4.1 6.3 3.1

has ____ ____ ____ ____ ____ you leadership
4.1 4.3 8.3 3.2 6.2

____ ____ ____ ____ ____ ____ ____, take the responsibility
2.1 2.2 4.3 5.3 4.3 8.1 9.3

____ ____ ____ ____ ____ ____ ____ ____ ____. And if you have a
7.4 3.2 7.3 4.3 6.3 8.2 7.4 5.3 9.3

____ ____ ____ ____ for ____ ____ ____ ____ ____ ____ ____
4.1 4.3 3.3 8.1 7.4 4.2 6.3 9.1 4.3 6.2 4.1

____ ____ ____ ____ ____ ____ ____ ____ to
5.2 4.3 6.2 3.1 6.2 3.2 7.4 7.4

____ ____ ____ ____ ____ ____, do it ____ ____ ____ ____ ____ ____.
6.3 8.1 4.2 3.2 7.3 7.4 4.1 5.3 2.1 3.1 5.3 9.3

How can you live this verse today?

Answer: If your gift is to encourage others, be encouraging. If it is giving, give generously. If God has given you leadership ability, take the responsibility seriously. And if you have a gift for showing kindness to others, do it gladly. (Romans 12:8)

thinking it through

The Bible includes examples of both righteous and ungodly people from whom we can learn. What lessons can you learn from Jezebel? How can you make sure your life counts here on earth?

Jezebel: The Queen's Death

The LORD cares deeply when his loved ones die.
PSALM 116:15

It's a sad time when loved ones die. We grieve because we miss them, but at the same time we know we will see them again in heaven if they believed in Jesus. The Bible says God himself cares when one of his loved ones dies.

Jezebel was not a believer in God. She killed his prophets. She killed innocent people. She was ruthless and unrepentant. God's people did not grieve when she died.

Jezebel's death was prophesied when she had Naboth killed. Elijah appeared to Ahab in Naboth's vineyard and told him that dogs would lick Ahab's blood where they had licked the blood of Naboth, and dogs would devour Jezebel's body at the plot of land in Jezreel (where the vineyard was located).

Ugh. That prophecy sounds like something from a horror movie you wouldn't even think of watching. But this wasn't a movie; it was real. When Jehu became king of Israel, he went to Jezebel's house. She taunted him from her upstairs window. At Jehu's command, two of her servants threw her from the window, and dogs devoured her as prophesied. All that was left was her skull, feet, and hands. What a horrible end!

How much better it is to be a believer in Jesus and know that both your life and death are important to God, and you have a heavenly home waiting for you. John 14 is often read in funerals because of the hope it offers. John 14:2-3 says, "There is more than enough room in my Father's home. . . . When everything is ready, I will come and get you, so that you will always be with me where I am." How much better to have this hope than to die in vain like Jezebel. If Jesus is Lord of your life, you know no matter when or how you die, you will be instantly at home with him in heaven.

Widow with Oil: Faith in Action

When all the jars were full, she said to her son, "Bring me another one." But he replied, "There is not a jar left." Then the oil stopped flowing.

2 KINGS 4:6, NIV

One day a widow with two boys went to find Elisha, a prophet of God, to get his help. The woman owed money, and the creditor was going to take her sons as slaves in payment.

Elisha asked the woman what she had in her home, and she told him she had only a little oil. Elisha instructed her to ask the neighbors for as many empty jars as were available. He told her to then go into her house, shut the door, and pour her oil into the pots. The widow did as Elisha said. She poured from her oil jar, filling each pot until there were no more. Then the oil stopped. Elisha told the woman to sell the oil, pay her debt, and use the rest to live on.

The widow sought out Elisha because he was a man of God, and she believed he could help solve her problem, but she didn't know how he would do it. His instructions to her may have seemed strange, but she did exactly as he said. The woman went house to house borrowing empty jars. I wonder what she told the neighbors when she borrowed them. "The man of God said I should borrow these"? "I'm expecting a miraculous flow of oil"? We don't know what she said, but we know she had faith that what Elisha said really would happen.

The widow's faith saved her from her creditor. It kept her from losing her sons, who would have become servants to the creditor. Her faith not only paid her debts, but it also gave her money to support herself and her sons until they were grown and could care for her.

What does your faith accomplish? Would your faith take you door-to-door collecting as many jars as you could? Or would you just collect one or two jars to test whether the oil really would keep flowing and fill all the borrowed pots?

thinking it through

What do you think would have happened if the widow had collected only a couple of jars to test the oil first, planning to collect more later once she knew what Elisha said would come to pass? When is the last time you stepped out in faith, trusting God for something specific?

thinking it through

What do you have that can be used for God or to help yourself or others? A hammer to help with repairs? A musical instrument to take part in praise? A computer to design brochures for an upcoming youth event?

Or how about talents you have that can help others or yourself, like a gift of working with children to babysit, a singing voice to use in the choir or to help lead worship, or computer skills to teach an older adult how to use the Internet?

Widow with Oil: Using Your Resources

Elisha replied to her, "How can I help you? Tell me, what do you have in your house?" "Your servant has nothing there at all," she said, "except a little oil."

2 KINGS 4:2, NIV

The widow went to Elisha because she needed help. Her sons were going to be taken as slaves to pay her debt. She knew Elisha would be able to help her.

Elisha, being a prophet of God, didn't receive a weekly paycheck—or any kind of money. Prophets didn't make money from prophesying, so he didn't have money stashed away he could give the woman in order to pay her debts. Elisha didn't magically make money appear to pay the woman's debt either. He asked her what she had in her house. He wanted her to use her own resources—plus faith and a miracle—to solve her problem. The oil the woman had at home miraculously multiplied and filled all the jars she had collected. If she'd collected more jars, there would have been more oil and more money to live on. If she'd collected fewer jars, then the flow of oil would have ended sooner.

God often chooses to use the resources already on hand to meet needs. Jesus took one small boy's lunch of fish and bread and multiplied it to feed thousands. God had Shamgar use the ox goad in his hand to slay hundreds of Philistines. God used the rod in Moses' hand to show his power to Pharaoh by changing it into a snake and back into a rod.

All of us have talents or possessions that we can use for God and to help ourselves and others. What resources do you have that God can use?

Shunemite Woman: Hospitality in Action

One day Elisha went to the town of Shunem. A wealthy woman lived there, and she urged him to come to her home for a meal. After that, whenever he passed that way, he would stop there for something to eat.

2 KINGS 4:8

A rich and prominent woman and her husband lived in Shunem, a village in the hills about seven miles south of where Jesus would grow up in Nazareth. Although she and her husband were better off than most, they were humble worshipers of God.

From her home, the woman often saw Elisha trudging along the road as he traveled wherever God sent him. The woman could tell there was something different about this traveler who she came to believe was a holy man of God. One day the woman decided to ask Elisha in for a meal as he passed by, and Elisha gratefully accepted. The woman extended an invitation for Elisha to stop and dine with them anytime he passed by, and Elisha became a welcomed guest.

The woman was under no obligation to provide for Elisha, but she took the opportunity to care for a prophet of God who was in need of her hospitality. We don't have prophets who travel city to city by foot anymore, but there are servants of God, or even people who don't yet know God, who are in need of our care.

Do you have a welcoming spirit about you? You might not be able to invite others in for a meal, but there are other ways you can make people feel welcome. It might be as simple as asking the lone girl to join you and your friends, or inviting another student over to study or work on a project together. Or perhaps your family could invite the pastor, a Sunday school teacher, or a missionary family over once a month for a meal. There are many ways to extend hospitality to others. Look around and see who you can reach out to today.

thinking it through

In February when you read about Rebekah, you were encouraged to talk to your parents about ways to extend hospitality to others. If you didn't do it then, or you've started reading this book since then, talk to your parents now about reaching out to one person in your church or community. Invite him or her for a meal, to watch a DVD, to share pizza, or for some other activity. Write down your ideas, and then share them with your parents.

thinking it through

In Matthew 25:40, Jesus says that anytime we care for someone's needs, it's as if we are caring for Jesus himself. Sometimes we get so busy we don't pay attention to those around us. We don't notice the needs they have. Take time this week to look around you for needs you can meet. Try to meet two needs this week. Write about them after you do.

Shunemite Woman: Seeing and Meeting a Need

She said to her husband, "I am sure this man who stops in from time to time is a holy man of God. Let's build a small room for him on the roof and furnish it with a bed, a table, a chair, and a lamp. Then he will have a place to stay whenever he comes by."

2 KINGS 4:9-10

Sometimes when I travel, I don't book a hotel room in advance because I'm not sure where I'll stop. I might find someplace interesting to explore along the way and cover fewer miles in a day. Or I make better time than I expected, so I'm farther along than I thought I'd be. When I do stop for the night, I am always a little anxious about finding a hotel with a vacancy. I feel relief when I find a nice room at a good price.

Elisha was a traveler who had to find places to stop at night sometimes too. He had been dining with the Shunemite woman and her husband for a while when the woman had an idea. She noticed Elisha was often weary from travel. The woman suggested to her husband that they fix up a small room in their house for Elisha to use. The woman lovingly cleaned the chamber and then added a bed, table, stool, and lamp.

The next time Elisha stopped by for a meal, the woman showed him the room and said it was for him to use as long as he liked, as often as he liked. The room gave Elisha a quiet place to rest on his journeys. He must have felt relief knowing he was always welcome at the Shunemite couple's home.

What led the woman to do this for Elisha? She saw the need—Elisha was often weary from travel. Then she found a way to meet the need. She built a room and furnished it for Elisha.

When did you last see a need and look for ways to meet it? It may be something as easy as helping a neighbor mow the lawn in the summer or even helping your brother finish a school project during the school year. What matters is that you meet the need out of love for God, not a sense of duty.

Shunemite Woman: Guarding Her Heart

"Next year at this time you will be holding a son in your arms!" "No, my lord!" she cried. "O man of God, don't deceive me and get my hopes up like that."

2 KINGS 4:16

My husband and I decided to adopt twins from Haiti. We excitedly prepared the paperwork, thinking our twins would be home in just a few short months. But adoption laws changed, paperwork was lost, and month after month passed without our twins coming home. Each time I'd get my hopes up, I was disappointed.

Then there was an earthquake in Haiti, and I was told all the children would be sent to their adoptive families. I'd been disappointed too many times already, so I was determined not to think about whether the twins would finally be coming home. However, there is a happy ending to this story because the twins did come home just two weeks after the earthquake.

Elisha wanted to do something nice for the Shunemite woman. His servant told him she'd never had a child and now her husband was old. Elisha went to the woman and told her God would send her a child. The woman told Elisha he shouldn't get her hopes up. She'd been without a child all her married life, and she had accepted it. She didn't want to get excited about a child now only to be disappointed. She was guarding her heart against hurt.

The woman did have a son, but then a few years later he died. The woman confronted Elisha. She told him it would have been better not to have a child than to have one and lose him so soon. Her heart was full of hurt. But Elisha was able to raise the child from the dead. If she had never given birth to the son, she wouldn't have gone through the painful hours of his loss, but she also wouldn't have had a child to love.

Sometimes when we avoid facing or accepting things to guard our hearts from hurt, we really are shielding our hearts from some of God's blessings.

thinking it through

It's okay to be cautious, but sometimes we avoid decisions because we are protecting ourselves. Perhaps you reached out to someone and she turned on you later, or you helped someone with homework and she shunned you in the lunchroom. Those things hurt. But if you decide you will never help anyone again, you might be missing out on making a new friend.

In what ways do you guard your heart from hurt? How can you open your heart today?

thinking it through

Do you make the best of the situations that come your way and let God use you in them? Allow God to work in your heart to help you accept circumstances you can't change. Ask God to give you a gracious spirit when things don't go your way.

Young Servant Girl: Making the Best of Situations

At this time Aramean raiders had invaded the land of Israel, and among their captives was a young girl who had been given to Naaman's wife as a maid.

2 KINGS 5:2

Naaman was the commander of the Syrian army. Although he was a mighty man, it was his young Hebrew servant who is the hero of this story. All we know about her is what this verse tells us: "Among their captives was a young girl." No name. No specific age.

The young servant was an Israelite being raised by godly parents. During a raid on the Israelites, the girl was taken, and she ended up in Naaman's house as a personal servant to his wife. The girl was treated kindly and came to care about Naaman and his wife.

Though Naaman was an important man, he had leprosy, a skin disease. One day the young servant remarked to her mistress she wished Naaman would go see the prophet in Samaria so he could be cured of his disease. Naaman told his king what the girl had said, and the king told him to go. This was the first spark of hope for a cure for Naaman.

The young servant was a captive, taken from her parents and brought to a foreign land. The servant girl could have been bitter. She could have wondered why God didn't either rescue her or punish those who captured her. She even could have rejoiced that Naaman had leprosy—but she didn't. She had God's love in her heart and a strong faith instilled by her parents. She knew no matter where she was, God was looking out for her. She trusted he would fulfill his plan for her, whether it was to go home or to stay in Naaman's house. The young servant accepted her situation and made the most of it because of her faith in God.

Quiz Time

You can determine you will make the best of the situations that come your way and allow God to use you in them. Take the quiz below to see how well you do that.

Read each sentence, and circle A for always, S for sometimes, or N for never.

1. I understand when I have to change my personal plans due to family plans.

   A S N

2. I handle it with dignity when I am left out of a friend's plans.

   A S N

3. I realize things don't have to revolve around me.

   A S N

4. I let my brother or sister have his or her way some of the time without complaining.

   A S N

5. I can deal with it when plans are canceled or changed due to rain, sickness, or lack of money.

   A S N

How did you do?

Give yourself 2 points for each A, 1 point for each S, and 0 points for every N.

7-10 points: Good for you. You understand there are things you can't control, and you accept the disappointments and changes graciously.

3-6 points: You try to accept the disruptions and changes to your plans, but you sometimes react negatively to those things. Learn to accept the things that can't be changed. Trust God to work through those things.

0-2 points: Allow God to work in your heart to help you accept circumstances you can't change. Ask God to give you a gracious spirit when things don't go your way.

Young Servant Girl: Sharing Your Faith

One day the girl said to her mistress, "I wish my master would go to see the prophet in Samaria. He would heal him of his leprosy."

2 KINGS 5:3

Naaman's young servant was taught about God from her Hebrew parents. She knew God could work miracles, and he could heal Naaman of the dreaded skin disease leprosy.

The king agreed Naaman should go see the king of Israel. Naaman journeyed to Israel, taking with him a letter from his own king asking for his healing, 750 pounds of silver, 150 pounds of gold, and 10 sets of clothing. When Israel's king read the letter asking him to heal Naaman, he was dismayed. He said, "Am I God, that I can give life and take it away?"

Elisha heard the king was distraught. He said, "Why are you so upset? Send Naaman to me, and he will learn that there is a true prophet here in Israel" (2 Kings 5:8).

Naaman went to Elisha's house. Naaman was an important man, and he expected to receive special treatment from Elisha, but the prophet sent a messenger to tell Naaman to wash himself seven times in the Jordan River instead.

Naaman was angry and stalked away. He didn't want to wash in a river, but if he was going to wash in a river, he wanted it to be one near his home.

His men reasoned with him, "Sir, if the prophet had told you to do something very difficult, wouldn't you have done it? So you should certainly obey him when he says simply, 'Go and wash and be cured!'" (2 Kings 5:13).

Naaman realized what the men said was true, so he went and did as the prophet said, and his leprosy disappeared. His skin was fresh like a child's.

Naaman was healed because the young Hebrew servant was brave enough to speak to Naaman's wife about the true God. She lived among people who didn't believe, but she stayed true to her faith.

thinking it through

If you, like the young servant girl, are often surrounded by peers who don't believe in God, you have a chance to talk with them about God. When did you last talk to a classmate or friend about God? Who can you bring up the subject with this week?

Athaliah: Family Influence

God showed his great love for us by sending Christ to die for us while we were still sinners.
ROMANS 5:8

Athaliah was a link in one of the most wicked families ever to live. Just take a look at her history.

Athaliah's grandfather was King Omri of Israel. First Kings 16:25 says, "Omri did what was evil in the LORD's sight, even more than any of the kings before him."

Athaliah's father was King Ahab of Israel. First Kings 16:31, 33 says about Ahab, "As though it were not enough to follow the example of Jeroboam, he married Jezebel, the daughter of King Ethbaal of the Sidonians, and he began to bow down in worship of Baal. . . . He did more to provoke the anger of the LORD, the God of Israel, than any of the other kings of Israel before him."

Athaliah's mother was Jezebel, the queen of mean who killed 150 prophets of God, murdered Naboth for a piece of land, and would have killed Elijah if God hadn't protected him.

Does coming from an ungodly family line mean you have to be ungodly? No, but in this case "like mother, like daughter" applies. Athaliah was as wicked and murderous as her mother. And worst of all, she brought idolatry from Israel, where her parents and grandparents reigned, to Judah, where the line of David reigned.

Athaliah chose to follow in her evil parents' steps, but she didn't have to. She could have chosen to serve the true God. The same is true today. No one has to choose to follow in ungodly footsteps. Christ died for everyone, but each person has to make his or her own decision to follow Christ. Being raised by unbelieving parents doesn't mean a person has to grow up to be unbelieving, and being raised by Christian parents doesn't automatically make someone a Christian. Each person must choose for himself or herself whether to follow Christ.

thinking it through

Parents have a strong influence on their children. There are some families where several generations in a row become doctors or police officers. There are some families where alcoholism is the heritage passed down from generation to generation.

How have your parents influenced your choices and beliefs? How can someone from an ungodly family break out of the mold?

Athaliah: An Evil Influence

Don't be fooled by those who say such things, for "bad company corrupts good character."

1 CORINTHIANS 15:33

Athaliah followed in her mother's steps in worshiping Baal, and she brought Baal worship from Israel to Judah. King Ahab of Israel and King Jehoshaphat of Judah arranged for their children to marry, so Baal-worshiping Athaliah was wed to God-worshiping Jehoram. Bad idea. Makes you wonder what King Jehoshaphat was thinking. Definitely not about what God wanted, because God never wants his children to marry those who don't honor him.

When Jehoram became king of Judah, Athaliah's bad influence corrupted him. Jehoram had six younger brothers. Their father gave them valuable gifts of gold and silver, as well as some of Judah's fortified towns. But once Jehoram became well established as king, he killed all his brothers and some of the other leaders of Judah.

With Athaliah's influence, Jehoram built pagan shrines and tried to lead the people away from God. Things got worse, so God stepped in and struck Jehoram with a painful disease. He died two years later.

Next on the throne was Jehoram and Athaliah's son Ahaziah. Did he decide to turn the kingdom back to God? No. He, too, was under Athaliah's influence. Second Chronicles 22:3 says, "His mother encouraged him in doing wrong."

Athaliah spread her wickedness to everyone around her. The Bible warns us that bad company corrupts good character. Sometimes young people think they can hang out with the bad kids and influence them to do good, but that rarely happens. Usually the good person either breaks away from the bad group or is pulled down into sin with them.

It's okay to want to influence others for good, but don't try to do it by associating with peers who are known as "bad kids." Be kind to them and talk to them about Christ, but don't hang out with them. Plant the seeds of faith in their hearts, and let God do the rest.

thinking it through

God will use you to influence others. He works in you to make you more like him; then those around you will notice that you are different and want to be like you. How do you know God is working in your life?

Athaliah: Taking the Throne

You want what you don't have, so you scheme and kill to get it. You are jealous of what others have, but you can't get it, so you fight and wage war to take it away from them. Yet you don't have what you want because you don't ask God for it.

JAMES 4:2

Ahaziah became king, and his mother, Athaliah, worked out her evil plans through him. Ahaziah had only ruled a short time when Jehu, who was trying to get rid of all of Ahab's family members, killed him.

When Athaliah heard her son was dead, she decided she wanted the throne. The problem was that Ahaziah had sons who were next in line for the crown. That didn't stop Athaliah. Taking a cue from her mother, the murderous queen of mean, Athaliah rounded up all the heirs and had them killed.

Athaliah didn't quite succeed, because a one-year-old boy was rescued and hidden. But Athaliah didn't know it and wouldn't find out for several years. In the meantime, Judah had a woman on the throne for the first time in its history.

Do you ever wonder why the Bible includes stories about wicked people like Athaliah? It's so we can learn from their examples. Maybe you don't feel like you can relate at all to Athaliah. After all, you'd never plot to take the throne or kill people to get what you want.

But all of us have been jealous of something someone else had. Perhaps we are overly ambitious, and although we wouldn't kill to get what we want, we plan how to get the same thing for ourselves. Our jealousy and ambitions don't lead to murder, but they may lead to bitterness or resentment, or maybe a desire to get even or to see another person put in his or her place. Those feelings make our hearts ugly before God.

Only when we surrender our desires to God can his peace and joy fill our hearts and replace any bad feelings we might have. Allow God to work in you. Ask him to take away any bad feelings you have and replace them with his peace.

thinking it through

None of us wants to think we are anything like Athaliah. Yet all of us at times suffer from jealousy or want what others have.

What happens when you allow jealousy to take over your life?

Ask God to clean any bad feelings out of your heart and replace them with his love. Take James's advice, and ask God to give you what you want instead of plotting to get it yourself.

thinking it through

James 3:16 says that "jealousy and selfish ambition" lead to "disorder and evil of every kind." What's the alternative? How can you have a positive influence on those around you today?

Athaliah: Right Ambition

Wherever there is jealousy and selfish ambition, there you will find disorder and evil of every kind.

JAMES 3:16

There is good ambition, and there is bad ambition. Athaliah was definitely driven by bad ambition. All her life Athaliah was either the daughter of a king, married to a king, or the mother of a king. As wife to a king and mother to a king, she was the true power behind the throne. She controlled her husband and son, so she really controlled the kingdom.

Once her son died, she was nobody. She was no longer the daughter, wife, or mother of a reigning king. Her power was ended. Athaliah couldn't stand not being in power. She couldn't deal with not being in charge. This was a woman with a real control issue—so much so that she killed her own grandchildren, who were the rightful heirs to the throne, and declared herself queen.

Ambition, when directed toward positive achievements, is a good thing. A student might set her mind on making the high honor roll, and her ambition pushes her to complete her homework, study for tests, and do more than required on projects. Or she might have the ambition of being on student council, which prompts her to think about ways she could help her classmates.

Those ambitions and goals could become wrong if the student decides to sabotage others who she feels are getting in her way. She might destroy the science project of someone who might get the blue ribbon instead of her or start a vicious rumor about a student running against her for class president.

When it comes to ambition and goals, it's good to examine your motives. Are you trying to better yourself and others? Do you share the work and the glory? Are your desires in line with God's Word?

Athaliah was filled with selfish ambition and destroyed her own family. Use your ambition to accomplish good in your corner of the world.

Athaliah: God Always Wins

The LORD's plans stand firm forever; his intentions can never be shaken.

PSALM 33:11

Athaliah had a wicked plan: to kill off all the heirs to the throne and become queen. And she almost accomplished that. If she had managed to kill all the heirs, she would have wiped out the line of David. But it was through this line that the Savior, Jesus, was to be born years later. Athaliah didn't know this, of course. She just wanted to get rid of anyone who might worship the true God and turn the country back to him. But God's plans never fail.

Athaliah thought she was winning against God. She believed for several years that she had wiped out the rightful heirs. Why didn't God act against her right away? Because he had another plan.

One of Athaliah's grandsons had been rescued by Jehosheba, Ahaziah's half sister, and taken to live in the Temple. He and his nurse stayed safely hidden there for several years. The grandson, Joash, was under the care of Jehosheba and her husband, Jehoiada, the high priest, who taught the boy, Joash, about God.

When Joash was seven, Jehoiada called together a group of military men and showed them Joash, the rightful heir to the throne. Later, those same men surrounded Joash while Jehoiada put the crown on him and declared him king in front of the people. The people clapped and shouted, and the noise brought Athaliah to see what was going on.

Second Kings 11:14 says, "When Athaliah saw all this, she tore her clothes in despair and shouted, 'Treason! Treason!'" How very like Athaliah to accuse the people of treason when they were actually welcoming the rightful king to the throne!

The people killed Athaliah, and Joash reigned as king. God's plans prevailed. And the people were more than happy to have Athaliah off the throne and to be able to worship God again.

thinking it through

People can try to stop others from worshiping God. They can take away freedom, but they can't get rid of God. He is in control and he always wins.

How do you think Athaliah felt when she realized who Joash really was? How might Athaliah have felt seeing the people give their allegiance to Joash?

Does it ever seem to you like evil has the upper hand? God's plans stand firm forever!

thinking it through

We don't know much about Jehosheba other than she lived a godly life in an ungodly family, and she was willing to be part of God's plan for saving Joash and the line of David. Why do you think God chose Jehosheba to rescue Joash? Are you willing for God to use you to do something remarkable for him?

Jehosheba: A True Hero

Ahaziah's sister Jehosheba, the daughter of King Jehoram, took Ahaziah's infant son, Joash, and stole him away from among the rest of the king's children, who were about to be killed. She put Joash and his nurse in a bedroom to hide him from Athaliah, so the child was not murdered.

2 KINGS 11:2

I like reading stories or watching movies where there is a clear distinction between good and evil. You know who the heroes and villains are, and good always triumphs. Unfortunately real life isn't always like that. The lines between good and evil are blurred, and sometimes heroes have major flaws. But in the story of Athaliah and Jehosheba, it's easy to tell good from evil and the hero from the villain.

Athaliah, the villain, was trying to wipe out all the heirs to the throne. She would have succeeded if it hadn't been for the hero—Jehosheba. She was Jehoram's daughter by a different wife from Athaliah. Even though Jehosheba was part of the royal family, she was nothing like them. She didn't worship Baal or take part in the evil practices that went on in the royal family. In fact, Jehosheba married Jehoiada, the high priest.

God knew that this princess, who followed him rather than the pagan religion of her family, would be in the right place at the right time to rescue Joash. By doing this she preserved the line of David so the prophecy, which said the Savior would come from this line, could be fulfilled.

Since God knows ahead of time what will happen, he can have the right person available to do something great for him, but she has to be willing. Jehosheba was quick thinking and willing to act as she snatched her nephew from death and hid him until it was time for him to be king.

You might be the one in the right place at the right time to be used by God at home or in your community this week. Are you ready and willing?

Puzzle Page

We learned this week that Athaliah was a bad influence on the people around her. If we follow God, though, we can be a good influence on others. Solve the puzzle below to find out what happens when we follow God.

Directions: The words in the word bank fit into the boxes below. The best way to solve these puzzles is to start with the longest words first. Then if you have many short words with the same number of letters left, you can fill them in by what word makes sense in each box. Give it a try.

For	to	you	pleases	power	God	the
giving	do	you	desire	working	what	him

____ ____ is ______________ in

_____, ____________ _____ the

__________ and _____ __________

___ ___ ______

___________ _____.

Answer: For God is working in you, giving you the desire and the power to do what pleases him. (Philippians 2:13)

thinking it through

How can having a parent who believes in God help you in your own faith walk?

Proverbs 22:6 says, "Direct your children onto the right path, and when they are older, they will not leave it." What does this verse say about a parent's positive influence?

Abijah: A Mom's Good Influence

[Hezekiah's] mother was Abijah, the daughter of Zechariah. . . . Hezekiah trusted in the LORD, the God of Israel. There was no one like him among all the kings of Judah, either before or after his time.

2 KINGS 18:2, 5

Hezekiah was twenty-five years old when he took the throne in Judah. We don't know much about Hezekiah's mother other than her name, but we can guess that she was a godly woman who influenced her son to walk with the Lord, because Hezekiah's father, King Ahaz, was not a follower of God. He worshiped idols, and he closed the Temple of God in Jerusalem.

When Hezekiah became king, his mother's godly influence on his life led him to be a king who walked with the Lord. Hezekiah started a religious revival. He took down pagan shrines and smashed the sacred pillars. He destroyed the bronze serpent Moses had made, because the people of Israel had turned it into an idol. The people started worshiping God again. Hezekiah obeyed all of God's commands and was faithful to the Lord in everything he did. Because of this God made him successful in all he did.

How different Abijah and her son Hezekiah are from Athaliah and her son Ahaziah. Both men were strongly influenced by their mothers, but Abijah was a godly mom married to an idol-worshiping husband, while cruel Athaliah turned her husband from worshiping God to worshiping Baal.

You are not yet a mother, but it's still easy for you to see the influence these mothers had on their sons. Parents do have a big influence on children, but that doesn't mean all children will be like their parents. Individual personalities, life experiences, and talents all help make someone who she is, but many children do share their parents' values and beliefs, especially if the parents have been active in teaching those things. Is this true in your family? Do you and your siblings share your parents' values?

Huldah: Knowing God's Word

Hilkiah and the other men went to the New Quarter of Jerusalem to consult with the prophet Huldah. She was the wife of Shallum son of Tikvah, son of Harhas, the keeper of the Temple wardrobe.

2 CHRONICLES 34:22

Even though Hezekiah was a godly king, his son who reigned after him rejected his father's faith, and for half a century the kings of Judah were not loyal to God. They turned to paganism, and the people worshiped idols. Then Josiah began to reign at the age of eight years old. Josiah tried to follow God, and he began to get rid of all the idols in the land. He tore down the pagan shrines, idols, and incense altars. After Josiah purged the land of all the false gods, he arranged to have the Temple of God repaired.

During this time Hilkiah the priest found the law of God written by Moses. King Josiah read the law and tore his clothing as a sign of despair. He realized the people had not been keeping the laws of God. Josiah wanted to know more about the law and about what would happen to the land of Judah for not following God's laws.

Hilkiah and some other men went to find Huldah, a prophetess of God. They sought her out because Huldah had a reputation for speaking words of truth from God, and Josiah wanted to hear the truth. She was the right person for the job.

How about you? Are you someone people can turn to when they want to hear God's truth? Are you able to give good answers from the Bible to friends who have questions? There were lots of people around the Temple while it was being repaired, including the priest himself, yet the priest found Huldah and asked her to speak for God.

thinking it through

God wants us to be students of his Word and to be able to explain it to others. Look up 2 Timothy 2:15. After you read your Bible today or tomorrow, find someone you can talk to about what you learned. Or find a friend to read the same passage with and talk about what you learned together.

thinking it through

Ephesians 4:15 says, "We will speak the truth in love, growing in every way more and more like Christ, who is the head of his body, the church." God wants us to share his truth in a loving way. When is the last time you shared God's truth with someone else? How can you do that this week?

Huldah: Boldly Speaking the Truth

She said to them, "The LORD, the God of Israel, has spoken! Go back and tell the man who sent you, 'This is what the LORD says: I am going to bring disaster on this city and its people. All the curses written in the scroll that was read to the king of Judah will come true.'"

2 CHRONICLES 34:23-24

Josiah was trying to do what was right. He had rid the land of idol worship and was repairing the Temple of God. Josiah sent men to find out what God would do because his law had not been followed and the kings before him had worshiped idols.

The men went to find the prophetess Huldah because they knew she would speak the truth to them, but the message she gave them from God was not good news. Huldah told the men God was going to punish the land of Judah for walking away from him, and he was angry with them for offering sacrifices to false gods. His anger would be poured out on them.

The only good news Huldah gave them from God was that since Josiah had humbled himself before God and repented when he heard the words of the law, the disaster would not happen during his lifetime but after he was dead.

Huldah did not shy away from telling the men the true message from God, even though it was not a pleasant message. She boldly spoke the truth. Sometimes it's hard for us to tell people unpleasant things or the things they don't want to hear. Not everyone wants to hear that they must accept Jesus to go to heaven. The alternative is unpleasant to think about, and many people think they should go to heaven for all the good works they've done. Telling them otherwise would not make you popular—but it would be the truth.

God can use you to speak his truth. God's truth isn't all bad news. In fact, it's good news. Jesus died so everyone can have eternal life with him in heaven and peace and joy in their hearts here on earth. What better news could you give?

Vashti: Disobeying the King

When it was all over, the king gave a banquet for all the people, from the greatest to the least, who were in the fortress of Susa. It lasted for seven days and was held in the courtyard of the palace garden.

ESTHER 1:5

King Xerxes ruled over 127 provinces from India to Ethiopia, ruling from his throne at the fortress of Susa. He decided he wanted to show off the grandeur of his palace and gardens, so he invited all the nobles, officials, military officers, and princes of the provinces for a celebration that went on for 180 days—six months straight! After it was over, the king gave a banquet for all the people in the fortress of Susa. This was held in the courtyard of the palace garden, which was decked out with elaborate decorations. There was plenty of royal wine for everyone, and there were no limits on drinking for those seven days.

King Xerxes liked showing off all his fine things, and at the end of the seven days of drinking, he decided he wanted to show off his wife. Men and women couldn't be at the same celebration, so while King Xerxes was entertaining the men, Queen Vashti was hosting the women. The king sent some men to have Vashti put on her crown, come out, and show off her beauty.

People criticize Vashti for not obeying the king's command, but consider the situation. The men had been drinking for seven days, and the king had encouraged them to enjoy themselves however they liked. We don't know what Vashti was wearing or asked to wear for her appearance, but she knew it would be unacceptable for her to parade among these men, even dressed in her royal robes. It was an inappropriate request because it wasn't acceptable for her to mix with the men in that culture, and Vashti was right to refuse the king. Her dignity was worth more to her than anything the king could offer.

thinking it through

The king loved to show off all his riches and possessions. He even wanted to show off his queen as though she were another possession. How did the queen feel about that? What do you think you would have done in Vashti's place?

Vashti: Saying No

When they conveyed the king's order to Queen Vashti, she refused to come. This made the king furious, and he burned with anger.

ESTHER 1:12

The first chapter of Esther reads like a drama. The stage is set. The actors are in place—King Xerxes and the men partying for a week, and the women with Queen Vashti at a smaller banquet.

The king, proud of all he owns and looking for attention from all his friends, decides it's now time to show off his most beautiful "possession" of all—his wife.

In the next scene, the women watch as several men tell the queen what the king expects. Rising tension here. The women wait to hear what Vashti will do. They recognize that it is a downright disgusting request, but the request also comes from the king. Refusing will surely have serious consequences.

Vashti, with more concern for her dignity and integrity than her royal standing, refuses to go to the king. The women around her are stunned but pleased by her brave stance. Similar dramas play out around you daily. The key players are you and your peers. Every day you face decisions, and this will be even truer in the new school year. Will you make fun of someone else to secure your position with the in-crowd, or risk being ignored? Will you go to a classmate's party to raise your social status even though you know the DVDs they plan to watch aren't appropriate? Will you take a peek at the answer key someone passed around before the science test because it might be your only chance to pass? Will you hang out with a group in the neighborhood just to have friends even though the things they talk about embarrass you?

Queen Vashti decided her dignity and integrity were more important than the riches she had as queen. Are you willing to make the right choices and be a role model even though it might mean losing social status or being alone more than you'd like? Or could you find someone to make the right choice with you and make a new friend in the process?

thinking it through

"Just say no" is more than just a slogan; sometimes it's a necessity for keeping your life pure and right. Do you think Vashti struggled with her decision to say no? Can you think of a time when you said no even though it wasn't the popular thing to do?

Vashti: Living with Dignity

She is clothed with strength and dignity, and she laughs without fear of the future.

PROVERBS 31:25

What is dignity? Most dictionaries say it's the state of being worthy of honor, esteem, or respect. Surely this is true of Queen Vashti. She conducted herself in a way that was above reproach or criticism. The other ladies looked up to her. That's why the king's request was so repulsive.

The king wanted Vashti to lower herself to parade among the men so her husband could show off her beauty. How could Vashti, someone worthy of honor, esteem, and respect, fulfill such a request from the king?

When the women heard the queen turn down a request from the king, it's likely their respect for her increased. They understood what it meant for her to turn down the king. It just wasn't done, and there were sure to be consequences.

The king didn't know what to do when Vashti refused him. He asked his advisers. They said, "Before this day is out, the wives of all the king's nobles throughout Persia and Media will hear what the queen did and will start treating their husbands the same way. There will be no end to their contempt and anger" (Esther 1:18).

So the king made a decree that Vashti could no longer appear before him. Vashti lost her crown, riches, and social position, but she kept her dignity and self-worth, which were far more important.

How about you? Is being worthy of respect and honor more important to you than anything you might gain by making a poor choice or allowing someone to treat you disrespectfully? Be a young woman of honor like Vashti.

thinking it through

Look at Proverbs 31:25 above. How do you think living with dignity can help you not to be afraid of the future, even when you don't make a popular decision?

Vashti: Stand Up for Yourself

Dear children, don't let anyone deceive you about this: When people do what is right, it shows that they are righteous, even as Christ is righteous.

1 JOHN 3:7

Vashti stood up for herself. She refused to lower herself by doing what the king asked her to do. Standing up for herself cost her position and crown, but she kept her self-worth and dignity intact.

What would Vashti be like if she were here today? She would not be one to give in to peer pressure. Sometimes it's hard not to do what others are doing, but Vashti would be the one to resist—especially when it came to doing something wrong.

The desire to dress like others is harmless enough as long as the styles are modest, but wearing clothes that are too tight or show too much skin just because they are popular isn't honoring God—or standing up for your dignity. And going along with peers who are choosing to break rules, bully another girl, or smoke is harmful. Go beyond just acknowledging that those things are wrong, and take steps to do what is right.

Not only would Vashti have avoided doing those things that are wrong, but she also would have been the one to influence those around her to do right. She was a positive influence in her own court. Vashti would be the one who was a trustworthy friend. She'd be the one who confidently chose her own styles and wore them with pride. She'd choose activities that allowed her to accomplish the most good, and she wouldn't be afraid to try new hobbies, sports, or service projects.

Vashti wouldn't just be confident in her own choices and activities, but she'd encourage her peers to stand up for themselves. She'd tell them to choose what they liked no matter what others thought and to be true to their beliefs even if others laughed.

We need more Vashtis to be positive influences at home, school, and in the community. How about you? Are you up to the challenge?

thinking it through

You have the chance to influence those around you every day. You can make a difference wherever you are. Do others know you are righteous because they see that you do what is right (1 John 3:7)? What is one way you can be a positive influence today? Are there areas where you need to take a stand for yourself? How can you do that?

Quiz Time

re you a young woman of dignity? Read each statement below, and circle A for always, S for sometimes, or N for never.

1. I do what I know is right even if it's not popular.

   A S N

2. I stand against negative peer pressure.

   A S N

3. I am not swayed by friends trying to get me to go along with wrong plans.

   A S N

4. In my life I have strong women who are good role models.

   A S N

5. I am a good role model for other girls.

   A S N

Give yourself 2 points for every A, 1 point for every S, and 0 points for every N. Add up your points.

7-10 points: Doing what's right and keeping your self-worth and dignity are more important to you than peer approval. You stand up for right even if it's not popular. Good for you!

4-6 points: You are sometimes swayed by others' opinions. You want to do right but you also want to follow the crowd. Your self-worth is more important than peer approval. Stand for right.

0-3 points: You go along with the crowd and seldom go against what they choose. You might be more popular because of it, but it would be better to ask God for wisdom in knowing what to do and for the courage to do it.

thinking it through

Sometimes self-esteem lags while you are trying to figure out who you are, which group of friends you belong with, and what your true talents are. God can help you find those answers. Do you think you have good self-esteem or poor self-esteem? Why?

Ephesians 2:10 says, "We are God's masterpiece. He has created us anew in Christ Jesus, so we can do the good things he planned for us long ago." How can this encourage you to have a positive self-image?

Vashti: Improving Self-Esteem

He wanted the nobles and all the other men to gaze on her beauty, for she was a very beautiful woman.
ESTHER 1:11

Vashti was beautiful. She probably knew it from seeing her own reflection and from other people's comments. All of us have a picture of ourselves in our minds. A person may think she is beautiful, average, or ugly. She may view herself as talented or as a loser.

Your self-esteem is based on how you see yourself and on how much you feel loved, valued, or accepted. If you have good self-esteem, you take pride in your abilities and accomplishments. Vashti had good self-esteem. That's why she was able to turn down the king's request. She didn't need his approval to feel good about herself.

Sometimes people with low self-esteem take part in risky or wrong activities to gain approval from others. Usually those activities just make them feel worse, though. A girl may date a guy she knows she shouldn't date because he flatters her and makes her feel pretty and loved. Someone else may try drinking alcohol with classmates to find acceptance.

Why is it important to have good self-esteem? Because if you feel good about yourself, you'll have better relationships and be more willing to accept positive challenges and try new things. Like Vashti, you'll be able to make the hard choices.

If you have low self-esteem, you may be spending too much time criticizing yourself for mistakes or for things you can't change. Instead, look for your good points. Not everyone has the same talents, academic ability, or looks. Don't expect to excel in every area. It's okay to want to improve yourself, but don't demand things of yourself you aren't capable of doing.

Perhaps you just haven't found your niche yet. You may want to be on the gymnastics team when really you'd be excellent at pottery. Work on building up your self-esteem so you are prepared to face challenges and stand up for right just as Vashti did.

Vashti: A Good Reputation

Choose a good reputation over great riches; being held in high esteem is better than silver or gold.

PROVERBS 22:1

Of all the lessons Vashti teaches us, perhaps the most important one is to do what is right no matter the cost. Doing that lost Vashti her position as queen but earned her a good reputation with the women in her court. When the king asked her to do something that was repulsive, she said no in spite of the consequences.

At the time the king made his request, Vashti was having a weeklong banquet for the women. We don't know how many were there, but it's likely they all knew about the request—and about her refusal. With the women looking on, Vashti refused to parade around in front of her husband's drinking friends even if he was the king. Because of it, the women admired her courage and dignity.

If Vashti had given in to her husband's request, it would have changed what the women thought of her. She wouldn't have been known for her courage to stand up for right or for the honor and dignity she'd shown.

What's your reputation worth to you? It takes only one mistake for people to change what they think of you, fair or not. One incident of yelling at someone in the school hallway can earn you the reputation of being bad tempered. One swear word can earn you the reputation of being foulmouthed.

It's easy to react to situations or emotions without thinking of how others will see you. You might not care at the time what others think, but it's better to bite your tongue and not react rather than try to repair your reputation later. It's harder to overcome a bad reputation than to guard your good name in the first place.

Take a cue from Vashti, and guard your reputation by choosing to do right even in difficult situations.

thinking it through

You know peers who have good reputations and those who have bad reputations. Think of one person who has a good reputation. Why does she have that reputation? Think of someone who has a bad reputation. How is she different from the person you identified with a good reputation? What kind of reputation do you have? Do you need to fix it?

thinking it through

Has anything bad happened in your life that God later used for good? How can that encourage you about any future events you face? If you can't see any way that a negative event in your life could be used for good, talk to God about it. Tell him why you feel discouraged, and ask him to reassure you that he is in control. Then reread Romans 8:28 above.

Vashti: Working Out for Good

We know that God causes everything to work together for the good of those who love God and are called according to his purpose for them.

ROMANS 8:28

When Vashti failed to appear before the king, it made the king look foolish in front of the other men. What kind of king couldn't even get his wife to obey him? The king's advisers suggested he banish Vashti. They were fearful that when all the other women in the kingdom heard she'd refused the king, they would refuse to do what their husbands asked them to do also. So Vashti was no longer queen.

With Vashti gone, the king searched for a new queen, and Esther was selected. The choice of queen shows God's hand in the lives of his people, because Esther, a Jew, was on the throne at just the right time to save her people from harm. God used for good what seemed like a tragedy—Vashti being banished.

This wasn't the first time God intervened in a negative situation to save the lives of his people. We talked about the story of Joseph in February and March. His brothers sold him into slavery, but he ended up in Egypt, where he was able to warn the pharaoh of a coming famine and was eventually able to save his father and brothers from starvation.

God is able to take a bad situation and turn it around in order to accomplish good. Sometimes it's hard to see how any good could come out of a situation, and we may not always know what God is up to. Vashti probably didn't see how any good would come from her being sent away, but God could see the whole picture.

Vashti didn't drop completely out of sight, either. Her son Artaxerxes became king, and she had the role of queen mother.

God is in control even when we don't see it. Sometimes we just have to accept it by faith and go on, trusting God to work things out.

Esther: No Turning Back

After Xerxes' anger had subsided, he began thinking about Vashti and what she had done and the decree he had made.

ESTHER 2:1

You remember that King Xerxes, also known as King Ahasuerus, had asked Queen Vashti to come and parade among his drunken guests and show off her beauty. She refused. He was angry that his own wife wouldn't listen to him. His advisers told him to send her away so all the other wives would know not to disobey their husbands. So that's what he did.

Once the king had time to think, he realized what he'd done. In anger he'd sent his queen, his prized possession, away, and his decision could not be changed.

Acting while angry is almost always a bad idea. When you're angry, you don't think clearly and don't consider the consequences of your actions. You might quit a sports team because you are angry at a call against you, a coach's decision, or something another player said or did. You might drop out of the school newspaper because the editor didn't let you use your idea for a story or because someone else got to write the front page article you wanted. Once you've quit, you may regret it, and sometimes it's too late or you have too much pride to rejoin.

Don't react to things while you are angry. Walk away or ask for a break. Leave for the day, but don't quit. Give yourself time to cool down. The situation may not seem so bad once you've removed yourself from it. If you still feel the same way after a few days, you can inform others of your decision calmly rather than in anger.

thinking it through

Do you tend to control your anger? Or do you have a hot temper? Ask God to give you his understanding so you will be slow to react in anger.

thinking it through

James 1:19 says we must "be quick to listen, slow to speak, and slow to get angry." How can being quick to listen and slow to speak help you control your anger? Ask God to help you do this today.

Esther: Dealing with Anger

Understand this, my dear brothers and sisters: You must all be quick to listen, slow to speak, and slow to get angry.

JAMES 1:19

King Xerxes made a mistake by acting in anger and lost his queen. Even though this devotion is supposed to be about Vashti, we can learn from Xerxes, too. Acting in anger is not a good choice. It's better to deal with your anger and then make decisions once you've calmed down.

When you get angry, be aware of what you are feeling. If you watch infants or toddlers when they are angry, you'll probably see them have a tantrum. They may throw a toy at or bite the person who angered them. As a young adult, you are more aware of your feelings. You might realize you are angry because someone embarrassed you in front of your friends or because you failed to live up to your own expectations in a sporting event or performance. Being aware of your feelings will help you understand why you are angry.

Sometimes it doesn't take a lot to trigger anger. Changes in hormones and higher stress levels can make you feel more emotional than usual. Things that might not have bothered you before can now cause you to feel embarrassed or angry.

You can also work on developing more self-control. That is what allows you to stop and think before reacting. Think about why you are angry, and then try to think of a way to handle the problem that doesn't include blowing up at someone. Once you've thought of possible solutions, consider the consequences of each.

King Xerxes didn't use self-control. If he'd waited until the next day when his pride wasn't stinging so badly, he would have made a better decision than banishing his queen.

Be smarter than King Xerxes. Next time you start to react in anger, stop and take an inventory of your feelings. Then decide on a better course of action to solve the problem.

Esther: The Book of Esther

This is what happened during the time of Xerxes, the Xerxes who ruled over 127 provinces stretching from India to Cush.

ESTHER 1:1, NIV

Esther is a much-loved book, although at first people didn't want to include it in the Bible because it doesn't mention God's name. But even though it doesn't mention his name, his working in the lives of his people is obvious in the book of Esther.

Why is the story of Esther so popular? Part of the reason is Esther herself. She is innocent, beautiful, brave, and wise. And she is a heroine for saving her people.

The book of Esther reads like a novel in some ways. It has an exotic setting. Much of it takes place in a grand palace in Persia. There is fast-paced action as one queen is banished and a search takes place for a new queen. An assassination attempt is foiled, and a plot against the Jews is exposed.

There is humor as the one who acts lofty to another ends up having to honor him, followed by intrigue and suspense as the plot against the Jews is discovered and it looks like there is no way out. There is a sudden reversal as the villain is hung on the gallows he built to hang the good guy, and there is a happy ending as the Jews are allowed to fight their enemies and win.

Esther is a fun book to read, and I hope you'll take time to read it over the next few weeks. But more than that, it's a book that shows God is in control, and he has a purpose for everything that happens.

That is still true today. You might find yourself in just the right spot to carry out part of God's plan. It may not be as dramatic as Esther approaching the king to save her people. However, it's not the greatness of the act that counts but the willingness. Are you willing to be used to carry out God's plans today?

thinking it through

Have you read the book of Esther before? If so, what is your favorite part and why? What did the book teach you about God, or how did he use it to speak to you? If you haven't read it before, read a few verses a day until you've read through the whole book. Then come back and answer these questions. Even if you have read Esther before, you might find that your answers change this time around.

thinking it through

In what areas might God use you to do something for him? (Church, school, sports, clubs, and extracurricular activities are some possibilities.) What opportunities do you have to do work for God? (Think about your church, youth group, ministry group, and club activities.)

Esther: A Young Orphan

[Mordecai's] family had been among those who, with King Jehoiachin of Judah, had been exiled from Jerusalem to Babylon by King Nebuchadnezzar.

ESTHER 2:6

The kingdom of Judah had many kings who worshiped idols and turned from God, so God allowed his people to be taken captive. Nebuchadnezzar, the king of Babylon, went to Judah and first took a small group of captives. Daniel, who was thrown into the lions' den for praying, was in this group. About ten years later, Judah tried to rebel against Nebuchadnezzar, so the Baylonian king returned to Judah, killed the king there, destroyed Jerusalem and the Temple, and took the rest of the people captive.

Many of the captives settled along the Euphrates River in Babylonia. Babylon, the capital of Babylonia, is one of the oldest cities in the world. It's where the tower of Babel was built. The city had temples, palaces, and the Hanging Gardens of Babylon, one of the Seven Wonders of the Ancient World.

The Medes and Persians conquered the Babylonian Empire. Now the people of Judah were under Persian rule. Seventy years after the first Jews were taken captive, one of the Persian kings said the people of Judah could return home, but many of the Jews didn't want to go back. It was a long journey, and they'd built homes and lives for themselves in Babylonia, which was now part of the Persian Empire.

Why is all this history important? Because it's the backdrop for Esther's story. Esther was one of the Jews living in Babylonia. Esther's parents had been among the captives taken to Babylonia, but they had died, and an older cousin, Mordecai, raised Esther, whose Hebrew name was Hadassah.

Esther was just a young orphaned Jewish girl, but God chose her to save his people. You don't have to have the right parents or grand qualifications to be used by God. You just have to be willing. God may have you where you are today because he has something special for you to accomplish.

Quiz Time

Do you react in anger? Read each question below, and circle the letter in front of the statement that best completes the sentence for you.

1. Your volleyball serve goes right into the net. The other team gets the ball—and the winning point. One teammate says, "Way to lose the game!" Several teammates laugh and give her high fives. You

   A. tell them they can just finish the season without you.
   B. go home and write the teammate's name on the ball, then practice serving it against your garage door.
   C. tell the coach you want to talk to her tomorrow.

2. You find out two of your friends are going shopping without you. They tell you you're no fun to shop with because you are bossy and always decide which stores to visit. You

   A. write a mean letter to both of them, then tear it up.
   B. tell them you don't need friends like them.
   C. go home, lie on your bed, and wonder if you really are bossy.

3. You just finish your daily job of mopping the kitchen floor when your little brother spills red Kool-Aid on it. You

   A. chase him with the mop and threaten to hit him with it.
   B. make new mop water, and ask him to help you mop up the mess.
   C. do one hundred jumping jacks to calm down before you remop the kitchen floor.

Answers:

1. B is a good way to burn off your anger. You could leave the teammate's name off the ball, though. C is a good choice too because you're giving yourself time to cool down before you talk to the coach either about quitting or how to improve your serve.
2. A is a good way to get your feelings out. Just don't deliver the letter. Rip it up so you won't dwell on it. C is a good choice too. Often when people criticize us, there is at least a bit of truth to it. Rather than write them off as mean, decide if there is any merit to their accusations.
3. B is an acceptable answer. He made the mess, so it's fair to ask him to help clean it up within his ability. C is a good answer too. Sometimes doing something physical like running, jumping, or throwing or kicking a ball is a good way to get rid of anger before dealing with the problem.

thinking it through

The king used a beauty contest to choose his new queen. What might have been a better way to choose Vashti's replacement? How can you use your outward and inward beauty for God?

Esther: The First Beauty Contest

His personal attendants suggested, "Let us search the empire to find beautiful young virgins for the king."

ESTHER 2:2

Kaitlyn had been entered in all sorts of pageants since she was eighteen months old. At age fifteen Kaitlyn realized most of her childhood was gone and she'd spent it living her mother's dream for her rather than doing the things she most wanted to do—play on sports teams, sleep over with friends, and just be a normal teen. She knew her mother dreamed of the day she'd be Miss Florida, but the ribbons and titles meant nothing to Kaitlyn. She refused to take part in any more pageants.

After Vashti was banished from the kingdom, the king needed a new queen. This led to what was probably the world's first beauty contest. Beautiful young virgins were gathered from all over the kingdom to be considered. The promising ones received special foods and beauty treatments before the final choice was made.

Does this seem like a good way to choose a queen? Probably not. Having outward beauty doesn't mean you are inwardly beautiful; or you are intelligent, wise, or compassionate; or you possess the inner character to be a good role model or leader.

But being beautiful doesn't mean you have none of those other characteristics. Sometimes being outwardly beautiful can open doors and allow you to make a difference, such as in the case of Esther. The king chose her for her beauty, but God put her in a position to save her people.

Kaitlyn made a good choice to pursue her own interests instead of her mother's. There can be a good side to spending some time in the limelight for beauty, though. Being in that position allows someone a chance to be a good role model or to speak out about her faith. The important thing is to acknowledge that beauty, as well as talents and abilities, comes from God and should always be used for his glory.

Esther: Thinking about Beauty

O LORD, you are our Father. We are the clay, and you are the potter. We all are formed by your hand.

ISAIAH 64:8

Have you ever heard the expression "Beauty is only skin deep"? When people say that, they mean that how you look is based only on your outward appearance. It isn't about your inner character, personality, or who you really are. Physical beauty is all about appearances—but real beauty starts in the heart and works its way outward. That doesn't mean what you look like outwardly isn't important. It just means your heart beauty is more important.

Sometimes people get mixed-up ideas about what physical beauty is. Models are thought to be the standard for beauty, but not too many people are five feet eleven inches and 110 pounds with perfect hair, eyebrows, lips, and teeth. That's just not realistic. And many of those models end up with eating disorders and mental health issues from trying to keep up an appearance.

So if you are an average height—or even a little short and have an athletic or stocky build rather than being superthin—or if you have hair that is oily one day and frizzy the next, and have braces, you are pretty normal. No matter how you look on the outside, you are the person God created you to be. You can be sure of that because Isaiah 64:8 says, "O LORD, you are our Father. We are the clay, and you are the potter. We all are formed by your hand."

Esther was outwardly beautiful, but God was able to use her to save her people because she was beautiful on the inside, too. People tend to judge by outward appearances, but God judges the heart. (See tomorrow's devo.)

thinking it through

Every day you are bombarded by media messages that tell you that you need to be taller, thinner, have shinier or thicker hair, or have a clearer complexion. But God accepts you just as you are. After all, he created you in his image.

What message does the media give about beauty? How does that compare to God's message in Isaiah 64:8?

Esther: Mirror, Mirror on the Wall

The LORD said to Samuel, "Don't judge by his appearance or height, for I have rejected him. The LORD doesn't see things the way you see them. People judge by outward appearance, but the LORD looks at the heart."

1 SAMUEL 16:7

The words in the verse above were spoken by God to Samuel when Samuel was getting ready to anoint a king for the Israelites. God was telling him not to choose by looks as many people do because it's what's in the heart that's more important.

King Xerxes had all the most beautiful young women brought to his palace so he could choose from among them for his new queen. But beauty isn't what makes someone a qualified queen. In this case God intervened and sent Esther, who was beautiful both on the outside and in her heart.

You might be thinking that even though God made you in his image, other people don't necessarily look for your inner qualities. After all, the guy who sits behind you in math says your shoes could be canoe paddles, and the girls who dress out with you in PE ask you if your mom bought your bra in the toddler department. That hurts. But thankfully, you're still growing. And no matter what you look like, you can make the best of what you have.

If you aren't sure how to make the best of the looks God gave you, ask a trusted adult to give you some ideas. But don't try to change who you are. If you do, you'll be shortchanging yourself because God gave you your own special looks and personality. He loves you the way you are.

thinking it through

Take a good look at yourself in the mirror. If you're honest about what you see, you'll admit you have good points—and those you want to change. Despite what other kids say, no one is a loser. And even the girls who are considered the most beautiful have flaws.

God sees you the way you truly are—the way he made you. Thank God for the strengths he gave you. How can you focus on them rather than the things you can't change?

Esther: Making the Most of Your Looks

Let the king appoint agents in each province to bring these beautiful young women into the royal harem at the fortress of Susa. Hegai, the king's eunuch in charge of the harem, will see that they are all given beauty treatments.

ESTHER 2:3

The media is full of beautiful faces. Just look at any teen magazine. Is there a plain- or average-looking teen on the front? Probably not. Teen stars have an image to keep, and they invest a lot of time and money in their looks. The rest of the world spends time and money trying to copy the hair and clothing styles, makeup, and mannerisms of the stars.

It's okay to want to make the most of your looks. God created you in his own image, and he wants you to enjoy how he made you. This doesn't mean you should spend hours on your appearance every morning; just be the best you can be.

The beautiful young women brought for consideration by King Xerxes spent a year in beauty treatments. They were given six months' treatment with oil of myrrh, followed by six months with special perfumes and ointments. That's not a typical beauty routine for today's teen girl, but it was what was chosen for those young ladies.

You can accept yourself for who God made you to be and desire to change at the same time. However, it's important to accept what you can't change. Take care of your appearance, but be glad about who God made you to be. Esther didn't have anything to do with her natural looks. She looked exactly how God created her to look.

Here's the bottom line. Don't play the comparison game. Don't try to look like your favorite television star or even your best friend. Look like you. The best you. What does this really mean? It means looking in the mirror again and accepting the things you see there. Be honest about it. Then decide what you'd like to improve. Improve—not change.

thinking it through

It's easy to get caught up in looks and lose sight of the fact that inner beauty is far more important than outward appearance. What things around you might make you feel that outward appearance is more important than inner beauty? Ask God to help you focus on the things that are most important.

thinking it through

What do you spend your time focusing on?

Do you worry about your looks? If so, remember that you are made in God's image and that your identity comes from who you are in Christ.

Esther: Your Natural Beauty

This man had a very beautiful and lovely young cousin, Hadassah, who was also called Esther. When her father and mother died, Mordecai adopted her into his family and raised her as his own daughter.

ESTHER 2:7

Esther was naturally beautiful. We don't know whether her appearance was important to her, or how much time she spent on her looks. I doubt that Esther spent much time worrying about how her looks compared to anyone else's or fretting about any flaws she thought she had.

The problem is that today you are bombarded by messages from the media about how you should look. Just flip through the pages of a teen magazine. You'll find it packed full of ads for shampoo, makeup, clothes, shoes, and other things that all claim they'll make you look prettier, older, or thinner. They send the message that you aren't okay the way you are. The problem is, those magazines are wrong. They want you to obsess about your looks—and buy the products advertised, of course.

You don't need products to make you beautiful. God has already created you in his own image. It can be hard to accept that when there's so much pressure to look a certain way. Look at the girls around you: you might notice that a lot of them have the same hair and clothing styles. Sometimes your self-esteem takes a blow when you don't look like everyone else. But your real worth doesn't come from your looks. It comes from who you are in Christ Jesus.

Esther was beautiful, but that wasn't the focus of her life. She was too busy trying to please God to worry about how she looked. And because of her obedience, she was able to save her people.

Esther: Beauty Inside Out

Don't be concerned about the outward beauty of fancy hairstyles, expensive jewelry, or beautiful clothes. You should clothe yourselves instead with the beauty that comes from within, the unfading beauty of a gentle and quiet spirit, which is so precious to God.

1 PETER 3:3-4

Esther was beautiful on the outside. But she was equally beautiful inside. What does it mean to be beautiful inside? A key to the answer is found in Proverbs 4:23: "Guard your heart above all else, for it determines the course of your life."

Remember the verse from August 22? It talks about how to choose a king, but you can pick out a principle for your life from it: "The LORD doesn't see things the way you see them. People judge by outward appearance, but the LORD looks at the heart" (1 Samuel 16:7). Do you see a common theme between these two verses?

Now look at today's verse. What concept do you see in all three verses? Real beauty comes from inside, from the heart.

So how's your heart? Is it filled with beautiful things? One test of that is the fruit of the Spirit: "love, joy, peace, patience, kindness, goodness, faithfulness, gentleness, and self-control" (Galatians 5:22-23). The fruits of the Spirit aren't qualities you are born with; they are characteristics you develop as God works in your life. And they are the true test of your inner beauty.

If you don't see those characteristics in your life, allow God to work in your heart to develop them. Try to do the things you know God wants you to do each day, and listen for his voice as he speaks to your heart.

thinking it through

Which fruit of the Spirit do you see most in your life? Which one is most lacking? How can you change that? Ask God to work in your heart this week to develop these characteristics in you.

thinking it through

Do you have a friend who is like Brianna? What advice would you give her?

If you or a friend of yours struggles with some of the issues talked about in this devo, talk to a parent, youth leader, school counselor, or other trusted adult about it.

Look at the verse for today. What does it mean to you that God calls you by name and claims you as his own?

Esther: Beautiful to God

Do not be afraid, for I have ransomed you. I have called you by name; you are mine.

ISAIAH 43:1

In all this talk about beauty, it's important to remember that God created you in a way that is special to him, just as he did with Esther. Because you are already beautiful to God, it doesn't really matter if others judge your beauty by their standards.

The problem with trying to follow the world's standard for beauty is that it's often destructive. Many girls your age or not much older struggle with eating disorders, cutting, depression, and substance abuse. Why? Because they are trying to live up to an unrealistic standard. They are sacrificing who they are inside to be what everyone else thinks they should be.

Brianna had always been overweight as a child. As she entered the elementary years, students began calling her "Fatty" and other names. The year before middle school, Brianna almost totally stopped eating and began exercising almost constantly, even though she hated it.

Brianna lived in fear that if she let up on her routine for even one day, she'd gain back all the weight. She became so consumed by it that she let everything else go—her grades, her activities, and her friends. If it hadn't been for her mother, who noticed what was going on and got her help, Brianna might have fallen into a deep depression or have had to be hospitalized if her weight got too low.

The real key to being happy with who you are and how you look is to see yourself the way that God sees you—as someone loved and redeemed by Jesus and a valuable member of God's family. Sure, it's okay to want to look your best and to be physically fit. It's okay to want to lose weight as long as you really need to (don't decide this on your own). But you don't have to do those things to be accepted by God. He loves you just the way you are.

Awesome Activity

We've been learning this week about Esther's beauty—both inside and out. Facial masks are a fun way to take care of your outer beauty. Did you know you can make your own facial mask . . . with ingredients from your kitchen? It's easy—just follow these simple steps:

Wash your face with mild soap and warm water.
Mash up an avocado or a cucumber and spread the paste evenly on your face.
Keep the paste on your face for about fifteen minutes.
Gently wash off the paste. Your skin should feel soft and pampered!

thinking it through

What does it mean to you to be a friend of God? How can knowing you are a friend of God help you face your problems? How can it help you feel beautiful and valued?

Esther: Beauty Is . . .

The king loved Esther more than any of the other young women. He was so delighted with her that he set the royal crown on her head and declared her queen instead of Vashti. To celebrate the occasion, he gave a great banquet in Esther's honor for all his nobles and officials, declaring a public holiday for the provinces and giving generous gifts to everyone.

ESTHER 2:17-18

When King Xerxes saw Esther, he found her more desirable than all the other young women, and he chose her to be the new queen. He gave a great banquet in her honor and declared a public holiday.

You might be thinking, "Of course he found her more desirable than the others. She was beautiful. But no one would ever choose me." Not true. God already did. I know you mean that no handsome young man would choose you. After all, it's not like God can sit with you at lunch or at the pep rally. He can't be at your side when you walk down the hall, and you can't show him off to your friends.

But the amazing thing is that the same God who hung the sun, moon, and stars and who holds the earth in place not only created you in a unique and awesome way, but he considers you his friend. Romans 5:11 says, "We can rejoice in our wonderful new relationship with God because our Lord Jesus Christ has made us friends of God."

Can you imagine that—friends with the creator of the universe? Having a bad day? No problem. Just talk it over with God, your friend. Someone making fun of you? Tell it to God, your friend. After all, he created you, so when someone is making fun of you, he cares about how you feel.

Having God as your friend won't magically solve your problems, but knowing that you are beautiful to God can help you through them. Your real worth comes from being created and redeemed by God. And that's your true beauty.

Esther: Haman's Prejudice

Haman approached King Xerxes and said, "There is a certain race of people scattered through all the provinces of your empire who keep themselves separate from everyone else. Their laws are different from those of any other people, and they refuse to obey the laws of the king. So it is not in the king's interest to let them live."

ESTHER 3:8

Haman was the most powerful official in the kingdom. When he'd pass by, the other officials would bow before him. All but one—Esther's cousin Mordecai. And this made Haman furious. Haman knew that Mordecai was a Jew, so he decided to get rid of not only Mordecai but all the Jews.

Haman decided to cast lots—or throw dice, called *purim*—to determine on what day to destroy the Jews. The date chosen was almost a year later. A decree was sent throughout the kingdom that all Jews of every age were to be killed on a certain day, and their belongings would go to whoever killed them.

Prejudice and hatred between races has been a problem ever since there was more than one race. And it remains a problem today. Just think of all the horrible events in history that took place because of hatred between races. There have been wars, riots, and all kinds of violence spurred by prejudice and hatred.

You can't stop wars or violence, but you can make a difference in your corner of the world. Show acceptance of those around you. A person's color, country of origin, or ethnic background shouldn't determine how she is treated. Neither should a person's disabilities or special needs. Don't be afraid to get to know someone who is different from you. Friends come in all colors and sizes and with differing challenges and abilities.

thinking it through

Sometime in the next few days, find a way to reach out to someone who is different from you or whom you wouldn't normally spend time with. She may look different from you, have different interests, or simply be part of a different group of friends. Look for an opportunity to do something kind or friendly; you may just make a new friend!

Esther: For Such a Time as This

If you keep quiet at a time like this, deliverance and relief for the Jews will arise from some other place, but you and your relatives will die. Who knows if perhaps you were made queen for just such a time as this?

ESTHER 4:14

Esther's cousin Mordecai found out about Haman's plan to kill all the Jews. Mordecai told Esther she had to speak to the king and get him to help the Jews. He told Esther that God might have put her in the palace for just that reason.

God arranged for Esther to be right where she needed to be when she needed to be there. God could have just zapped Haman for his evil plan, but that's not the way he works. If God wiped out everyone who had a wicked thought, the world would be empty. God allows bad things to happen because we live on a sinful earth. Haman followed his own sinful nature. But God also had a plan to save the Jews, and the plan centered on Esther. She was in the palace "for just such a time as this."

Each of us is created with a purpose. Our purposes may not seem as grand as Esther's, but they are important just the same. Living as though God has a purpose for you will change the way you live. Instead of moping around doing nothing, you will be engaged in seeking out what he wants you to do. There's no secret formula to finding out his plan for you. You just need to be willing to be used, stay attentive to God's voice in your heart, and then do the things you think God wants you to do.

God created you with a purpose, and he gave you what you need to fulfill that purpose. You might have insight into how people feel or give special attention to details. You might have the ability to work with computers or to learn other languages.

God has a purpose for you, just as he did for Esther and the other women you have read about in this book. He will help you find it if you ask him.

thinking it through

Not sure what your purpose might be? These questions may help you get an idea of what you could accomplish for God:

What do you like to do? What concerns you most in life? What world problem would you change if you could? What would you change about your school? What's your dream? What makes you feel the most useful? What would you do for those around you if you could? What makes you feel sad or brokenhearted?

Esther: Living Your Life with Purpose

"I know the plans I have for you," says the LORD. "They are plans for good and not for disaster, to give you a future and a hope."

JEREMIAH 29:11

God had a plan for Esther before she was ever born. He knew one day she would be married to the king and be in a position to save her people. He knew it would require courage and the ability to speak calmly and decisively, and God equipped her to do that.

God also made a plan for you before you were born. You may not know all the details right now, but you can be sure God has given you all the skills and talents to carry out that plan, because his plan is tailor made for you. And the best part is, you don't have to wait until you are an adult to live out his plan for you. You can live your life with purpose right now.

In order to live God's purpose for you, it's important to talk to God daily. Tell him about the things that bother you and the things you are passionate about. Ask him to show you what he wants you to do each day.

Read from the Bible every day. Look for things that speak to you. You can also learn from the Bible women in this book. Listen to God as he speaks to you through his Word, through other people, and through your own heart.

There's no mystery to finding God's plan for you. Just ask yourself how you are living for God right now at home, at school, at church, on your volleyball team, in your dance company, at club meetings, and at other activities. God will work through your everyday life to lead you to what he wants you to do.

Don't go through each day aimlessly. Ask God to show you what he wants you to accomplish today, and look for ways to do it.

thinking it through

Not sure what you should be doing each day? Look up these verses and jot down what they say you should do:

Deuteronomy 6:5
Micah 6:8
Colossians 3:12-15
Galatians 5:13

Think about these verses this week as you go to school and church and spend time with your family and friends.

thinking it through

Are you facing a situation where you need courage? How can you prepare for it? How can Esther's example help you?

Esther: True Courage

Go and gather together all the Jews of Susa and fast for me. Do not eat or drink for three days, night or day. My maids and I will do the same. And then, though it is against the law, I will go in to see the king. If I must die, I must die.

ESTHER 4:16

Haman devised a plan to kill all the Jews, including Mordecai and possibly Esther (she had kept her Jewish heritage a secret). Mordecai told Esther that she needed to talk to the king and plead for her people. But you couldn't just walk up to the king and ask him for a favor. You had to wait for him to send for you. If Esther approached the king without being summoned, she could be killed.

Esther agreed to approach the king, but she told Mordecai to gather the Jews and have them fast and pray for her for three days. And in a moment of true courage she declared, "If I must die, I must die."

Esther had courage because she knew she was doing the right thing. Approaching the king was necessary to save herself and her people. Perhaps there has been a time when you had to stand up to peers who wanted you to do something wrong. Or maybe you befriended another student, knowing that others might ignore you or make fun of you for it. You can do those things bravely, knowing they are the right choices.

Esther also had courage because she was prepared when she faced the king. Esther didn't impulsively run to the king and blurt out her problem. She stopped to think things through and make a plan. Maybe you have a speech contest or play audition coming up, or you plan to ask the principal for permission to start a Bible club. When you are prepared, you can approach the situation with courage.

Finally, Esther had courage because she knew the outcome was in God's hands. Knowing that God is in control gives you added courage to face the tough times in your life.

Follow Esther's example next time you have to do something that requires courage.

Esther: Facing Fear

God has not given us a spirit of fear and timidity, but of power, love, and self-discipline.

2 TIMOTHY 1:7

Esther had every right to be afraid—of the extermination of her people and of her own death from appearing before the king without being summoned first. She wasn't a great leader or warrior; she was a young Jewish girl, alone except for an older cousin. She was the queen only because the king was taken with her beauty. It was normal for her to be afraid.

Fear is natural, but like Esther, you don't have to let it keep you from doing what you need to do. Sometimes fear is helpful. It's an emotion that's programmed into your nervous system and alerts you when there is danger. Your brain kicks into gear and causes your body to respond by making your heart beat faster and your breathing become more rapid. Blood pressure rises and skin sweats to keep the body cool. Your muscles prepare to run or fight. The fear prepares you to face the approaching danger.

Fear becomes a problem when it keeps you from doing what you need to do. Esther felt afraid when Mordecai told her she needed to approach the king, but it didn't keep her from acting.

Rather than avoiding what you are afraid of, face it head-on. Name your fear. Then prepare for situations when you might face your fear. Afraid to share your faith? Practice different methods that are comfortable for you, like telling a peer what God has done for you.

Scared of the dark? Think of the reason you might be afraid. If you know you will be outside in the dark, bring a flashlight with extra batteries.

Afraid to speak in front of others? Practice giving your report to your family or a group of friends until you can do it with ease.

Fill your mind with Scripture, and ask God to fill your heart with courage.

thinking it through

What's your biggest fear? What is one way you can face your fear head-on and prepare for it?

thinking it through

Which Bible woman listed in this devo can you relate to most? Why? Find her story in the Bible or in this book, and read it. What can you learn from her about facing your fears?

Esther: Women Who Overcame Fear

Be strong and courageous! Do not be afraid and do not panic before them. For the LORD your God will personally go ahead of you. He will neither fail you nor abandon you.
DEUTERONOMY 31:6

Esther wasn't the only Bible woman who faced and overcame fear. If you've been reading this book since January, you can probably think of several women who faced fearful situations:

Eve had to leave her beautiful garden sanctuary for a less desirable and unknown home.

Mrs. Noah had to leave her home and board a boat filled with animals, knowing that everything around her would be destroyed and she'd be facing a new and unfamiliar world when the Flood ended.

Sarah faced two moves to new places.

Hagar fled into the desert, where she feared that she and her son would die.

Rebekah traveled hundreds of miles to marry a man she'd never met.

Shiphrah and Puah disobeyed an order to kill all the Hebrew baby boys, which could have meant their own deaths if they were found out.

Jochebed placed Baby Moses in a basket in the river because she feared for her young son's life.

Ruth traveled with her mother-in-law to a new country with unfamiliar customs.

The widow of Zarephath feared that both she and her son would starve to death.

All of these women had their own fears and anxieties, but all of them trusted in God and knew that whatever happened was part of God's plan for them. They had faith in the face of danger, change, or the unknown. And in every case, God blessed them because of it.

Are you facing a situation that is causing you to be anxious or afraid? Think of the brave Bible women you've read about and trust God to work things out for you just as he did for each of them.

Quiz Time

Haman tried to get rid of all the Jews during the time of Esther. You have no plans to go to that extreme, but do you treat everyone fairly? Read each sentence below, and circle A for always, S for sometimes, or N for never.

1. I have friends who are a different skin color or have a different ethnic background from me, or I would being willing to have these friends if possible.

   A S N

2. When I see someone who is different from me, I think he or she is pretty much like me on the inside.

   A S N

3. Students who are different from me are welcome to sit with me at lunch or join my team in PE.

   A S N

4. I try to see behind what a person looks like to who he or she really is.

   A S N

5. I believe that our differences are what make us unique and special.

   A S N

Give yourself 2 points for every A, 1 point for every S, and 0 points for every N. How did you do?

8-10 points: You are accepting of other people. You befriend students who are different from you and don't judge them by color, race, or background.

5-7 points: You make an effort to accept others, but you are more comfortable with those who are most like you. Don't miss out on a great friendship by avoiding someone different from you.

0-4 points: You are missing out by avoiding people who may look or act differently from you. Be open to new friendships. God loves everyone, not just one race or one color.

If you've been guilty of avoiding anyone different from yourself, take steps to change that this week.

Esther: Steps to Problem Solving, Part 1

When he saw Queen Esther standing there in the inner court, he welcomed her and held out the gold scepter to her. So Esther approached and touched the end of the scepter.

ESTHER 5:2

Esther knew she had to face the king, but she didn't just rush in without thinking. She was wise in how she approached both the problem and the king. In that way she was similar to Abigail, who knew that unless she took action, David and his men would kill all the male members of her household. But Abigail had to plan and act quickly, whereas Esther took more time to come up with a plan.

For both Abigail and Esther, the first step in dealing with the problem was to understand the problem and consequences. In Abigail's case, her foolish husband, Nabal, had refused to give David and his men food after they had helped guard his flock. So David was going to get revenge. In Esther's case, Haman was going to kill all the Jews on a certain day, and even she wasn't safe if someone found out she was a Jew.

The next step for both Abigail and Esther was deciding what needed to be done to solve the problem. Abigail needed to prepare enough food to feed David and all his men, and she needed to deliver it in time to prevent them from murdering the men in her house. Esther needed to go before the king to ask for help for the Jews, but appearing before the king unasked could get her killed.

Once Esther knew what she needed to do, she asked Mordecai to have all the Jews fast and pray. She knew she needed God's help in approaching the king. Abigail didn't have three days to fast and pray, but she trusted God to help her do the right thing when she faced David.

Do you need to solve a problem? Like Abigail and Esther, make sure you understand the problem and the consequences, decide what needs to be done, and pray about what to do next.

thinking it through

What problem are you facing today? A sticky friendship issue or girl bully problem? Difficulty with schoolwork or a schedule conflict? The need to raise money for something? Describe the problem as specifically as you can.

What needs to be done to solve the problem?

Take time to talk to God about possible solutions for the problem. He will give you wisdom in knowing how to deal with it.

Esther: Steps to Problem Solving, Part 2

If I have found favor with the king, and if it pleases the king to grant my request and do what I ask, please come with Haman tomorrow to the banquet I will prepare for you. Then I will explain what this is all about.
ESTHER 5:8

Esther was a successful problem solver because she identified the problem and what needed to be done to solve it. She knew that unless she went and talked to the king, no one would be able to stop Haman from killing the Jews. Esther knew she needed God's help. She asked the Jews to fast and pray for her.

Esther carefully planned how to approach the king. The timing had to be just right for her to bring up such an important matter. She could actually be killed for appearing before him without being summoned. Thankfully the king was glad to see her and asked what he could do for her.

Instead of telling the king about Haman's plot, Esther asked the king and Haman to attend a banquet she had prepared. At the banquet, the king again asked Esther what he could do for her, and she asked him to attend another banquet the next day. Perhaps the time wasn't quite right to tell him about Haman's plot.

Esther was not only wise in planning how to approach the king, but careful in her choice of words. At the second banquet, she was very respectful when she asked that her life and the lives of her people be spared. The king heard her request and ordered that Haman be killed. He couldn't change the decree that the Jews would be killed on a certain day, but he said that they could defend themselves.

Esther's tactics can help you solve problems. Take your time, and use wisdom in planning how to deal with a problem. Don't approach someone in anger and expect to get positive results. Wait until you are calm, then use care in choosing your words.

If you follow these principles for problem solving, you'll have a much better chance of success.

thinking it through

You can learn a lot from Esther about problem solving. What is the most important lesson you have learned? What will you do differently from now on when problem solving?

Proverbs 15:1 says, "A gentle answer deflects anger, but harsh words make tempers flare." How can this verse guide you when approaching someone to talk about a problem?

thinking it through

How do you celebrate special occasions with your family and friends? What special ways do you celebrate Jesus' birth and resurrection?

Start a new "festival day." Think of a time when God worked in your life or in your family. Write it on the calendar, and when that day comes around, have a celebration to remember what God did for you. It could be a party with your family or just a time when you thank God and share what he's done for you.

Esther: Remembering

These days would be remembered and kept from generation to generation and celebrated by every family throughout the provinces and cities of the empire. This Festival of Purim would never cease to be celebrated among the Jews, nor would the memory of what happened ever die out among their descendants.

ESTHER 9:28

Esther was a hero to the Jews because she talked to King Xerxes about Haman's plot to destroy them. The king gave the Jews permission to defend themselves against their enemies, and when the time came, the king allowed them two days to fight their enemies. Instead of the Jews being annihilated, they defeated those who wanted to kill them.

Mordecai said that the Jews should hold a celebration each year on the two days when the Jews defeated their enemies. The celebration is called the Festival of Purim, named after the lots, or dice, that Haman cast to choose the day to kill the Jews. Celebrating the Festival of Purim helps the Jews remember Esther's story as they retell it each year.

It's important to have times to give thanks, remember special events, and celebrate spiritual victories in your life. For Christians, Christmas and Easter are two days of remembering. Christmas is a time to remember the birth of the Savior, and Easter is a time to celebrate the day he rose from the dead. Birthdays are a celebration of your life. You may have other special days that your family celebrates.

Remembering special events is important because it shows God's work in our lives. The Jews celebrate Purim to remind them of God's deliverance during the time of Esther. What has God done for you that you want to remember?

Mrs. Job: Failing to Trust God

He said, "I came naked from my mother's womb, and I will be naked when I leave. The LORD gave me what I had, and the LORD has taken it away. Praise the name of the LORD!"

JOB 1:21

Before we look at Job's wife, let's take a look at who Job (rhymes with *robe*) was. Job, who lived around the same time as Abraham and Isaac, was the richest man around. He had a large family and many servants and owned thousands of animals. But he was also righteous. Job 1:1 tells us, "He was blameless—a man of complete integrity." When his sons and daughters had celebrations, he would offer burnt sacrifices to the Lord just in case his children had sinned in any way. The sacrifices were how people at that time paid for their sins, and Job took his faith—including sacrificing—very seriously.

Satan told God that Job loved and served him only because God had always protected Job and made him rich. So God allowed Satan to test Job. In a true series of unfortunate events, Job lost his flocks, servants, and children. Then Job was afflicted with terrible boils.

While he sat in ashes and scraped his skin with a piece of broken pottery, his wife said to him, "Are you still trying to maintain your integrity? Curse God and die." Job answered her, "You talk like a foolish woman. Should we accept only good things from the hand of God and never anything bad?" (Job 2:9-10).

Mrs. Job didn't have her husband's faith that God was in control. Her feelings were normal, but they stand in contrast to Job's strong faith.

Are you more like Job or Job's wife when bad things happen? Do you accept that God is in control even when it doesn't seem that way, or do you want to give up on your faith and walk away? After losing everything, Job was able to say, "The LORD gave me what I had, and the LORD has taken it away. Praise the name of the LORD!"

thinking it through

Whether or not you've been in his shoes, you probably know what it feels like to be Job; losing a friend, having to move, or even getting yelled at by your mom can make you feel like your whole world has fallen apart. The next time it feels like everything is going wrong, read Job's words out loud. Praise the God who can comfort and strengthen you.

Mrs. Job: What Mrs. Job Forgot, Part 1

We are pressed on every side by troubles, but we are not crushed. We are perplexed, but not driven to despair.

2 CORINTHIANS 4:8

Job's wife was used to a life of wealth. Being married to the richest man around gave her a prestigious position among her peers. God had protected and blessed Job, and things had always gone well for the family.

Then God allowed Satan to test Job's faith by taking away his flocks, servants, and children. Job's body was covered in boils. His wife felt it would be better if he gave up and died. But Mrs. Job forgot a few things.

The first thing Mrs. Job forgot is that bad things happen to good people. God never promised our lives will be without pain or disappointment. He just promised that nothing can separate us from his love, and he will be with us no matter what happens. Romans 8:38 says, "Not even the powers of hell can separate us from God's love." It's easy to love and trust God when everything is going right, but it's when hard times come that we really grow in our faith.

The second thing Mrs. Job forgot is that God is beyond our understanding. We can't begin to guess why things happen, but he knows, and that's what matters. Isaiah 55:9 says, "Just as the heavens are higher than the earth, so my ways are higher than your ways and my thoughts higher than your thoughts." Since we can't begin to know God's thoughts, our job is just to trust.

The third thing Mrs. Job forgot is that God is always close even if it doesn't seem like it. Psalm 145:18 says, "The LORD is close to all who call on him." Job and his wife probably didn't feel God was near during the time they were being tested, yet Job chose to trust God and was comforted by it.

We all face times of trouble, and although we don't understand why, we can know God is near and find comfort in that.

thinking it through

Why do you think Job trusted God through his tough times, while Mrs. Job lacked faith? Is it easier for you to trust God when everything is going well or when hard times come?

Which of the verses in this devo is the most comforting to you? Write it down on a card or piece of paper, and put it on your bedroom wall as a reminder when you encounter tough times.

Mrs. Job: What Mrs. Job Forgot, Part 2

The godly may trip seven times, but they will get up again. But one disaster is enough to overthrow the wicked.

PROVERBS 24:16

Mrs. Job forgot important truths about God. She forgot that her job was to follow God and obey him. God expects this even in hard times. Proverbs 3:5-6 says, "Trust in the LORD with all your heart; do not depend on your own understanding. Seek his will in all you do, and he will show you which path to take." It wasn't up to Mrs. Job to decide what to do. She just had to follow, and God would lead. God will lead you, too, if you seek him through reading your Bible, praying, and talking to godly people in your life.

Mrs. Job also forgot that God gives us comfort in hard times. She was distraught and asked Job why he didn't just give up and die. But Job knew his comfort came from God. He prayed and was comforted even though he'd lost everything. Psalm 94:19 says, "When doubts filled my mind, your comfort gave me renewed hope and cheer." Turning to God for comfort provides hope for the future. God cares about each thing that happens in your life. He will be near you in tough times.

Mrs. Job forgot God is the giver of hope. Even when it looks like there is no reason to go on, God gives renewed hope. Hebrews 10:23 says, "Let us hold tightly without wavering to the hope we affirm, for God can be trusted to keep his promise." The Job family was definitely in need of hope. Job knew where to look for it, but his wife didn't trust God to make the future brighter. The hard times you are going through now are temporary. It may not seem like things will ever get better, but they will. Ask God to give you the strength to hang on until brighter days come.

thinking it through

If you had the chance to tell Mrs. Job one thing, what would it be? Write it as a letter to her. Do you need to take any of that advice? Ask God for hope and strength to get through the tough times.

thinking it through

Is there a specific verse from this devo that would help you through tough times? How can it help you to deal with hard times? How can you put it into practice this week?

Mrs. Job: What Mrs. Job Forgot, Part 3

Praise the LORD! Give thanks to the LORD, for he is good! His faithful love endures forever.

PSALM 106:1

Mrs. Job has taught us several things about how not to handle tough times in our lives. There are three more things Mrs. Job forgot that would have helped her have hope in spite of her circumstances.

Mrs. Job forgot that we must always look forward. Looking back at the riches she once had and longing for the life that was taken from her were normal, but that didn't accomplish anything. When you face difficult times, don't fall into the trap of wishing you could go back and do things over, or wishing things hadn't changed. It's easy to do that, but it's not helpful. Look ahead toward what God still has for you in the future.

Another thing Mrs. Job forgot is that we need to encourage others. Mrs. Job was not an encourager to her husband. She told him to give up and die. Galatians 6:2 instructs us to "share each other's burdens, and in this way obey the law of Christ." You can be the one to reach out to a friend who is going through a tough time. You can listen, and if needed, you can get help for her.

The last thing Mrs. Job forgot was that we must praise God in every circumstance. Job knew this. He said, "I came naked from my mother's womb, and I will be naked when I leave. The LORD gave me what I had, and the LORD has taken it away. Praise the name of the LORD!" (Job 1:21). Job acknowledged that all he had came from God. Even though it was all gone, Job still praised God. His faith in God didn't depend on what he had.

Hard times may come, but you can face them with God's help and look forward to a better tomorrow.

Puzzle Page

Mrs. Job faced hard times, but she didn't always deal with them in the best way. Below is some good advice for dealing with hard times. Solve the Telephone Puzzle to decode the verse.

Directions: This puzzle has two numbers under each line. The first number is for the phone button. Only button numbers 2-9 have letters on them. The second number tells which letter on the button to use. All the buttons except 7 and 9 have three letters on them. Numbers 7 and 9 have four letters. Look under the first line. You see 2.1. That means button #2. Then choose the first letter on that button. That is A. Write it on the line. Finish the puzzle, and check your answer below.

1	2 ABC	3 DEF
4 GHI	5 JKL	6 MNO
7 PQRS	8 TUV	9 WXYZ
*	0 OPER	#

___ ___ ___ ___ ___ ___ be ___ ___ ___ ___ ___ ___.
2.1 5.3 9.1 2.1 9.3 7.4 5.1 6.3 9.3 3.3 8.2 5.3

___ ___ ___ ___ ___ stop ___ ___ ___ ___ ___ ___ ___.
6.2 3.2 8.3 3.2 7.3 7.1 7.3 2.1 9.3 4.3 6.2 4.1

Be ___ ___ ___ ___ ___ ___ ___ ___ in all
8.1 4.2 2.1 6.2 5.2 3.3 8.2 5.3

___ ___ ___ ___ ___ ___ ___ ___ ___ ___ ___ ___ ___
2.3 4.3 7.3 2.3 8.2 6.1 7.4 8.1 2.1 6.2 2.3 3.2 7.4 ,

for this is ___ ___ ___ ' ___ ___ ___ ___ ___ for
4.1 6.3 3.1 7.4 9.1 4.3 5.3 5.3

___ ___ ___ ___ ___ ___ ___ ___ ___ ___ ___ ___ to
9.3 6.3 8.2 9.1 4.2 6.3 2.2 3.2 5.3 6.3 6.2 4.1

___ ___ ___ ___ ___ ___ ___ ___ ___ ___ ___.
2.3 4.2 7.3 4.3 7.4 8.1 5.1 3.2 7.4 8.2 7.4

Answer: Always be joyful. Never stop praying. Be thankful in all circumstances, for this is God's will for you who belong to Christ Jesus. (1 Thessalonians 5:16-18)

thinking it through

What makes you special? How are you using your talents and personality traits for God and others?

Pray Psalm 139:14 as a prayer of thanks to God—and really mean what you say. Next time you find yourself wishing you were more like someone else, think of these words.

Old Testament Women: God Created You to Be Unique

Thank you for making me so wonderfully complex! Your workmanship is marvelous—how well I know it.

PSALM 139:14

We've looked at many Old Testament women. Some were examples of how to live, and some were examples of how not to live. But there is something to be learned from each Bible woman. The next nine devotions are going to look at principles from these women that apply to your life right now, right where you are. It doesn't matter whether you are homeschooled or in public or private school. It doesn't matter if you've been a follower of Jesus most of your life or if faith is new to you. These principles are for you.

The first one is this: God created you to be unique. Remember Eve? God created her as a full-grown woman in the Garden of Eden in his own image. Eve was the first woman, so of course she was individual, but so are you. God doesn't have a limited set of molds he uses to create people. He makes each one with his or her own looks, personality, talents, and strengths.

Think about your friends. One might be short, red haired, musical, and love roller coasters. Another might be tall with dark skin and dark hair and be a math whiz. You may look totally different from both of them and have some shared and some different interests.

God made you your own person. When you try to be like someone else, you cheat yourself of the individuality God gave you. Sure, it's okay to try the same hairstyle as one of your friends or to want an outfit similar to hers, but you shortchange yourself when you try to be her and not yourself.

Look for the things that make you unique and special. Are you outgoing? thoughtful? good at planning? Can you sing? identify all the constellations? decorate cakes? God gave you the looks, talents, and personality traits he wants you to have. It's up to you to develop them and to be willing to use them for him.

Old Testament Women: God Has a Special Plan Just for You

Trust in the LORD with all your heart; do not depend on your own understanding. Seek his will in all you do, and he will show you which path to take.
PROVERBS 3:5-6

Just as God created you to be unique, he also has a special plan tailor made for you. Sometimes it's easy to fall into the trap of being and doing what everyone else is—or doing what others think you should do, not what you really want to do. It's important to look for God's plan for you and follow it rather than copying others. Each person's plan is different. Think of the plans he had for these Old Testament women:

- God created Eve to be the mother of all living things.
- God planned for Mrs. Noah to step out in faith with her husband and save her family. She led her family into a new world after the Flood.
- God planned for Sarah to be the mother of the child who would fulfill God's promises to Abraham.
- God chose for Jochebed to save her young son, Moses, who would lead his people out of bondage.
- God planned for Ruth to move to a foreign country and be part of Jesus' family tree.
- God put Esther in the right place at the right time to save her people.

God has an equally special plan for you. It doesn't matter to God if you're popular or a superbrain or if your parents are rich. It doesn't matter if you live with two parents or are being raised by a single mom or a grandparent. God's plan is designed just for you, and you are the only one who can fulfill it.

Ask God to guide you each day, and be willing to do what he asks. As you read your Bible, look for God's instructions to you. Listen to his voice speaking to your heart. He will keep you on the path to fulfilling his plan for you.

thinking it through

Read Proverbs 3:5-6. What wisdom does this verse give for finding God's plan for you? Ask God to show you his plan for you today, and follow as he guides you through his Word and his Spirit speaking to your heart.

thinking it through

Which of the women mentioned to the right stands out to you the most? Why? What can you learn from her story that can help you in your own life?

Old Testament Women: God May Call You to Do Hard Things

Don't be afraid, for I am with you. Don't be discouraged, for I am your God. I will strengthen you and help you. I will hold you up with my victorious right hand.

ISAIAH 41:10

God wants you to be willing to follow his plan for your life, but he doesn't promise it will be easy. In fact, I can't think of any Bible woman who had an easy, comfortable life and still made a difference to those around her. The Bible women who stand out are those who struggled with fear, discouragement, change, or hardship.

The midwives Shiphrah and Puah risked death by disobeying the pharaoh's orders to kill the Hebrew baby boys. Deborah went into battle with the army. Jael killed an enemy in her own tent. The widow of Zarephath faced starvation. These women stand out because of the way they handled difficult situations with courage.

Rebekah traveled hundreds of miles to a new home to marry a man she'd never met. Naomi left home because of a famine and returned, having buried her husband and two sons. Ruth left her homeland to live in Naomi's. These women stand out because of the noble way in which they faced the changes in their lives.

Hagar was mistreated. Leah wasn't loved. Jephthah's daughter could never marry due to her father's rash vow. Hannah longed for a baby and was taunted by her husband's other wife. We remember these women for their strength of character despite their difficulties.

Each of these women had problems, but God worked through those difficulties to make them stronger. God may ask you to do something that is hard. Or you may face difficulties God allows. These don't catch God by surprise. He already knew you'd face them, and he knows how to help you through them. The important thing is to have faith in God during both the good times and the difficult ones.

Old Testament Women: God Equips You to Do the Things He's Called You to Do

May he equip you with all you need for doing his will. May he produce in you, through the power of Jesus Christ, every good thing that is pleasing to him. All glory to him forever and ever! Amen.

HEBREWS 13:21

God has a plan just for you, and he's given you the talents and abilities to fulfill that plan. Each of the Bible women called to fulfill a specific task already had what she needed to do it. Rebekah was strong and full of initiative and hospitality. This helped her when it was time to move to a new place. Abigail was wise. This helped her when she needed to confront David. Mrs. Noah was filled with faith. This helped her stand firm against ridicule and prepare for her new life after the Flood.

God has given you what you need to live out his plan for you, too. If you can't carry a tune, chances are God isn't going to call you to be a singer. If you don't understand equations or formulas, it's unlikely God will call you to be a math teacher or scientist.

Some people are good at art, drama, music, or physical activities. They may illustrate books, act in plays that make others aware of God, or minister to others through music or sports.

Some people excel in logic and reasoning. They may be instrumental in making new discoveries or in showing others the hand of God in nature.

Some people enjoy writing or speaking. They may change the world through the written or spoken word.

Some people have a good understanding of themselves and others. They can give wise advice or counsel.

Some people have the gift of leadership. They can influence people to live for God and to make good choices.

God isn't going to pick a plan for your life that you aren't capable of living out. He'll lead you in doing the things he has already equipped you to do and given you a passion for.

thinking it through

Go back and read the devotions for January 4–5. Retake the quiz that follows January 7 (or take the quiz for the first time). If you took the quiz before, see if you come out the same now as you did then. Then read the ways to use those talents and abilities for God, or think of your own ways to use them for God and others.

Make Hebrews 13:21 your prayer today. Thank God for giving you just what you need to carry out his plans for you.

thinking it through

When has God given you courage to do something hard? What might it look like for you to "put your hope in the LORD"?

Old Testament Women: God Gives You Courage to Do the Things You Need to Do

Be strong and courageous, all you who put your hope in the LORD!

PSALM 31:24

I am amazed at the courage of the Old Testament women. I'm not sure I could do the things they were called to do. And I know I couldn't do them in my own strength. Neither could they. God gave them the courage to act when they needed to.

Mrs. Noah had to spend a year on a boat with the animals before making a home in the new world. Shiphrah and Puah saved lives by refusing to obey Pharaoh's order to kill any baby boys born to Israelite women, even though it could mean their own lives. These things took a lot of courage.

Barak, an army general, wouldn't go into battle unless Deborah went with him. She had the courage he lacked. She knew God would give them the victory, so there was no need to fear.

Vashti had the courage to say no to the king when he asked her to show off her beauty for the drunken men at his banquet. She knew saying no could have serious consequences, but her dignity meant enough to her to risk the consequences.

All of these women had courage to do the things they needed to do. You won't have to worry about refusing the king a request, but you may face peer pressure to do something you know to be wrong. You won't have to disobey an order from the pharaoh to kill babies, but you may find yourself having to take a stand for babies' rights or human life. You won't be called on to live in a floating zoo for a year, but you may have to move several times in your life and face new places and situations. Just as God gave these women the courage to do what they needed to do, he'll give you the courage to do what he calls you to do.

Old Testament Women: God May Ask You to Wait

Hope deferred makes the heart sick, but a dream fulfilled is a tree of life.

PROVERBS 13:12

Sometimes it's hard to understand why answers to prayer are so delayed. Abraham and Sarah loved God and obeyed him wholeheartedly. When God told them to move to a place he'd show them, they packed up and went. Yet Sarah's plea for a baby went unanswered, while her servant Hagar was able to give Abraham a son. Sarah didn't have a child until she was long past the age to have a baby.

Rebekah also longed for a child and was unable to have one. God finally answered Isaac's prayer and sent Rebekah not one son but twin boys. Rachel, too, was unable to have children at first. Her older sister, Leah, her husband's first wife, had several. After many years God allowed Rachel to have a son. She died giving birth to a second son later. These women were all told "wait" by God.

You may have some waiting time in your life too. Right now you might be praying for one of your friends to become a Christian, but it isn't happening. Or you may be praying for a new best friend to replace the one who moved over the summer, but no new friend has come along.

Why does God ask people to wait? We may never know why he asks us to wait for specific things, but he knows the right time for each event to happen in our lives. He may also ask us to wait for something so it will be more special to us when we finally receive it, or he may give us time to grow in our faith first. We may not be ready to receive what we've asked for. Or God may want us to spend more time praying and seeking his will.

If you're waiting for something, don't give up. God knows the perfect time to answer your prayer.

thinking it through

If there is something that you're waiting for, take some time today to talk to God about how you feel. He has a reason for your waiting, so don't give up.

Old Testament Women: God Sees the Whole Plan

The LORD's plans stand firm forever; his intentions can never be shaken.

PSALM 33:11

Ever do a jigsaw puzzle? At first you have one hundred or more colorful pieces scattered on the table. Then you start assembling the border. You get the framework in place for the puzzle. Then one piece at a time you start putting the picture together using the box cover as a guide. Have you ever tried to assemble a puzzle without the picture as a guide? It might not be too difficult with a one-hundred-piece puzzle, but just try it with a five-hundred-piece puzzle! Without knowing what the puzzle should look like, you'd just have hundreds of colorful pieces. Is that blue piece part of the sky? a lake? flowers in a field?

Sometimes life feels like a jigsaw puzzle with no picture. You see bits and pieces of your life, but you don't know what the whole picture looks like. You have a problem with a teacher. You finally get a B on a math test. Your grandmother gets sick. You find out you're moving. You score the winning soccer goal. All these pieces are part of your life, but you only see them a piece at a time. God sees the whole thing. He knows what the picture of your life looks like and how all the pieces fit together.

Esther is a good example of this. Vashti refused to follow the king's order and was banished. The king held an elaborate beauty contest to choose a new queen. A young Jewish woman was chosen. Then her cousin Mordecai found out about a plot to kill all the Jews. He told Esther she had to tell the king. He said she might have been chosen just so she'd be in place to save her people. That's how God works. He sees the whole picture of our lives, and he arranges the pieces so they all fit together to form that picture.

You see your life one piece at a time. You live your life one day at a time. God will lead you day by day on the path he wants you to take if you ask him to.

thinking it through

Can you think of examples of how other Old Testament women lived out God's plan one day at a time?

Puzzle Page

Some of the Old Testament women we've been reviewing this week had to wait for things. Sarah, for instance, waited years for a baby. Solve the Speedometer Puzzle below to read a verse about waiting.

Directions: Each blank line has a number under it. Those numbers correspond to letters on the speedometer. Look at the number under the first line. It is 50. Look at the speedometer. The letter with 50 is L. Write L on the line. Finish decoding the words, and check your answer below.

But if we ____ ____ ____ ____ ____ ____ ____ ____ ____ ____ ____ to
50 65 65 45 25 65 75 100 5 75 15

____ ____ ____ ____ ____ ____ ____ ____ ____ we ____ ____ ____ ' ____
80 65 55 20 85 35 40 60 30 15 65 60 85

yet ____ ____ ____ ____, we must ____ ____ ____ ____
35 5 95 20 100 5 40 85

____ ____ ____ ____ ____ ____ ____ ____ ____ and
70 5 85 40 20 60 85 50 105

____ ____ ____ ____ ____ ____ ____ ____ ____ ____ ____.
10 65 60 25 40 15 20 60 85 50 105

Answer: But if we look forward to something we don't yet have, we must wait patiently and confidently. (Romans 8:25)

thinking it through

Is there a mean girl in your life? How do you react to her? What changes do you need to make? How can you make an effort to be united, "binding yourselves together with peace"?

Old Testament Women: There Will Always Be Mean Girls

Make every effort to keep yourselves united in the Spirit, binding yourselves together with peace.

EPHESIANS 4:3

Brooke hid in a stall in the girls' bathroom at school, trying to avoid Sierra. On the first day of school Brooke had accidentally bumped into Sierra, making her drop her books. That same day she and Sierra both tried out for the volleyball team. Brooke made the team but Sierra didn't. Four weeks into school Sierra and her group were still going out of their way to be mean to Brooke. They made fun of her clothes, her hair, the way she walked—anything they could think of. Brooke looked forward to volleyball practice at the end of the day. That was one time when Sierra and her clones couldn't bother Brooke.

There have always been mean girls, and unfortunately there probably always will be. As long as there are comparisons, jealousy, and rivalry, there will be girls who are angry and bitter. Bible women weren't much different. When Hagar got pregnant after Sarah couldn't, she taunted Sarah. Sarah reacted by treating her unkindly, causing Hagar to run away.

Jacob was tricked into marrying Leah when it was Rachel he loved. That caused all sorts of problems. Leah was plain and unloved, but she had baby after baby. Rachel was beautiful and was loved by Jacob, but she couldn't have children. Comparisons and jealousy between the sisters strained their relationship.

Elkanah had two wives—Hannah and Peninnah. He loved Hannah more, but just like Rachel, she couldn't have children. Peninnah could, and she made fun of Hannah because of it.

Mean girls grow into mean women and make life miserable for those around them. You can't change them, but you can change how you respond to them. Ask God to give you the grace to ignore them and to see them as girls in need of God's love and forgiveness.

Old Testament Women: Sin Doesn't Pay

The wages of sin is death, but the free gift of God is eternal life through Christ Jesus our Lord.

ROMANS 6:23

In addition to the honorable Old Testament women, we find some evil women too. The good girls aren't perfect. They struggle. They question God. They make mistakes. But the difference is that they love God and strive to trust and serve him. When they mess up, they ask forgiveness and go on. Not so with the wicked women. They either don't believe in God or choose not to follow him.

Jezebel and her daughter Athaliah are two examples of wicked Bible women. Jezebel worshiped Baal. She tried to kill all the prophets of God. She especially hated Elijah, who won a showdown against her false prophets and then had them all killed. She came to an end when she was thrown from a window and eaten by dogs.

Athaliah followed in her mother's footsteps. She had all the heirs to the throne killed so she could rule. She didn't know a one-year-old grandson, Joash, was rescued and raised in the Temple. When he took the throne a few years later, the people killed Athaliah.

No one mourned the deaths of Jezebel and Athaliah. They had helped no one. They hadn't improved their kingdoms. They hadn't influenced anyone for good. Their lives were wasted.

Sometimes it might seem like the bad kids have all the fun, have the most friends, and own more things than anyone else, but it's temporary. Only the things you do for Jesus will last. Others may have more worldly goods, but they lack peace and the assurance of a home in heaven.

If living the right way seems boring, add some excitement. Talk to a parent or youth leader about how to make a difference in your town. Can you and some friends form a club that does service projects, like collecting food or planting flowers? Can you get involved with a community program that helps the poor? Find one way to put your faith into action this week.

thinking it through

In Psalm 73, the psalmist Asaph struggles with the way the wicked seem to have such easy lives while he goes unrewarded for trying to be godly. After Asaph's complaint (verses 3-14), he realizes that the wicked won't win in the end (verses 17-26).

Do you ever feel like Asaph? How can this psalm help you think through your feelings?

thinking it through

Many Bible women are good examples for you today. They were women who were courageous, compassionate, wise, dependable, faithful, devoted to family, and full of initiative. Which Bible woman do you admire most? Why? What can you learn from her?

Old Testament Women: God's Way Is the Best Way

My old self has been crucified with Christ. It is no longer I who live, but Christ lives in me. So I live in this earthly body by trusting in the Son of God, who loved me and gave himself for me.

GALATIANS 2:20

The Old Testament women have shown that God created each of us in a unique and wonderful way. He has a special plan tailor made for you that uses the talents and personality he has already given you. God may ask you to do hard things or to wait on his timing, but he will give you the strength and courage to do that. You may run into mean or ungodly girls along the way. They might make your life miserable for a while, but they never win in the end. God's way is the best way. Following the plan he has for you is the only way to be truly successful and to have peace even in the midst of troubles.

If you can realize God's way is the best way and remember that throughout your life, you will do great things for God. You might be like Vashti and stand strong against pressure to do wrong. You might be like Shiphrah and Puah and defend human life. You might be like Jochebed, protecting your own family, or Deborah, leading others to victory. You might be a women's leader like Miriam or speak wise words to solve problems like Abigail.

Allow God to lead you and use you, and you will be amazed at all you can accomplish for him.

Elizabeth: A Godly Heritage

When Herod was king of Judea, there was a Jewish priest named Zechariah. He was a member of the priestly order of Abijah, and his wife, Elizabeth, was also from the priestly line of Aaron.

LUKE 1:5

Zechariah and Elizabeth were a godly couple who lived in the hill country of Judea. Zechariah served in the Temple, and both were known for their righteous lifestyles.

Zechariah and Elizabeth were both raised to serve God from their earliest years. Elizabeth was a descendant of Moses' brother, Aaron, who was a priest, so she grew up in a family of priests. Zechariah also grew up in a priestly family and became a priest. They both knew God's law and what was required of them as Jews, and they were careful to obey each of God's commandments.

Zechariah and Elizabeth would have been the perfect parents to raise children who loved and served God. The problem was that they didn't have any children, and now they were too old to have children—until God sent a miracle their way. In many ways their story was like Abraham and Sarah's. Both were righteous couples who loved and served God. Both families prayed for a child and were given a miracle baby in their old age. Both Sarah's and Elizabeth's sons were raised to love God and obey his commands, and both played very special roles in history.

Whether you come from a godly family like Elizabeth and Zechariah's or from a family that doesn't know God, you can love and serve God. It's sometimes easier to follow Jesus when you come from a home where everyone believes in him, but if that's not true of your family, don't despair. Look for Christian women who can be role models for you and encourage you. Find other Christians at school or in your neighborhood, and take part in Christian clubs. You can do the same if you come from a godly home. Look around for someone who needs encouragement in her Christian walk, and be a friend to her.

thinking it through

Is your family like Zechariah and Elizabeth's? How have your parents passed on their faith to you? If no one else in your family believes in God, who shared his or her faith with you?

Who can be a role model and encourager for you? Who can you encourage in her faith?

thinking it through

How do you think Elizabeth responded to the news she would have a child?

Is there anything you've been praying about for so long that it doesn't seem like God will ever answer you? How can Zechariah and Elizabeth's story encourage you?

Elizabeth: The Angel's Message

The angel said, "Don't be afraid, Zechariah! God has heard your prayer. Your wife, Elizabeth, will give you a son, and you are to name him John."

LUKE 1:13

Being unable to have children in Bible times was shameful. People usually thought of it as a sign of God's displeasure. Zechariah and Elizabeth obeyed God in all they did, yet they hadn't had any children in all the years they'd been married. They were probably perplexed by why God hadn't sent them children.

Zechariah was doing a very special job at the Temple. He was chosen by lots (like dice) to burn incense in the Temple, while the crowd outside prayed. This was an honor a priest normally had only once or twice in a lifetime. While he was doing this, the angel Gabriel appeared to him and told him he and Elizabeth were going to have a son. But Zechariah had doubts God would really send them a child in their old age. Because of that, the angel told him he wouldn't be able to speak until the child was born.

Certainly Zechariah knew the stories of God parting the Red Sea for Moses and causing the walls of Jericho to fall for Joshua. He knew of God's miracles in the history of his people, but he doubted God would give him and his wife a child. In his human thinking, it wasn't possible. But God doesn't have to work within natural laws. He created the whole world in six days, so he could certainly give a childless couple a baby despite their ages.

We aren't told how Elizabeth accepted the message once Zechariah was able to convey it to her, possibly by writing down the angel's message for her to read. But we do know Elizabeth was soon pregnant with a very special child, known to us as John the Baptist, who would be the one to declare that Jesus was the Messiah.

Elizabeth: Praising God

Soon afterward his wife, Elizabeth, became pregnant and went into seclusion for five months. "How kind the Lord is!" she exclaimed. "He has taken away my disgrace of having no children."

LUKE 1:24-25

Zechariah and Elizabeth soon learned the angel's message was true. A baby was on the way. Today when a woman becomes pregnant, she often calls her closest friends right away with the news. They discuss when the baby will arrive, what its name will be, and how the nursery will be decorated. They may even go shopping together for baby clothes or cute toys. Soon everyone knows a baby is expected.

It wasn't the same in Elizabeth's day. People often didn't know a woman was expecting until near the time the baby would be born. A woman would tell only her family and closest friends. But Elizabeth didn't even do that. She stayed to herself for five months. What did she do during that time? We know she spent much of it praising God for this miracle he'd performed for her. Not only was she going to have a child after all these years, but she was going to give birth to a special child with a holy mission. He would be great in God's eyes, and he would turn many toward the coming of the Lord.

Most of us have no need to hide away for five months, but we could do better at praising God. How much time do we really spend each day sincerely praising God? That doesn't include that thirty-second prayer before lunch or the one thanking God that the history project deadline was rescheduled for a week later. We need to spend time just praising and thanking God for who he is and what he has done in our lives. Elizabeth spent five months marveling at God's blessing and praising him—why not set aside just five minutes each day this week to spend praising God?

thinking it through

What can you praise God for this week? Try to think of five things and write them down. If you can't think of anything, read a psalm to the Lord. Try Psalm 48, 66, or 68.

thinking it through

Have you ever seen something you would call one of God's "wonders"? Or have you heard a friend tell about one of God's "wonderful deeds" in her life? How are you doing with spending time praising God each day (see yesterday's "Thinking It Through")? Use the words from today's verse to praise God for the things he's done for you.

Elizabeth: God's Timing

O LORD my God, you have performed many wonders for us. Your plans for us are too numerous to list. You have no equal. If I tried to recite all your wonderful deeds, I would never come to the end of them.

PSALM 40:5

There are a lot of lessons repeated over and over in the Bible. "God's timing is not our timing" is a lesson Sarah, Rebekah, Rachel, Hannah, and Elizabeth all found to be true.

Like the Old Testament women before her, Elizabeth pleaded with God for a child. But many years passed, and she did not get pregnant. Although disappointed not to have children, she and her husband stayed faithful to God and were busy serving him. Then, like Sarah and Abraham, an angel delivered surprising news. Elizabeth would have a baby even though she was past the age when it seemed possible.

Why did God make such a godly couple wait so long to have a child? We don't know. It may have been so they would cherish their son even more after waiting so long. It may have been so they would be mature in their faith and well established in the Temple. It may have been so they would be single-mindedly focused on raising John the way God wanted him to be raised.

Whatever the reason, God sent a baby to Elizabeth at the exact time he'd planned. It wasn't an afterthought. He didn't suddenly change his mind and decide to send a child after all. It was part of his plan from the beginning. God's thoughts and ways are far beyond ours, so we can't always understand why he does the things he does. God just wants us to trust him to work in our lives and wait on him. This doesn't mean we should just sit and wait. We can be busy serving him while he reveals his plan for us one day at a time.

Puzzle Page

It may seem like sinful people get away with doing wrong, but they don't. Solve the Telephone Puzzle to read what the Bible says about sinful people.

Directions: This puzzle has two numbers under each line. The first number is for the phone button. Only button numbers 2-9 have letters on them. The second number tells which letter on the button to use. All the buttons except 7 and 9 have three letters on them. Numbers 7 and 9 have four letters. Look under the first line. You see 7.1. That means button #7. Then choose the first letter on that button. That is P. Write it on the line. Finish the puzzle, and check your answer below.

____ ____ ____ ____ ____ ____ who ____ ____ ____ ____ ____ ____ ____
7.1 3.2 6.3 7.1 5.3 3.2 2.3 6.3 6.2 2.3 3.2 2.1 5.3

their ____ ____ ____ ____ will not ____ ____ ____ ____ ____ ____ ____,
7.4 4.3 6.2 7.4 7.1 7.3 6.3 7.4 7.1 3.2 7.3

but if they ____ ____ ____ ____ ____ ____ ____ and ____ ____ ____ ____
2.3 6.3 6.2 3.3 3.2 7.4 7.4 8.1 8.2 7.3 6.2

from ____ ____ ____ ____, ____ ____ ____ ____ will
8.1 4.2 3.2 6.1 8.1 4.2 3.2 9.3

____ ____ ____ ____ ____ ____ ____ ____ ____ ____ ____ ____.
7.3 3.2 2.3 3.2 4.3 8.3 3.2 6.1 3.2 7.3 2.3 9.3

Answer: People who conceal their sins will not prosper, but if they confess and turn from them, they will receive mercy. (Proverbs 28:13)

thinking it through

Every life God creates is special. Praise God today for the special and unique way he made you, and for the plans he has for you.

Elizabeth: Children of Purpose

At the sound of Mary's greeting, Elizabeth's child leaped within her, and Elizabeth was filled with the Holy Spirit.

LUKE 1:41

The angel Gabriel delivered two unusual announcements just a few months apart. First, he told Zechariah that Elizabeth, who was past childbearing years, would have a son. When Elizabeth was six months along in her pregnancy, Gabriel told Mary, a young virgin, that she was going to have a baby who would be the Savior of the world. Mary was a young relative of Elizabeth's, possibly a cousin. The angel also told Mary that Elizabeth was pregnant.

Mary decided to visit Elizabeth, so she made the long journey to the hills of Judea. When Mary arrived and greeted Elizabeth, Elizabeth's baby jumped inside her. The baby recognized the mother of the Savior. Perhaps he already sensed that his mission was to turn others to Jesus and to proclaim him as the Savior.

Even though Mary hadn't told Elizabeth about her own pregnancy, "Elizabeth gave a glad cry and exclaimed to Mary, 'God has blessed you above all women, and your child is blessed. Why am I so honored, that the mother of my Lord should visit me?'" (Luke 1:42-43).

God chose two holy women, one young and one old. He performed two miracles so two special babies would be born, and the lives of the babies would be intertwined.

Jesus and John were miracle babies who had missions from God. God has a plan for each baby born. They won't be the Savior of the world or the one who prepares people for his coming, but they may be missionary doctors, counselors, or musicians. They may work in a restaurant or run a car wash. It doesn't matter if the job is great or small. It matters only that they live out God's plan for them. Each life God creates is sacred because each person has a special purpose to fulfill.

Elizabeth: Equipped for the Job

Everyone who heard about it reflected on these events and asked, "What will this child turn out to be?" For the hand of the Lord was surely upon him in a special way.

LUKE 1:66

Elizabeth knew her baby would be special because God had performed a miracle in order for her to become pregnant. Her son had a special mission, and she was given specific instructions about how to raise him. Zechariah was told these things by the angel:

- You are to name him John. (Normally children were named for a relative, but there was no one named John in Zechariah's family.)
- You will have great joy and gladness.
- Many will rejoice at his birth.
- He will be great in the eyes of the Lord.
- He must never touch wine or other alcoholic drinks.
- He will be filled with the Holy Spirit, even before his birth.
- He will turn many Israelites to the Lord their God.
- He will be a man with the spirit and power of Elijah.
- He will prepare the people for the coming of the Lord.
- He will turn the hearts of the fathers to their children.
- He will cause those who are rebellious to accept the wisdom of the godly.

When God chooses someone to do a job for him, he makes sure that person is equipped to do the job. John the Baptist had the important mission of preaching about the Savior in order to prepare people to accept Jesus as the Savior. Zechariah and Elizabeth had the righteousness and maturity to raise their special son.

When God asks you to do something for him, you can be confident, knowing he has already prepared you for the job.

thinking it through

God equips us for each job he gives us to do.

In what ways was Elizabeth equipped to be John's mom? What made her the best choice?

What are you doing for God that he has equipped you for? Or what can you do for God based on your talents and abilities?

thinking it through

If you have a Bible nearby, read Psalm 139:13-16 for yourself. Fill your own name in the verses as you read it. What does this passage mean to you today?

Elizabeth: The Value of Life

He will be great in the eyes of the Lord. . . . He will be filled with the Holy Spirit, even before his birth.

LUKE 1:15

Babies are important to God. They are unique individuals even before they are born. While Elizabeth was still pregnant with John, John heard Mary's voice and jumped inside Elizabeth. Luke 1 says he was filled with the Holy Spirit even before he was born. John was very much an individual with God-given abilities, looks, and mission before birth.

All life has value, including the life of an unborn child. Here is what Psalm 139:13-16 says about all of us:

- God made all the delicate, inner parts of our bodies.
- God knit us together in our mothers' wombs.
- God made us wonderfully complex.
- God's workmanship is marvelous.
- God watched us as we were being formed before birth.
- God saw us before we were born.
- Every moment of our lives was planned before we were ever born.

Usually when a baby is born, the parents are excited. They call and share the news with relatives, and they answer questions about how big the baby is and who he or she looks like. Elizabeth and Zechariah were excited to share their news too. Luke 1:58 says, "When her neighbors and relatives heard that the Lord had been very merciful to her, everyone rejoiced with her."

Parents may have special dreams for their babies. Some even have a certain college in mind for when the baby is old enough! God has plans and dreams for each child too. All life is valuable to God, and you are no exception.

Mary: Meet Mary

In the sixth month of Elizabeth's pregnancy, God sent the angel Gabriel to Nazareth, a village in Galilee, to a virgin named Mary. She was engaged to be married to a man named Joseph, a descendant of King David.

LUKE 1:26-27

The place was Nazareth, a small village in the region of Galilee. The person was Mary, a young woman probably in her teen years. She was poor and unknown to most of the world. Her parents were unknown. Yet this was the woman chosen by God to give birth to his Son.

No woman in history is so well known as Mary, mother of Jesus. She is depicted in paintings, stained-glass windows, and statues around the world. We sing about her in Christmas carols. All of these things make it appear Mary was honored, even exalted, for giving birth to Jesus, but this wasn't true during the time in which she lived.

Mary never wore fancy clothes or had many possessions. She was a small-town peasant girl who married a carpenter. They didn't have much money. They traveled only when they had to, first for a census, then to Egypt for Jesus' safety, and yearly to the Temple.

Being chosen to give birth to Jesus wasn't easy for Mary. At the time, she was young, a virgin, and unmarried. Most people assumed she had sinned and gotten pregnant by Joseph or some other man. Even Joseph was thinking of ending their engagement, until an angel appeared to him to tell him Mary was carrying the Son of God.

The most important thing about Mary was that she loved God, and she was willing to do whatever he asked of her, even if it seemed hard or impossible. She called herself a servant of the Lord.

Do you have the same attitude? Do you consider yourself a servant of God ready to do whatever he asks? That's why Mary was chosen for one of the most important jobs in history, and God will use you, too, if you have the same willingness.

thinking it through

Why do you think God chose Mary out of all the women in history to be the mother of his Son?

What's your attitude about yourself and God's ability to use you? Do you feel like you aren't special enough or good enough to do important work for God? Don't be afraid to say yes to God when he chooses you. He won't give you a task that he can't help you to do.

thinking it through

Reread 1 Samuel 2:26 in today's devotion, and then read Luke 2:52: "Jesus grew in wisdom and in stature and in favor with God and all the people." These verses describe Samuel and Jesus as they were growing up. You're never too young to start growing in favor with God and the people around you (notice how those two things go hand in hand).

Mary: Finding Favor with God

"Don't be afraid, Mary," the angel told her, "for you have found favor with God!"

LUKE 1:30

Mary was young. She was poor. She had no social status. She was unknown outside of her little village. But Mary found favor with God.

Mary wasn't the first one to find favor with God. "Noah found favor with the LORD" (Genesis 6:8), and God spared Noah and his family when he destroyed the rest of the world. God told Moses, "I look favorably on you, and I know you by name'" (Exodus 33:17), and God used Moses to deliver his people from slavery. "The boy Samuel grew taller and grew in favor with the LORD and with the people" (1 Samuel 2:26), and he became a great prophet.

When God favored people, it meant he approved of the way they loved and worshiped him, and he singled them out to do a special job. Noah and his family were the only survivors of the Flood, and everyone born after the Flood would be their descendants. Moses led the Israelites out of slavery and to the Promised Land. Samuel served in the Tabernacle and anointed the first two kings of Israel. Mary gave birth to God's Son.

Are you living in a way that God can show you favor? Like Noah, Moses, Samuel, and Mary, you don't have to be rich or well known. You don't have to be important in your community. You don't have to have certain talents or abilities. You just have to be living the way God wants you to live. Do the things God tells you to do in his Word. Listen to his voice as he speaks in your heart, and be willing to say yes when he asks you to step out in faith and accomplish something for him.

Mary: Nothing Is Impossible with God

Nothing is impossible with God.
LUKE 1:37

Mary was willing to be used by God, but it seemed impossible to her that she could give birth to God's Son. Mary asked, "How can this happen? I am a virgin" (Luke 1:34). Mary wasn't married, and she'd never slept with a man.

The angel had the answer for her: "The Holy Spirit will come upon you, and the power of the Most High will overshadow you. So the baby to be born will be holy, and he will be called the Son of God. What's more, your relative Elizabeth has become pregnant in her old age! People used to say she was barren, but she has conceived a son and is now in her sixth month. For nothing is impossible with God" (Luke 1:35-37).

For either Mary or Elizabeth to be pregnant was impossible as far as people were concerned. But God doesn't have to work within human limits. Sometimes people use this verse to say they can do anything with God's help, but what it really says is that God can do anything. He created the earth; he set the laws of science in place. He can override them if he chooses.

One reason God caused Elizabeth and Mary to become pregnant when it was impossible, humanly speaking, was so it would be obvious it was God's work. Elizabeth didn't just happen to get pregnant. God caused it to happen because he needed a very special mother and father to raise John the Baptist. Neither did Mary just happen to get pregnant. God chose her out of all the women in the world to be the mother of Jesus, God's very own Son.

God created the world, he created people and animals, he caused a worldwide Flood, he confused people's languages so they could no longer understand each other, he shut the lions' mouths when Daniel was trapped in their den, and the list goes on. The births of John and Jesus were just two more miracles God performed in order to carry out his plan of salvation for us.

thinking it through

What parts did Elizabeth and Mary play in the salvation story (the story of God sending his Son to save us from our sins)? Take time today to thank God for Elizabeth's and Mary's parts in his plans for us.

thinking it through

God has a plan for each of us just as he did for Mary. And like Mary, the only qualifications we need are hearts that love God and a willingness to be used. Take some time today to pray to God, telling him that you love him and are willing to be used for his plans.

Mary: Accepting God's Plan, Part 1

Mary responded, "I am the Lord's servant. May everything you have said about me come true." And then the angel left her.

LUKE 1:38

Mary was an ordinary girl whose life was probably much the same as any other girl's in the small village of Nazareth. She never dreamed that in one day her whole life would change. Mary may have been grinding grain or preparing a meal, or she may have been getting ready for bed or daydreaming about her upcoming marriage to Joseph when an angel appeared to her and told her she would be the mother of the Savior.

This was shocking news to Mary. She loved God and believed the prophecies that the Messiah would one day be born, but she never dreamed she would be the one to give birth to him. Yet she accepted the angel's news and only asked how she, a virgin and unmarried girl, could give birth to the Son of God. It would have been understandable if she had asked more questions like, "What will I tell people when they realize I'm pregnant but not married?" and "How do I explain this to Joseph?" But Mary simply acknowledged she was God's servant and would do as he asked.

Mary accepted God's plan for her even though it meant having to explain her pregnancy to friends and family, risking people thinking she had sinned, having her friends fail to believe her news, making a long journey to talk things over with her relative Elizabeth, making another long journey for a census right at the time the baby would be born, and watching her son grow up to be rejected and crucified. Of course, Mary didn't know all this ahead of time, but certainly she sensed her life would be anything but easy and typical from this point on.

Mary accepted God's plan for her because she had a strong faith in him and trusted him totally. Are you able to accept and willingly do the things God asks of you, knowing his plan for you is best?

Puzzle Page

God has good plans for us, just as he had good plans for Mary. Solve the puzzle below to see what the Bible says about our part in God's plans.

Directions: The words in the word bank fit on the lines below. The best way to solve the puzzle is to start with the longest words first. Then if you have many short words with the same number of letters left, you can fill them in by what word makes sense in each box. Give it a try.

planned	has	good	can	are	created	masterpiece	
For	ago	God's	Jesus	things	for	us	anew
we	Christ	long					

___ ___ ___ we ___ ___ ___ ___ ___ ___ ___' ___

___ ___ ___ ___ ___ ___ ___ ___ ___ ___ ___. He ___ ___ ___

___ ___ ___ ___ ___ ___ ___ us ___ ___ ___ ___ in

___ ___ ___ ___ ___ ___ ___ ___ ___ ___ ___, so ___ ___

___ ___ ___ do the ___ ___ ___ ___ ___ ___ ___ ___ ___ ___ he

___ ___ ___ ___ ___ ___ ___ ___ ___ ___ ___ ___ ___ ___ ___ ___

___ ___ ___.

What has God done for us?

Answer: For we are God's masterpiece. He has created us anew in Christ Jesus, so we can do the good things he planned for us long ago. (Ephesians 2:10)

thinking it through

Obeying God with your actions is important, but so is being willing to obey him in your mind and the attitude of your heart. In 1 Chronicles 28:9, David instructs his son Solomon to "worship and serve [God] with your whole heart and a willing mind. For the LORD sees every heart and knows every plan and thought." How can you have a willing heart and mind? Read the verse for the day, Romans 12:2. What does it say about the way God can change our hearts and minds?

Mary: Accepting God's Plan, Part 2

Don't copy the behavior and customs of this world, but let God transform you into a new person by changing the way you think. Then you will learn to know God's will for you, which is good and pleasing and perfect.

ROMANS 12:2

Mary didn't know what God's plan for her was, other than to love and serve him, learn the Scriptures, and obey them. That is what Mary was doing when God chose her to give birth to Jesus.

When Mary learned that God's will for her was to be the mother of Jesus, it was a major, life-changing event. But most of the time, knowing and doing God's will is a day-by-day experience. Mary was chosen for the big task because she was faithful to obey God in little things. This showed God she had a willing heart. If she wasn't willing to obey God in the small things, it wasn't likely that God would ask such a big thing of her.

The same is true today. God has a plan for you, but he may not reveal it to you all at once. Are you willing to accept God's will for your life? God may want you to be a missionary or a teacher. He may plan for you to be a professional singer or athlete. God may choose you to create computer programs or sell clothing. He probably won't send an angel to give you the plan in person, but he will lead you toward this plan day by day, step by step. The things you are learning in school and at home this week may be the very things you'll need to know to fulfill God's plan for you.

Each morning, ask God to show you his plan for you for that day, and then try to do the things you know he wants you to do. It may be as easy as asking a new student to be your partner in PE class or obeying your mom when she asks you to do the dishes. When you are faithful to do these little things, God will see your willingness and will give you bigger things to do for him.

Mary: A Long Journey

At that time Mary got ready and hurried to a town in the hill country of Judea, where she entered Zechariah's home and greeted Elizabeth.

LUKE 1:39-40, NIV

When the angel visited Mary and told her she would give birth to the Christ child, he also told her that Elizabeth was pregnant. Elizabeth was too old to have a child, but God had answered her prayer.

As Mary thought about all the angel had said, she needed someone to talk to. Who would believe that an angel had appeared to her and told her she'd become pregnant with the Son of God? Who could she talk to about what to expect? Who would share her secret? Who would offer advice? Mary decided to visit Elizabeth. After all, Elizabeth was pregnant with a miracle child of her own. Surely Elizabeth would understand Mary's feelings. And since Elizabeth was much older, raised in a family of priests, and now married to a priest, she had the maturity and spiritual insight to offer Mary counsel.

The Bible doesn't say much about Mary's trip to visit Elizabeth, but it must have been a hard journey, close to eighty or eighty-five miles and into hill country. Mary most likely made the trip by foot, although she may have ridden a donkey. Or perhaps she walked but had her supplies for the journey on a camel. No matter how she traveled, it was a long journey without the luxuries of a car or air-conditioning, and no convenience stores to stop at for a soda or snacks. She may have journeyed alone or with a group going in the same direction part of the way. Mary was young and healthy, but she was also secretly pregnant.

If you've ever gone on a road trip, you know how long it can feel, even when you are in a car and have plenty of snacks and things to do. Mary's journey was long and tiring, but it was worth it to be able to talk to Elizabeth.

thinking it through

What do you think Mary thought about during her journey? What emotions might she have been feeling? Why?

When something unexpected happens in your life, how can it be helpful to spend time with an older friend who has experienced the same thing?

thinking it through

Proverbs 16:24 says, "Kind words are like honey—sweet to the soul and healthy for the body."

Someone near you today may need a word of encouragement. Who can you speak kind words to today?

Mary: Meeting of the Moms

Elizabeth gave a glad cry and exclaimed to Mary, "God has blessed you above all women, and your child is blessed. Why am I so honored, that the mother of my Lord should visit me? When I heard your greeting, the baby in my womb jumped for joy. You are blessed because you believed that the Lord would do what he said."

LUKE 1:42-45

After her long journey, Mary found herself at Elizabeth's door. Perhaps she hesitated, wondering how to explain why she had come. But it's obvious from the verses above that Elizabeth was happy to see her young relative. Elizabeth's baby even jumped for joy at the sound of Mary's voice.

Elizabeth excitedly acknowledged that both Mary and her baby were blessed—and this was before Mary had shared her news with Elizabeth. God allowed Elizabeth to know that Mary was pregnant with the Messiah. What an encouragement Elizabeth's greeting must have been to Mary. God had sent her to a relative who not only believed Mary was pregnant with God's Son, but who also knew the truth of the situation and was a part of the story. Elizabeth would soon give birth to John the Baptist, whose job it would be to prepare people to accept Jesus as the promised Messiah.

These two women, one young and one old, must have found a lot to talk about. Both were expecting miracle babies. Perhaps they talked about how other people would accept their pregnancies. Maybe Mary shared her fears that people would think she had sinned. Mary hadn't yet told Joseph about her pregnancy. She may have asked Elizabeth for advice on how to share the news with her fiancé.

Elizabeth was happy to see Mary and acknowledged that both Mary and her baby were blessed. What a relief that must have been for Mary. We, too, can encourage others by being welcoming and kind.

Mary: Mary's Song of Praise

Mary responded, "Oh, how my soul praises the Lord."
LUKE 1:46

When Mary arrived at her relative Elizabeth's house, Elizabeth was overjoyed to see her. She blessed Mary and her unborn baby. Then Mary responded with a song of praise for God. It is a song that tells of God's faithfulness, righteousness, and justice.

Mary had probably been taught the Scriptures all her life, so when she wanted to praise God for what he was doing in her life, she was able to recall those Scriptures and include them as she sang this song out of the depths of her heart. Mary's song not only shows her knowledge of Scripture, but it also reveals her emotions and her heart response to God's work in her life. She praises God for acting on behalf of the righteous in the past and for noticing and choosing her.

Mary had listened to what the angel told her concerning Jesus' birth. She kept his message in her heart and thought about it over and over. Her heart was filled with wonder at being chosen and with praise for God.

Proverbs 4:23 says, "Guard your heart above all else, for it determines the course of your life." That means it's important what you put in your heart because the things in your heart are the things that fill your mind and life.

If you were to sing a song of all that's in your heart, what would the song contain? Would it be filled with praise for God and what he did for you by sending Jesus as Savior? with words of praise for what you have and how your needs are met? Or would it be filled with negative feelings—feelings of anger toward a sibling or jealousy toward a classmate? Thoughts of how much you dislike a certain teacher or of how unfair your parents are? Consider what's in your heart today, and decide if it would make a good song of praise to God.

thinking it through

What are you thinking about and filling your heart with today? Try writing a short song or poem to God, expressing what's in your heart.

Philippians 4:8 says, "Dear brothers and sisters, one final thing. Fix your thoughts on what is true, and honorable, and right, and pure, and lovely, and admirable. Think about things that are excellent and worthy of praise." List the things it says you should think about. How can you concentrate on these types of things today?

thinking it through

Why is Mary blessed among women?

What is the difference between honoring someone and worshiping her? Do you worship God alone, or is there anyone else you're tempted to put on a pedestal?

Mary: Called Blessed

He took notice of his lowly servant girl, and from now on all generations will call me blessed.

LUKE 1:48

Mary was a young girl of exceptional faith. God chose her to be the mother of Jesus, and performed the miracle that caused her to become pregnant with his Son.

Over the years some churches have exalted Mary, making her almost an equal with Jesus, but in truth she isn't. Mary was born with a tendency to sin just as everyone since Adam and Eve has been. Romans 3:23 says, "Everyone has sinned; we all fall short of God's glorious standard." Mary was a sinner in need of a Savior just like the rest of us.

Mary was the earthly mother of the Savior, but Mary herself plays no part in our salvation. Acts 4:12 says, "There is salvation in no one else! God has given no other name under heaven by which we must be saved." Believing in Jesus is the only way to be saved. Jesus himself said, "I am the way, the truth, and the life. No one can come to the Father except through me" (John 14:6).

Why does Elizabeth say Mary is blessed by God, and why does Mary say she will be called blessed? Because out of all the women in the world who could have given birth to Jesus, God chose Mary. God wasn't looking for someone considered beautiful or rich. He was looking for someone with a heart that worshiped him and who would be willing to accept his will. Mary knew what a privilege it was that God found her worthy. She acknowledged that honor in her song of praise.

Many Christmas hymns mention the important role Mary had in the birth of the Savior, and it's good to acknowledge that. But always keep in mind that it is Jesus alone who lived a sinless life and gave himself as a sacrifice to save us from our sins.

Mary: The Importance of Supportive Friends

Mary stayed with Elizabeth about three months and then went back to her own home.

LUKE 1:56

Despite their differences in age and experiences, Elizabeth and Mary spent three months together at Elizabeth's house, sharing the common bond of miraculous pregnancies.

During this time Elizabeth probably served as a spiritual mentor for Mary. Elizabeth had a long life of service to the Lord to draw on so she could offer encouragement and guidance to her much younger relative, and Mary had a teachable spirit. She welcomed Elizabeth's wisdom. The older woman was someone Mary could talk to about her amazing news and what it might mean for her. God told Mary she would give birth to the Savior, but only God knew what was ahead for Jesus. Elizabeth and Mary probably had long talks about what it would mean for Mary to raise Jesus as her own son. God brought these women together for a period of time for them to help and encourage each other.

Do you have a Christian woman you can talk to and get advice from? Perhaps there is a Sunday school teacher or youth leader you feel close to. God brings different people into your life at different times so you can learn and grow in order to serve him better. Or you may be the one God chooses to reach out to someone else to offer support and encouragement.

thinking it through

Who do you turn to for advice and encouragement? Your parents and friends are great sources of support, but it's also healthy to have the perspective of someone who is a little older and who isn't in your family. Ask God to bring the right person to you when you need her.

Who can you encourage? Maybe a family with younger girls just started going to your church, or maybe you're in seventh grade and a sixth grader could use some support in her first year of middle school. Ask God for opportunities to encourage and mentor others.

thinking it through

How do you think Joseph felt when he first heard the news that Mary was pregnant? When you hear a rumor about someone, do you think the worst of that person? Or do you wait to find out the truth before judging?

How is it encouraging to know that God knew the place you would be born—and all the places you would live—before your life began?

Mary: The Census

Joseph also went up from the town of Nazareth in Galilee to Judea, to Bethlehem the town of David, because he belonged to the house and line of David.

LUKE 2:4, NIV

Sometime after Mary returned from her visit with Elizabeth, Mary told Joseph about the angel appearing to her and about her pregnancy. Joseph didn't know what to make of it. He loved Mary, and he didn't want to hurt or embarrass her. He thought about quietly ending their engagement. Then an angel appeared to him and told him the baby Mary was going to have was indeed the promised Messiah. The angel told Joseph to go ahead and wed Mary.

After this, there was a census, and Joseph had to go to his hometown to register. This was so the Roman emperor would know how many people lived in the empire. Joseph and Mary had to travel from Nazareth to Bethlehem, about ninety miles away.

Recently a census form showed up in our mailbox, and I had to complete it by filling in the names of everyone in our family and some information about each one. But Joseph didn't have this option. For him a census meant a journey to his hometown.

This census was important to Jesus' birth because in the Old Testament it was prophesied that the Savior would be born in Bethlehem, but Mary and Joseph lived in Nazareth. God knew from the beginning the census would occur, and Jesus' earthly family would be required to travel to Bethlehem. He knew Jesus would be born while they were still there.

God knew the details of Jesus' birth from the beginning, and he knows the details of our lives too. He knew where each of us would be born, and he knows where we live now. He knows how all the details of our lives will work together to fulfill his plan. Mary and Joseph trusted God's plan, and we can too.

Quiz Time

re you willing to have someone like Elizabeth in your life to help guide you? Read each sentence below. Circle A for always, S for sometimes, or N for never.

1. When I have a problem, I talk to a trusted adult.

   A S N

2. I ask for advice when I need it.

   A S N

3. If someone gives me unasked-for advice or criticism, I consider whether it's true and then make needed changes.

   A S N

4. I have someone in my life I can pray with, or I would be willing to have someone like that.

   A S N

5. I try to learn all I can from the mature women in my church, home, or community.

   A S N

Give yourself 2 points for every A, 1 point for every S, and 0 points for every N.

8-10 points: You realize it's important to have someone like Elizabeth in your life to offer advice and guide you. You welcome helpful suggestions and try to learn from others. You have a teachable spirit, just as Mary did.

4-7 points: You don't regularly seek out advice from others but you might listen if they offer you suggestions. You may prefer to talk about your problems to friends your age rather than mature adult Christians. Don't overlook Sunday school teachers or youth leaders as a source of encouragement and wisdom.

0-3 points: You deal with your problems on your own. You often miss out on good advice others might offer because you aren't open to their suggestions. There is much you can learn from older and wiser Christians. Find one you feel comfortable talking to when you need advice or help.

thinking it through

How does Mary's second journey compare to the first? Do you think her feelings about the trip were the same or different? What might have been Mary's biggest challenges?

Can you think of a situation in your life that seemed like bad timing? Even if you're still waiting to learn God's purpose for those events, you can be sure that he will use them for good in your life. Ask him to help you trust his plans.

Mary: Traveling

[Joseph] went there to register with Mary, who was pledged to be married to him and was expecting a child.

LUKE 2:5, NIV

Mary had already made a trip to see Elizabeth in the hills of Judea. Now she was making another long journey, and this time she was very pregnant. It wasn't long until the baby would be born, but there was no choice about traveling to Joseph's hometown for the census. It was required.

There were probably a lot of preparations for the trip. Mary may have baked bread or dried meat. Water needed to be stored. Mary may have realized she could have the baby while in Bethlehem and packed the things she would need for her newborn.

The journey from Nazareth to Bethlehem was ninety miles. Mary probably rode on a donkey and perhaps walked when she needed a change of position. Neither may have been comfortable this late in her pregnancy. During the long hours of travel, Joseph and Mary perhaps shared their dreams of a life raising Jesus. He would learn carpentry at Joseph's side. He would be trained in the Scriptures and God's laws.

The roads were dusty and crowded as many travelers made their way to Bethlehem to be counted. The inns were full, and there wasn't a room to be found anywhere. Knowing the baby was close to being born, Joseph must have pleaded with innkeepers to give them a place to stay until one finally said he could have shelter in the stable with the animals. At this point, Mary and Joseph were probably grateful to have any shelter at all. Joseph quickly got Mary settled as comfortably as possible as they anxiously awaited the birth of their firstborn.

It must have seemed like terrible timing to have to travel to Bethlehem just when Mary's baby was due. Yet this wasn't a mistake—it was an important part of God's plan. When things seem difficult or even impossible for us, God has them under control.

Mary: The Savior Is Born

She gave birth to her firstborn, a son. She wrapped him in cloths and placed him in a manger, because there was no room for them in the inn.

LUKE 2:7, NIV

The time had come. The long-awaited Messiah was born in a stable in Bethlehem, because all the inns were full. Jesus' arrival wasn't a grand birth into a noble or rich family. Just young Mary and Joseph the carpenter were there, alone in a stable. The only eyewitnesses to the birth were the barn animals that may have been present. But this is how God planned it from the beginning. Second Corinthians 8:9 says, "Though he was rich, yet for your sakes he became poor, so that by his poverty he could make you rich." Jesus chose to give up his heavenly riches to come to earth for you. He didn't come to save just the rich or famous but the everyday people who work hard to make ends meet.

God often works through the lowly things of life to accomplish his will. First Corinthians 1:27 says, "God chose the foolish things of the world to shame the wise" (NIV). God chooses the weak and lowly because they know they need him. The rich and powerful may take credit for their own successes rather than acknowledging God's work in their lives.

We are encouraged to have the same attitude Jesus had on earth, that of a servant. Philippians 2:5-8 says, "You must have the same attitude that Christ Jesus had. Though he was God, he did not think of equality with God as something to cling to. Instead, he gave up his divine privileges. . . . He humbled himself in obedience to God and died a criminal's death on a cross."

Jesus, God's own Son, came to earth through a lowly birth and lived a servant's life in order to be the sacrifice for our sins. He didn't set himself up as an earthly king with great riches. He became part of Mary and Joseph's family because they were willing to lay aside their own plans and expectations to live out God's will.

thinking it through

Reread Philippians 2:5-8 (these verses are included in today's devo). What does it mean to have the same attitude that Jesus had? What could that look like in your life?

thinking it through

How do you think the shepherds felt when the angels appeared to them? How do you think Mary felt when the shepherds arrived?

Each person has to decide for himself or herself whether to believe that Jesus is the Son of God who died for all our sins. Do you believe that Jesus is the Savior?

Mary: The Angel Choir and the Shepherds

Suddenly, the angel was joined by a vast host of others—the armies of heaven—praising God and saying, "Glory to God in highest heaven, and peace on earth to those with whom God is pleased."

LUKE 2:13-14

Even though Mary gave birth to Jesus in a stable and placed him in a manger, his birth didn't go unnoticed. God sent a heavenly choir to announce the birth to shepherds in a nearby field. Just as God chose a lowly birth for his Son, he chose to announce the birth to shepherds, not kings or nobility.

Can you imagine the scene? Just like on any other night, the shepherds were out with their sheep, talking or just quietly watching the herd, when an angel suddenly appeared, and the night was bright with heavenly light. The shepherds were terrified. But then the angel spoke to them, telling them not to be afraid but to go find the Savior in Bethlehem, lying in a manger.

More angels appeared, proclaiming Jesus' birth. Then they returned to heaven, and all was dark and quiet again. The shepherds were astounded by all that had taken place in just a few minutes' time. They hurried to town and found baby Jesus just as the angels had said.

Now imagine what it must have been like for Mary, quietly taking care of her infant son in the stable, when some shepherds rushed in looking for the Messiah. After all that had happened to her, she probably wasn't surprised by their story of an angel choir, but it was another example of how different and special it was to be Jesus' mother. As the shepherds spread the news throughout the town, "Mary kept all these things in her heart and thought about them often" (Luke 2:19).

The shepherds were the first to see the Messiah, and they were changed by their encounter with the angels and the baby. Mary's life continued to change by becoming the mother of the Savior. Two thousand years later people are still changed by an encounter with Jesus.

Mary: Simeon's Prophecy

Simeon blessed them, and he said to Mary, the baby's mother, "This child is destined to cause many in Israel to fall, but he will be a joy to many others. He has been sent as a sign from God, but many will oppose him. As a result, the deepest thoughts of many hearts will be revealed. And a sword will pierce your very soul."

LUKE 2:34-35

Simeon was an elderly, righteous man who was eagerly awaiting the coming of the Messiah. God had revealed to him that he wouldn't die until he'd seen the Savior. One day God urged him to go to the Temple. It was the same day that Joseph and Mary took Jesus to the Temple to present him as the law required. Simeon recognized Jesus as the Messiah and took him in his arms. He praised God, and then he said something that must have caused Mary concern: "A sword will pierce your very soul."

Mary knew that nothing could happen to Jesus that his heavenly Father didn't allow, but God hadn't told her what Jesus' future held. Simeon, under God's direction, opened Mary's eyes to some of the suffering Jesus would face when he declared that "many will oppose him."

At this time, Mary didn't know that many would despise Jesus, or that an angry mob would nail her son to a cross and she'd watch as he died. Even as a sword pierced Jesus' side, pain would pierce Mary's heart. As she stood at the foot of the cross, did Mary think of Simeon's prophecy given over thirty years earlier?

Jesus chose to die for our sins so we can spend eternity in heaven, but the joy of salvation and the pain of the Cross are inseparable. Mary watched in agony as Jesus died, but joy came to her later as she learned that he had risen from the dead.

When the angel first gave Mary the news that God had chosen her, she knew it wasn't going to be an easy life, but she agreed to it, not knowing what was ahead. And because of that she had a privilege no one else has ever had—to be the earthly mother of our Lord.

thinking it through

How do you think Mary felt when Simeon made his prophecy? What might she have thought he meant?

You probably won't hear a prophecy about suffering you'll face in the future, but you can be sure that God will bring joy to your life no matter what sorrow you have to face.

thinking it through

In which of the ways below can you worship God this week?

- Sing or listen to praise music.
- Participate in a church choir.
- Read Scripture.
- Write prayers or psalms of praise in a journal.
- Make a list of people in your life to praise God for.
- Do a good deed in Jesus' name to show your love for him.

Mary: The Gifts

They entered the house and saw the child with his mother, Mary, and they bowed down and worshiped him. Then they opened their treasure chests and gave him gifts of gold, frankincense, and myrrh.

MATTHEW 2:11

Wise men, or magi, from the east were among Jesus' early visitors. The wise men brought gifts of gold, frankincense, and myrrh to the holy family. Why were these particular gifts given to Jesus? People have made guesses over the years. Some say that those gifts were commonly given to a king in those days. Gold was a valuable metal, frankincense was used to make perfume, and myrrh was an anointing oil.

Other people say that the gifts were prophetic. Gold was a symbol of royalty, frankincense was a symbol of priesthood, and myrrh, sometimes used as an embalming oil, was a symbol of death. Some people believe the gifts were symbolic, with gold representing virtue; frankincense, prayer; and myrrh, suffering.

Why the magi brought these gifts isn't nearly as important as why they came, and that was to worship Jesus. They had seen a special star in the sky and knew it meant that a special king had been born. God used the star to guide them to Jesus, and when they finally found him, they bowed and worshiped him.

Mary was with Jesus when the wise men arrived. We aren't told what her response was; perhaps she was surprised that these wealthy nobles had come to visit her lowly family. Or maybe having seen others worship and prophesy about her son had prepared Mary for these distinguished guests. Either way, it was an honor the young king deserved.

The wise men brought gifts with special significance to Jesus, and they worshiped him. It's important to take time to do both of those things today and over the next couple of months as you celebrate the holiday season. Gifts don't have to cost money to be significant. You can give the gifts of your time and talents. And God especially wants your worship.

Mary: Journey to Safety

After the wise men were gone, an angel of the Lord appeared to Joseph in a dream. "Get up! Flee to Egypt with the child and his mother," the angel said. "Stay there until I tell you to return, because Herod is going to search for the child to kill him."

MATTHEW 2:13

This is the third time an angel appeared to Mary or Joseph concerning Jesus. And it is the third journey for Mary since finding out she would be the earthly mother of the Messiah. God put a special star in the sky to alert the wise men that the new King had been born. They traveled a long distance and then stopped to ask King Herod where to find the new King. This made King Herod angry and jealous. God warned the wise men in a dream not to return to Herod, so they went home a different way. When the king realized the wise men were not going to return to tell him where to find the young King, he became even angrier. He decided to kill all the baby boys in Bethlehem who were the right age to be the child the wise men had inquired about.

Sadness and grieving filled the land as families lost their precious sons, but the Messiah was safe in Egypt. The holy family stayed there until Herod died. Then they returned to Nazareth.

Mary must have been a very courageous young woman to handle all that happened to her in such a short amount of time. She was a young virgin chosen to give birth to the Messiah. She made a long journey just when her baby was due, delivered her infant in a stable, and then had to flee to Egypt. Mary wasn't alone, though. Joseph was with her, and God knew Joseph would take good care of Mary and baby Jesus. God himself was also with Mary, giving her the strength and courage to face the things she encountered.

When God gives someone a job to do, he gives her people who can guide and help her, and he is with her too.

thinking it through

The Christmas story focuses mostly on Mary, but Joseph also had an important role. How do you think Joseph felt about being chosen to be Jesus' earthly father and taking care of both Mary and Jesus?

In difficult times, how have you seen God guiding you? Are there special people in your life who have helped you?

thinking it through

Ephesians 6:1-3 says, "Children, obey your parents because you belong to the Lord, for this is the right thing to do. 'Honor your father and mother.' This is the first commandment with a promise: If you honor your father and mother, 'things will go well for you, and you will have a long life on the earth.'" How well do you follow these instructions? What does the verse say will happen when you obey your parents?

Mary: At the Temple

His parents didn't know what to think. "Son," his mother said to him, "why have you done this to us? Your father and I have been frantic, searching for you everywhere."

LUKE 2:48

When Jesus was twelve, Mary and Joseph made the long journey to Jerusalem for the Passover festival as they did each year. People normally traveled in large groups for safety, so Mary, Joseph, and Jesus would have been part of a throng of people on the road, some on foot and some on donkeys. After the festival, Mary and Joseph journeyed with the group on the way home. When they stopped for the night, they realized that Jesus wasn't with them or among the other travelers.

Mary and Joseph turned back to Jerusalem to search for Jesus. They finally found him at the Temple, talking with the religious teachers, who were amazed at his knowledge and understanding. Mary, like any mother, expressed the anguish she and Joseph had felt as they searched for him.

Jesus answered, "But why did you need to search? . . . Didn't you know that I must be in my Father's house?" (Luke 2:49). Jesus wasn't being disrespectful; he had been caught up in learning, discussing religious matters, and asking questions. Jesus expected his parents to know he'd be at the Temple.

Luke 2:51 says, "Then he returned to Nazareth with them and was obedient to them." Even though Jesus was the Son of God, Mary was his earthly mother, and he was obedient to her and Joseph all through his childhood years. Being obedient to his earthly mother was part of being obedient to God. Mary may not have always made the best choices, but she did the best she could to guide her Son in the right path.

Families are important, and God is in charge of choosing the right parents for each child. Parents aren't always perfect, but God still requires obedience. Even his own Son was obedient to earthly parents. It's good to follow Jesus' example in this.

Quiz Time

How well do you obey? Read each question below, and circle A for always, S for sometimes, or N for never.

1. I obey the first time I'm told to do something.

   A S N

2. I follow my parents' rules even if they won't know the difference.

   A S N

3. I accept my parents' decisions even if I don't agree.

   A S N

4. If I disagree with a rule, I talk it out respectfully with my parents.

   A S N

Give yourself 2 points for every A, 1 point for S, and 0 points for every N.

6-8 points: You do a good job of obeying your parents. God is pleased with this.

3-5 points: You try to obey, but there is room for improvement. Be sure to obey the first time you're asked to do something.

0-2 points: You need to work on obedience. Jesus obeyed his earthly parents even though he was the Son of God.

Mary: Pondering

Mary treasured up all these things and pondered them in her heart.

LUKE 2:19, NIV

Have you ever been in a situation where someone said or did something, and you played it over and over in your mind? You could still hear every word, and you replayed your reactions and response. You might have wished you'd said or done something different, or you might have been glad you walked away without saying anything.

Mary, mother of Jesus, must have had lots of memories like that—when the angel told her she'd been chosen to give birth to Jesus, when the shepherds arrived and said they'd seen a choir of angels announcing Jesus' birth, when Simeon prophesied that a sword would pierce her soul, when Jesus stayed behind in the Temple, and many more times during Jesus' life.

Mary was a human mother raising the Son of God. There was no way to prepare for the job, and there was no way to know what was coming. But Mary had a genuine desire to understand all that being mother to the Son of God meant. She wanted to understand why he'd come to earth and what his mission was. She wanted to know how God could become man and how he'd provide salvation. God hadn't told her these things ahead of time. God showed her only pieces of his plan for her day by day.

In just about a month, the world will start preparing to celebrate the Savior's birth. Some do it in very holy ways by focusing on Jesus during the holiday season, and others ignore the true meaning of Christmas and get caught up in gifts and parties. As the season approaches, be like Mary and ponder Jesus in your heart. Think about what it meant for Mary to give birth to Jesus and what it means to you that Jesus lived on earth and died for you.

thinking it through

Make it a point to set aside time between now and Christmas to think about what Christmas really means. Write down your observations, or pretend you are Mary and write it from her point of view.

Mary: Mary's Role Changes

The wine supply ran out during the festivities, so Jesus' mother told him, "They have no more wine."
JOHN 2:3

Mary and Jesus were at a wedding in Cana of Galilee when the host ran out of wine. Mary knew that Jesus could solve the problem, even though he hadn't yet performed a miracle, so she went and found him.

Jesus responded, "Dear woman, that's not our problem. . . . My time has not yet come" (John 2:4). Jesus was addressing her as a woman, not his mother. He was pointing out that she had no control over his mission on earth. He had to pull away from her and become involved in the purpose for which he'd come to earth: the work of salvation.

Jesus went ahead and performed the miracle of turning water into wine. This may be what he had planned all along, but it had to be his choice and his decision.

Mary isn't included in Scripture much after this miracle, which launched Jesus' earthly ministry. One other story is recorded, when Jesus was very busy, and his mother and brothers were concerned for him. When someone told him that his mother and brothers were outside wanting to speak with him, he answered, "Who is my mother? Who are my brothers? . . . Anyone who does God's will is my brother and sister and mother" (Mark 3:33, 35). Again Jesus was pointing out that his earthly family could not control his heavenly mission.

Mary must have realized her relationship with Jesus had changed. For the most part, her involvement in his life was over. She could only support him with love and prayer. He now had to do what he'd been sent to do.

As you grow up, your relationship with your parents changes too. The older you get, the less dependent you will be on your parents. But you should always respect them and receive their support.

thinking it through

Mary's job of being Jesus' earthly mother was pretty much over. Jesus' focus now was on his ministry. How do you think Mary felt about that? How had Mary's relationship with her son changed?

How has your relationship with your parents changed as you've gotten older? How can you continue to show them love and respect as you gain more freedom?

thinking it through

Why do you think it was important that Mary acknowledged Jesus as her Savior, not her son? Do you think it was harder or easier for Mary to acknowledge Jesus as her Savior after having raised him?

How can you acknowledge Jesus as your Savior?

Mary: Responding to the Savior

When Jesus saw his mother standing there beside the disciple he loved, he said to her, "Dear woman, here is your son." And he said to this disciple, "Here is your mother." And from then on this disciple took her into his home.

JOHN 19:26-27

Mary no longer filled the role of Jesus' earthly mother. He didn't need to be cared for, and he had a mission to fulfill. Mary had become a devoted disciple of Jesus during the years he traveled around preaching and performing miracles. Then came the day Jesus was crucified. Mary had probably heard Jesus speak of his own death. Throughout his whole life she'd known he'd come to be the Savior of the world.

Mary stood near the cross as Jesus was crucified. His last act of being her earthly son was when he looked on her and gave her to John. Jesus knew John would care for her the rest of her life. Mary was chosen to be the earthly mother of Jesus, but he was dying in order to be her Savior and Lord.

There is only one more mention of Mary in the Bible after that. She is listed as being with the early believers who met together for prayer in Acts 1:14.

In some ways Mary had a joyful and rich life, but in other ways it was filled with pain and sorrow. She had the privilege of raising Jesus until adulthood. She must have had the same pride as any other mother when Jesus took his first step or said his first word. At the same time she knew this was no ordinary child that she was raising. She knew he was the Savior, but she didn't know how the plan would play out. She must have been filled with grief as she watched him die on the cross, but then she rejoiced with the news that he'd risen from the dead. She acknowledged him as her Savior along with the other early believers.

Mary holds a special place of honor as mother of the Savior. And just as she said in her song of praise, people still call her blessed.

Anna: Devoted to God

[Anna] lived as a widow to the age of eighty-four. She never left the Temple but stayed there day and night, worshiping God with fasting and prayer.

LUKE 2:37

There are only three verses mentioning Anna in the Bible, but those verses say a lot about her. Her name means "gracious," and that is a good word to describe her. Her life was filled with grace.

Anna was married, but her husband died after only seven years of marriage. Anna was still young at the time, but she never remarried. Instead, she dedicated herself to fasting and prayer. At the age of eighty-four, Anna had a lifetime of devotion to God behind her.

Anna was constantly at the Temple. Some people believe she actually lived on the Temple grounds or that she may have been a caretaker at one time. Others believe she lived nearby and spent most of her time at the Temple. Either way, she was dedicated to God and his laws.

Some people are Sunday-morning Christians. They attend church and may even put a little money in the offering plate. That's the extent of their involvement in spiritual things until the next Sunday. Others may go to church again on Sunday or Wednesday night but keep their faith separate from their everyday lives. Others are fully committed to God. Their faith spills over into everything else they do. They seek to honor God in every decision they make.

How about you? Do you go willingly when it is time to attend church? Are you so dedicated to learning about God that you eagerly look forward to hearing the sermon or Sunday school lesson? Do you take your faith out of the church door with you, or do you leave it parked there until next Sunday? You can't be like Anna in spending all your time at church, but you can be like her in seeking God above all else. And don't stop with church attendance; make God part of everything you do during the week.

thinking it through

How does your willingness to take part in church activities reflect your devotion to God? Is your faith for Sunday only, or is it a part of all you do?

Anna: Recognizing the Savior

She came along just as Simeon was talking with Mary and Joseph, and she began praising God. She talked about the child to everyone who had been waiting expectantly for God to rescue Jerusalem.

LUKE 2:38

Anna spent so much time in the Temple that she probably already knew Simeon. She was there when Simeon took baby Jesus into his arms and made his prophecy concerning the child. She had been waiting for the Messiah and looking forward to his coming for so long that she immediately recognized the baby. Perhaps God allowed her to know the Messiah on sight because she had been faithful to God for so many years.

Few people actually recognized Jesus as the Messiah because most were looking for some great political or military leader. They expected him to set up a grand earthly kingdom. But instead of arriving with great pageantry, he was born in a stable. Only the shepherds, magi, Simeon, and Anna truly recognized Jesus for who he was. They were all waiting for his appearance or were actively seeking him.

After seeing the Messiah face-to-face, Anna praised God. This wasn't a onetime thing where she said a brief prayer of thanksgiving. Anna continually praised God for sending the Messiah. What's more, she went out and began telling everyone that she'd seen him. She kept this up until her death.

Anna was continually in the Temple, praying. God allowed her to recognize the Messiah. She told everyone she could about him. Many people today still don't accept Jesus as the Son of God. They don't believe he is the Savior, even though he reveals himself in Scripture and in nature to those who truly want to find him.

thinking it through

Jeremiah 29:13 says, "If you look for me wholeheartedly, you will find me." How can you seek God wholeheartedly today?

What does it mean to continually praise God? Today, think of one thing you can praise God for, and try to praise him for it all day long.

Samaritan Woman: Jesus Sees Our Needs

A Samaritan woman came to draw water, and Jesus said to her, "Please give me a drink."

JOHN 4:7

One day Jesus was traveling with his disciples, and they stopped along the road in Samaria. The road through Samaria was the shortest and most direct route to travel from Jerusalem to Galilee, but many people avoided it. The Jews did not associate with the Samaritans because they were a mixed race. The few Jews from the northern kingdom who weren't taken captive had intermarried with pagans, and they became the Samaritans. Jesus was above racial prejudice, so he chose to travel through Samaria.

Jesus sat by Jacob's well resting while his disciples went into town to find food. A woman came to draw water. Most women drew their water early in the morning or in the evening when it was cooler. This nameless woman may have chosen to come at noontime to avoid the other women, who probably gossiped about her sinful lifestyle.

When she arrived at the well, Jesus spoke to her and asked for water. This surprised the woman. She recognized him as a Jew by both his clothing and his speech.

Jesus told her, "If you only knew the gift God has for you and who you are speaking to, you would ask me, and I would give you living water" (John 4:10). Jesus meant he could fill the inner longing in her heart. He saw her true need—forgiveness and a cleansed heart.

It may seem like this was a chance encounter between Jesus and the Samaritan woman at a time when no one else was at the well, but more likely it was a God encounter. God knows all things, and he knew this woman needed to hear the message Jesus gave her. God brought the woman to the well at just the right time.

Jesus saw the Samaritan woman's need for forgiveness. He sees your needs and is able to meet them just as he did for the woman at the well.

thinking it through

Jesus talked with the Samaritan woman one-on-one. He discussed her personal need for living water. What one person can you reach out to this week to share God's love?

thinking it through

Jesus sees your heart. What does he see in it? A need for forgiveness? A need for love or acceptance? Cut out a paper heart. Then write your needs on it. Keep it as a reminder that Jesus knows your needs, and ask him to meet those needs.

Samaritan Woman: Jesus Sees Our Hearts

"Go and get your husband," Jesus told her. "I don't have a husband," the woman replied. Jesus said, "You're right! You don't have a husband—for you have had five husbands, and you aren't even married to the man you're living with now. You certainly spoke the truth!"

JOHN 4:16-18

The day had started out like any other. The woman probably prepared breakfast for herself and the man who lived with her. She did her morning chores. Then around noon she decided to go to the well. She expected to fill her water jug and return home to her normal routine.

When the woman reached the well, a man was resting there. He spoke to her, and that's when everything changed. This man not only promised her water that would quench her thirst forever, but he knew all about her. He knew her sin, yet he still spoke to her. The woman was probably used to being gossiped about or called names. She may have expected the same from Jesus, but that wasn't his style.

Jesus knew she didn't have a husband, yet he told her to go get her husband. He was testing her to see what she would say. Jesus knew her heart. He knew her sin. Best of all, he alone had the cure for her sin.

The conversation continued, and the woman said she knew the Messiah would come. He would explain everything they needed to know. Then Jesus did something he didn't normally do. He told her, "I AM the Messiah!" (John 4:26). Jesus didn't often declare himself to be the Messiah, so he must have thought this woman needed to be told outright. Perhaps it was the final step in opening her eyes to her need for forgiveness. And because he was the Messiah he was able to offer her that forgiveness.

Jesus sees your heart and knows your needs. If you haven't accepted his gift of forgiveness, don't put it off. Talk to someone about it today.

Puzzle Page

On October 19, we learned that Anna recognized baby Jesus as the Savior because she had been seeking him for years. Solve the Balloon Puzzle below to find out what will happen when we seek God.

Directions: Each balloon has both a scrambled word and a number in it. There are also numbers next to the blank lines in the verse. Look at the number next to the blank. Find the balloon with the same number. Unscramble the word in that balloon, and write it on the line. Check your answers at the bottom.

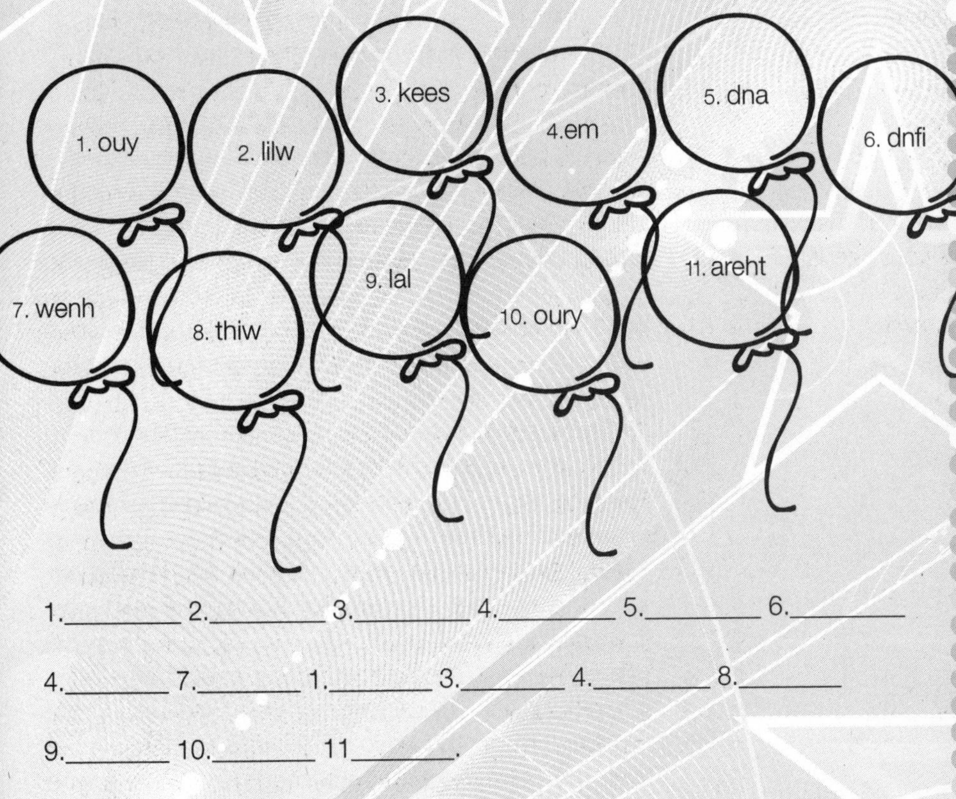

1.________ 2.________ 3.________ 4.________ 5.________ 6.________

4.________ 7.________ 1.________ 3.________ 4.________ 8.________

9.________ 10.________ 11________.

Answer: You will seek me and find me when you seek me with all your heart. (Jeremiah 29:13, NIV)

thinking it through

If Jesus were here today, who do you think he'd reach out to? Where would he hang out? How can you and your family do the same?

Samaritan Woman: Clueless

His disciples came back. They were shocked to find him talking to a woman, but none of them had the nerve to ask, "What do you want with her?" or "Why are you talking to her?"

JOHN 4:27

The disciples were Jesus' followers on earth. They traveled with him, ate with him, and spent almost all their time with him, but they often didn't understand him. They didn't grasp why he did the things he did. Jesus came to save sinners, but the disciples had their own ideas about who Jesus should talk to.

We don't know how many of the disciples were with Jesus in Samaria or even if they were the twelve closest disciples Jesus chose. But when they found Jesus talking to the woman at the well, they were surprised because Jesus was talking with a woman, and in that time men didn't often talk to women in public. The woman was also a Samaritan, and the Jews didn't have anything to do with Samaritans. Finally, the woman was a sinner.

Throughout his ministry, Jesus reached out to those who needed him most. He helped the blind, the crippled, those with leprosy, widows, and children. He dined with sinners—much to the dismay of the religious leaders. Jesus knew these people needed not only physical healing or help but also spiritual guidance.

Jesus was often criticized—sometimes even by his disciples—for talking to the wrong people or healing people considered outcasts, but this didn't bother him. He didn't follow the world's guidelines for hanging out with the right people. He reached out to those who needed him most.

Today, some people are still clueless. They will minister to those in fancy churches but wouldn't think of reaching out to the homeless man on the street. They sing in the choir and serve on committees, but you won't catch them serving in a soup kitchen. Yet it's to the people often considered outcasts that Jesus ministered, and we can follow his steps in that.

Samaritan Woman: Bringing Others to Jesus

The woman left her water jar beside the well and ran back to the village, telling everyone, "Come and see a man who told me everything I ever did! Could he possibly be the Messiah?"

JOHN 4:28-29

Jesus revealed to the woman at the well that he was the Messiah. The woman left her water jar there and ran back to the village with the news. Most of the people knew her story and normally shunned her. They were probably astonished to see her running to the village, talking excitedly about a Jewish man she'd met at the well.

The woman's excitement was contagious, and the people flocked to the well to meet Jesus. There isn't a record of what Jesus said to the people, but we can assume that he spoke to them of God and the laws they already knew. He probably shared the same things with them that he'd shared with the woman about salvation and worshiping God. The people may have been filled with questions, and Jesus would have patiently answered them. The Samaritans were so open to the gospel that Jesus stayed for two days talking to them.

Many of the people in the Samaritan village of Sychar believed in Jesus during those two days. The entire village was changed by Jesus' visit, and it began with a woman considered an outcast by her neighbors. She was probably the least likely prospect to become a believer in Jesus, yet she is the one Jesus approached. Her heart was receptive to the message, perhaps because she realized she was a sinner and in need of a Savior. If Jesus had approached a more religious person, he or she may not have seen the need for a Savior.

When we share the gospel, we often avoid people who look less open to the gospel. We shy away from people with lots of piercings and tattoos or who look like they would never talk to us. Yet it may be the tough girl who most needs to hear Jesus' message.

thinking it through

Why do you think Jesus chose to talk to the woman at the well out of all the people in the town?

Is there a student or neighbor you've avoided who needs to hear the gospel message? How can you approach her?

thinking it through

The Samaritan woman was a witness for Jesus to the other villagers. We are called to be witnesses too. What is your job as a witness for Jesus? How can you tell others about Jesus this week?

Samaritan Woman: Changed Lives

They said to the woman, "Now we believe, not just because of what you told us, but because we have heard him ourselves. Now we know that he is indeed the Savior of the world."

JOHN 4:42

Jesus approached the Samaritan woman, and she realized that he was the Messiah. She believed in him and then brought the other villagers to hear him too. The people first went to the well with the woman out of curiosity. They could see that she was a changed person. She was excited and told them she'd found the Messiah. They had to see him for themselves.

The woman brought the people to Jesus, but it was Jesus himself who caused them to believe. They heard his words and realized he spoke with wisdom and authority. This was no ordinary prophet or rabbi; he was the Son of God, the promised Messiah.

Maybe you bring people to Jesus just as the Samaritan woman did. You might invite them to church or a special youth activity or concert. You might share your story with them by telling them how you first met Jesus, just as the woman did. Those things are good. God wants you to be a witness for him. But it is God himself who does the work of salvation. When you share the gospel or take a classmate to church where she hears the salvation message, God's Spirit works in her heart. She either responds to God and accepts his gift of salvation, or she doesn't.

The village people told the Samaritan woman that they'd gone to see Jesus because of what she said, but they believed in him because of the things he said to them. When you share the gospel, it is like planting a seed. Someone else may share more with that person, and that is like watering the seed. But only God can cause it to grow.

Peter's Mother-in-Law: Expressing Gratitude to Jesus

When Jesus arrived at Peter's house, Peter's mother-in-law was sick in bed with a high fever. But when Jesus touched her hand, the fever left her. Then she got up and prepared a meal for him.

MATTHEW 8:14-15

Peter's mother-in-law moved into Peter's house when her husband died. She was a gracious woman who encouraged Peter in his ministry, and many people loved her. Peter, his brother Andrew, Jesus, and the other disciples who visited Peter's home were blessed by his mother-in-law's welcoming ways. That's why everyone was concerned when she had a high fever and was unable to leave her bed.

Peter told Jesus about her, and Jesus went to Peter's house. He touched the woman's hand, and she was healed instantly. What did she do next? She went to the kitchen and prepared a meal for Jesus. She showed her gratitude by serving and being hospitable.

Jesus healed many other people. Some openly praised him, but others were like the ten lepers he healed, who went on their way with only one turning back to thank Jesus. Peter's mother-in-law chose to show her gratitude by serving Jesus and meeting his need for nourishment.

Jesus isn't with us physically anymore, but he still hears prayers for healing and answers them. He also answers prayers for safety, peace, and more. How do you show your gratitude to Jesus for the things he's done for you? You can't prepare him a meal like Peter's mother-in-law did, but you can show your thankfulness by reaching out to someone else in Jesus' name. You might donate outgrown clothing to the homeless shelter or help collect canned goods for the food bank. You might mow the lawn for an elderly church member or babysit for a busy mom. You can also thank Jesus by reading a psalm of thanksgiving to the Lord or writing a prayer of thankfulness in a journal.

Peter's mother-in-law immediately expressed her gratitude to Jesus. Let's do the same this week.

thinking it through

What is one way you can show Jesus you are thankful for the things he's done for you? Try to do that this week.

thinking it through

Why do you think Jesus met the woman's need without being asked? What need do you have that you'd like Jesus to take care of?

Widow of Nain: Jesus' Compassion

When the Lord saw her, his heart overflowed with compassion. "Don't cry!" he said.

LUKE 7:13

A woman was in despair. First her husband had died, leaving her alone with her son. Then her son had died. She faced a bleak future with no one to care for her. Jesus and his followers were passing by as the funeral procession took place. The woman didn't call out to him. Perhaps she didn't notice Jesus or know who he was. And at that time, people didn't realize he had the power to raise the dead.

Jesus saw the woman, and he was filled with compassion—not for the son who was already dead but for the woman who had no one left to care for her. Jesus touched the coffin and said, "Young man . . . , I tell you, get up" (Luke 7:14).

The boy sat up and began to talk. Can you imagine the shock of those in the funeral procession? They were in the midst of grieving, and then with a few simple words Jesus caused the boy to live again. They wondered who this man was who could bring the dead to life. Then they praised God, saying that Jesus was a mighty prophet sent to them by God.

We aren't told the widow's reaction to this, but her heart must have been filled with joy when she saw her son sit up and begin to talk. There was no more need to grieve, because she was no longer alone. The woman was probably one of Jesus' followers from that day on because of the gift he'd given her. Her life was forever changed by his compassion, and every time she saw her son she would have been reminded of it.

Jesus still looks with compassion on people. He still sees people's needs and often meets them without being asked. He is still a God who cares.

Woman Who Anointed Jesus: Expressing Repentance and Faith

She knelt behind him at his feet, weeping. Her tears fell on his feet, and she wiped them off with her hair. Then she kept kissing his feet and putting perfume on them.

LUKE 7:38

Do you remember the story of the Samaritan woman Jesus talked to at the well (from October 20–24)? That woman and this one were alike in some ways and different in others. They were alike in that they were both looked down on as being sinners. The Samaritan woman had been married five times, but she wasn't married to the man living with her when she met Jesus. The woman who anointed Jesus was immoral. The Bible doesn't say specifically what she did, but everyone knew she was living a sinful life, and they were surprised to see her enter the house where Simon, a Pharisee, was hosting a banquet. The Pharisees were a group of educated religious people who prided themselves on keeping all the Jewish laws. They looked down on those who didn't.

The woman at the well asked Jesus questions and listened to his answers. The woman who anointed Jesus didn't say a word. She approached Jesus weeping. She knew she was guilty of sin and that he was able to help her. Her tears fell on Jesus' dusty feet, and she wiped his feet with her hair. She kissed his feet and then opened a small alabaster container holding precious perfume and poured it over his feet. Only a small drop was needed for fragrance, but she poured out her whole container.

The Samaritan woman talked with Jesus and went away a believer. The woman who anointed Jesus' feet with perfume showed her repentance and worship by her actions. Both women received forgiveness and went away changed.

How you express your repentance and belief isn't as important as actually believing in Jesus and acknowledging him as your Savior.

thinking it through

How did both women show that they believed in Jesus?

Which woman are you most like—the one who held a conversation with Jesus or the one who showed her repentance and faith by her actions?

thinking it through

If your heart doesn't feel at peace today, there may be something you need to talk to God about. Pray this prayer that the psalmist prayed long ago: "Search me, O God, and know my heart; test me and know my anxious thoughts. Point out anything in me that offends you, and lead me along the path of everlasting life" (Psalm 139:23-24).

Woman Who Anointed Jesus: The Greater Debt

Jesus told him this story: "A man loaned money to two people—500 pieces of silver to one and 50 pieces to the other. But neither of them could repay him, so he kindly forgave them both, canceling their debts. Who do you suppose loved him more after that?"

LUKE 7:41-42

The scene was a dinner at Simon the Pharisee's house. It had taken a surprising turn when a sinful woman washed Jesus' feet with her tears and dried them with her hair before anointing his feet with expensive perfume.

Simon didn't say anything aloud, but he was thinking that if Jesus were really a prophet, he would know the woman was a sinner.

Jesus knew what Simon was thinking and answered his thoughts. He asked Simon a question: A man loaned one person five hundred pieces of silver and another fifty pieces, but neither could repay him. The man canceled both debts. Who would love the man more? Simon correctly chose the man who had the greater debt canceled.

Jesus pointed out that Simon hadn't offered him water to wash his feet when he arrived—a common courtesy because the people wore sandals and walked on dusty roads. The woman had washed Jesus' feet with her tears. Simon hadn't given him a brotherly kiss on the cheek, a common greeting, but the woman had kissed his feet. Simon hadn't anointed his head with some olive oil as was the custom, but the woman had poured costly perfume on his feet.

Jesus told Simon, "Her sins . . . have been forgiven, so she has shown me much love. But a person who is forgiven little shows only little love" (Luke 7:47).

Jesus told the woman, "Your sins are forgiven. . . . Go in peace" (Luke 7:48, 50). Forgiveness and peace go hand in hand. If you try to cover up sin, you won't have peace, but once you confess it to God and ask for his forgiveness, you'll experience peace in your heart.

Puzzle Page

Solve the Telephone Puzzle below to find out how you can be a witness for Jesus.

Directions: This puzzle has two numbers under each line. The first number is for the phone button. Only button numbers 2-9 have letters on them. The second number tells which letter on the button to use. All the buttons except 7 and 9 have three letters on them. Numbers 7 and 9 have four letters. Look under the first line. You see 9.3. That means button #9. Then choose the third letter on that button. That is Y. Write it on the line. Finish the puzzle, and check your answer below.

For ____ ____ ____   ____ ____ ____ to be ____ ____ ____
9.3 6.3 8.2   2.1 7.3 3.2   4.2 4.3 7.4

____ ____ ____ ____ ____ ____ ____, ____ ____ ____ ____ ____ ____ ____
9.1 4.3 8.1 6.2 3.2 7.4 7.4   8.1 3.2 5.3 5.3 4.3 6.2 4.1

____ ____ ____ ____ ____ ____ ____ ____ what you ____ ____ ____ ____
3.2 8.3 3.2 7.3 9.3 6.3 6.2 3.2   4.2 2.1 8.3 3.2

____ ____ ____ ____ and ____ ____ ____ ____ ____.
7.4 3.2 3.2 6.2   4.2 3.2 2.1 7.3 3.1

Paul said that God had called him to be a witness of all he had seen and heard. God wants you to do the same.

Answer: For you are to be his witness, telling everyone what you have seen and heard. (Acts 22:15)

Woman Who Anointed Jesus: Saving Sinners

God loved the world so much that he gave his one and only Son, so that everyone who believes in him will not perish but have eternal life.

JOHN 3:16

Simon the Pharisee was upset when a known sinner, and a woman on top of that, showed up uninvited at his dinner. When Jesus told the woman that her sins were forgiven, all the men asked each other, "Who is this man, that he goes around forgiving sins?" (Luke 7:49). Jesus heard what they said, but he ignored it. The people who most needed a Savior recognized him as the promised Messiah.

The uninvited woman was known as a sinner. She was probably gossiped about, shunned, and treated rudely. The other women may have gone out of their way to avoid her. The woman was an outcast with little hope or happiness. Perhaps someone had told her about Jesus' power to heal the sick, blind, and crippled. Maybe she'd heard his message of love, healing, and forgiveness. Then she heard Jesus would be at Simon's dinner.

Did the woman make plans to enter the dinner uninvited to meet Jesus, or did she plan to just catch a glimpse of him from a distance? We don't know. Maybe she planned only to take a peek or try to hear him speak some words of wisdom. Perhaps she felt drawn to him until she found herself beside him crying tears of repentance at his feet.

And at the feet of Jesus she found forgiveness and healing for her troubled heart. This happened right in front of Simon's eyes, but he was blind to it. All he saw was a sinful woman crashing his party and making an emotional scene. He didn't realize that Jesus was the Son of God, who came to earth to be the Savior of the world.

So few people recognized Jesus for who he was, but this woman did, and she found forgiveness and new life at Simon's dinner party.

thinking it through

If you were to throw a party for Jesus, is there anyone you would be embarrassed to have show up uninvited? How do you think Jesus would respond to that person's presence? The next time you see this person, try to treat him or her the way Jesus would.

Mary Magdalene: A Misunderstood Woman

Among them were Mary Magdalene, from whom he had cast out seven demons.

LUKE 8:2

Mary Magdalene is a woman about whom much wrong information has been given over the years. Some people believe she is the woman who anointed Jesus' feet. They believe this because she is mentioned right after that story in the book of Luke, but Luke was telling two separate stories. In no way was he saying Mary Magdalene was the sinful woman from the earlier story.

Others believe she was the woman caught in adultery, mentioned in John 8 (see November 16), but there is no reason to believe that, either. Since Mary Magdalene was always called by name in the Gospels, it's unlikely she would also be talked about as a nameless woman.

Another belief is that Mary Magdalene and Jesus were secretly married. Although this is totally false, the belief was made popular by books and television shows in past years.

So who was Mary Magdalene? She was a remarkable woman from the fishing village of Magdala, which was on the northwest shore of the Sea of Galilee. Her name was Mary, but the name of her hometown was often added to her name to distinguish her from the other women named Mary in the Bible.

Mary Magdalene was possessed by seven demons. We'll talk more about what that means tomorrow, but for now, it's just important to know she was probably unhappy, shunned by others, and tormented. In general, her life was bleak. Then Jesus came along and changed her life by casting out the demons. Mary was free, and she became a close follower of Jesus.

Mary had been freed, and her life transformed. Because of this she joined the group of women who followed the Lord. Her gratitude showed through her devotion to Jesus.

thinking it through

Do you remember the story about the two debtors that Jesus told Simon the Pharisee? You can read it in the October 28 devo, or in Luke 7:41-47. Jesus' point was that the sinful woman loved him more than Simon did, because she had been forgiven for more. Do you think this story is also true of Mary Magdalene? Why or why not?

How does your commitment to Jesus reflect the debt he has forgiven you of?

thinking it through

Why do you think some people play around with the occult? Why is it dangerous?

In Galatians 5:20, Paul includes sorcery in a list of results that come from following our sinful nature. But then he adds a list of contrasting characteristics that come from following the Spirit: "love, joy, peace, patience, kindness, goodness, faithfulness, gentleness, and self-control" (Galatians 5:22-23). How can you respond with these traits when a friend asks you to join her in playing around with occult practices?

Mary Magdalene: Seven Demons

That evening many demon-possessed people were brought to Jesus. He cast out the evil spirits with a simple command, and he healed all the sick.

MATTHEW 8:16

During Jesus' ministry, he cast demons out of many people. Demons weren't a superstition; they were actual evil spirits that could take over a person's body. They could make the person blind, deaf, or mute, or they could cause people to have seizures. Sometimes the demons spoke through the people they possessed. The Bible refers to demon possession as an affliction, not a sin. Those possessed weren't willing participants. They were victims and became miserable outcasts. Demon possession wasn't a disease or a mental illness that they could be treated for.

Mary Magdalene was possessed by seven demons, and they had complete control of her. There wasn't much hope for her apart from Jesus. When he cast the demons out of her, she recognized Jesus as the Messiah, the Son of God, and became a believer.

People don't talk about demons and evil spirits much in our culture. Most of us haven't encountered anyone possessed by an evil spirit. But Satan and his demons do exist in our world. Do you have to worry about demons and evil spirits? Not if you have God's Spirit in you. God's Spirit and an evil spirit can't exist in the same place, and God's Spirit is stronger than Satan or any of his demons.

Just because you have the Spirit of God doesn't mean it's okay to experiment with the occult and evil spirits. Steer clear of anyone who wants you to try a Ouija board or tarot card reading or take part in a séance. These aren't things to play with, and they don't honor God.

Mary Magdalene chose to honor Jesus. He delivered her from her demons and forgave her sins, and she became one of the women who followed the Messiah the rest of his days on earth.

Mary Magdalene: A Changed Life

He took his twelve disciples with him, along with some women who had been cured of evil spirits and diseases. Among them were Mary Magdalene, from whom he had cast out seven demons; Joanna, the wife of Chuza, Herod's business manager; Susanna; and many others who were contributing from their own resources to support Jesus and his disciples.

LUKE 8:1-3

Sometimes people walk down an aisle at church and pray to accept Jesus as their Savior, but then they return to their old way of life. They keep the same friends, lifestyles, and habits. Little or nothing changes in their lives. Not so with Mary Magdalene. Everything changed for her.

Mary didn't return to her home in Magdala after she met Jesus; she traveled with him and his twelve disciples and some other women. Perhaps Mary felt if she returned home, everyone would remember her as the woman who'd been possessed by demons. They knew her as a wild-eyed, mad woman. Or maybe Mary wanted to stay close to Jesus to make sure the demons didn't return. Or she may have just followed him out of love for her Savior. That love wouldn't let her turn back or return to her old home.

Not only did Mary leave everything behind to follow Jesus, but she helped support his ministry financially. Jesus and the disciples left their jobs behind. They didn't have any worldly possessions. They needed to eat and have a place to stay while they traveled and ministered. Mary willingly gave her money to support the Lord's work.

When you accept Jesus as your Savior, your life changes. Mary's changed more than most since she had been controlled by seven demons, but every person's life should be transformed when he or she meets the Savior. Love and gratitude for salvation moved Mary to support her Lord and to follow him to the end. Love and gratitude for salvation should do the same for each person who calls Jesus his or her Savior.

thinking it through

How has your life been changed by Jesus? True or false:

1. My love for Jesus often motivates me to help others.
2. My Christian values affect the activities and actions I choose.
3. I attend church out of gratitude to Jesus for my salvation.
4. I eagerly read my Bible and pray.

If most of the above statements are true, your faith in Jesus makes a difference in your life.

If most of the above statements are false, let Jesus change your heart, and actively seek to do his will.

Mary Magdalene: The Women Who Followed Jesus

Some women were there, watching from a distance, including Mary Magdalene, Mary (the mother of James the younger and of Joseph), and Salome. They had been followers of Jesus and had cared for him while he was in Galilee. Many other women who had come with him to Jerusalem were also there.

MARK 15:40-41

Mary Magdalene and several other women followed Jesus throughout his ministry. They traveled with him and helped support him financially.

These brave women didn't leave Jesus and return home when things got tough. They remained with Jesus as the religious leaders cried out against him. They stayed nearby as he was sentenced to death. They followed as he made the walk to Calvary, where he was crucified. They were there even after other followers fled.

The women who loved Jesus, many of whom he had healed from illnesses or delivered from bondage to demons, watched for six hours as Jesus hung on the cross and died.

They must have been filled with grief. Jesus had totally changed their lives. They knew who he truly was. They were devoted followers and stood together near the one they loved.

Even after Jesus died and everyone else left, Mary Magdalene and another woman called Mary stayed. They followed as Jesus' body was taken down, prepared for burial, and then laid in a tomb.

Mary Magdalene stayed at Jesus' tomb for as long as she could before having to leave to observe the Sabbath. This must have been the saddest Sabbath she had ever kept. But her sadness would soon be turned to joy.

thinking it through

How do you think the women at the cross felt watching their Messiah be put to death? What might they have talked about during those six hours, or do you think they remained silent?

Do you think you would have stayed with the women at the cross, or would you have been tempted to run away with the other disciples?

Since Jesus has totally changed your life, devote yourself to him today.

Mary Magdalene: Seeing the Risen Lord

The angel spoke to the women. "Don't be afraid!" he said. "I know you are looking for Jesus, who was crucified. He isn't here! He is risen from the dead, just as he said would happen. Come, see where his body was lying."

MATTHEW 28:5-6

The Sabbath was over, and Mary Magdalene, filled with sorrow, made her way to Jesus' tomb along with some other women. What a surprise awaited them there! The large stone covering the entrance was rolled away, and the tomb was empty. The women ran back to Jerusalem and told Peter and John that Jesus had risen. The men raced to the tomb to see for themselves, then left.

Mary Magdalene stayed to grieve. She was crying alone at the tomb when she had a privilege no one else got. She was the first to see the risen Lord. At first, she thought he was the gardener. But when Jesus said her name, she recognized him.

It's interesting that Jesus didn't appear first to some of his twelve disciples or to his own mother. He appeared first to Mary Magdalene, a faithful follower ever since Jesus delivered her from demon possession. Why did she get this privilege? Perhaps because her devotion was greatest. Jesus called the twelve disciples to follow him, and God chose Mary to be his mother, but Mary Magdalene chose to follow Jesus out of love and gratitude.

With one word, her name, "Mary," her world was made right again. Her Savior was alive. Death hadn't conquered him. He'd defeated death and sin.

Jesus called Mary by name, and he calls you by name too. Jesus knows all about you—your needs, your desires, your hopes, and your plans. You can't see him physically as Mary Magdalene did, but you can see his work in your life, hear his voice as he speaks to your heart, and be filled with his peace as you leave your worries with him.

thinking it through

How do you think Mary Magdalene felt when she first saw the empty tomb? How did those feelings change when Jesus spoke her name? Has there been a time when you've been aware of Jesus' presence with you? What does it mean to you that Jesus knows you by name?

thinking it through

We don't have to be evangelists or preachers to share the hope we have in Christ. How can you be ready to explain your hope in Christ to others?

Mary Magdalene: Telling the Good News

Mary Magdalene found the disciples and told them, "I have seen the Lord!" Then she gave them his message.

JOHN 20:18

After Jesus appeared to Mary, he told her to tell his disciples he was going to his Father. Mary took the message to Jesus' followers. She probably repeated the story over and over as each of them questioned her. And she probably continued telling the story of her resurrected Lord for the rest of her life. He'd made such a change in her, and she'd been the first one to see him after he rose from the dead. That was something worth sharing.

When Jesus changes someone's life in such a dramatic way, it's only natural they tell others about it. The Samaritan woman ran and told the townspeople about her meeting with Jesus. She got them to return to the well to hear Jesus for themselves.

Jesus wants us to tell others about our encounter with him too. We don't literally meet him face-to-face as the Samaritan woman and Mary Magdalene did, but in a spiritual sense all of us who claim him as Savior come face-to-face with him, and one day we will see him personally in heaven. In the meantime, he has appointed us to take the gospel to those around us.

Mary Magdalene wasn't a preacher or evangelist; she was just a woman sharing what she'd seen and experienced. That's the best way to share the Good News of salvation. Has Jesus changed your life? Have you experienced his forgiveness? Simply tell others how you met Jesus and how he's changed your life. If you can't think of anything to say, you may not be paying attention to God's work in your life. Keep your testimony fresh as you open yourself to what God wants for you, and grow in your faith by daily reading God's Word, praying, and seeking to follow God's plan. If you do those things, you'll always have something to share with others about the difference Jesus makes in your life.

Puzzle Page

We should always be ready to share our Christian faith, just like Mary Magdalene was. Solve the Balloon Puzzle to find out what the Bible says about sharing our faith.

Directions: Each balloon has both a scrambled word and a number in it. There are also numbers next to the blank lines in the verse. Look at the number next to the blank. Find the balloon with the same number. Unscramble the word in that balloon, and write it on the line. Check your answers at the bottom.

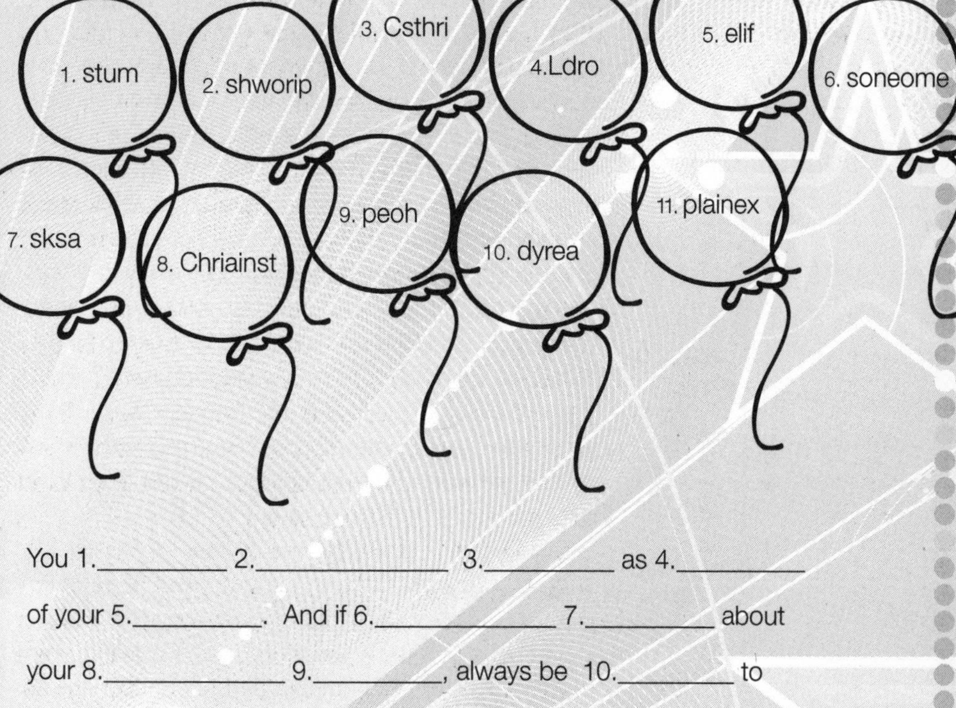

You 1.__________ 2.________________ 3.__________ as 4.__________

of your 5.__________. And if 6.______________ 7.__________ about

your 8.______________ 9.__________, always be 10._________ to

11.______________ it.

Answer: You must worship Christ as Lord of your life. And if someone asks about your Christian hope, always be ready to explain it. (1 Peter 3:15)

thinking it through

In Matthew 10:42, Jesus said, "If you give even a cup of cold water to one of the least of my followers, you will surely be rewarded." What is one way you can reach out to someone in Jesus' name this week?

Mary Magdalene: Lessons from Mary Magdalene

They worshiped together at the Temple each day, met in homes for the Lord's Supper, and shared their meals with great joy and generosity—all the while praising God and enjoying the goodwill of all the people. And each day the Lord added to their fellowship those who were being saved.

ACTS 2:46-47

Jesus' ministry made a big difference in Mary Magdalene's life. After he delivered her from seven demons, her life instantly changed, and she left behind all she knew to follow him.

Mary Magdalene isn't mentioned again after the Resurrection story, but it appears that all the believers stayed together. First they waited together until God sent his Spirit to them. Then they formed a community where they ate together, and all the believers shared what they had with the group. These believers shared a close bond because of their association with Jesus while he was on earth, and new converts were added to the group as the disciples preached the Good News.

What can we learn from Mary Magdalene? First, Jesus is the Son of God, and he is more powerful than any demon—even Satan himself. He delivered Mary from demons, and he also delivers people from their sins.

Second, Jesus changes lives. Whether you decide to believe in Jesus at a young age or after years of living for yourself, God transforms your heart. The change was dramatic in Mary's life because she'd been possessed by demons, but anyone who accepts Jesus as Savior becomes a new person inside.

Third, we should feel love and gratitude to Jesus for saving us, and those feelings should result in living our lives for him. Mary followed Jesus, ministering to him and his disciples, and supported his ministry with her money. We can't minister to Jesus like Mary did, but we can reach out to others in Jesus' name, and we can give part of our money to the church and to others who take the Good News throughout the world.

Joanna: Following Jesus

Among them were Mary Magdalene, from whom he had cast out seven demons; Joanna, the wife of Chuza, Herod's business manager; Susanna; and many others who were contributing from their own resources to support Jesus and his disciples.

LUKE 8:2-3

Joanna had either been healed of a disease or, like Mary Magdalene, had demons cast out by Jesus. She followed Jesus out of a grateful heart, ministering to his needs and those of the disciples.

Joanna was the wife of Chuza, Herod's business manager. Chuza was in charge of Herod's estate. This job required intelligence and discretion. Chuza and Joanna lived in comfort in Herod's palace, yet Joanna chose to follow Christ rather than enjoy her position. She used her wealth to provide for the Lord's needs. Some people believe that Chuza had already died before Joanna met Jesus and that's why she was free to travel with him. If Chuza was still alive, he must have seen that Jesus was important to her and allowed her to travel with the group of women who followed Jesus.

Joanna gave up a comfortable life, either in the palace or in a home provided by money her husband had left her, to travel with Jesus, never knowing where she would be lodging or what she would be eating.

Would you be willing to give up the comfort of your home to follow Jesus, never knowing where you'd travel from day to day? Never knowing what or when you'd next be eating, or where you'd be sleeping? Of course, Jesus no longer lives here on earth in physical form, so you can't travel with him. But as you follow his leading you may find yourself out of your comfort zone on occasion. God may lead you to talk to a student you aren't comfortable talking with or to share the gospel with someone who seems unapproachable. The good news is, you don't have to do it alone. He is always with you and will give you the strength to do what he calls you to do.

thinking it through

What does Jesus require of those who want to follow him? Luke 9:23-24 says, "If any of you wants to be my follower, you must turn from your selfish ways, take up your cross daily, and follow me. If you try to hang on to your life, you will lose it. But if you give up your life for my sake, you will save it." What does it mean to give up your life for Jesus? What could that look like for you?

thinking it through

What does it mean to you to be committed to Jesus? How can you live that out in your daily life?

Susanna: A Life Committed to Jesus

Anyone who wants to be my disciple must follow me, because my servants must be where I am. And the Father will honor anyone who serves me.

JOHN 12:26

All that is known about Susanna is that she was one of the women who was healed by Jesus, and she became part of the group of women who followed him as he traveled. She was with him through his death and resurrection, and she was probably one of the group who stayed together sharing all they had after Jesus went back to heaven.

The Bible says anyone who wants to be Jesus' disciple needs to leave everything behind and follow him. Susanna left her old life and her worldly goods behind. Or perhaps she sold what she had to help support Jesus' ministry before following him, because she is listed among the women who both ministered to Jesus and supported him financially.

Jesus said that following him required commitment. For some people that meant actually following him as he taught; for others it meant supporting him or ministering to him when he was in their town. The same is true today. God wants us to be totally committed to him, but that doesn't mean each believer will leave his or her home and become a missionary in a foreign country. You can be totally committed to God and be a teacher, doctor, or store clerk. There is no limit to the possibilities of where God may call you to serve. The important thing is that you are willing to do whatever it is he calls you to do.

Mary Magdalene, Joanna, and Susanna had the privilege of following Jesus to minister to him and support him while he was on earth. You don't have that privilege, but you do have the ability to serve him with just as much commitment as those women did. The story of your life is still being written. Make sure it is the story of a life committed to Jesus.

Jairus's Daughter: Alive Again

A leader of the local synagogue, whose name was Jairus, arrived. When he saw Jesus, he fell at his feet, pleading fervently with him. "My little daughter is dying," he said. "Please come and lay your hands on her; heal her so she can live."

MARK 5:22-23

Jairus was a ruler in the synagogue, and he was respected among the people. His only daughter was twelve years old, and she was very ill. Jairus had heard how Jesus healed people, so he hurried to Capernaum, where Jesus was, and urged him to come and heal his daughter.

A crowd of people surrounded Jesus as he headed to Jairus's house. As he stopped to speak to a woman, servants came and told Jairus that his daughter had already died. Jesus told Jairus, "Don't be afraid. Just have faith" (Mark 5:36). He left the crowd behind and continued to Jairus's house with only Jairus, Peter, James, and John.

The group arrived at the house to find it filled with people. Mourners were weeping, and musicians had gathered to play funeral music. Jesus asked, "Why all this commotion and weeping? The child isn't dead; she's only asleep" (Mark 5:39). The people laughed at Jesus because the girl was obviously dead. He sent the people outside.

Jesus went to where the girl lay and took her hand. He said, "'*Talitha koum*,' which means 'Little girl, get up!'" (Mark 5:41). The girl got up and began to walk around. She was not only alive again; she was totally healed.

We don't know the girl's name or what her life was like after Jesus healed her, but we can imagine that she realized Jesus was the Messiah and believed in him. It would be hard to experience such a great miracle without being changed by it. Most likely the whole family was transformed by the miracle Jesus performed that day.

thinking it through

Many people came to Jesus because they'd heard he could heal them, and they had nowhere else to turn. They turned to him in desperation. How do you think their feelings changed after Jesus healed them? How might Jairus's family have changed after Jesus performed the miracle?

Have you ever witnessed or experienced God's healing? If so, how did your feelings change afterward?

thinking it through

Jesus often told people that their faith had healed them. What did he mean by that? What would it look like for you to have that kind of faith?

Sometimes people ask Jesus for things, but they don't really expect an answer. If you have time today, look up the following verses: Matthew 21:22; Mark 11:24; James 1:6. What do they say about prayer? Think about these verses as you share your requests with God this week.

Woman Who Touched Jesus: Healed by Faith

She had heard about Jesus, so she came up behind him through the crowd and touched his robe. For she thought to herself, "If I can just touch his robe, I will be healed."

MARK 5:27-28

While Jesus was making his way to Jairus's house, a crowd surrounded him. In the crowd was a woman who had been bleeding for twelve years. She'd gone to several doctors, but they hadn't helped her. Her hope was gone. Then she heard Jesus could heal people.

The woman joined the crowd that thronged Jesus. Her plan was to touch his robe in hopes his healing power would cure her. With that purpose in mind, she inched forward until she was able to reach out and touch his garment. As soon as she did, she felt the bleeding stop, and she was immediately well. Imagine her relief after having lived with her infirmity for twelve years. She didn't have to take medicine for weeks or have repeated follow-up visits. She was able to do all the things she hadn't been able to do for many years as her condition made her weaker and weaker with each passing year.

When the woman touched Jesus' robe, he felt the healing power go out from him and asked, "Who touched my robe?" (Mark 5:30).

The disciples thought this was a strange question. With so many people crowding against him, how could anyone know who'd touched him? They didn't realize someone had been healed by touching him.

The woman dropped to her knees in front of Jesus and told him what had happened. Perhaps she was worried Jesus would be angry or he'd cause her illness to return, but Jesus told her, "Daughter, your faith has made you well. Go in peace. Your suffering is over" (Mark 5:34). The woman was overjoyed. She knew she really was healed.

The woman was healed because of her faith in Jesus. Lives are still changed through faith in him.

Herodias and Her Daughter: Bad Babe of the Bible

John also publicly criticized Herod Antipas, the ruler of Galilee, for marrying Herodias, his brother's wife, and for many other wrongs he had done.

LUKE 3:19

Herodias is one bad Bible babe. Her name is the female version of the name *Herod*. Herod was the name of the ruling family during the time of Christ. The name means "heroic," but the family didn't live up to that name. They were the family that was most responsible for causing trouble for Jesus and his followers. Herodias was a descendant of Herod the Great, who wanted to kill baby Jesus when the wise men inquired about a new king.

Herodias was a scheming, vindictive person who liked power. And she liked getting her own way. It can be confusing to keep track of who's who in Herodias's life because of all the step and half relationships. She was first married to her half uncle, Herod Philip, and they had a daughter most commonly known as Salome. During the time Herodias was married to Philip, his half brother, Herod Antipas, visited. Antipas was step-brother to her father, and he was tetrarch of Galilee and Perea, which made him much more important than Philip. Then something unthinkable happened. Antipas talked Herodias into leaving Philip and becoming his wife. But, under Jewish law, a woman couldn't marry the brother of a living husband or get divorced.

John the Baptist spoke out against the couple. He told them their marriage wasn't lawful. It was sinful in God's eyes. Herodias didn't like to hear that. She wanted her husband to use his authority and kill John, but Herod didn't agree. However, he did have John imprisoned.

Herodias is a Bible woman you don't want as a role model. Her desire for power and her need to get her own way were a dangerous combination. She began plotting ways to get rid of John the Baptist, and with Antipas's birthday approaching, she came up with the perfect plan.

thinking it through

Herodias left her husband, Philip, to illegally marry his brother Antipas because Antipas had a better position and more power. Does she remind you of any other Bible women? What character traits would you use to describe Herodias? Now list the opposite of those traits. Which of the positive traits would you want to have?

thinking it through

Zechariah 8:16-17 reminds us to "tell the truth to each other" because God hates scheming and telling lies. What is the opposite of plotting and scheming? What can you do to bring peace instead of getting your own way?

Herodias and Her Daughter: The Birthday Dance

At a birthday party for Herod, Herodias's daughter performed a dance that greatly pleased him, so he promised with a vow to give her anything she wanted.
MATTHEW 14:6-7

Herodias was furious at John the Baptist for publicly calling her marriage sinful because she had left her husband, Herod Philip, and married his half brother, Herod Antipas. People were listening to John, and it was hurting her status. She was afraid her husband might listen to John and repent. Then she'd lose all she'd gained by marrying him.

Antipas had John thrown in prison, but he refused to kill him. So Herodias came up with another plan. Antipas's birthday was coming up. There would be a grand party with high government officials, army officers, and leading citizens of Galilee. There would also be plenty of wine, so Antipas and the other men would be drinking a lot.

Herodias told her daughter, Salome, to dance before her stepfather. Antipas was pleased by the dance and told Salome she could have whatever she wanted, up to half of his kingdom.

This was the chance Herodias was waiting for. She told Salome to ask for the head of John the Baptist on a tray. The king was very saddened by this, but he couldn't go back on his promise to Salome.

Herodias had a wicked heart. She lived for power. She was driven by the need to have her own way. We'd all like to think we have nothing in common with Herodias, but have you ever schemed to get your own way? Maybe plotted how to get a sibling in trouble or how to choose the TV show when it's not your turn? Or perhaps you manipulated your friends into letting you choose what to do on the weekend? These things aren't as serious as what Herodias did, but they're not good, either. Scheming or manipulating about little things can lead to plotting about bigger things down the road. Watch for it in your life, and weed it out.

Quiz Time

Do you manipulate or scheme? Read each sentence below, and circle A for always, S for sometimes, or N for never.

1. I am fair about taking turns when it comes to choosing television shows, chores, and family activities.

   A S N

2. I do my jobs myself and don't try to get someone else to do them through guilt, promises, or pouting.

   A S N

3. If someone offends me, I let it go and don't try to get even.

   A S N

4. When it comes to doing things with my friends, I don't try to get my way more often than is fair.

   A S N

5. I refrain from using pouting, anger, guilt, or games to get my own way.

   A S N

If you circled mostly A's, good for you. You make sure everyone gets a say when it comes to choosing activities, and you don't use emotional games to get your own way.

If you circled mostly S's, check your life for ways you might be manipulating others. Be sure to let others have their way just as much as you do. Be fair when it comes to making choices.

If you circled mostly N's, you are treading on dangerous ground. It's not just about you. Let others have first choice just as much as you do. Manipulating others or getting even will keep you from living out God's awesome plan for your life.

thinking it through

It can be hard to take criticism sometimes. When someone criticizes you, try these steps:

1. Listen to the criticism, and make sure you understand what the person is really saying.
2. Avoid becoming angry or reacting to the criticism.
3. Ask yourself if any of what was said was true.
4. Fix what you can.
5. Let go of unfair criticism.
6. Remember the truth found in Proverbs 27:6: "Wounds from a sincere friend are better than many kisses from an enemy."

Herodias and Her Daughter: Accepting Correction

John had been telling Herod, "It is against God's law for you to marry your brother's wife." So Herodias bore a grudge against John and wanted to kill him. But without Herod's approval she was powerless.

MARK 6:18-19

Antipas and Herodias had done a sinful thing by leaving their first spouses and getting married. John the Baptist told them it was wrong. In fact, he told them often and loudly. Antipas had sometimes listened as John preached and found him interesting, but Herodias was angry. She didn't like being told she was wrong. She didn't take the criticism well at all. Herodias held a grudge against John and looked for a way to get even.

All of us make mistakes. That's why God gave us parents, pastors, counselors, and teachers to learn from. It's good to listen to their advice and to pay attention if they point out an error or flaw in our lives.

Sometimes it's hard to hear criticism, but it's important to pay attention to it. Listen to what is being said. Avoid reacting in anger if someone gives you counsel or correction. It's better to wait and think things through. Ask yourself if any part of the criticism is true. Perhaps your mom says your room looks like a pigsty. You think that's unfair. But when you look around your room, there are clothes on the floor and papers all over your desk. Empty soda bottles adorn your dresser. Maybe your room's not a pigsty, but it could be improved.

If you are criticized and it's true or partly true, fix what you can. Maybe you haven't committed any great sin, but you do need to start your homework sooner or be better about finishing your chores. Change the things that need changing, and ignore false criticism.

Herodias and Her Daughter: Greedy for Power

Royal power belongs to the LORD. He rules all the nations.

PSALM 22:28

Cynthia was determined to be the next class president. She was tired of the baby activities this year's class president planned. She had her campaign all mapped out.

There was one person who stood between her and her goal—Marissa, a girl who'd transferred to the school last May. Marissa was instantly popular. Cynthia found it sickening the way the other girls flocked around Marissa in the hall. She'd heard some of them ask Marissa to run for class president.

Cynthia wasn't worried, though. Marissa's aunt and Cynthia's mom volunteered together at the hospital. Cynthia had heard enough of a phone conversation between them to know Marissa had gotten expelled from her private school for stealing an exam and passing it around. If Marissa ran against her for class president, a few well-placed comments should take care of the competition.

Cynthia was a bit like Herodias, who was greedy for power. But Herodias wouldn't stop at spreading some gossip. She held a grudge against John the Baptist until she finally got him killed. She was afraid her husband might listen to John when he said their marriage was wrong. If Antipas believed John, he might send her back to her legal husband. The people they ruled might turn on her too. Either way, she'd lose her power. She couldn't let that happen. She used her only daughter to put Herod in a position where he had to kill John or go back on his word in front of a lot of important people.

It's okay to want to be in a leadership position, as long as you get the position in an honorable way and use it for good. Many Christian leaders have accomplished good things through the years. Who knows? Your name may be added to that group one day.

thinking it through

What kind of a leader would Cynthia make? Why is her attitude harmful? What kind of attitude should a leader have?

thinking it through

Salome may have been just about your age. Put yourself in her shoes. How do you think she felt about her mother's request? Why do you think she didn't question it but just repeated it to Herod as though it were her own request? What would you have asked for?

Herodias and Her Daughter: Being Used

She went out and asked her mother, "What should I ask for?" Her mother told her, "Ask for the head of John the Baptist!" So the girl hurried back to the king and told him, "I want the head of John the Baptist, right now, on a tray!"

MARK 6:24-25

We aren't told much about Herodias's daughter, Salome. In fact, it's the historian Josephus, not the Bible, who tells us her name. The Bible only tells us that she danced for her stepfather and his guests and won his favor. When he asked her what she wanted, her mother told her to ask for the head of John the Baptist. That's not a reward any girl would want, no matter her age.

But Salome went along with her mother's request. She even added that it should be "on a tray" and "right now." Perhaps she sensed her mother's urgency. Herodias was afraid that if Antipas had time to think about it or if the onlookers were gone, he might not grant the grisly request. Or perhaps being raised by a cruel and vindictive mother had turned Salome into the same, even at a young age.

An executioner brought the head of John the Baptist on a platter, and Salome handed it to her mother. This raises a lot of questions:

What did this do to the party spirit?

What did knowing that her request caused John's death and seeing John's severed head do to Salome?

Were the other partygoers shocked and appalled?

Did Salome have nightmares because of this?

How did Salome turn out?

We don't know because nothing more is written about Herodias and Salome. We are told that John's followers came and got his body and buried it. Then they went and told Jesus.

My heart goes out to young Salome, whether she was an innocent pawn in her mother's scheme or she was as evil as her mother. Most young girls imitate their mothers, and Salome may not have been any different.

Syrophoenician Woman: A Determined Mother

When she arrived home, she found her little girl lying quietly in bed, and the demon was gone.

MARK 7:30

The Syrophoenician woman, also called the Canaanite woman, was a Gentile (non-Jew) with a demon-possessed daughter. It was hard for the mother to care for her child, and sometimes the situation seemed hopeless. There was nothing that could be done to free the girl from her torment.

The mother had heard of Jesus' power to heal and went to him. She told him about her daughter and asked him to heal the little girl. Jesus said, "First I should feed the children—my own family, the Jews. It isn't right to take food from the children and throw it to the dogs" (Mark 7:27). Jesus meant he should care for the Jews first, and this woman was a Gentile.

The woman was desperate. She wasn't willing to give up so easily, because Jesus was the only hope for her daughter. The woman answered, "That's true, Lord, but even the dogs under the table are allowed to eat the scraps from the children's plates" (Mark 7:28).

Jesus told the woman she'd given a good answer. He instructed her to go home, because the demon had left her daughter. The woman hurried home, now filled with hope. When she got there, she saw it was true. Her daughter was resting quietly because the demon was gone.

The mother believed Jesus could heal her daughter. She never doubted. She didn't give up, either, even when it looked like Jesus would deny her request. The hopeful mother wasn't going to let go of this chance to have her child freed from the demon. Perhaps Jesus was testing her faith or her persistence. If it was a test, she passed. Jesus didn't even journey to her home as he had with Jairus. Jesus healed the girl without even seeing her.

thinking it through

The woman wasn't willing to give up. She told Jesus that even dogs deserve the crumbs. If she'd accepted Jesus' first answer and left, her daughter would have remained demon possessed. What one thing will you persistently ask God for?

thinking it through

Were any of the religious teachers worthy of throwing the first stone? Can any of us claim we are sinless? What hope does Jesus' response to the woman give us, no matter what sins we've committed?

Forgiven Woman: Self-Righteousness

As he was speaking, the teachers of religious law and the Pharisees brought a woman who had been caught in the act of adultery. They put her in front of the crowd.

JOHN 8:3

Back in Jesus' time there were groups of men who prided themselves on following all the Jewish laws. These groups failed to recognize Jesus as the Messiah. They often criticized him.

One day the men dragged a woman before Jesus and a whole crowd of people. She had been caught with a man who wasn't her husband.

The religious leaders were testing Jesus. Under the law of Moses, this woman—and the missing man—should be stoned to death. But Jesus taught of love and grace. The men figured that if he said to stone her, he'd be going against his teachings; but if he said to let her go, he'd be violating the law of Moses.

Jesus was too wise to be caught in their trap. He stooped down and wrote in the dust. When the men kept asking whether the woman should be stoned he answered, "All right, but let the one who has never sinned throw the first stone!" (John 8:7). Then he went back to writing in the dust.

Why did Jesus write in the dust? Some people feel it was to avoid looking at the woman, who may have been only partially dressed. Others say the second time, he wrote the sins of all the men standing there. There's no way to know if that's true, but it would have been an eye-opener for sure.

The men left one by one, starting with the oldest. When Jesus looked up, only the woman was left.

The men had prided themselves on being righteous, but Jesus turned the situation around. Jesus was the only one there qualified to throw the first stone, but he didn't. He hadn't come to earth to condemn sinners but to save them. And he's still in the business of saving sinners.

Forgiven Woman: Jesus Forgives Sins

Jesus stood up again and said to the woman, "Where are your accusers? Didn't even one of them condemn you?" "No, Lord," she said. And Jesus said, "Neither do I. Go and sin no more."

JOHN 8:10-11

When the Pharisees dragged the woman caught in sin to Jesus, it was more about trapping Jesus than it was about the woman herself. The law of Moses said she should be stoned, but Jesus believed in forgiveness. He came to earth to find and save the lost. This woman knew she was sinful. The Pharisees thought of themselves as righteous. But when Jesus said that the man without sin should cast the first stone, none of them was foolish enough to claim to be sinless. They all left.

Jesus and the woman were the only ones remaining. Jesus told the woman to "go and sin no more." Did she do that? We don't know, but her life was surely changed by that encounter with Jesus. The Pharisees were harsh and judgmental. Jesus showed her love and compassion. It's possible she recognized him as the promised Messiah and was forever changed by the knowledge she'd been forgiven by the Son of God.

Under Moses' law, different sins had different penalties. But God views every sin as bad enough to condemn us to a life apart from him. The good news is that every sin can be forgiven because of Jesus' death and resurrection. Sometimes you might feel like you've really blown it. You find yourself doing the same wrong thing over and over and wonder how God can keep forgiving you for the same sin. Or you do something that seems so bad God won't want to forgive it. Neither is true. If you have a repentant heart, God will forgive you. And he doesn't remember your sin either. That doesn't mean your peers will forgive and forget, or that there won't be earthly consequences. But you can have peace knowing that God's forgiven you and will give you the strength to overcome temptation in the future.

thinking it through

First John 1:9 tells us that "if we confess our sins to him, he is faithful and just to forgive us our sins and to cleanse us from all wickedness." Is there anything you need to confess right now?

thinking it through

What do you think Jesus meant when he said there was only one thing worth being concerned about? How did Jesus show kindness to Martha at the same time as rebuking her?

Mary and Martha: Two Sisters

As Jesus and the disciples continued on their way to Jerusalem, they came to a certain village where a woman named Martha welcomed him into her home. Her sister, Mary, sat at the Lord's feet, listening to what he taught.

LUKE 10:38-39

In the 1970s many people watched a show called *The Odd Couple*. It was about two roommates who were so opposite that they often drove each other crazy. Felix was a neat freak, while Oscar was a slob. In the show the situation is humorous, but in real life the situation would lead to irritation and conflict.

Mary and Martha were two sisters who were opposite in some ways too. Jesus often stopped by their home in Bethany, a small town east of Jerusalem. It appears that all three adults were single. Some people believe their brother, Lazarus, inherited the house from their father, while others believe Martha was widowed, and the house had originally belonged to her husband.

One day Jesus stopped for a visit. Martha welcomed him but became busy with preparations because she wanted to make him a nice meal. As she worked, her irritation at Mary, who sat listening to Jesus, built. She said, "Lord, doesn't it seem unfair to you that my sister just sits here while I do all the work? Tell her to come and help me" (Luke 10:40).

Jesus said, "My dear Martha, you are worried and upset over all these details! There is only one thing worth being concerned about. Mary has discovered it, and it will not be taken away from her" (Luke 10:41-42).

Jesus understood that Martha was trying to do a nice thing for him, and he wasn't criticizing her for wanting to serve him, only for letting it distract her from spending time with him.

Jesus loved both sisters, and they loved him, too. People often remember that Jesus rebuked Martha for being too busy to sit at his feet listening. But there is much more to Martha, as you'll see in the next devotion.

Puzzle Page

The religious leaders were stopped in their tracks when Jesus told them, "Let the one who has never sinned throw the first stone" (John 8:7). Use the Box Code below to help you decode the verse and find out what the Bible says about those who claim they have not sinned.

sinned	claim	we	place
word	have	liar	calling
hearts	his	that	our
God	showing		

If ________ ________ ________ ________ not ________,

________ are ________ ________ a ________ and ________

________ ________ ________ has no ________

in ________ ________.

Answer: If we claim we have not sinned, we are calling God a liar and showing that his word has no place in our hearts. (1 John 1:10)

thinking it through

How do you think Martha felt as she worked hard to prepare the meal without any offer of help from her sister? Have you ever had to do all the work while someone else was sitting around? How did that feel?

What does today's verse say about serving the Lord? How can you apply this to your life this week?

Mary and Martha: Dependable Martha

My dear brothers and sisters, be strong and immovable. Always work enthusiastically for the Lord, for you know that nothing you do for the Lord is ever useless.

1 CORINTHIANS 15:58

Gracyn hurried around straightening the room. She could hardly believe it—a famous Christian football player was visiting their middle school club for Christian athletes. One of the club members' grandparents had gone to school with the athlete's father and arranged for the football player to visit. Gracyn quickly vacuumed the classroom floor and set up chairs. Then she started putting out snacks.

Gracyn looked up to see what the others were doing to get ready. She couldn't believe what she saw. The football player had already arrived. The club members were gathered around listening as he told about a great play he'd made in his last game. Gracyn was angry. The club members knew there was work to do to get ready for the meeting, but they'd left it all to her!

Gracyn felt a lot like Martha in the story. It wasn't that Gracyn didn't want to spend time with the football player or that Martha didn't want to spend time with Jesus; they were just task-oriented individuals who liked organizing and serving. There is nothing wrong with doing these things, but Jesus wanted Martha to realize he wouldn't always be with her, so it was important that she spent time listening to him and learning.

It's the Marthas in our churches who organize the banquets, collect food for needy families, provide housing and meals for visiting missionary families, and paint the nursery. They are hardworking, hospitable, welcoming, and dependable.

Martha was showing her love for Jesus through welcoming him in her home and preparing a meal for him. Martha loved Jesus, and she had great faith in him. She just got her priorities out of order and forgot that it's more important to find a balance between spending time with Jesus and spending time serving for him.

Mary and Martha: Mary Worships Jesus

God is Spirit, so those who worship him must worship in spirit and in truth.

JOHN 4:24

While Martha was task oriented and focused her energy on caring for Jesus' physical needs, Mary sat at Jesus' feet. She wanted to learn from him. Mary understood who Jesus was, and she worshiped him. This doesn't mean that Martha didn't worship him; she was just distracted by all that needed to be done. It also doesn't mean that Mary was lazy; she just knew it was more important to spend the time with Jesus. Mary was concerned about food for the soul, while Martha was concerned about food for the body.

Are you more like Martha or Mary? Martha loved and worshiped Jesus, but she often got too busy doing good things for Jesus to spend time with him. Martha didn't lack faith or love Jesus any less than Mary; she just had to be reminded of the right priorities. Mary probably helped Martha with the work when Jesus and his disciples weren't there, but when Jesus was with them, she wanted to spend the time listening to him. Mary may have been more spiritually sensitive and emotional than Martha.

It's easy to get so caught up in school, homework, family situations, friendships, relationships, sports, and clubs that there isn't much time left to spend time with God. Even church activities can take away from time with God. Going out on an evangelistic team, taking part in choir and youth group, and doing service projects shouldn't replace time alone reading God's Word, talking to God, and listening as he speaks to you.

Jesus commended Mary because she didn't let preparations or pressure keep her from sitting peacefully at his feet listening. That's what he still wants today.

thinking it through

Look at the verse for the day. What do you think it means to worship God "in spirit and in truth"?

Do you worship God more often with your actions or with time set aside just to be with him? Which one can you work on more this week?

thinking it through

When the Pharisees and priests saw what Jesus did, they were upset and didn't want the people to believe in Jesus. How could people see this miracle and still not believe? What do you think keeps people today from believing in Jesus?

Even if you believe that Jesus can help you through any problem, you'll probably still be amazed by some of the ways he'll take care of you throughout your life. Thank him today for his love and his gift of everlasting life.

Mary and Martha: The Sisters' Faith

"Yes, Lord," [Martha] told him. "I have always believed you are the Messiah, the Son of God, the one who has come into the world from God."

JOHN 11:27

Mary and Martha were worried. Their brother, Lazarus, was very sick. The sisters sent a messenger to Jesus asking him to come. Jesus waited a couple of days, even though he knew Lazarus would die while he was away.

Jesus and his disciples went to Bethany, where Mary and Martha lived. Martha went out to meet him, while Mary waited in the house. Martha said, "Lord, if only you had been here, my brother would not have died. But even now I know that God will give you whatever you ask" (verses 21-22).

Jesus told Martha that Lazarus would rise again. Martha said, "Yes . . . he will rise when everyone else rises, at the last day" (verse 24).

But Jesus meant he was going to bring Lazarus back to life. Jesus said, "I am the resurrection and the life. Anyone who believes in me will live, even after dying. Everyone who lives in me and believes in me will never ever die" (verses 25-26).

Martha believed this. She and Mary knew that Jesus was the Son of God. Mary and Martha showed Jesus where Lazarus was buried. Jesus ordered the stone moved aside. He prayed, and then he shouted, "Lazarus come out!" (verse 43). Jesus wanted everyone to hear and believe.

Lazarus walked out of the tomb, still wrapped in his graveclothes. Many people believed in Jesus when this happened.

Martha believed that Jesus was the Messiah and that he could help her, but she had no idea what he was going to do for her family that day. Even if we believe in Jesus, we don't always realize the extent of his power and love. Jesus can raise the dead, and he can help you through your difficulties in ways you can't even imagine.

Mary and Martha: Mary Anoints Jesus

Mary took a twelve-ounce jar of expensive perfume made from essence of nard, and she anointed Jesus' feet with it, wiping his feet with her hair. The house was filled with the fragrance.

JOHN 12:3

There is some confusion about this story of Mary anointing Jesus with oil. It's very similar to the story of another woman who anointed Jesus, told in Luke 7 (see the devos for October 27–29). Sometimes people think it's the same story, and that Mary is that woman, but that's not true.

In the story mentioned in today's verse, it was just a few days before the Passover celebration was to begin. Jesus had raised Lazarus from the dead, and he was at Mary, Martha, and Lazarus's home, where they were having a special dinner in his honor.

Mary took a twelve-ounce jar of expensive perfume and anointed Jesus' feet with it, then wiped them with her hair. The fragrance filled the whole house. Judas, who later betrayed Jesus, immediately criticized Mary. "That perfume was worth a year's wages. It should have been sold and the money given to the poor" (John 12:5). Judas didn't really care about the poor; he only cared about money. He was in charge of the disciples' money and often stole from it.

Jesus was quick to defend her: "Leave her alone. She did this in preparation for my burial. You will always have the poor among you, but you will not always have me" (John 12:7-8). Once again Mary showed a spiritual sensitivity beyond what the others displayed. She honored Jesus by anointing him with perfume worth a year's pay. Some considered it a waste, but not Mary—and not Jesus.

Different people have different ways of honoring God today. Some do it through gifts of money, others through acts of service. What's important to God is the heart attitude. Mary's act was an unselfish one motivated by love, and ours should be also.

thinking it through

What are some different ways you can think of to honor God? Which are you most comfortable with? Why?

thinking it through

Think of three ways to both spend time with God and serve him this week. Ask a friend to join you.

Mary and Martha: Finding Balance

Whatever you do, do it all for the glory of God.

1 CORINTHIANS 10:31

Kara and Tanya are modern-day sisters who are much like Mary and Martha. Kara is part of a prayer group that meets before school once a week. She likes to listen to the Bible on her MP3 player, sitting on her bed so she can really think about what she's hearing. She also listens on the school bus and while she walks.

Tanya helps out with the gym night at church. She supervises games for the younger groups. Tanya went on a mission trip to fix roofs on houses damaged by a hurricane. She's the first one to volunteer when there's work to be done.

Both Kara and Tanya love Jesus, but they show it in different ways. Like Mary and Martha, they are learning to find balance in their spiritual lives. Kara sometimes gets so caught up in listening to the Bible she neglects putting her faith into action. Tanya volunteers Kara to help with some of the youth group projects, or she'd probably never get involved. Kara often asks Tanya what she read from the Bible that day. That reminds Tanya to spend at least a few minutes with God so she has an answer for Kara.

It's important to find a balance between spending time alone with God and serving. The most important thing is to worship God, but your love for the Lord should result in wanting to do good things for others and reaching them for him. Perhaps you will go on a mission trip like Tanya did. Make sure to set aside time at the beginning and end of each day to spend alone with God, reading Scripture and praying. Look for ways to both listen to God and serve, especially as the birth of our Savior draws near. The Christmas season often provides opportunities to reflect on God's great sacrifice in sending Jesus and to be involved in helping those in need. Take time to do both.

Mary and Martha: Family Ties

Make allowance for each other's faults, and forgive anyone who offends you. Remember, the Lord forgave you, so you must forgive others. Above all, clothe yourselves with love, which binds us all together in perfect harmony. And let the peace that comes from Christ rule in your hearts. For as members of one body you are called to live in peace. And always be thankful.

COLOSSIANS 3:13-15

Mary and Martha were sisters with different personalities just like girls today. They probably became irritated with each other and argued as they grew up together. The people in the Bible were ordinary people like you. They had the same problems and feelings you have. They experienced happiness and sadness. They had hopes and dreams. And they fought with their siblings.

But Mary and Martha had something that was stronger than their differences. They both loved Jesus and believed he was the Messiah, the Son of God. Even though Mary and Martha were different, neither was totally right or wrong. There is no one Christian personality. God made us all unique and wants us to use our own individual personalities to express our love to him.

The sisters also had a strong family tie. They are most often mentioned together in the Bible. They each had their own responsibilities but spent their free time together. While Jesus lived on earth, he was a welcomed friend and guest at their house.

We don't know what happened to Mary and Martha after the dinner where Mary anointed Jesus. They may have been standing at the cross with Jesus' other followers when Jesus was crucified. They may have been among those who met together after Jesus went back to heaven. One thing is certain: Mary's and Martha's lives were changed forever because of their time spent with Jesus. If you are a Christian, when you get to heaven one day, you just may see Mary sitting at the feet of her Savior.

thinking it through

Do you have a sibling? If not, are there any friends or relatives you spend a lot of time with? How are you similar? How are you different? How do your differences allow you to help each other? When you argue or have a conflict about something, how can the words of Colossians 3:13-15 help you?

What's the most important lesson you've learned from Mary and Martha? Is there anything you've seen that needs to be changed in your life after reading about these sisters?

thinking it through

Do you know Christians who are judgmental rather than compassionate? They are like the synagogue ruler. How about you? Does it bother you when someone breaks a "rule" like not wearing the right clothes to church or walking in late every week? Have you ever been the subject of someone's judgmental attitude? What did it feel like? This week, try to see everyone through Jesus' eyes, with love and compassion.

Crippled Woman: Jesus Is Compassionate

When Jesus saw her, he called her forward and said to her, "Woman, you are set free from your infirmity." Then he put his hands on her, and immediately she straightened up and praised God.

LUKE 13:12-13, NIV

One Sabbath Jesus was speaking in a synagogue when he noticed a woman who had been crippled by a spirit for eighteen years. During that whole time she had not been able to stand up straight or walk without difficulty. Though there's no good reason for it, many times when people see someone with a disability, it makes them uncomfortable, so they turn away. But not Jesus. He called her up to the front. Then he said, "Woman, you are set free from your infirmity," and he put his hands on her. She stood up straight and began praising God. In just a moment of time she went from crippled to completely well.

The ruler of the synagogue was indignant. How dare Jesus heal on the Sabbath! That broke the rule about not working on the Sabbath. Instead of being happy for the woman, he criticized Jesus. A few others agreed with him. But as always, Jesus knew what to say. "You hypocrites! Doesn't each of you on the Sabbath untie his ox or donkey from the stall and lead it out to give it water? Then should not this woman, a daughter of Abraham, whom Satan has kept bound for eighteen long years, be set free on the Sabbath day from what bound her?" (Luke 13:15-16, NIV).

Jesus' opponents were humiliated by the answer; they were very concerned about keeping every little part of the law, but Jesus followed the law of love, grace, and mercy. He thought people were more important than rules.

There are still those today who find rules more important than people. They criticize others for how they look, dress, or act. But being judgmental doesn't win people to Jesus—loving does. It's better to see people through God's eyes and extend a little grace than to judge them based on how they dress or act.

Quiz Time

You can't physically sit at Jesus' feet like Mary did, but you can spend time with him. Are you more of a Mary or a Martha? Read the list below. Put a check by each statement that applies to you.

___ 1. I am one of the first to sign up for youth group service projects (or other projects).
___ 2. I start or end my day by reading my Bible.
___ 3. My Sunday school teacher or youth leader knows he or she can depend on me to help clean up after a class or activity.
___ 4. I have a prayer list that I use when I pray each day.
___ 5. If I hear of a need someone has, I do what I can to meet that need.
___ 6. Sometimes I sit quietly listening for what God has to say to me or listening to praise music that focuses my mind on God.
___ 7. I have gone on or would like to go on a mission trip during the summer.
___ 8. I memorize Bible verses and often repeat them to myself.

Did you check mostly odd numbers (1, 3, 5, 7) or even numbers (2, 4, 6, 8)?

If you checked mostly odd numbers, you are like Martha. You see what needs to be done, and you do it. That's okay, but make sure you take time to do the even-numbered things above too.

If you checked mostly even numbers, you are like Mary. You like to spend time with God through Bible reading and prayer. That's good. Time with God is the most important thing, but make sure you don't use it as an excuse to get out of work.

thinking it through

Jesus told his disciples in Matthew 20:26-28, "Whoever wants to be a leader among you must be your servant, and whoever wants to be first among you must become your slave. For even the Son of Man came not to be served but to serve others and to give his life as a ransom for many." How does that apply to you today?

Salome, Mother of James and John: A Mother's Request

The mother of Zebedee's sons came to Jesus with her sons and, kneeling down, asked a favor of him.

MATTHEW 20:20, NIV

Salome came to Jesus with a special request. She wanted her sons to sit at Jesus' side in heaven. Salome didn't hesitate in making this request of Jesus, because she was one of his followers too. She is listed by name in Mark 15:40 as one of the women who ministered to Jesus. She was also among the women at the cross and those who took spices to Jesus' tomb.

Even though Salome loved her sons and wanted the best for them, it was probably James and John who asked her to make the request. Jesus addressed the brothers, not Salome, when he said that the places next to him in heaven were for the ones God had chosen. And the other disciples were angry with James and John, not Salome, for asking.

James and John's request to be elevated above others shows they didn't really understand all Jesus taught. Jesus said the first would be last, and the last would be first. He taught that whoever wanted to be first should be a servant to all.

Many people today have it backwards too. They push their way to the top by hurting or using others. They try to be more important by earning more money or owning more possessions.

Salome was a good example of someone who had it right. She ministered to Jesus, but she never tried to be important. She was a servant caring for her Messiah. The request she made for her sons was out of character for her, which is why Jesus and the disciples knew the request most likely came from the brothers themselves.

If you want to get ahead in God's eyes, follow Salome's example. Be a servant, and don't worry about being important.

Widow with Two Coins: The Woman Who Gave All Her Money

Jesus called his disciples to him and said, "I tell you the truth, this poor widow has given more than all the others who are making contributions. For they gave a tiny part of their surplus, but she, poor as she is, has given everything she had to live on."

MARK 12:43-44

Picture this: People are filing in to church one at a time. There are several businessmen, city officials, and one lone woman in front of you. The businessmen and city officials are acting haughty. They have their heads held high as though they expect everyone to recognize them and their importance. There's an offering box by the door. The first man unrolls a wad of bills and drops several twenties in the box. The next man, not to be outdone, drops in some fifties. And so it goes until the woman reaches the box. She's dressed in a clean but worn dress. It stands in contrast to the men's brand-name suits. She has something in her hand, but you can't see what it is as she drops it in the box. There's a peaceful look on her face as she takes her place in a pew.

This might be a modern-day equivalent of what happened in Jesus' time. Jesus was watching as many rich people filed by the Temple box and dropped in generous offerings. Then a poor widow walked by the box and dropped in two small coins. Jesus called his disciples over and told them the woman had given more than all the others. The disciples looked at him in surprise. How could she have given more than all the rich men?

But of course Jesus wasn't talking about the actual amount; he meant she had given all she had as compared to the rich men who gave only a small percentage of their money.

Sometimes we hesitate to give 10 percent, but the woman in this story gave 100 percent of what she had.

thinking it through

Do you give 10 percent of what you have? Why do you think it's important for us to give what we have back to God?

thinking it through

Are you a generous giver? Are there changes you need to make to your giving or your attitude?

Widow with Two Coins: Heart Watching

Jesus sat down near the collection box in the Temple and watched as the crowds dropped in their money.

MARK 12:41

Do you ever people watch? You know, sit in the food court at the mall and observe everyone walking by. There's a couple pushing twins in a stroller. Then a teen with spiked hair goes by. Next is a dad trying to keep up with three young children. Then a giggling group of teen girls strolls by. If you're with a friend or your mom, you probably make comments about the more unusual people who walk by, or even snicker at a few of the untraditional outfits you see people wearing.

Jesus was sitting near the collection box in the Temple people watching. But he wasn't looking at their hairstyles or clothes; he was looking at their hearts. The attitude of a person's heart is much more important to Jesus than his or her appearance. Jesus didn't like what he saw in the rich men's hearts. They were giving large offerings for show, but the money was only a small bit of what they had. They didn't sacrifice anything to give to God. But Jesus saw the poor woman's heart and knew she was making a big sacrifice to give her two small coins.

Jesus was more pleased by the woman's offering than that of the rich men. God doesn't really need anyone's money. He created everything, and he owns everything. We are just caretakers of his money. But the rich men didn't see it that way. They were proud of their money, and they wanted everyone to see their big offerings. Other people might have been impressed, but Jesus wasn't.

Jesus still people watches, and he still sees heart attitudes. What does Jesus see when he looks at you? Does he see a generous heart willing to give or a stingy heart holding on to money and possessions?

Widow with Two Coins: God Supplies Our Needs

Let's not get tired of doing what is good. At just the right time we will reap a harvest of blessing if we don't give up.

GALATIANS 6:9

Back in July we talked about the widow of Zarephath. There was a drought, and nothing would grow. She was almost out of food. The widow was gathering sticks to prepare one last meal for herself and her son when Elijah asked her for food. He told her not to fear, because her flour and oil would last until the drought was over and crops could grow again.

The widow with two coins had a lot in common with the widow of Zarephath. Both women had lost husbands and had no one to care for them. They had to live on whatever they had. Both were generous—they were willing to give the rest of what they had. But the widow of Zarephath had Elijah's promise that her oil and flour wouldn't run out until crops could grow again, and the widow with the coins didn't have that promise. She gave the rest of her money probably not knowing what she would live on.

Perhaps the widow went home wondering if she would starve when her meager food supply was gone. Maybe she trusted God to take care of her. Philippians 4:19 says, "This same God who takes care of me will supply all your needs from his glorious riches, which have been given to us in Christ Jesus." The verse hadn't been written when the widow gave all she had, but it's one of God's promises, and those never change.

I like to think that when Jesus saw the woman give all she had left, he did a special miracle for her like the miracle the widow of Zarephath received. Perhaps she went home and made a meal only to find the same amount of food was still left. Maybe an anonymous basket of fish and loaves was sitting at her door. I'm sure Jesus rewarded her generous heart in some way.

thinking it through

What do you think motivated the woman to give all she had left? What do you think she expected to happen?

How does Philippians 4:19 motivate you to be more generous? (See verse on the left.)

Widow with Two Coins: Giving Eagerly

Whatever you give is acceptable if you give it eagerly. And give according to what you have, not what you don't have.

2 CORINTHIANS 8:12

Meaghan sat on her bed, her money spread out in front of her. She had twenty dollars in birthday money, twelve dollars from babysitting, and eight dollars from her allowance. Meaghan knew she could buy something nice with her forty dollars, but she wasn't sure what she wanted. Some friends were going to the mall on the weekend to Christmas shop, but Meaghan didn't want to go. It wasn't that Meaghan didn't want to buy Christmas presents for other people, but she didn't usually have this much money, and some of it was gift money. She wanted to spend it on something for herself.

Then there was the special youth group project at church. Each teen was buying a toy to be donated to a foster child. Meaghan groaned. She didn't want to spend her money on that, but how could she decline without looking selfish? Meaghan sighed. Why did having money have to be so complicated?

Both the widow of Zarephath and the widow with two coins fulfilled the above verse. They gave what they had. The widow of Zarephath gave the last of her oil and flour to feed Elijah; the poor widow put her last two coins in the Temple box. The oil and flour and the two coins weren't given reluctantly but willingly and in faith.

Meaghan isn't at the point where she's willing to give eagerly. Since she was given some money as a present and earned some herself, she wants to spend it all on herself. What advice would you give Meaghan about her money? Save some, spend some, give some? That's a good rule, but we should make sure we follow God's leading, not just a rule. He wants the money to be given willingly, not grudgingly. Everything we have comes from God in the first place. He's just asking us to be willing to give some of it back to him.

thinking it through

What does it mean to give eagerly, not grudgingly? How can you make sure you have the right attitude about giving? Talk to God about it today. Ask him to help you decide how much money to give and to help you have the right attitude about it.

Pilate's Wife: Being Ignored

As Pilate was sitting on the judgment seat, his wife sent him this message: "Leave that innocent man alone. I suffered through a terrible nightmare about him last night."

MATTHEW 27:19

Pilate's wife may not have been a follower of Jesus, or she may have been a secret believer. Either way, she had a nightmare about the things that were happening to Jesus as he was arrested and put on trial. Sometimes God speaks to people through dreams, and this may have been an attempt to get Pilate's wife to speak up on Jesus' behalf. She believed Jesus was innocent and didn't want her husband to be involved in deciding against him. She sent a message to her husband early in the morning during Jesus' trial.

Pilate knew the religious leaders had arrested Jesus only out of envy. They had no cause to arrest or punish him. Pilate could have freed Jesus, but he feared the mob of people gathered there.

It was the custom to release one prisoner during the Passover celebration. There was a vile prisoner named Barabbas, who was known as a rebel against the government, a murderer, and a robber. Pilate asked the people if they wanted him to release Barabbas or Jesus. The people chose to let Barabbas walk free and go back into a life of crime rather than release Jesus. During this time Pilate received his wife's message—and ignored it. Pilate ordered Jesus flogged and turned over to the Roman soldiers to be crucified.

Pilate's wife spoke out on Jesus' behalf, but no one listened. Her note to her husband was read but ignored. There may be times when you speak out for Jesus, but those around you aren't willing to listen or aren't ready to hear. Don't give up. Ask Christian friends to pray for you or to join you as you speak out for Jesus just as Pilate's wife did.

thinking it through

How do you think Pilate's wife felt when she found out her husband had ignored her warning? Have you ever tried to share the gospel, but no one would listen? How did that feel?

Ask a friend or two to help you stand up for Christ. Spend some time praying together, and ask God to lead you to the right people to share the Good News about Jesus.

thinking it through

Which Mary stands out most to you? Why?

What does it look like to be a faithful follower of Jesus today? Does this describe you? If not, what changes could you make?

Mary, Mother of James and Joseph: How Many Marys?

Many women who had come from Galilee with Jesus to care for him were watching from a distance. Among them were Mary Magdalene, Mary (the mother of James and Joseph), and the mother of James and John, the sons of Zebedee.

MATTHEW 27:55-56

Mary is the most often used name in the New Testament. There are at least seven different Marys mentioned in the New Testament. We've already talked about three of them: Mary of Nazareth, who was the mother of Jesus; Mary Magdalene, from whom Jesus cast out seven demons; and Mary of Bethany, sister to Martha.

There is some confusion about the other Marys. There is Mary the mother of James and Joseph, and there is Mary the wife of Cleophas (also called Alphaeus). Some people believe she was the sister of Mary, mother of Jesus, but others don't think two sisters would have the same first name. They believe Salome was the one referred to as the sister of Jesus' mother. Salome isn't mentioned by name in the verse above but is just called the mother of James and John.

There is also Mary of Jerusalem, the mother of John Mark. You'll read about her on December 12 and 13. And there is Mary of Rome, whom Paul referred to in his epistle to the Romans.

It's easy to get the Marys mixed up, especially since they all loved Jesus. With the exception of Mary of Rome, they all fed Jesus, ministered to him, and followed him as he went place to place preaching, or they were at the cross and the tomb.

Women in those times were not given much value, but women are important to Jesus. He doesn't think of them as less worthy than men. And at times the women were braver than Jesus' twelve disciples, who sometimes deserted him when things got tough.

The Marys were all faithful followers of Jesus. Are you known as a faithful follower?

Puzzle Page

God wants you to give, just like the widow with two coins did in the November 27 through November 30 devotions. Solve the Balloon Puzzle to find out what the Bible says about giving.

Directions: Each balloon has both a scrambled word and a number in it. There are also numbers next to the blank lines in the verse. Look at the number next to the blank. Find the balloon with the same number. Unscramble the word in that balloon, and write it on the line. Check your answers at the bottom.

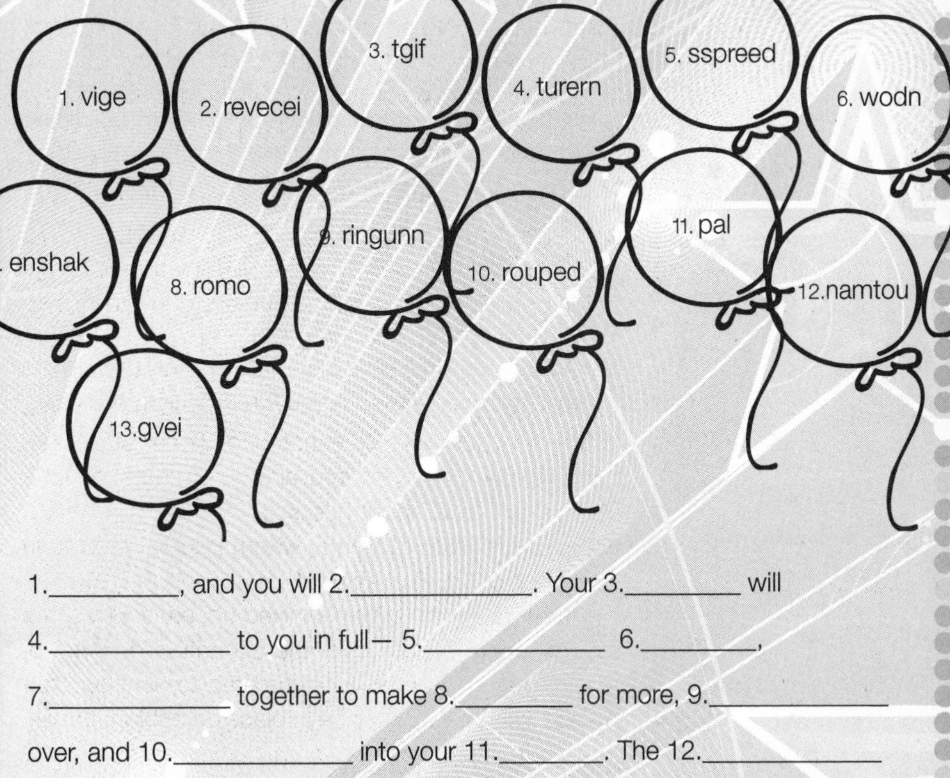

1.__________, and you will 2.______________. Your 3.________ will

4.______________ to you in full— 5.______________ 6.________,

7.______________ together to make 8.________ for more, 9.______________

over, and 10.______________ into your 11.________. The 12.______________

you 13.________ will determine the 12.______________ you get back.

Do you think this verse was just for the people Jesus was talking to at the time or for us today too? Why?

Answer: Give, and you will receive. Your gift will return to you in full—pressed down, shaken together to make room for more, running over, and poured into your lap. The amount you give will determine the amount you get back. (Luke 6:38)

Mary, Mother of James and Joseph: Faithful Follower

Saturday evening, when the Sabbath ended, Mary Magdalene, Mary the mother of James, and Salome went out and purchased burial spices so they could anoint Jesus' body.

MARK 16:1

Mary, the mother of James and Joseph, was one of the faithful women who followed Christ. What did this Mary do?

- She followed Jesus from Galilee, caring for him.
  Many women who had come from Galilee with Jesus to care for him were watching from a distance. Among them were Mary Magdalene, Mary (the mother of James and Joseph), and the mother of James and John, the sons of Zebedee.
  Matthew 27:55-56
- She went to visit Jesus' tomb.
  Early on Sunday morning, as the new day was dawning, Mary Magdalene and the other Mary went out to visit the tomb.
  Matthew 28:1
- She saw the empty tomb and the angels.
  As they stood there puzzled, two men suddenly appeared to them, clothed in dazzling robes.
  Luke 24:4
- She told Jesus' disciples what she'd seen.
  It was Mary Magdalene, Joanna, Mary the mother of James, and several other women who told the apostles what had happened.
  Luke 24:10

Mary was devoted to following Christ while he was on the earth ministering to men and women. Her testimony is recorded in the Bible for everyone to see. What a legacy of faith she left behind for us today!

thinking it through

What kind of legacy are you leaving behind? Are you numbered with those who faithfully follow Christ?

Sapphira: A Unique Community of Believers

All the believers met together in one place and shared everything they had. They sold their property and possessions and shared the money with those in need. They worshiped together at the Temple each day, met in homes for the Lord's Supper, and shared their meals with great joy and generosity—all the while praising God and enjoying the goodwill of all the people. And each day the Lord added to their fellowship those who were being saved.

ACTS 2:44-47

Often all we hear about Sapphira is that she sinned and God struck her dead, but there was more to her than that. Let's look at who Sapphira was before we look at the wrong she did.

When Jesus went back to heaven, his followers became like a family, and they shared everything they had. Many of these early believers sold their property and put the money into a fund for those who needed it.

Peter and the other disciples, also called apostles, were preaching, and the Holy Spirit was working in people's hearts so they'd believe the message and become followers of Christ too. The church was growing at a rapid rate. Sapphira and her husband, Ananias, loved Jesus and were an active part of this group.

One day Barnabas sold his property and brought the entire amount he received for the land to Peter to add to the fund. Word got around about Barnabas's generosity, and people praised him for it. Barnabas didn't sell the land and give the money to receive praise; he did it because he knew the things done for Christ are what last for eternity.

The praise Barnabas received might be what prompted Ananias and Sapphira to do what they did. They wanted others to think they were generous too. So Ananias came up with a plan that we'll talk about in the next devo, and Sapphira agreed with it. And that's where things went wrong. But they appeared to be sincere believers, adding to the community before they planned their deception.

thinking it through

Do you think having a community of believers who shared everything would work in our society? Why or why not? If God asked you to give up all your possessions for him, how hard would it be for you?

thinking it through

The money from the sale of their land was Ananias and Sapphira's to do with as they pleased. They didn't have to give any to the church, but they gave so they could be praised. Are you ever tempted to give so you'll receive praise from others for what you've done? Ask God to give you a humble heart, and ask him what he would want you to do with the money and possessions he gives you.

Sapphira: A Deceitful Plan

There was a certain man named Ananias who, with his wife, Sapphira, sold some property. He brought part of the money to the apostles, claiming it was the full amount. With his wife's consent, he kept the rest.

ACTS 5:1-2

Ananias and Sapphira decided to sell their land. No one forced them to. It was their land, and they could do with it as they pleased. They decided between them that they'd give the money to Peter. Since it was their money, they could give however much they wanted. If they wanted to give part of it and keep part of it, that was acceptable. Any money they gave would be a help to others in need. They did decide to give part of the money to Peter for the church—and also to keep some of it. The bad choice was that they decided to tell Peter the money they gave him was the whole amount they received for selling their land.

Why did they lie to Peter rather than just say they were keeping some of it? Perhaps it was because of all the attention Barnabas received for selling his land and giving 100 percent of the money to the church. Ananias and Sapphira may have wanted to receive praise for doing the same. Maybe they thought people would think them less generous if they gave only half of the money and saved half for themselves. It might have been seen as a lack of faith in God if people knew they kept part of the money.

For whatever reason they decided to do it, Ananias and Sapphira were in agreement on the deceitful plan. And as you'll see in the next devotion, it had serious consequences and served as a wake-up call for any other believer who might be thinking about doing the same.

Sapphira: Defeating Temptation

The temptations in your life are no different from what others experience. And God is faithful. He will not allow the temptation to be more than you can stand. When you are tempted, he will show you a way out so that you can endure.

1 CORINTHIANS 10:13

Ananias and Sapphira were well-known believers in the early church. They sold their land, and Ananias took the money to Peter for the early believers in need. The problem was that Ananias told Peter he was giving him all the money when really he'd kept part of it for himself. It was okay to keep part for himself but not to lie about it to Peter.

The Bible says Sapphira agreed to the plan. Ananias and Sapphira must have had a strong marriage to be in agreement with the plan to deceive the early believers. It's too bad Sapphira didn't use her good relationship with her husband to try to talk him out of his plan. She may have been able to convince him they didn't need to keep any of the money, or to tell Peter the truth that they were giving only part of the money.

Ananias and Sapphira probably agreed to lie so the other believers would praise their generosity. It sounds silly, but we do the same thing today. We might do a good deed so others will see it and think we are more spiritual or generous with our time than we are. Pretending to be something we aren't is deceitful too.

The good news is, God can help us make a better choice. He can help us overcome the temptation to sin in any area of our lives. Today's verse says there's always a way. But we have to look for the way and be willing to take it. If you're tempted to gossip, you might need to walk away from the group you're with. If you're at a friend's house and are tempted to watch a DVD you know you're not allowed to watch, you might need to ask your friend to choose a different DVD, or you may need to leave. There is always a way out of temptation.

thinking it through

What are some things you can do when you're tempted to sin? (Walk away, talk to a trusted adult, or read Scripture are some ideas.) Write a list of your ideas on one side of a small card and the verse for the day on the other side. Keep the card in your purse or backpack to remind yourself to look for the way out when you are next tempted to sin.

thinking it through

Can you think of a time when you were honest and got rewarded for it? How about a time when you were honest but didn't get rewarded? How did each of those situations make you feel?

Write today's verse on a small strip of paper, and tape it to your lip balm or lip gloss. Then each time you use it, you'll be reminded to keep your words pure.

Sapphira: Honesty

Keep your tongue from speaking evil and your lips from telling lies!

PSALM 34:13

Sapphira and her husband, Ananias, figured they had a lot to gain from telling Peter they were giving the believers all of the money from their land, when really they were keeping some money for themselves. They would earn a good reputation among the believers, and they'd have some extra cash. But their deception caught up with them.

God has a lot to say about lying. In fact, it's mentioned in Proverbs 6:16-19 as one of the seven things the Lord detests: "haughty eyes, a lying tongue, hands that kill the innocent, a heart that plots evil, feet that race to do wrong, a false witness who pours out lies, a person who sows discord in a family."

Many times several of these sins go hand in hand when we start being deceitful. Sometimes when we lie, we are plotting to do evil, or our feet are racing to do wrong. For instance, maybe a friend talks you into sneaking out of the house when you're grounded and telling your mom you're going to bed early so she won't come to check on you. Deceit and wrongdoing are going on when you plan something like that.

The better thing is to be completely honest in all you do. If the cashier gives you a dollar too much change, give it back. If a teacher grades your test wrong, show her. Even though these aren't your mistakes, your integrity is worth more than a dollar or a few extra points.

I was given back a test once where the teacher had taken off only ten points, even though he'd marked five points off four different answers. I decided to be honest and hoped he'd let me keep the extra ten points. Not so. He erased the 90 and replaced it with an 80 faster than I'd seen him move all year. I had a clear conscience but a lower test grade.

We don't always get rewarded for honesty here on earth, but God sees our hearts and he knows when we try to honor him with our honesty.

Sapphira: Sin Costs

People who conceal their sins will not prosper, but if they confess and turn from them, they will receive mercy.

PROVERBS 28:13

Sin has consequences. For Ananias and Sapphira, it was a deadly consequence. Ananias left to take the money to Peter at the church. He told Peter it was all the money he'd received for the sale of his land.

Peter said, "Ananias, why have you let Satan fill your heart? You lied to the Holy Spirit, and you kept some of the money for yourself. The property was yours to sell or not sell, as you wished. And after selling it, the money was also yours to give away. How could you do a thing like this? You weren't lying to us but to God!" (Acts 5:3-4).

When Ananias heard what Peter said, he fell to the floor dead! Some young men wrapped him in a sheet and took him away to bury him. About three hours passed, and Sapphira showed up. Perhaps she wondered why Ananias wasn't home yet. Or maybe she thought he was being praised for his generosity and wanted in on it.

When Peter asked her if Ananias had given him the full price for the land, she said yes. Then Peter rebuked her, just as he had her husband, and she died instantly.

When the believers saw what had happened, they were filled with fear, as we all would be. It's not often someone sins and is immediately struck dead.

God's punishment seems harsh, but he always has reasons for what he does. God did not take Ananias and Sapphira's lies lightly. Even though God struck them dead, they were still his children. Their sin didn't change that.

God forgives us of our sins, but they may still have consequences. God doesn't normally override natural consequences. If you lie to your parents and confess it or are caught, God will forgive you, but you may still be grounded. Ask God to keep your heart from deceit and your lips from lying so he'll be able to use you each day.

thinking it through

Do you need to work on truthfulness? Ask God to help you overcome the temptation to lie or deceive, and to always help you speak the truth.

thinking it through

Dorcas was known for her kindness and good deeds. What do others know you for? What is one kind thing you can do for someone else this week?

Dorcas: Making a Difference

There was a believer in Joppa named Tabitha (which in Greek is Dorcas). She was always doing kind things for others and helping the poor.

ACTS 9:36

Ivy was an older church member who'd made a big difference throughout her lifetime. She wasn't a famous evangelist, preacher, or missionary. But Ivy knitted, and she prayed. In fact, she usually did both things together.

While Ivy knitted baby booties and hats for a missionary, she prayed for the missionary and for the babies who would wear the booties and hats. While she knitted baby afghans to give to the new mothers in the church, she prayed for each baby who would be wrapped in one. While she knitted scarves and caps for the children in one of the poorer schools in town, she prayed for each child who would wear them.

Ivy was a modern-day Dorcas. Dorcas, also called Tabitha, was a believer who lived in the seaport town of Joppa, now called Jaffa, outside Tel Aviv. Dorcas owned her own house and probably had plenty of money to live on, but that wasn't what she was known for. She had a reputation for kindness and helping the poor. She made them robes and tunics and coats.

Many people used what was in their hands for God. Moses used the rod he carried to show Pharaoh God's power. Shamgar used his ox goad to defeat the Philistines. The widow of Zarephath used her flour and oil to feed Elijah. And Dorcas used her sewing needle to help clothe the poor and the widows.

Not all of us can be famous Christian singers, missionaries, or speakers, but all of us can use what we have to help others. What do you have that you can use? Knitting needles to make things like Ivy did? A computer to create a newsletter for your church youth group or Christmas cards for the local nursing home? A shovel to clear the sidewalks for older church members? Look around and find something you can use for good.

Puzzle Page

nanias and Sapphira would have needed a verse like this before they decided to lie about their financial gift. Solve the Thermometer Puzzle to read the verse for yourself.

Directions: Look at the thermometer. Each temperature has a corresponding letter. Look at the temperatures under the lines below. On each line, write the letter that goes with the temperature. Check your answer below.

You ____ ____ ____ ____ each ____ ____ ____ ____ ____ ____
50° 85° 75° 80° 15° 20° 10° 40° 15° 20°

in your ____ ____ ____ ____ ____ how ____ ____ ____ ____
35° 20° 5° 70° 80° 50° 85° 10° 35°

to ____ ____ ____ ____. And don't ____ ____ ____ ____
30° 40° 90° 20° 30° 40° 90° 20°

____ ____ ____ ____ ____ ____ ____ ____ ____ ____ ____ or in
70° 20° 45° 85° 10° 80° 5° 55° 80° 45° 95°

____ ____ ____ ____ ____ ____ ____ ____
70° 20° 75° 65° 60° 55° 75° 20°

to ____ ____ ____ ____ ____ ____ ____ ____. "For God
65° 70° 20° 75° 75° 85° 70° 20°

____ ____ ____ ____ ____ a ____ ____ ____ ____ ____ ____
45° 60° 90° 20° 75° 65° 20° 70° 75° 60° 55°

who ____ ____ ____ ____ ____
30° 40° 90° 20° 75°

____ ____ ____ ____ ____ ____ ____ ____ ____ ____."
10° 35° 20° 20° 70° 25° 85° 45° 45° 95°

95-Y
90-V
85-U
80-T
75-S
70-R
65-P
60-O
55-N
50-M
45-L
40-I
35-H
30-G
25-F
20-E
15-D
10-C
5-A

How might this verse have applied to Ananias and Sapphira? How does it apply to you?

Answer: You must each decide in your heart how much to give. And don't give reluctantly or in response to pressure. "For God loves a person who gives cheerfully." (2 Corinthians 9:7)

thinking it through

Proverbs 31:19-21 says, "Her hands are busy spinning thread, her fingers twisting fiber. She extends a helping hand to the poor and opens her arms to the needy. She has no fear of winter for her household, for everyone has warm clothes." How did Dorcas live out these verses? How can you do the same?

Dorcas: Touching Lives

About this time [Dorcas] became ill and died. Her body was washed for burial and laid in an upstairs room. But the believers had heard that Peter was nearby at Lydda, so they sent two men to beg him, "Please come as soon as possible!"

ACTS 9:37-38

Dorcas touched many lives. The people in her church and community loved her because she was kind and generous to everyone, especially the poor and widowed. Dorcas herself may have been a widow, but she was grateful for all she had and shared it with others.

Dorcas sewed clothing for people, but she didn't distribute it in a way that made the recipients feel looked down on. Sometimes when people serve dinner at a homeless shelter or give clothes to the needy, they do it to look good to others or be praised for it. They view the homeless and poor as being less valuable than themselves. Dorcas wasn't like that—and neither was Jesus. Both of them treated the poor, sick, and widowed kindly.

You can help those in need too. Ask your youth pastor if your church already has a ministry to the poor or homeless where you can be involved. If not, talk to him about what the youth in your church can do to help out. You might be able to have a food or clothing drive or serve a meal at a homeless shelter. You may want to organize a group to sing Christmas carols at a nursing home and visit with the residents. It might feel uncomfortable, but sometimes it's good to go out of your comfort zone to bless those who are lonely or in need. Just make sure you are with an adult when you take part in these kinds of ministries.

During the holidays, many groups visit prisons, hospitals, homeless shelters, and nursing homes, but once the Christmas season is over, they are often forgotten. Make a commitment to visit once a month throughout the whole next year.

Dorcas: Acts of Kindness

Peter returned with them; and as soon as he arrived, they took him to the upstairs room. The room was filled with widows who were weeping and showing him the coats and other clothes Dorcas had made for them.

ACTS 9:39

Everyone loved Dorcas, but she became sick and died. The people were sad. She'd touched all their lives with her kindness and unselfish ways. They carried her upstairs to await burial. Two men went and found Peter and brought him to the house.

When Peter arrived at the house, it was full of people grieving for Dorcas. People she had helped over the years gathered around Peter, and they showed him carefully stitched robes, coats, and other garments she'd made for them. They probably wondered who else would care for them as Dorcas had. Who would reach out to the poor and needy?

Peter asked everyone to leave the room. Once he was alone, he knelt and prayed. Then he looked at Dorcas and said, "Get up." Dorcas opened her eyes. She looked around and saw Peter. Then she sat up. Peter called all the people together and showed them that Dorcas was alive again.

Peter's miracle, done by God's power, filled Dorcas's friends with joy, but it did more than that. Many people believed in Jesus that day because of the miracle Peter did. More people were added to the church in Joppa.

We don't read anymore about Dorcas after this, but we can assume she spent many more years blessing people with her kindness and generosity. Dorcas was probably remembered many years after she was gone because of the impact she made on her community.

How will we be remembered when we're gone? Will people talk about us in glowing terms, remembering acts of kindness we performed? Will we be remembered and desperately missed because of the contribution we made and the lives we touched? Let's live in such a way that our lives make a difference too.

thinking it through

What are you known for now? If you aren't sure, ask a friend. Or if you want a real answer, ask someone who isn't a close friend! What can you do to add to your legacy and make a difference in someone's life today?

thinking it through

Ever shy away from sharing your faith because of what people might think? After all, if word gets out you're a Christian, people might not think you're cool. Take a lesson from Mary, and live out your faith without worry about what others will think. Start today.

Mary of Jerusalem (Mother of John Mark): A Brave Believer

About that time King Herod Agrippa began to persecute some believers in the church.

ACTS 12:1

Today's verse isn't a very pleasant one, but persecution was a fact of life for the early believers. Mary of Jerusalem lived in a time when it was dangerous to be a believer. She and her family members were very active in the early church. Her son, John Mark, became an evangelist after a rough start. And her brother Barnabas traveled with Paul on his first missionary trip.

As long as the Herod family was in control, believers weren't safe. Herod the Great murdered all the young boys in Bethlehem in an attempt to kill the new King, Jesus. Herod Antipas beheaded John the Baptist as a reward for his stepdaughter. Herod Agrippa had the apostle James killed for preaching about Jesus. When Agrippa saw how happy some of the Jews were that James had been killed, he seized Peter and imprisoned him, too. He planned to have a public trial after the Passover celebration. Chances are Agrippa planned to increase his popularity with the people by killing Peter.

None of this frightened Mary, who opened her home to the believers so they could meet for fellowship and prayer. With all the believers coming and going, it wouldn't have been surprising if Agrippa's soldiers had shown up at the door to drag Mary and the other Christians off to prison to join Peter. But that didn't worry Mary. She knew Jesus, and she'd seen the miracles he'd done, and seen or heard of the ones Peter had done. She knew God's Spirit was with them. Her faith was stronger than the fear of persecution.

We probably don't live with the reality of being killed for our faith, and sometimes we take our faith for granted. But not the early believers. Their faith was very real to them, and they were willing to die for it if needed.

Mary of Jerusalem: Mary Opens Her Home to Believers

Peter finally came to his senses. "It's really true!" he said. "The Lord has sent his angel and saved me from Herod and from what the Jewish leaders had planned to do to me!" When he realized this, he went to the home of Mary, the mother of John Mark, where many were gathered for prayer.

ACTS 12:11-12

Mary the mother of John Mark was a widow who owned a large house in Jerusalem. She offered her home as a meeting place for believers. Legend has it that the upper room where Jesus served the Last Supper was in Mary's home. We don't know if that's true, but we know her large home was a place where many met together to talk and pray. They probably did have meals there from time to time too.

Peter had been imprisoned for his faith and was awaiting public trial. It likely would have been one of his last nights on earth if Herod Agrippa had gotten his way. Agrippa had already had James killed. The believers gathered at Mary's home to pray for Peter and stayed late into the night.

While the believers prayed, an angel appeared to Peter in his cell. As the guards slept, the angel told Peter to get up. His chains fell off. The angel told Peter to get dressed and follow him. Peter followed the angel out of the cell. He thought he was having a vision and didn't realize this was really happening. Peter and the angel walked by the guards, and the gate of the city opened by itself for them. Then the angel left Peter, and Peter realized this wasn't a vision. He was really free!

Peter must have known that everyone would be gathered at Mary's house praying for his release, so that's where he went.

Mary was brave to open her home to believers when it could have had serious consequences, but her love for the Lord and her faith in him were stronger than any anxiety she might have felt.

thinking it through

Do you think it would have been exciting or scary to live during the early church years? What would have been some advantages to living then? What advantages do you have today that they didn't have?

thinking it through

Read Hebrews 11:6: "It is impossible to please God without faith. Anyone who wants to come to him must believe that God exists and that he rewards those who sincerely seek him." What is necessary to please God? Why do you think that's true?

Rhoda: Believing in Prayer

He knocked at the door in the gate, and a servant girl named Rhoda came to open it. When she recognized Peter's voice, she was so overjoyed that, instead of opening the door, she ran back inside and told everyone, "Peter is standing at the door!"

ACTS 12:13-14

Rhoda served in Mary's large house and was there when the believers gathered to pray for Peter, who was in prison. Even though it was late at night, Rhoda was either still serving or was there to pray with the group.

Then a knock sounded at the door. Rhoda hurried to see who it was. She hoped it wasn't Herod's soldiers wanting to make trouble for the believers gathered there. A knock sounded again, and a man spoke. It was Peter! Rhoda was so overjoyed—and stunned—that she left Peter still knocking and ran to tell the others, "Peter is standing at the door!"

You would expect people who were gathered to pray for that very thing to be overjoyed that their prayers had been answered. Instead, they didn't believe her. They told her she was crazy! But the knocking continued, so they finally went to the door and found Peter standing there just as Rhoda had said. The Bible says they were amazed to find him there.

The group of believers gathered to pray, but when their prayer was answered, they didn't have the faith to believe it. It's like a story often told about a church that called a special meeting to pray for rain during a time of drought—yet only one person brought an umbrella to the meeting.

Sometimes people pray because it's what they know they should do, but they don't really expect an answer. God doesn't always answer prayers on the spot, but he does answer, and he knows who really has faith when they pray. The people at Mary's house failed to believe it when Rhoda told them Peter was there. How sad that in a day when the apostles were performing miracles and many of the people gathered had walked with Jesus, they didn't believe he would answer their prayers.

Lydia: Sharing the Gospel in Your Home

One of them was Lydia from Thyatira, a merchant of expensive purple cloth, who worshiped God. As she listened to us, the Lord opened her heart, and she accepted what Paul was saying.

ACTS 16:14

Lydia was possibly the most wealthy and influential woman in Philippi. She was originally from Thyatira, a city famous for its purple dye. The dye was hard to produce, so it was expensive, as was the purple fabric made from it. Lydia made a good living selling it.

Philippi was a thriving Roman colony without enough Jewish men to have a synagogue. Jewish law said there must be ten men to form a synagogue, but the women could meet together to pray without a formal place.

A group of Jewish women met at the riverside to pray. The Bible doesn't say if Lydia was Jewish or a Gentile who joined them, but many believe she was a Gentile who was seeking God.

God sent Paul and his traveling companions, Silas, Timothy, and Luke, to Philippi, where they found the group of women. Paul shared with them how Jesus, God's Son, had come to earth, how he was crucified, rose again, and now lives in heaven. Paul told the women they could be saved from their sins by believing in Jesus. Lydia became a believer that day. And as she shared what she'd learned, the other members of her household became believers too. Many believe Lydia was a widow and that the others in her household might have been her grown children or servants. The Bible doesn't say. The important thing is that, once Lydia was a believer, she shared the gospel with them.

Sometimes it's harder to talk about Jesus to your own family than to strangers. They know you well and might point out things you do that are less than Christian. Or they may think you are implying they aren't as good as you are or that you're trying to change them into different people. If this is true for you, don't give up. Ask God to show you the best way to reach your family.

thinking it through

If you have people in your home who aren't believers, do you share the gospel with them? What about extended family members? Is it easy or hard for you to talk to your family about Jesus?

Romans 1:16 says, "I am not ashamed of this Good News about Christ. It is the power of God at work, saving everyone who believes—the Jew first and also the Gentile." Does it give you courage to know that God's power is at work when you share the gospel?

thinking it through

God chose Lydia to be part of beginning the church at Philippi. Sometimes we take churches for granted. What can you do to show appreciation for your church? Help with church maintenance—wash the nursery toys, wipe the tables in the preschool room, or help clean up the grounds? Volunteer to help with a program for the younger children? Greet visitors or hand out bulletins? Send a note of encouragement to a pastor, teacher, or staff worker? Instead of just attending church this week, see what you can contribute.

Lydia: The Beginning of a Church

When Paul and Silas left the prison, they returned to the home of Lydia. There they met with the believers and encouraged them once more. Then they left town.

ACTS 16:40

After Lydia became a believer, she asked Paul and his mission team—Silas, Timothy, and Luke, and possibly more—to stay at her house. Like Mary in Jerusalem, Lydia probably had a large house, so there was room enough for everyone. And like Mary, Lydia wasn't afraid to take the risk of hosting believers in her home.

One day the mission team met a slave girl possessed by a demon. She earned a lot of money for her master by telling fortunes. She followed the mission team, shouting, "These men are servants of the Most High God, and they have come to tell you how to be saved" (Acts 16:17). Finally Paul turned to the girl and said to the demon within her, "I command you in the name of Jesus Christ to come out of her" (verse 18). The demon left the girl, and she was no longer able to tell fortunes—or make money for her master. This made the master angry. He dragged Paul and Silas into the marketplace and turned the mob against them. They were beaten and thrown into prison.

But even though they were bound in prison and in pain from the beating, Paul and Silas prayed and sang songs to God. Around midnight there was an earthquake; the whole jail shook, and the prisoners were freed. The guard knew he'd be blamed for the prisoners' escape, so he got out his sword to kill himself. Paul said, "Stop! Don't kill yourself! We are all here!" (verse 28). He shared the gospel with the man and his family, and they all became believers that night.

Then Paul and Silas returned to Lydia's house, where the believers were gathered. Because Lydia believed and was willing to open her home, she hosted the beginnings of the church at Philippi. It was an exciting time as the first Christian church there was formed.

Quiz Time

Lydia immediately started sharing her faith. Are you a soul winner like Lydia? Read each sentence below, and circle A for always, S for sometimes, or N for never.

1. I share my faith with at least one person each week.

   A S N

2. I tell my peers that knowing Jesus is what gives life meaning.

   A S N

3. When discussions about religion come up, I confidently and politely share my views.

   A S N

4. I live in such a way that others can tell I belong to Jesus.

   A S N

5. I encourage my family in their Christian walk if they are believers, and try to reach them for Jesus if they aren't.

   A S N

Did you circle mostly A's? If so, you are like Lydia in sharing your faith with others. If you circled mostly S's, you have a good start but need to be more bold about sharing your faith. If you circled mostly N's, ask yourself why you are hesitant to share your faith. Ask God to help you overcome any obstacles to witnessing.

thinking it through

Make a list of classes you attend, activities you're involved in, and any other opportunities you have to interact with different people. Who could you talk to about Jesus in each of these contexts? Ask God to bring to mind some names of people he wants you to talk to. Then ask for his help in approaching them.

Lydia: Sharing the Truth Where You Are

Never be lazy, but work hard and serve the Lord enthusiastically.

ROMANS 12:11

Lydia was a successful businesswoman. She was influential, organized, and knew how to take charge. When she became a believer, she didn't lose those characteristics, and she didn't give them up. She used them for the Lord.

Because of Lydia's ability to run her business and her ambition in making it successful, she was able to use her money and her home to help the early believers. Her large, comfortable house was the meeting place for the church of Philippi when it began, and her house was the home base for Paul and his team when they were in town.

When a person believes in Jesus, her heart changes. Her lifestyle may change too, because God makes her a new creation. But that doesn't mean her talents and abilities change. After believing in Jesus, Lydia was still the person she was before, but now she used her talents and possessions for the Lord.

God needs doctors, lawyers, businesswomen, teachers, mechanics, and pilots who are living for him. He needs anyone who will take the gospel into her work area and share it with others. Not everyone is called to full-time Christian service, but everyone is called to share the truth right where he or she is.

Today's verse tells us not to be lazy but to work hard and serve the Lord enthusiastically. God doesn't need couch-potato Christians. He needs young women who will get excited about their faith and take the gospel to their gymnastics classes, their soccer teams, their dance companies, their honor clubs, their science classes, their drama clubs, and everywhere they go.

God needs you to enthusiastically share the gospel wherever you go today. Where will that be?

Lois and Eunice: Influencing Others

I remember your genuine faith, for you share the faith that first filled your grandmother Lois and your mother, Eunice. And I know that same faith continues strong in you.

2 TIMOTHY 1:5

Lois and Eunice are known for being Timothy's grandmother and mother. We first meet Eunice in Acts 16 when Paul asks Timothy to accompany him on a missionary trip. Timothy's mother isn't mentioned by name there, but we're told she was a Jewish believer, and his father was Greek.

Lois and Eunice were familiar with the Old Testament Scriptures, and they taught these to Timothy from the time he was a very young child. Timothy was an eager learner, and he loved God. But even though Lois, Eunice, and Timothy loved God and the Scriptures, they didn't know about Jesus. They probably became believers in Jesus when Paul traveled through their city of Lystra, in the hill country of present-day Turkey, on an earlier trip.

Lois and Eunice went about their daily work of cooking, cleaning, and raising Timothy. They were just living out their lives, but they were also leaving a legacy of faith that started with Lois and passed to Eunice and then to Timothy.

Lois and Eunice influenced Timothy while they raised him, but you influence people too without even knowing it. Every time you tell someone about Jesus, you plant a seed in her heart. When you say a kind word to a classmate, you brighten her day. When you take a few minutes to help a sibling with a chore, you encourage him or her. Every time you smile at a cashier or a stranger you pass in the mall, you make a difference.

The more time you invest in someone, the more you influence her. If you want to make a difference in a friend's or sibling's life, shower her with kindness every day. Share what you learn in your daily Bible reading. Listen as she talks and offer godly advice. You never know what difference you may make in her life.

thinking it through

Think about who you might be influencing without even knowing it. What are some ways you can make a difference in someone's life today?

Has anyone passed a legacy of faith to you? Maybe a parent, grandparent, neighbor, or pastor? Thank God for this person and the important role he or she has in your life.

thinking it through

What talents do you have that you can use in your church? Try one of the following ideas, or talk to your parents, Sunday school teacher, or youth leader, and ask them how you can be more involved.

- Sing in the choir or be part of a worship team.
- Welcome visitors to your youth group.
- Join a prayer group, or get one started.
- Take part in an outreach program or community service project.

Phoebe: A Brave Church Worker

I commend to you our sister Phoebe, who is a deacon in the church in Cenchrea. Welcome her in the Lord as one who is worthy of honor among God's people. Help her in whatever she needs, for she has been helpful to many, and especially to me.

ROMANS 16:1-2

Phoebe lived in Cenchrea, a seaport near the city of Corinth. Since Paul introduces Phoebe to the Christians in Rome within his letter, it's likely she was the one who delivered it to them.

A woman taking a journey to deliver a letter doesn't sound uncommon to us, but around AD 57, it was highly unusual. People still lived pretty much in isolation. Few people had the chance to travel, yet Phoebe journeyed by land and water to another country to deliver Paul's letter. This gave her a chance not only to visit another country but also to meet Christians in another church. It's likely Phoebe was single, because women rarely traveled due to responsibilities at home.

Phoebe was a deacon in her own church. She was known for helping many people, including Paul, who spoke highly of her. Phoebe probably taught the women at church. She probably made sure the poor and widows had enough money to live on. She may have opened her home to other believers and provided food and shelter to travelers.

Phoebe wasn't the kind of Christian who went to church and then went home and forgot about her faith until the next church service. She held an office at church and was well known there. She was also known for her good deeds and helpfulness to others.

Do people at church know who you are? Do you attend services because your parents make you, or do you go so you can be actively involved? Perhaps you're reluctant to go to church because it seems boring and meaningless to you. What can you do to change that? Try to be involved like Phoebe by helping out at your church. Give of your energy and talent to make your church a better place.

Priscilla: Serving God Together

Give my greetings to Priscilla and Aquila, my co-workers in the ministry of Christ Jesus. In fact, they once risked their lives for me. I am thankful to them, and so are all the Gentile churches. Also give my greetings to the church that meets in their home.

ROMANS 16:3-5

In Scripture, Priscilla and her husband, Aquila, are always mentioned together. They are one of many sets of names we've come to know as Bible spouses—Adam and Eve, Abraham and Sarah, Mary and Joseph. When both spouses love and honor God, they can accomplish a lot together for the Lord.

Before they sinned, Adam and Eve served God together by taking care of their garden home and the animals that resided there. They were the beginning of the human race. By faith Abraham and Sarah followed God to a new country where they gave birth to the child God had promised them, and they were the beginning of God's chosen people. Mary and Joseph were chosen to parent the Messiah, the Son of God.

God can use couples who are willing to serve him together. That's why it's important to be discerning about who you date, and especially who you marry. When God's people are married to spouses who don't love him, things don't go well. Look at Abigail and Nabal. Abigail worshiped God, but Nabal was a fool. He denied David and his men the food they asked for and deserved. Only by acting quickly was Abigail able to salvage the situation and prevent the murder of the men in her household. And what about Samson and Delilah? Samson was one of God's chosen deliverers, but the ungodly Delilah betrayed him for money.

Right now marriage may seem light years away, but it's not. You may enter a dating relationship in a few years. Don't date just to say you have a boyfriend, but date only guys who love and honor God. Be like Priscilla and Aquila and the other couples who served God together, or you could find yourself married to a Nabal instead!

thinking it through

Do you think it's okay to date whomever you want as long as you marry someone with similar beliefs, or is it better to date only someone you would consider marrying? If you aren't sure, can you think of any Scripture verses on the subject? Ask God to give you wisdom to determine the answer. It's good to decide these things before you date, so your feelings don't make the decision for you.

thinking it through

What does the Bible say about work? Read Romans 12:11: "Never be lazy, but work hard and serve the Lord enthusiastically." Though you aren't responsible for supporting yourself right now, you can do a lot to help out at home and make the responsibility easier for your parents or those you live with. Come up with three different ways you can help out at home this week that are different from your usual chores. See what you can do to help out.

Priscilla: Be a Hard Worker

[Paul] became acquainted with a Jew named Aquila, born in Pontus, who had recently arrived from Italy with his wife, Priscilla. They had left Italy when Claudius Caesar deported all Jews from Rome. Paul lived and worked with them, for they were tentmakers just as he was.

ACTS 18:2-3

Like Paul, Priscilla and Aquila were tentmakers. All Jewish boys were taught a trade. Aquila was taught the craft of cutting and sewing rough goat hair fabric or other cloth or leather into tents. Aquila probably taught Priscilla how to make tents too. This was how they supported themselves, and they continued even after they began traveling to start churches. They didn't want to be a burden on others while they shared the gospel. When Paul stayed with the couple, they likely sat together sharing their day while making or repairing tents. They worked hard, and they were proud of the tents they sold.

Priscilla and Aquila were valuable coworkers of Paul. After hosting Paul for a year and a half in their Corinth home, the couple went to Ephesus with him. Paul left them there to establish a church, and they began a church in their home. During their ministry, the couple met Apollos, who was enthusiastic in his teaching but didn't know the whole gospel. He was still waiting for the promised Messiah. The couple took him in and told him about salvation through Christ. They taught him all the things they had learned, and Apollos went on to preach about Jesus.

Priscilla and Aquila went back to Rome, and soon a church was meeting in their house there. They eventually moved back to Ephesus, possibly to avoid persecution in Rome.

Throughout all their travels, ministry, and starting churches, Priscilla and Aquila continued their tentmaking trade. This was an honorable way to support themselves as they served Jesus, sometimes side by side with fellow tentmaker Paul.

Women in the Church: Being a Church Worker

Give my greetings to Tryphena and Tryphosa, the Lord's workers, and to dear Persis, who has worked so hard for the Lord.

ROMANS 16:12

There are many women who are mentioned only briefly by name in the New Testament. Many of them helped in the churches where Paul preached. Here are a few of them:

- Damaris is listed among those in Athens who became believers (Acts 17:34).
- Persis, Tryphena, and Tryphosa are listed as hard workers in the Roman church (Romans 16:12).
- Julia and Nereus's sister are included with those who faithfully gathered with other believers in Rome (Romans 16:15).
- Junia was in prison with Paul, and he singles her out in his letter to the Romans as being highly respected among the apostles (Romans 16:7).
- Some members of Chloe's household were upset enough about the quarreling in the Corinthian church to contact Paul about it (1 Corinthians 1:11).
- Rufus's mother, a woman in the Roman church, was like a mother to Paul (Romans 16:13).
- Mary of Rome was a hard worker in the Roman church (Romans 16:6).

These women are singled out because they tirelessly served the Lord. There is usually one small group of people in every church who teach Sunday school, work with the youth, lead VBS, serve as camp counselors, lead the children's choir, and work in the nursery. Although the early church didn't have all those programs, there was work to be done, and it was one small group of people who took charge in each church.

Which group are you in? Do you help out wherever you can, or do you leave the work to someone else?

thinking it through

Sometimes people don't get involved because they don't know what needs to be done. Are you among the workers at your church? If so, consider asking a friend or two to help you. You'll have fun serving together, and you'll be helping to get more people involved. If you don't know what you can do to contribute, ask a pastor or staff member for some ideas.

thinking it through

Have you accepted Jesus as your Lord and Savior and given your life to him? If you've never taken that step, it's not too late. Ask Jesus to forgive you for your sins, and believe that he died and rose again for you. You'll be part of his family forever!

If you have chosen to believe in Jesus, how diligent are you about sharing God's Good News with those around you? Who can you share the gospel with this week?

Drusilla and Bernice: Enemies of the Gospel

A few days later Felix came back with his wife, Drusilla, who was Jewish. Sending for Paul, they listened as he told them about faith in Christ Jesus.

ACTS 24:24

Drusilla and Bernice were enemies of the gospel. They were part of the brutal Herod family. They were the daughters of Herod Agrippa I and granddaughters of Herod the Great, who had all the baby boys killed in an attempt to get rid of baby Jesus. They were also nieces of Herod Antipas, who had John the Baptist beheaded.

Although the Bible doesn't tell us much about these wicked sisters, history records that they hated each other. Drusilla was the younger sister and more beautiful than Bernice. Bernice was very unkind to her sister. But there's one thing they had in common—they both had the chance to hear the apostle Paul share the gospel, and they both rejected it.

Drusilla had married Aziz, King of Emesa, at a young age. She left him for Felix, a Gentile. When Paul was imprisoned in Caesarea, Felix sent for him. Paul shared his faith in Jesus with the couple. Both rejected the message, and Felix sent him away, hoping Paul would offer him a bribe for his freedom.

Paul later appeared before Bernice and her brother Agrippa II. Paul told them about his salvation through Jesus and how they could experience it too. Like her sister, Bernice rejected his message.

There are many today who hear the gospel preached in their churches or on television but don't accept the message. They choose not to accept God's gift of salvation through Jesus.

Tradition says Drusilla was near Pompeii when Mount Vesuvius erupted, and she was killed trying to escape. None of us know when we will die. Some reject Jesus, thinking they can always accept his gift of salvation later, but sometimes later never comes. If you've never responded to God's message of salvation, don't let another day go by before you do.

Quiz Time

The Bible women we've read about have been hardworking and enthusiastic, and most of them had faith in God that saw them through difficult times. A few were strongly opposed to God. They were very energetic in making trouble for those who believed in God. Can you match each hardworking woman below with what she did?

a. Dorcas
b. Mrs. Noah
c. Martha
d. Abigail
e. Nurse Deborah
f. Rachel
g. Peter's mother-in-law
h. Rebekah
i. Widow of Zarephath
j. Anna

___ 1. She went to the well for water for her family. She offered to water a stranger's camels.
___ 2. She gathered enough food for her family and all the animals to last many months.
___ 3. She helped her mistress prepare for a long trip and then went along on the trip.
___ 4. She sewed clothing for the poor and widowed.
___ 5. She watered her family's flocks.
___ 6. She worked hard to prepare a meal for Jesus when he visited.
___ 7. She prepared a meal for Jesus after he healed her.
___ 8. She dedicated her life to serving in the Temple.
___ 9. She prepared meals for Elijah, as well as for herself and her son.
___ 10. She prepared enough food for David and all his men.

Answer: 1. h, 2. b, 3. e, 4. a, 5. f, 6. c, 7. g, 8. j, 9. i, 10. d

thinking it through

Are you like Euodia and Syntyche? Have you let little things come between you and a friend? Or are you the one who always has to patch things up between two other friends? How can you encourage peace among you and your friends?

Euodia and Syntyche: Get Along

I appeal to Euodia and Syntyche. Please, because you belong to the Lord, settle your disagreement. And I ask you, my true partner, to help these two women, for they worked hard with me in telling others the Good News. They worked along with Clement and the rest of my co-workers, whose names are written in the Book of Life.

PHILIPPIANS 4:2-3

Euodia and Syntyche were part of the church at Philippi. They may have been among the women who met at the river with Lydia and became believers when Paul stopped there.

Euodia and Syntyche put a lot of time and effort into the church at Philippi. They weren't afraid to tackle the tough jobs or to do menial work. They were active in telling others about Jesus and bringing them to church.

Even though both women were working together in the church, it appears they didn't always get along. Faithful believers don't agree on everything, and many times it's personal preferences that cause the problem. That was true in Paul's day, and it's still true today. Churches have had terrible fights over what color the new carpet, the choir robes, or the church kitchen should be. In fact, churches have even divided over these things! The blue-carpet people leave the maroon-carpet Christians and start their own little church.

What were Euodia and Syntyche arguing about? We don't know. It could have been over what day to meet and pray. Perhaps it was over differing beliefs. Whatever it was, it hindered their friendship and their work.

I imagine both women were embarrassed to see their names in Paul's letter to the church. Maybe they didn't realize news of their disagreement had reached him. They may have wished he had sent them a personal letter rather than bringing it up in the letter to the church. Chances are, once they saw their names in that letter, they fixed whatever the problem was between them and went on to be faithful church workers.

Christmas: Jesus' Family Tree, Part 1

Salmon was the father of Boaz (whose mother was Rahab). Boaz was the father of Obed (whose mother was Ruth). Obed was the father of Jesse.

MATTHEW 1:5

Have you ever researched your family history? Maybe you've heard stories about your great-grandparents or seen a family tree showing the names of your ancestors.

Earlier in the year you read about a few of the women in Jesus' family tree. Let's take another look at them and at one we didn't read about earlier—Tamar.

Tamar was married to Er, Jacob's grandson and Judah's oldest son, but Er was wicked and God caused him to die. When a husband died, it was the next brother's responsibility to marry the widow. So Onan, the next son, married Tamar. But Onan wouldn't allow her to have children because they would be counted as Er's sons. So God caused him to die.

Judah sent Tamar back to her own home and told her she could marry his third son, Shelah, when he grew up. But Judah didn't keep his promise. He was afraid this son would die also. When Tamar realized she wasn't going to be allowed to marry Shelah, she dressed like a prostitute and tricked Judah into getting her pregnant. That way she could carry on the family line and would be provided for. Tamar gave birth to twins, and one of the twins, Perez, continued the line that led to Jesus.

Another woman from Jesus' family tree is the prostitute Rahab, who helped the Israelite spies escape from Jericho and was saved when the Israelites conquered the city (see the devotions for April 7–13). Rahab later gave birth to Boaz, the great-grandfather of David, putting her in Jesus' ancestral line.

You wouldn't be where you are today without the people in your family tree. Even if some of your ancestors made poor choices, you don't have to follow in their steps. With God's help, you can make choices that will grow you into the woman God wants you to be.

thinking it through

If you're spending time with family this week, ask your grandparents or aunts and uncles to tell you some stories about when they were growing up. You'll learn a lot about your family's past.

As you reflect on Jesus' birth today, thank God that he can use anyone to accomplish his plans. Ask him to show you how you can fulfill his plans too.

thinking it through

Why do you think God didn't choose only the best women from the best families to be part of Jesus' family tree? How can God use you this Christmas season?

Christmas: Jesus' Family Tree, Part 2

Jesse was the father of King David. David was the father of Solomon (whose mother was Bathsheba, the widow of Uriah).

MATTHEW 1:6

If you read the devotions at the end of May, you'll remember that Ruth was from Moab, a country that was one of Israel's enemies. She married an Israelite, one of Elimelech and Naomi's sons. After Elimelech and both sons died, Ruth went with Naomi back to Israel, where she cared for her mother-in-law. Ruth gathered leftover grain from Boaz's field to provide for both of them. Boaz saw Ruth in his fields and instructed his men to leave extra for her. Eventually Boaz and Ruth were married. Ruth gave birth to Obed, David's father—another step forward in Jesus' line.

We talked about Bathsheba in July. She was married to Uriah, but one day while Uriah was off in battle, David saw Bathsheba and wanted her. He sent his men to bring her to him. Bathsheba became pregnant with David's child. When she told David, he had Uriah sent home from battle. He tried to get Uriah to go to Bathsheba so Uriah would think the baby was his. But Uriah wouldn't stay with Bathsheba while the other men were still fighting. David was getting desperate to cover up his sin, so when his first plan failed, he had Uriah sent to the front of the battle where Uriah was killed. After that, David and Bathsheba were married. Their first child died, but later they had another son, Solomon, who was also in Jesus' line.

Why do you suppose God allowed women like Tamar, Rahab, Ruth, and Bathsheba to be part of Jesus' family tree? Why didn't he choose Jewish women from the best families, or those who were righteous and holy? Perhaps God chose the unlikely women he did to encourage us that no matter who we are, where we're from, or what sins we've committed in the past, God can use us for good.

Women of the Bible: God Uses Unlikely People

Remember, dear brothers and sisters, that few of you were wise in the world's eyes or powerful or wealthy when God called you. Instead, God chose things the world considers foolish in order to shame those who think they are wise. And he chose things that are powerless to shame those who are powerful.

1 CORINTHIANS 1:26-27

One lesson that has appeared over and over as we've looked at different Bible women is that God chooses and uses unlikely people. Sometimes we think God would choose holy, righteous people who are talented and smart. But the people God really chooses are those who are willing. Think back to the women in this book.

God chose Pharaoh's daughter to raise Moses. She was the daughter of the very person who wanted Moses dead. Yet she took Moses into her own home. Moses grew up to lead the Israelites out of slavery.

God chose Esther, an orphaned Jewish girl, to become the queen of Persia. God gave her the courage to approach the king and tell him of the plot to destroy the Jews.

God chose Sarah and Elizabeth to have babies in their old age. Sarah's son was the child who fulfilled God's promises to Abraham and began the Israelite nation. Elizabeth's son was the person chosen to prepare the people for the Messiah.

God chose Mary, a poor, young girl, to be the mother of the Savior. She was unknown among people, but known to God for her faithfulness.

God chose to use the Samaritan woman, the woman who anointed Jesus, and the woman caught in adultery to demonstrate his grace and forgiveness. They were witnesses for him after meeting Jesus.

God uses unlikely people. Maybe sometimes you feel you don't have any talents he can use, or you don't come from the right kind of family to be used—just think of the women you've read about. Be open to God's leading, and he will use you, too.

thinking it through

Are you willing to be used? Write God a letter and let him know!

thinking it through

Are you willing to say yes to God's adventure for you as you go into the New Year? Ask a friend to join you in seeking God and his plans for each of you this year.

Women of the Bible: Say Yes to God

I can do everything through Christ, who gives me strength.

PHILIPPIANS 4:13

God can use anyone who is willing, but that doesn't mean he'll always call you to do easy things. It doesn't work that way. God may call you to do some difficult tasks, but he will give you what you need to succeed.

Just imagine how some of the Bible women felt when God gave them a task to do. Mrs. Noah was told the world was going to be destroyed, but she and her family would be saved . . . by spending a year on a boat full of animals. God gave her the grace to survive her time on the boat and the courage to start over in a new world.

Rebekah left her home to travel hundreds of miles to marry a man she'd never met. What did she think about as she traveled farther and farther from her home and everything she knew? Did she dream about Isaac and wonder if she would find true love? God gave her the courage and strength she needed to leave everything behind and make the long journey to her future.

The widow of Zarephath was sure she and her son were going to starve when Elijah asked her to feed him. She had no guarantee his promise of unlimited oil and flour throughout the famine was true. She didn't even worship the true God at this point, yet he chose her to feed his prophet.

Mary of Jerusalem and the other early church women opened their homes to the apostles and believers, even though there was the risk of persecution. God gave these women the courage to meet with other believers and to support the church.

God may call you to do something that seems hard, but he'll give you the courage, wisdom, and ability to do it just as he did for the Bible women. Don't miss out on the adventure by being afraid to say yes to God.

Women of the Bible: Jesus Came to Call Sinners, Not the Righteous

Go and learn the meaning of this Scripture: "I want you to show mercy, not offer sacrifices." For I have come to call not those who think they are righteous, but those who know they are sinners.

MATTHEW 9:13

While Jesus lived on earth, he didn't always act the way the religious leaders thought he should. He talked to women, even those who were considered immoral. He healed on the Sabbath. He talked to those who were the "wrong" race. And he didn't show favoritism toward those who thought themselves righteous.

Jesus came to earth to save sinners. He had many followers who were grateful recipients of both his healing and forgiveness. After he cast seven demons out of her, Mary Magdalene became one of Jesus' most faithful followers.

The Samaritan woman Jesus met at the well was a changed person after meeting Jesus. He talked to her even though she was a Samaritan and a woman and a sinner, offering her his gift of eternal life. She told everyone she met about Jesus.

Another sinful woman crashed Simon the Pharisee's dinner party. She cried tears of repentance and gratitude on Jesus' feet, then dried the tears with her hair and anointed his feet with expensive perfume. Jesus told Simon that people who have been forgiven more love their Savior more.

The Pharisees dragged a woman caught in adultery to Jesus. They were trying to trick him into saying something wrong. But Jesus quietly reminded them of their own sin, and he forgave the woman.

Jesus didn't come to earth for the people who thought themselves righteous on their own. He came to save sinners. Many of Jesus' enemies didn't consider themselves sinners because of their own good works, and they hated Jesus. But those Jesus healed and forgave loved him. They became faithful followers.

thinking it through

Read Titus 3:5: "He saved us, not because of the righteous things we had done, but because of his mercy. He washed away our sins, giving us a new birth and new life through the Holy Spirit." How and why does Jesus save us? Do you consider yourself a good person or a sinner? What do you think Jesus would say? What would he do in response?

thinking it through

In the verse for today, Paul tells Timothy that everyone who wants to live a godly life will face suffering. But later in his letter to Timothy, he tells him, "You should keep a clear mind in every situation. Don't be afraid of suffering for the Lord. Work at telling others the Good News, and fully carry out the ministry God has given you" (2 Timothy 4:5). How could this help you when you face suffering and rejection for standing up for Christ?

Women of the Bible: There Will Always Be Those Who Oppose Christians

Everyone who wants to live a godly life in Christ Jesus will suffer persecution.

2 TIMOTHY 3:12

Jesus had enemies when he lived on earth. The religious leaders didn't like the things he did or the things he said. They didn't like that he said they needed a Savior like everyone else. Jesus' enemies crucified him.

Some women in the Bible followed Jesus despite the risks. Mary the mother of Jesus, Mary Magdalene, Mary the mother of James and Joseph, Salome, Joanna, Susanna, and others traveled with Jesus. They followed him clear to the cross. While some of the disciples fled, the women stayed. They were among the first to find out Jesus had risen.

After Jesus died, rose from the dead, and ascended into heaven, the people who hated Jesus started persecuting his followers. James was killed. Peter was thrown into jail. Mary, Rhoda, Lydia, and Phoebe were among the brave women who made up the early church. None of these women hesitated to spread the gospel, host the apostles when they traveled, or open their homes for meetings.

It's not likely you'll face the risk of death for sharing your faith, but sometimes it's hard to speak out for Jesus. Some of your peers may reject you because of the things you stand for. Others may write you off as being old fashioned or just not cool. That hurts, but don't let that stop you. Find other Christians for support. Try to join a Christian club at school or become more involved in youth activities at church. Don't back down on your beliefs or hide them just because some people might not like you. And if they don't, you are in good company with all the women of the Bible who stood up for their faith no matter the cost.

Quiz Time

Euodia and Syntyche had trouble getting along. How well do you get along with others? Read each sentence below, and circle A for always, S for sometimes, or N for never.

1. When a friend and I disagree, we come to a compromise.

   A S N

2. It's okay if my friend gets her way, as long as I get my way sometimes too.

   A S N

3. I try not to let differences in personal preferences bother me.

   A S N

4. I accept that my friend and I have differences in our likes and dislikes.

   A S N

5. If I argue with a friend, I make sure to talk it through later.

   A S N

How did you do?

If you circled mostly A's, you realize it's okay to have differences, but they shouldn't damage your friendship. After all, variety is what keeps things interesting. Arguments happen, but you are able to work them through and not let them damage your friendship.

If you circled mostly S's, you need to work harder at not allowing differences to harm your friendships. There has to be give-and-take in any relationship. No one person should get her way all the time. Take turns choosing, compromise, and be willing to overlook faults.

If you circled mostly N's, your friendships are in danger. Be willing to compromise and take turns. There will always be disagreements, so it's important to learn to deal with them. Practice doing that now so you won't be like Euodia and Syntyche and let differences harm your work for Jesus.

thinking it through

Which character traits will you work on developing in your life? How?

What Bible women can you think of who demonstrated those character traits? Go back and read their stories if you need ideas for how you can develop those traits in your own life.

Women of the Bible: Every Day Is a New Start

No, dear brothers and sisters, I have not achieved it, but I focus on this one thing: Forgetting the past and looking forward to what lies ahead, I press on to reach the end of the race and receive the heavenly prize for which God, through Christ Jesus, is calling us.

PHILIPPIANS 3:13-14

December 31 is a day when many people reflect on the past year. They think about the good they've done—and the bad. They think about all the things they've accomplished—and the things they wish they'd accomplished. Many times people resolve they'll do better in the coming year. They may even set goals to accomplish certain things.

Setting goals for the coming year is a good thing. One goal you might want to set is to develop in your own life the characteristics displayed by the Bible women you've read about this year. Perhaps you might pick one character trait per month and think of several ways to build up that trait during the month.

Here are some of the characteristics:

Obedience
Enthusiasm
Fairness
Diligence
Responsibility
Hospitality
Thankfulness
Faith
Trust
Kindness
Patience
Dependability
Friendliness
Dignity
Generosity
Perseverance
Humility
Initiative
Courage
Wisdom
Purity
Compassion

You're at the end of this devotion book, but don't stop learning about Bible women now. There's so much to learn from each of them. Choose one or two and research them more. Read their stories in the Bible, and find out all you can about their lives. Or, go back through and reread this book, and look for something new about each woman. Ask a friend or sister join you. Some things are more fun with two.

Scripture Index

Genesis 1:27 . . . . ***January 1***
Genesis 1:31 . . . . ***January 6***
Genesis 3:6 . . . . ***January 8***
Genesis 4:9, NIV . . . . ***March 24***
Genesis 6:18 . . . . ***January 15***
Genesis 7:1 . . . . ***January 17***
Genesis 8:16 . . . . ***January 18***
Genesis 11:31 . . . . ***January 22***
Genesis 12:1 . . . . ***January 23***
Genesis 15:5 . . . . ***January 24***
Genesis 16:5 . . . . ***January 29***
Genesis 16:7 . . . . ***January 31***
Genesis 19:26 . . . . ***February 5***
Genesis 24:15 . . . . ***February 6***
Genesis 24:57-58. . . . . ***February 11***
Genesis 24:59 . . . . ***February 20***
Genesis 25:23 . . . . ***February 18***
Genesis 29:6 . . . . ***February 23***
Genesis 29:20 . . . . ***February 21***
Genesis 29:25 . . . . ***February 24***
Genesis 29:33 . . . . ***March 4***
Genesis 30:1 . . . . ***February 26***
Genesis 39:3-4. . . . . ***February 27***
Genesis 39:9 . . . . ***March 7***
Exodus 1:15-16 . . . . ***March 8***
Exodus 1:17. . . . . ***March 9***
Exodus 2:3. . . . . ***March 16***
Exodus 2:4. . . . . ***March 23***
Exodus 2:6. . . . . ***March 22***
Exodus 2:10. . . . . ***March 20***
Exodus 2:16-17 . . . . ***April 6***
Exodus 13:21. ***March 31***
Exodus 15:1. . . . . ***March 30***
Exodus 15:20. . . . . ***April 1***
Exodus 15:21. . . . . ***April 2***
Numbers 12:15 . . . . ***April 5***
Numbers 27:5-7. . . . . ***April 14***
Deuteronomy 10:12 . . . . ***March 11***
Deuteronomy 31:6 . . . . ***March 18***
Deuteronomy 31:6 . . . . ***September 2***
Joshua 1:9. . . . . ***April 21***
Joshua 2:1 . . . . ***April 7***
Joshua 2:11 . . . . ***April 8***
Joshua 6:25 . . . . ***April 12***
Joshua 15:19 . . . . ***April 15***
Judges 4:4. . . . . ***April 16***
Judges 4:5. . . . . ***April 17***
Judges 4:8. . . . . ***April 22***
Judges 4:9. . . . . ***April 20***
Judges 4:10. . . . . ***April 24***

Judges 4:14 . . . . ***April 27***
Judges 4:21 . . . . ***April 30***
Judges 5:7 . . . . ***April 29***
Judges 5:13 . . . . ***April 26***
Judges 11:36 . . . . ***May 1***
Judges 13:24 . . . . ***May 2***
Judges 16:4-5 . . . . ***May 3***
Ruth 1:1 . . . . ***May 10***
Ruth 1:4 . . . . ***May 18***
Ruth 1:4-5 . . . . ***May 11***
Ruth 1:6 . . . . ***May 19***
Ruth 1:14-15 . . . . ***May 17***
Ruth 1:16 . . . . ***May 20***
Ruth 1:20-21 . . . . ***May 12***
Ruth 2:4 . . . . ***May 30***
Ruth 2:10, NIV . . . . ***May 22***
Ruth 2:14 . . . . ***May 31***
Ruth 2:23 . . . . ***May 21***
Ruth 3:9 . . . . ***May 23***
Ruth 3:14 . . . . ***May 29***
Ruth 4:13 . . . . ***May 25***
Ruth 4:17 . . . . ***May 16***
1 Samuel 1:2 . . . . ***June 1***
1 Samuel 1:6, NIV . . . . ***June 15***
1 Samuel 1:10, 15 . . . . ***June 2***
1 Samuel 1:11 . . . . ***June 3***
1 Samuel 1:19 . . . . ***June 10***
1 Samuel 1:27-28 . . . . ***June 13***
1 Samuel 2:1 . . . . ***June 8***
1 Samuel 2:3 . . . . ***June 9***
1 Samuel 2:26, NIV . . . . ***June 14***
1 Samuel 4:21 . . . . ***June 16***
1 Samuel 16:7 . . . . ***August 22***
1 Samuel 18:20-21 . . . . ***June 17***
1 Samuel 19:11-13 . . . . ***June 18***
1 Samuel 25:3 . . . . ***June 24***
1 Samuel 25:26 . . . . ***June 25***
1 Samuel 25:32-33 . . . . ***June 28***
1 Samuel 25:36 . . . . ***June 27***
1 Samuel 25:44 . . . . ***June 19***
1 Samuel 28:7 . . . . ***July 1***
2 Samuel 6:16 . . . . ***June 20***
2 Samuel 6:20 . . . . ***June 21***
2 Samuel 11:27 . . . . ***July 2***
1 Kings 1:29-30 . . . . ***July 3***
1 Kings 10:2 . . . . ***July 9***
1 Kings 16:31 . . . . ***July 17***
1 Kings 17:14 . . . . ***July 10***
1 Kings 17:24 . . . . ***July 16***
1 Kings 18:4 . . . . ***July 18***
1 Kings 19:2 . . . . ***July 20***
1 Kings 21:7 . . . . ***July 19***
2 Kings 4:2, NIV . . . . ***July 25***
2 Kings 4:6, NIV . . . . ***July 24***
2 Kings 4:8 . . . . ***July 26***
2 Kings 4:9-10 . . . . ***July 27***
2 Kings 4:16 . . . . ***July 28***
2 Kings 5:2 . . . . ***July 29***
2 Kings 5:3 . . . . ***July 30***
2 Kings 11:2 . . . . ***August 5***
2 Kings 18:2, 5 . . . . ***August 6***
2 Chronicles 34:22 . . . . ***August 7***
2 Chronicles 34:23-24 . . . . ***August 8***
Esther 1:1, NIV . . . . ***August 18***
Esther 1:5 . . . . ***August 9***
Esther 1:11 . . . . ***August 13***
Esther 1:12 . . . . ***August 10***
Esther 2:1 . . . . ***August 16***
Esther 2:2 . . . . ***August 20***
Esther 2:3 . . . . ***August 23***
Esther 2:6 . . . . ***August 19***
Esther 2:7 . . . . ***August 24***
Esther 2:17-18 . . . . ***August 27***
Esther 3:8 . . . . ***August 28***
Esther 4:14 . . . . ***August 29***
Esther 4:16 . . . . ***August 31***
Esther 5:2 . . . . ***September 3***
Esther 5:8 . . . . ***September 4***
Esther 9:28 . . . . ***September 5***
Job 1:21 . . . . ***September 6***

Psalm 19:7 . . . . *January 12*
Psalm 22:28 . . . . *November 13*
Psalm 27:4 . . . . *March 5*
Psalm 28:7 . . . .*April 25*
Psalm 31:24 . . . . *September 14*
Psalm 33:11 . . . .*March 12, September 16*
Psalm 34:13 . . . . *December 7*
Psalm 34:14, NIV . . . .*April 23*
Psalm 40:5 . . . . *September 23*
Psalm 68:5-6 . . . . *March 25*
Psalm 100:3 . . . . *March 1*
Psalm 106:1 . . . . *September 9*
Psalm 109:26 . . . . *February 2*
Psalm 116:15 . . . . *July 23*
Psalm 139:13-14 . . . . *January 2*
Psalm 139:14 . . . . *September 10*
Proverbs 2:6 . . . .*June 30*
Proverbs 3:5-6 . . . . *September 11*
Proverbs 3:9 . . . . *July 15*
Proverbs 6:16-19 . . . . *July 21*
Proverbs 11:3 . . . . *May 7*
Proverbs 11:14 . . . . *July 22*
Proverbs 13:12 . . . . *September 15*
Proverbs 16:7 . . . . *February 1*
Proverbs 17:17 . . . . *May 5*
Proverbs 18:4 . . . .*April 19*
Proverbs 18:24 . . . . *May 9*
Proverbs 20:6 . . . . *May 8*
Proverbs 22:1 . . . .*August 14*
Proverbs 22:4, NIV . . . . *March 10*
Proverbs 24:16 . . . . *September 8*
Proverbs 27:4 . . . . *January 26*
Proverbs 28:13 . . . . *December 8*
Proverbs 30:5 . . . . *January 9*
Proverbs 31:10 . . . . *May 24, July 4*
Proverbs 31:15 . . . . *July 5*
Proverbs 31:16 . . . . *July 7*
Proverbs 31:17 . . . . *March 19*
Proverbs 31:17-18 . . . . *May 27*
Proverbs 31:17, 25 . . . . *February 9*
Proverbs 31:20 . . . . *July 8*
Proverbs 31:25 . . . .*August 11*
Proverbs 31:28-29 . . . . *May 26*
Proverbs 31:30 . . . . *May 28*
Ecclesiastes 3:1 . . . . *February 15*
Ecclesiastes 3:1, 4 . . . . *February 25, May 15*
Ecclesiastes 9:10 . . . . *July 6*
Isaiah 40:31, KJV . . . . *January 25*
Isaiah 41:10 . . . . *September 12*
Isaiah 43:1 . . . .*January 5, August 26*
Isaiah 43:25 . . . . *February 19*
Isaiah 64:8 . . . .*February 28, August 21*
Jeremiah 1:5 . . . . *January 3*
Jeremiah 29:11 . . . .*January 4, August 30*
Lamentations 3:20-22 . . . . *May 14*
Micah 6:4, NIV . . . .*April 4*
Zephaniah 3:17 . . . . *March 3*
Matthew 1:5 . . . .*December 25*
Matthew 1:6 . . . .*December 26*
Matthew 2:11 . . . .*October 12*
Matthew 2:13 . . . .*October 13*
Matthew 5:16 . . . . *January 19*
Matthew 5:41-42 . . . . *February 8*
Matthew 6:21 . . . . *July 14*
Matthew 6:30 . . . .*June 22*
Matthew 7:7 . . . . *January 27, June 7*
Matthew 8:14-15 . . . .*October 25*
Matthew 8:16 . . . .*October 31*
Matthew 9:13 . . . .*December 29*
Matthew 14:6-7 . . . .*November 11*
Matthew 18:20 . . . .*June 11*
Matthew 2-0:20, NIV . . . .*November 26*
Matthew 27:19 . . . .*December 1*
Matthew 27:55-56 . . . .*December 2*
Matthew 28:5-6 . . . .*November 3*
Mark 5:22-23 . . . .*November 8*
Mark 5:27-28 . . . .*November 9*
Mark 6:18-19 . . . .*November 12*
Mark 6:24-25 . . . .*November 14*
Mark 7:30 . . . .*November 15*

Mark 12:41 . . . . ***November 28***
Mark 12:43-44 . . . . ***November 27***
Mark 15:40-41 . . . . ***November 2***
Mark 16:1 . . . . ***December 3***
Luke 1:5 . . . . ***September 20***
Luke 1:13 . . . . ***September 21***
Luke 1:15 . . . . ***September 26***
Luke 1:24-25 . . . . ***September 22***
Luke 1:26-27 . . . . ***September 27***
Luke 1:30 . . . . ***September 28***
Luke 1:37 . . . . ***September 29***
Luke 1:38 . . . . ***September 30***
Luke 1:39-40, NIV . . . . ***October 2***
Luke 1:41 . . . . ***September 24***
Luke 1:42-45 . . . . ***October 3***
Luke 1:46 . . . . ***October 4***
Luke 1:48 . . . . ***October 5***
Luke 1:56 . . . . ***October 6***
Luke 1:66 . . . . ***September 25***
Luke 2:4, NIV . . . . ***October 7***
Luke 2:5, NIV . . . . ***October 8***
Luke 2:7, NIV . . . . ***October 9***
Luke 2:13-14 . . . . ***October 10***
Luke 2:19, NIV . . . . ***October 15***
Luke 2:34-35 . . . . ***October 11***
Luke 2:37 . . . . ***October 18***
Luke 2:38 . . . . ***October 19***
Luke 2:48 . . . . ***October 14***
Luke 3:19 . . . . ***November 10***
Luke 5:19 . . . . ***March 17***
Luke 6:38 . . . . ***July 11***
Luke 7:13 . . . . ***October 26***
Luke 7:38 . . . . ***October 27***
Luke 7:41-42 . . . . ***October 28***
Luke 8:1-3 . . . . ***November 1***
Luke 8:2 . . . . ***October 30***
Luke 8:2-3 . . . . ***November 6***
Luke 10:38-39 . . . . ***November 18***
Luke 13:12-13, NIV . . . . ***November 25***
John 2:3 . . . . ***October 16***
John 3:7 . . . . ***August 12***
John 3:10 . . . . ***June 23***
John 3:16 . . . . ***January 21, October 29***
John 4:7 . . . . ***October 20***
John 4:16-18 . . . . ***October 21***
John 4:28-29 . . . . ***October 23***
John 4:24 . . . . ***November 20***
John 4:27 . . . . ***October 22***
John 4:42 . . . . ***October 24***
John 8:3 . . . . ***November 16***
John 8:10-11 . . . . ***November 17***
John 11:27 . . . . ***November 21***
John 12:3 . . . . ***November 22***
John 12:26 . . . . ***November 7***
John 19:26-27 . . . . ***October 17***
John 20:18 . . . . ***November 4***
Acts 2:44-47 . . . . ***December 4***
Acts 2:46-47 . . . . ***November 5***
Acts 5:1-2 . . . . ***December 5***
Acts 9:36 . . . . ***December 9***
Acts 9:37-38 . . . . ***December 10***
Acts 9:39 . . . . ***December 11***
Acts 12:1 . . . . ***December 12***
Acts 12:11-12 . . . . ***December 13***
Acts 12:13-14 . . . . ***December 14***
Acts 16:14 . . . . ***December 15***
Acts 16:40 . . . . ***December 16***
Acts 18:2-3 . . . . ***December 21***
Acts 24:24 . . . . ***December 23***
Romans 5:8 . . . . ***July 31***
Romans 6:23 . . . . ***September 18***
Romans 8:28 . . . . ***February 22, August 15***
Romans 8:37 . . . . ***March 6***
Romans 12:1 . . . . ***January 28***
Romans 12:2 . . . . ***February 13***
Romans 12:3 . . . . ***January 30***
Romans 12:10 . . . . ***March 29***
Romans 12:11 . . . . ***December 17***
Romans 12:12 . . . . ***June 4, October 1***
Romans 12:13 . . . . ***February 10***

Romans 12:18 . . . . *March 28*
Romans 16:1-2 . . . . *December 19*
Romans 16:3-5 . . . . *December 20*
Romans 16:12 . . . . *December 22*
1 Corinthians 1:9, NIV . . . . *January 7*
1 Corinthians 1:26-27. . . . *April 28, December 27*
1 Corinthians 10:13 . . . . *January 10, December 6*
1 Corinthians 10:31 . . . . *November 23*
1 Corinthians 13:13 . . . . *May 4*
1 Corinthians 15:33 . . . . *August 1*
1 Corinthians 15:58 . . . . *November 19*
1 Corinthians 15:55-57. . . . . *May 13*
2 Corinthians 4:8 . . . . *September 7*
2 Corinthians 5:17 . . . . *April 11*
2 Corinthians 6:14 . . . . *May 6*
2 Corinthians 8:5 . . . . *July 13*
2 Corinthians 8:12 . . . . *July 12, November 30*
2 Corinthians 10:12 . . . . *March 2*
Galatians 2:20 . . . . *September 19*
Galatians 6:9 . . . . *November 29*
Ephesians 1:7. . . . . *April 9*
Ephesians 4:2-3 . . . . *March 26*
Ephesians 4:3. . . . . *September 17*
Ephesians 5:1-2 . . . . *January 13*
Ephesians 5:31. . . . . *February 14*
Ephesians 6:13. *March 14*
Philippians 1:27 . . . . *March 13*
Philippians 2:1-4. . . . . *April 3*
Philippians 2:15 . . . . *February 7*
Philippians 3:13-14. . . . . *December 31*
Philippians 3:14 . . . . *February 12*
Philippians 4:2-3. . . . . *December 24*
Philippians 4:6-7. . . . . *February 16*
Philippians 4:12-13. *June 26*
Philippians 4:13 . . . . . . *February 3, December 28*
Colossians 1:10 . . . . *March 21*
Colossians 3:13-15 . . . . *November 24*
Colossians 3:12-13 . . . . *March 27*
Colossians 3:23 . . . . *January 20*
1 Timothy 5:8. . . . . *April 13*
2 Timothy 1:5. . . . . *December 18*
2 Timothy 1:7 . . . . *September 1*
2 Timothy 3:12. . . . . *December 30*
Titus 3:5. . . . . *April 10*
Hebrews 10:25. . . . . *June 12*
Hebrews 11:23. . . . . *March 15*
Hebrews 13:5. . . . . *January 14, February 4*
Hebrews 13:21. . . . . *September 13*
James 1:5 . . . . *April 18*
James 1:14-15. *January 11*
James 1:19 . . . . *August 17*
James 2:8-9. . . . . *February 17*
James 3:16 . . . . *August 3*
James 3:17 . . . . *June 29*
James 4:2 . . . . *June 6, August 2*
James 5:16 . . . . *June 5*
1 Peter 3:3-4 . . . . *August 25*
1 Peter 3:15-17 . . . . *January 16*

Women of the Bible Index

A

Abigail
- June 24
- June 25
- June 26
- June 27
- June 28
- June 29
- June 30

Abijah
- August 6

Acsah
- April 15

Anna
- October 18
- October 19

Athaliah
- August 1
- August 2
- August 3
- August 4
- July 31

B

Bathsheba
- July 2
- July 3
- July 4
- July 5
- July 6
- July 7
- July 8

C

Crippled Woman
- November 25

D

Deborah
- February 20
- April 16
- April 17
- April 18
- April 19
- April 20
- April 21
- April 22
- April 23
- April 24
- April 25
- April 26
- April 27
- April 28
- April 29

Delilah
- May 3
- May 4
- May 5
- May 6
- May 7
- May 8
- May 9

Dorcas
- December 9
- December 10
- December 11

Drusilla and Bernice
- December 23

E

Elizabeth
- September 20
- September 21
- September 22
- September 23
- September 24
- September 25
- September 26

Esther 347
- August 16
- August 17
- August 18
- August 19
- August 20
- August 21
- August 22
- August 23
- August 24

August 25
August 26
August 27
August 28
August 29
August 30
August 31
September 1
September 2
September 3
September 4
September 5
Euodia and Syntyche
December 24
Eve
January 1
January 2
January 3
January 4
January 5
January 6
January 7
January 8
January 9
January 10
January 11
January 12
January 13
January 14

F

Five Sisters 150
April 14 150
Forgiven Woman
November 16
November 17

H

Hagar 40
January 29
January 30
January 31
February 1
February 2
February 3
February 4
Hannah
June 1
June 2
June 3
June 4
June 5
June 6
June 7
June 8
June 9
June 10
June 11
June 12
June 13
June 14
Herodias and Her Daughter
November 10
November 11
November 12
November 13
November 14
Huldah
August 7
August 8

I

Ichabod's Mother
June 16

J

Jael
April 30
Jairus's Daughter
November 8
Jehosheba
August 5
Jephthah's Daughter
May 1
Jezebel
July 17
July 18
July 19
July 20
July 21
July 22
July 23
Joanna
November 6
Jochebed
March 15
March 16
March 17
March 18
March 19
March 20
March 21

L

Leah 83
February 28
March 1
March 2
March 3
March 4
March 5
Lois and Eunice
December 18
Lydia
December 15
December 16
December 17

M

Mary 403
September 27
September 28
September 29
September 30
October 1
October 2
October 3
October 4
October 5
October 6
October 7
October 8
October 9
October 10
October 11
October 12
October 13
October 14
October 15
October 16
October 17

Mary and Martha
November 18
November 19
November 20
November 21
November 22
November 23
November 24
Mary Magdalene
October 30
October 31
November 1
November 2
November 3
November 4
November 5
Mary, Mother of James and Joseph
December 2
December 3
Mary of Jerusalem
December 12
December 13
Medium of Endor
July 1
Michal
June 17
June 18
June 19
June 20
June 21
June 22
June 23
Miriam
March 23
March 24
March 25
March 26
March 27
March 28
March 29
March 30
March 31
April 1
April 2
April 3
April 4
April 5
Mrs. Job
September 6
September 7
September 8
September 9
Mrs. Lot
February 5
Mrs. Noah
January 15
January 16
January 17
January 18
January 19
January 20
January 21
Mrs. Potiphar
March 7

N

Naomi
May 10
May 11
May 12
May 13
May 14
May 15
May 16

O

Orpah
May 17

P

Peninnah
June 15
Peter's Mother-in-Law
October 25
Pharaoh's Daughter
March 22
Phoebe
December 19
Pilate's Wife
December 1
Priscilla
December 20
December 21

Q

Queen of Sheba
July 9

R

Rachel 71
February 21
February 22
February 23
February 24
February 25
February 26
February 27
Rahab
April 7
April 8
April 9
April 10
April 11
April 12
April 13
Rebekah
February 6
February 7
February 8
February 9
February 10
February 11
February 12
February 13
February 14
February 15
February 16
February 17
February 18
February 19
Rhoda
December 14
Ruth
May 18
May 19
May 20
May 21
May 22
May 23
May 24

May 25
May 26
May 27
May 28
May 29
May 30
May 31

S

Salome, Mother of James and John
November 26
Samaritan Woman
October 20
October 21
October 22
October 23
October 24
Samson's Mother
May 2
Sapphira
December 4
December 5
December 6
December 7
December 8
Sarah 29
January 22
January 23
January 24
January 25
January 26
January 27
January 28
Shiphrah and Puah
March 8
March 9
March 10
March 11
March 12
March 13
March 14
Shunemite Woman
July 26
July 27
July 28
Susanna
November 7
Syrophoenician Woman
November 15

V

Vashti
August 9
August 10
August 11
August 12
August 13
August 14
August 15

W

Widow of Nain
October 26
Widow of Zarephath
July 10
July 11
July 12
July 13
July 14
July 15
July 16
Widow with Oil
July 24
July 25
Widow with Two Coins
November 27
November 28
November 29
November 30
Woman Who Anointed Jesus
October 27
October 28
October 29
Woman Who Touched Jesus
November 9
Women in the Church
December 22

Y

Young Servant Girl
July 29
July 30

Z

Zipporah
April 6

About the Author

Katrina (Kathy) Cassel is author of *The Christian Girl's Guide to Being Your Best*, *The Christian Girl's Guide to the Bible*, and several other books for the teen/tween audience. Katrina has a BS degree in elementary education from Grace College, Winona Lake, Indiana, and an EdM with a reading specialty from the University of North Dakota. Katrina has worked with children of all ages in a variety of educational and church settings. She and her husband have eight children and live in Panama City, Florida.